T0301403

Central Banking, Monetary Policy and the Environment

THE ELGAR SERIES ON CENTRAL BANKING AND MONETARY POLICY

Series Editors: Louis-Philippe Rochon, *Full Professor, Laurentian University, Canada,* *Editor-in-Chief,* Review of Political Economy *and Founding Editor Emeritus,* Review of Keynesian Economics, Sylvio Kappes, *Assistant Professor, Federal University of Ceará, Brazil and Coordinator, Keynesian Economics Working Group, Young Scholars Initiative* and Guillaume Vallet, *Associate Professor, Université Grenoble Alpes and Centre de Recherche en Economie de Grenoble (CREG), France*

This series explores the various topics important to the study of central banking and monetary theory and policy and the challenges surrounding them. The books in the series analyze specific aspects such as income distribution, gender and ecology and will, as a body of work, help better explain the nature and the future of central banks and their role in society and the economy.

Titles in the series include:

The Future of Central Banking
Edited by Sylvio Kappes, Louis-Philippe Rochon and Guillaume Vallet

Central Banking, Monetary Policy and the Environment
Edited by Louis-Philippe Rochon, Sylvio Kappes and Guillaume Vallet

Future volumes will include:

Central Banking, Monetary Policy and Social Responsibility
Edited by Guillaume Vallet, Sylvio Kappes and Louis-Philippe Rochon

Central Banking, Monetary Policy and the Future of Money
Edited by Guillaume Vallet, Sylvio Kappes and Louis-Philippe Rochon

Central Banks and Monetary Regimes in Emerging Countries
Theoretical and Empirical Analysis of Latin America
Edited by Fernando Ferrari Filho and Luiz Fernando de Paula

Central Banking, Monetary Policy and Income Distribution
Edited by Louis-Philippe Rochon, Sylvio Kappes and Guillaume Vallet

Covid 19 and the Response of Central Banks
Coping with Challenges in Sub-Saharan Africa
Salewa Olawoye-Mann

Central Banking, Monetary Policy and the Political Economy of Dollarization
Edited by Sylvio Kappes and Andrés Arauz

Central Banking, Monetary Policy and Gender
Edited by Louis-Philippe Rochon, Sylvio Kappes and Guillaume Vallet

Central Banking, Monetary Policy and Financial In/Stability
Edited by Louis-Philippe Rochon, Sylvio Kappes and Guillaume Vallet

Central Banking, Monetary Policy and the Environment

Edited by

Louis-Philippe Rochon

Full Professor, Laurentian University, Canada, Editor-in-Chief,
Review of Political Economy *and Founding Editor Emeritus,*
Review of Keynesian Economics

Sylvio Kappes

Assistant Professor, Federal University of Ceará, Brazil and
Coordinator, Keynesian Economics Working Group, Young
Scholars Initiative

Guillaume Vallet

Associate Professor, Université Grenoble Alpes and Research
Fellow, Centre de Recherche en Economie de Grenoble
(CREG), France

THE ELGAR SERIES ON CENTRAL BANKING AND
MONETARY POLICY

 Edward Elgar
PUBLISHING

Cheltenham, UK • Northampton, MA, USA

Published by
Edward Elgar Publishing Limited
The Lypiatts
15 Lansdown Road
Cheltenham
Glos GL50 2JA
UK

Edward Elgar Publishing, Inc.
William Pratt House
9 Dewey Court
Northampton
Massachusetts 01060
USA

A catalogue record for this book
is available from the British Library

Library of Congress Control Number: 2022939157

This book is available electronically in the **Elgar**online
Economics subject collection
http://dx.doi.org/10.4337/9781800371958

ISBN 978 1 80037 194 1 (cased)
ISBN 978 1 80037 195 8 (eBook)

Printed and bound by CPI Group (UK) Ltd, Croydon, CR0 4YY

Contents

Figures

About the editors

Sylvio Kappes is Assistant Professor of Economic Theory at the Federal University of Ceará, Brazil. He has a PhD in Development Economics from the Federal University of Rio Grande do Sul, Brazil. His main areas of research are Central Banking, Monetary Policy, Income Distribution and Stock-flow Consistent models. His work has been published in a number of peer-reviewed journals, such as the *Review of Political Economy*, the *Journal of Post Keynesian Economics* and the *Brazilian Keynesian Review*. Sylvio is a co-editor of The Elgar Series on Central Banking and Monetary Policy, together with Louis-Philippe Rochon and Guillaume Vallet. He is the Books Review Editor of the *Review of Political Economy*, and sits on the editorial boards of the *Review of Political Economy* and the *Bulletin of Political Economy*. He is also a co-coordinator of the Keynesian Economics Working Group of the Young Scholars Initiative (YSI) of the Institute for New Economic Thinking (INET).

Louis-Philippe Rochon is Full Professor of Economics at Laurentian University, Canada, where he has been teaching since 2004. Before that, he taught at Kalamazoo College, in Michigan. He obtained his doctorate from the New School for Social Research, in 1998, earning him the Frieda Wunderlich Award for Outstanding Dissertation, for his dissertation on endogenous money and post-Keynesian economics.

In January 2019, he became the co-editor of the *Review of Political Economy* and its Editor-in-Chief in 2021. Before that, he created the *Review of Keynesian Economics*, and was its editor from 2012 to 2018, and is now Founding Editor Emeritus. He has been guest editor for the *Journal of Post Keynesian Economics*, the *International Journal of Pluralism and Economics Education*, the *European Journal of Economic and Social Systems*, the *International Journal of Political Economy*, and the *Journal of Banking Finance and Sustainable Development*. He has published on monetary theory and policy, post-Keynesian economics and fiscal policy.

Louis-Philippe is on the editorial board of *Ola Financiera*, the *International Journal of Political Economy*, the *European Journal of Economics and Economic Policies: Intervention*, *Problemas del Desarrollo*, *Cuestiones Económicas* (Central Bank of Ecuador) and *Bank & Credit* (Central Bank of Poland), the *Bulletin of Political Economy*, *Advances in Economics Education*,

Il Pensiero Economico Moderno, the *Journal of Banking, Finance and Sustainable Development* and *Research Papers in Economics and Finance*.

He is the Editor of the following series: The Elgar Series of Central Banking and Monetary Policy; and Elgar's New Directions in Post-Keynesian Economics series.

Louis-Philippe has been a Visiting Professor or Visiting Scholar in Australia, Brazil, France, Italy, Mexico, Poland, South Africa and the USA, and has further lectured in China, Colombia, Ecuador, Italy, Japan, Kyrgyzstan and Peru.

He is also the author of 150 articles in peer-reviewed journals and books, and has written or edited close to 35 books.

He has received grants from the Social Sciences and Humanities Research Council in Canada (SSHRC), the Ford Foundation and the Mott Foundation, among other places.

Guillaume Vallet is an Associate Professor of Economics at the University of Grenoble Alpes, France and a Research Fellow at Centre de Recherche en Economie de Grenoble.

He holds two PhDs, one in economics earned from the University Pierre Mendès-France (Grenoble, France) and the other in sociology obtained at the University of Geneva (Switzerland) and at the École des hautes études en sciences sociales (Paris, France).

Guillaume was awarded a Fulbright Award, in 2021, to explore the development of the social sciences during the Progressive Era (1892–1920), especially in light of economists' and sociologists' treatment of income inequality.

His research focuses on monetary economics, the political economy of gender and the history of economic thought during the Progressive Era. He is the author of 47 articles in peer-reviewed journals and books, and has written nine books. His work has appeared in several distinguished academic journals, such as *Revue d'Economie Politique, Economy and Society*. His work on Albion W. Small has appeared in *Business History* and the *Journal of the History of Economic Thought*. He has been invited to give talks by many institutions, such as the New School for Social Research (New York, USA), the Bank of Ecuador, the Bank of Hungary, the Bank of Israel, the Swiss National Bank and the United Nations in Geneva.

Contributors

Michel Aglietta is Emeritus Professor of Economics at Paris X Nanterre and teaches at the Hautes Etudes Ciommerciales (HEC, Paris). He is also Scientific Advisor at the Centre d'Etudes Prospectives et d'Informations Internationales (CEPII), a French research center in the field of international economics that produces studies, research and databases and analyzes major challenges of the world economy and its evolution. He is also an advisor to Groupama Asset Management. A specialist in the mechanisms of modern finance and a theoretician of money, Aglietta is also a member of the Economic Analysis Council to the Prime Minister of France and a member of the Institut Universitaire de France. He is the author of several authoritative works, including, most recently, *Crise et rénovation de la finance* with Sandra Rigot (Odile Jacob, 2009), *La Crise* (Michalon, 2008) and *Désordres dans le capitalisme mondial* with Laurent Berrebi (Odile Jacob, 2007).

Étienne Espagne is a senior economist at the Agence Française de Développement (AFD), the bilateral development bank for the French government. He develops and contributes to a research program on the modelization and evaluation of climate damages, adaptation and mitigation strategies in developing and emerging economies. He holds a PhD in Environmental Economics from the École des Hautes Études en Sciences Sociales (EHESS) and is also a graduate of the French École des Mines de Paris and the Paris School of Economics. He has published several papers in academic journals in the field of climate change and energy economics and regularly teaches at Paris 1 University, EHESS, École Polytechnique and ENSTA Paristech. He has previously worked at France Stratégie, the Centre d'Etudes Prospectives et d'Informations Internationales (CEPII) and the Centre international de recherche sur l'environnement et le développement (CIRED).

Giorgos Galanis is Associate Professor of Economics at Goldsmiths, University of London. As of September 2022 he will be Associate Professor (Senior Lecturer) in Applied Economics at Queen Mary University of London. He holds a PhD in Economics from the University of Warwick and a second PhD in Mathematical Methods and Systems from City, University of London. His current research interests lie at the intersection of economics with political philosophy, (international) political economy and sustainable development.

His work utilizes insights from behavioral science and different schools of thought within political economy and combines analytical and computational tools to answer questions related to political instability, social justice, global production and the social foundations of epidemics.

Robert Guttmann is Professor of Economics at Hofstra University (New York), and he is also affiliated with the Centre d'Économie Paris Nord (CEPN) of the Université Sorbonne Paris Nord in France. He studied in Vienna and at the University of Wisconsin–Madison, USA, before obtaining his PhD at the University of Greenwich, UK. He won Distinguished Teacher of the Year awards at Hofstra in 1989, 2004 and 2012. Guttmann teaches international economics, monetary economics, financial regulation and economic integration in the European Union. An expert in money and banking, international finance, and monetary theory, he has published numerous books and journal articles, including his bestselling books *How Credit-Money Shapes the Economy* (1994), *Cybercash* (2003), *Finance-Led Capitalism* (2016), *Eco-Capitalism* (2018) and *Multi-Polar Capitalism* (2021).

Eric Kemp-Benedict's research focuses on the macroeconomics of a sustainability transition. Working within post-Keynesian, structuralist and classical traditions, but viewing the economy through an ecological economics lens, he addresses questions around long-run growth, decoupling, structural change and economic development. His academic background is in physics, with a PhD from Boston University. He works at the Stockholm Environment Institute (SEI), which he first joined in 1997. He is based at SEI's US Center, where he directs the Equitable Transitions Program. He was director of SEI's regional Asia Center in Bangkok from 2013 to 2016.

Wesley C. Marshall received his undergraduate degree in Government from the College of William & Mary. He received his doctorate in Latin American Studies from the National Autonomous University of Mexico (UNAM) and completed post-doctorate studies at the Faculty of Economics of UNAM. Since 2009 he has been a professor-researcher at UAM Iztapalapa, where he is currently responsible for the Center for Financial and Economic Studies of North America, and Jefe of the Political Economy Area. He is a member of the national system of researchers (level 2), the Mexican Academy of Political Economy and the Mexican Academy of Science. He is a member of the Editorial Board of *Ola Financiera* and the *Review of Political Economy*, and is associate editor of the *International Journal of Political Economy*. He is author of the book *México desbancado: causas y consecuencias de la pérdida de la banca nacional.*

Basil Oberholzer received his PhD from the University of Fribourg, Switzerland, and is currently an associated researcher at the Centre for Development and Environment at the University of Bern, Switzerland. His research focus is on monetary economics, development macroeconomics and ecological economics. Moreover, Oberholzer is an economics officer at the Global Green Growth Institute, which supports governments and other stakeholders in developing countries regarding decarbonization strategies and green economic policies. His main publications include the books *Monetary Policy and Crude Oil: Prices, Production and Consumption* and *Development Macroeconomics: Alternative Strategies for Growth*, both with Edward Elgar Publishing.

Salewa Olawoye-Mann is Assistant Professor in the Business and Society Program of the Department of Social Science, York University, Canada. She has a PhD in Economics and Social Science Consortium (University of Missouri–Kansas City, 2016). Her research focuses on heterodox approaches to sustainable economic development through natural resources, and monetary theory. Her research mainly focuses on these issues in the sub-Saharan African region. She co-edited the book *Monetary Policy and Central Banking: New Directions in Post-Keynesian Theory* (Edward Elgar, 2012) and is currently working on a book on central banking responses to COVID-19 in sub-Saharan Africa (Edward Elgar).

Lilit Popoyan is Assistant Professor at the University of Naples "Partenope" (Naples, Italy) and Associate Researcher at Scuola Superiore Sant'Anna (Pisa, Italy). She is also a global lecturer at New York University (Florence, Italy). Her research is mainly focused on the nexus between financial regulations, financial stability, sustainable finance and macroeconomic dynamics. Part of her current scientific activity is in straight collaboration with central banks. Her research has contributed to such European research projects as DOLFINS, ISIGrowth and GROWINPRO and has been published in international peer-reviewed scientific journals.

Josh Ryan-Collins is Associate Professor in Economics and Finance at University College London's Institute for Innovation and Public Purpose. His research interests include money and banking, sustainable finance, and the economics of land and housing. His books include *Where Does Money Come From?* (New Economics Foundation, 2011), *Rethinking the Economics of Land and Housing* (Zed Books, 2017) and *Why Can't You Afford a Home?* (Polity, 2018). He has published in journals including *Socioeconomic Review*, *Ecological Economics*, *Nature Climate Change*, *Environment and Planning A: Economy and Space* and *The British Journal of Sociology*. He was previously Senior Economist at the New Economics Foundation (NEF), one of the

UK's leading progressive think tanks, and is a council member of the UK's Progressive Economy Forum.

Malcolm Sawyer is Emeritus Professor of Economics, University of Leeds, UK. He was the lead coordinator for the European Union-funded, 8-million-euro, 15-partner, five-year project on Financialisation: Economy Society and Sustainable Development. He was managing editor of the *International Review of Applied Economics* for over 30 years and has served on a range of editorial boards. He is the editor of the book series New Directions in Modern Economics (Edward Elgar) and co-edits (with Philip Arestis) the annual *International Papers in Political Economy* (Palgrave Macmillan). He is the author of 12 books, including *The Economics of Michał Kalecki* (Macmillan, 1985) and, most recently, *Can the Euro Survive?* (Polity Press, 2018). He is currently working on *The Power of Finance: Financialization and the Real Economy* (to be published by Agenda). He has edited or co-edited over 30 books. He has published over 140 papers in refereed journals and contributed over 160 book chapters on a wide range of topics, including financialization, the eurozone, fiscal policies and alternatives to austerity, money, public–private partnerships, and Kalecki and Kaleckian economics.

Romain Svartzman is a research economist at the Banque de France and a research associate at the Institute for Innovation and Public Purpose (IIPP, University College London). He focuses on the integration of nature-related financial risks (including climate and biodiversity) into monetary policy and financial supervision, and on the macroeconomics of the ecological transition. He previously worked as an environmental risk management officer for the International Finance Corporation (World Bank Group) and as an investor in "green" technologies for a French venture capital firm. Romain Svartzman completed his PhD in Ecological Macroeconomics at McGill University (Canada). He also holds a master's degree in Finance from the Institut d'Etudes Politiques de Paris (Sciences Po) and a degree in Economics and Law of Climate Change from FLACSO Argentina.

Giada Valsangiacomo is currently a PhD candidate in Economics at the University of Fribourg, Switzerland. Her dissertation addresses the analysis of the macroeconomic and financial effects of environmental change, both by reviewing standard macroeconomic models and by developing a novel framework that embeds the precepts of endogenous money theory. Her research is also concerned with the design of an effective economic policy to counteract ecological degradation on a global scale, as well as the analysis of its possible technical, ethical and social implications. She has an MA degree in Political Economy from the same university, obtained after a break dedicated to raising her three children.

Acknowledgments

In the making of this book, we would like to thank all the authors who contributed a chapter, therefore their time and energy. Written and put together during the worst of COVID-19, we appreciate it more knowing that many of the authors had urgent family commitments, and we all had to navigate more difficult work conditions.

We would also like to acknowledge, as always, the generous support of Alan Sturmer and the rest of the team at Edward Elgar Publishing for their continued and enthusiastic support of our work.

Introduction to *Central Banking, Monetary Policy and the Environment*

Louis-Philippe Rochon, Sylvio Kappes and Guillaume Vallet

INTRODUCTION

Since the 2007/08 financial crisis, central banks have been waking up to new realities concerning both the limitations of conventional policies, and the impact conventional and unconventional policies may have, only to face the possibility of aggregate demand secular stagnation. The task currently facing central banks is in identifying the challenges ahead and to respond to them with the right tools and policies.

This is a far cry from the Goldilocks years of the Great Moderation when central bankers and policymakers celebrated, thinking they had finally got things right. Business cycles had been vanquished, we were told, with huge and obvious implications for monetary policy. Keynes was a relic of a bygone era. However, this illusion was short lived.

With the financial and then the pandemic crises, central banks tested the limits of monetary policy. They pushed interest rates to near zero in many countries, but the results were disappointing as the policy had very limited or even no success in generating economic growth, thus disapproving neoclassical theory. It would appear that consumption and investment decisions rely on variables other than the rate of interest. Real interest rates were pushed to negative territory in the hope of stimulating demand. However, this was an instance of imposing a theory where the empirical evidence was clearly showing otherwise. As Storm writes, 'As the real interest [rate] *increased* from 1.6% in 1980 to 8.1% in 1984, the investment rate *increased*' (Storm 2019, n.p., original emphasis).

Nevertheless, there was still a belief in the loanable funds theory: if only real rates were pushed low enough, investment would pick up. This was how some, such as Lawrence Summers, interpreted secular stagnation: not as much as a crisis in aggregate demand, but instead as a crisis in loanable funds, easily solved by lowering interest rates.

This approach corresponded, for the past few decades, with the rise of the Austerian philosophy, where central banks have been made to carry most of the economic-policy burden, thereby contributing to the age of monetary policy dominance, during which fiscal policy was given up to the pursuit of economic growth. Governments, it was assumed, overburdened us and future generations with piles of public debt. They had to assure balanced or sound finances, and leave the challenge of fine-tuning economic activity to independent central bankers.

An important conclusion we can draw from the pair of crises is that central banks are unable to carry the whole burden of recovery. With the failure of both conventional and unconventional policies, many central banks resorted to asking governments to inject stimulus, given that they 'had done their job'. As Bernanke testified in front of Congress, on 5 June 2012, 'Monetary policy is not a panacea. ... I would feel much more comfortable if Congress would take some of this burden from us and address these issues.'

It was the return of Keynes, or rather, the 'Return of the Master' (Skidelsky 2009). Although Keynes did make an appearance in 2009, it was short lived as, by 2010, many countries had resorted back to sound finance. But the Master did return in a big way during the COVID crisis, when unprecedented fiscal stimulus, including in some countries the quasi-nationalization of private-sector wages, proved so historically important. Around the world, governments embraced deficit spending on a large and unprecedented scale: once again, Keynes rescued aggregate demand.

Central banks also went through a rethinking process of their own. Strict adherence to inflation targeting, which has been around since the early 1990s, started to wane, as some central banks started to adopt either dual mandates, for example, New Zealand which was ironically the first bank to inflation target, or a looser version of inflation targeting – average inflation targeting.

Of particular note, and following in the footsteps of a number of countries such as Canada, the Federal Reserve abandoned reserve requirements in 2020, in a further attempt to update their monetary framework. This is a clear statement that reserve requirements do not work in giving central banks control over the supply of credit by commercial banks. That is, the money multiplier is dead, and as a recently published paper by the Federal Reserve states, 'RIP money multiplier' (Ihrig et al. 2021).

THE OLD MODEL OF CENTRAL BANKING

Despite these seemingly positive changes over the past decade, has there been real change in monetary thinking, or has it been more cosmetic than anything else? The answer may be a little of both.

To answer this question, let us begin with a discussion of what we call the old model of central banking, most associated with Friedman's monetarism, pre-dating the new consensus model. Such an old model, we argue, is based on the following nine fundamental arguments:

1. Central banks control the supply of high-powered money or reserves.
2. Central banks exert control over the growth of monetary aggregates, the money supply.
3. Central banks control reserve requirements.
4. The money multiplier is at the core of the transmission mechanism.
5. Debate over rules versus discretion, favouring the former.
6. The natural rate of interest is a relevant variable for policy.
7. Money and inflation are linked.
8. Central banks must be independent.
9. The long-run neutrality of money.

Accordingly, central banks can control the money supply given their control over high-powered reserves and reserve requirements, a key element in the money multiplier. It is assumed that the money multiplier is stable. If central banks want to rein in money supply growth, they need only to either decrease the supply of high-powered money or increase reserve requirements. In both instances, the supply of money is assumed exogenous and therefore independent of whatever occurs in the economy, by definition. In accordance with the quantity theory of money, assuming stable velocity, the rate of growth of the money supply should be set according to the long-run, natural growth of the economy, also known as Friedman's rule.

According to this model, commercial banks are mere financial intermediaries, and their lending activities are at the mercy of central banks: they are severally constrained in their ability to lend – by the availability of reserves and deposits. Central banks can influence lending by increasing or decreasing the availability of high-powered money to the banking system and, through the (stable and predictable) money multiplier, will impact the supply of bank loans. That is, deposits create loans.

However, if the central bank can influence the supply of loans, this is only a short-run phenomenon. Indeed, monetary policy only has short-run effects. In the long run, money is neutral and has no impact on real variables. Money only affects prices in the long run. This is the standard way of reading the quantity theory of money equation: from left to right and, if money supply growth is appropriately set, then in the long run the price level remains constant.

This is an important function of central banks, and is seen as crucial given the notion that inflation is influenced by all things monetary: inflation is 'always and everywhere a monetary phenomenon'. Control of the growth of the money supply therefore becomes of paramount importance: if central banks cannot control the money supply, then they must as well give up on trying to control inflation.

The idea that inflation and money are linked was considered – and still is – a universal truth. This led Friedman to propose his monetary rule. There were in fact two main reasons for favouring rules over discretion: Friedman had a deep mistrust of central bankers, and in this sense always opposed the notion of independent central banks. At least, were they so independent, rules would ensure that central bankers would follow proper monetary policy etiquette.

THE NEW MODEL OF CENTRAL BANKING

In recent years, central banks themselves have come a long way in leaving at least parts of the monetarist story behind, and many have gone so far as to embrace some version of the post-Keynesian theory of endogenous money (even though post-Keynesian works and authors are seldom, if ever, cited). If the old model of central banking owed a debt to Friedman, the new approach owes a great deal to the work of Wicksell.

In this new model, most now readily admit that it is the rate of interest that is the control instrument, not some monetary aggregate, and that the setting of interest rates is independent of the quantity of reserves in existence – what Borio and Disyatat (2010) have termed the 'decoupling' effect. Former Bank of Canada Governor Gerald Bouey famously stated in 1982, 'We did not abandon the monetary targets: they abandoned us' (Dodge 2010). It is perhaps because of this that central banks turned to another monetary framework, careful, however, not to stray theoretically too far from orthodox monetary thinking. Indeed, 'the main change is that it replaces the assumption that the central bank targets the money supply with an assumption that it follows a simple interest rate rule' (Romer 2000, p. 154).

With that in mind, central banks then looked for a more suitable model to build, and turned to inflation targeting, a concept that goes back at least to Keynes (1923). This elegant, three-equation model (see Romer 2000; Taylor 1993; Woodford 2003) contains a Taylor rule, and well-behaved IS and Phillips curves. New Zealand was the first country in the world to adopt the new model, in 1990, followed by Canada the following year.

The model was widely popular with central banks and academics. Indeed, Goodfriend (2007, p. 59) claimed that 'the Taylor Rule became the most common way to model monetary policy', and Taylor (2000, p. 90), heralded that 'at the practical level, a common view of macroeconomics is now pervasive in policy-research projects at universities and central banks around the world'.

The inflation target itself became the anchor for inflation, and in Wicksellian fashion, we find embedded in the model the inescapable natural rate of interest determined by productivity and thrift, and a market-determined benchmark rate set by the central bank. The model was also based on some fine-tuning: whenever the rate of inflation was above target, central banks, via a Taylor rule, would raise the benchmark rate, hoping the economy would slow down just enough to bring inflation back down to target, via the well-behaved IS and Phillips curves. Without these, of course, the model falls apart.

The adoption of this new model corresponded also to the period of the Great Moderation, leading some to argue that 'In the years prior to August 2007, central banks had appeared to have almost perfected the conduct of monetary policy' (Goodhart 2011, p. 145).

Yet, with the financial crisis, the model began falling apart and a new search for a new monetary policy framework was under way. This model was confronted with the problem of the lower bound, where central banks were unable to push nominal interest rates below zero. Here, central banks were convinced the natural rate was below zero and hence why they needed to push the benchmark rate to such low levels. However, in their model, even a zero nominal rate was still too high: real rates were still above the natural rate given low levels of inflation. Interestingly, the secular stagnationist view was based precisely on this view: our economies were stagnating because the natural rate had fallen below zero; austerity had nothing to do with it. As stated previously, stagnation was interpreted as a crisis in loanable funds, not a crisis in aggregate demand per se. Owing to this, fiscal policy was not seen initially as a possible solution; austerity made sense, according to this view.

In the continued absence of fiscal policy, central banks were struggling to be seen as still relevant, and turned to unconventional means to foster economic growth – means that proved as uninspiring as the more conventional policies. Yet, the financial crisis would eventually reveal the degree to which the monetary new emperor had no clothes: the limits of this new view were starting to emerge. In a startling new paper, 'Whither central banking', Summers and Stansbury (2019) were now admitting 'the impotence' of the model: 'Simply put, tweaking inflation targets, communications strategies, or even balance sheets is not an adequate response to the challenges now confronting the major economies ... Central banks cannot always set inflation rates through monetary policy'.

THE HUMPTY-DUMPTYING OF THE NEW MODEL

There is no denying that the new consensus model has come under criticism in the past decade, since the financial crisis, and not just from post-Keynesians, but from a growing number of analyses from within central banks themselves.

The question remains as to whether all the central banks' guards and horses can put the model back together again.

In a Bank of England paper now almost a decade old, McLeay et al. (2014) go to great lengths to dispel some old myths surrounding monetary creation, and clarify the misconceptions of money creation from the reality. In particular, they argue that lending creates deposits: 'In the modern economy, those bank deposits are mostly created by commercial banks themselves' (McLeay et al. 2014, p. 15). More crucial, we believe, is the explanation of why reserves are not an important component of bank lending, and cannot 'be multiplied into more loans' (McLeay et al. 2014, p. 14).

In a second paper published at the Bank of England, Jakab and Kumhof (2018) argue that 'loans come before deposits' and that 'a new loan involves no intermediation. No real resources need to be diverted from other uses, by other agents, in order to be able to lend to the new customer' (Jakab and Kumhof 2018, p. 4), which they claim is a 'more realistic framework' which is 'supported by a long and growing list of central bank publications' (Jakab and Kumhof 2018, p. 1). Moreover, they specify that this view 'has always been very well understood by central banks' (Jakab and Kumhof 2018, p. 7).

The Bundesbank, of all banks, also contributed to this new central bank model, in 2017, with a paper entitled 'The role of banks, non-banks and the central bank in the money creation process'. A reference to the 'money creation process' is a very telling rejection of the exogenous money story where this process is absent, in the notion of helicopter money. The paper argues that:

> Sight deposits are created by transactions between a bank and a non-bank (its customer) – the bank grants a loan, say, or purchases an asset and credits the corresponding amount to the non-bank's bank account in return. Banks are thus able to create book (giro) money. This form of money creation reflects the financing and portfolio decisions of banks and non-banks and is thus driven by the same factors that determine the behaviour of banks and non-banks. (Deutsche Bundesbank 2017, p. 15)

In a 2018 speech, Christopher Kent, Assistant Governor of the Reserve Bank of Australia, discussed whether money was 'born of credit?' He makes clear that 'Money can be created, however, when financial intermediaries make loans. Accordingly, the concepts of money and credit are closely linked in a modern economy … The process of money creation requires a willing borrower … [and the bank must] satisfy itself that the borrower can service the loan' (Kent 2018, p. 4).

These are familiar themes for post-Keynesians, who will recognize the notion that loans create deposits, and that they are demand-determined by creditworthy borrowers; that is, money is seemingly endogenous.

Moreover, two papers recently published by the Federal Reserve show a very different side to the central bank model. In the first, Rudd (2022) argues that inflationary expectations are no ground for predicting future levels of inflation. According to the author, such an idea rests on 'extremely shaky foundations' (Rudd 2022, p. 25). The conclusions are devastating as anticipations of inflation certainly are a core principle of central banking today. The 'pugnacious paper' created a firestorm, leading *The Economist* (2021) to declare the paper 'a social-media sensation'.

In the second paper, by Ihrig et al. (2021), with the provocative subtitle 'R.I.P. money multiplier', the authors explain the changes to monetary policy in the USA, following the financial crisis and COVID. The paper is worth noting for a few reasons. First, in light of the Federal Reserve's elimination of reserve requirements in 2020, the authors warn professors of mistakes they still make when teaching money and banking. Second, the authors admonish textbooks for still teaching the ways of the old model. The subtitle of the paper is meant to be a definitive statement (and perhaps even a warning) to economists that they are doing a disservice to students by not correctly representing (or understanding) what central banks do. Both reasons are summarized by the title to one section of the paper: 'Make sure your teaching is current'.

Finally, in celebrating the twenty-fifth anniversary of the publication of Moore (1988), Bindseil and König (2013) – Bindseil works at the European Central Bank (ECB) – have acknowledged that 'the last 25 years have vindicated the substance of his thinking [Moore's] in a surprising way that could hardly have been anticipated in 1988. Central bankers have by now largely buried "verticalism", at least when it comes to monetary policy implementation' (Bindseil and König 2013, p. 385). This is an acknowledgement that the old model of central banking is dead.

Or is it? While many of the above quotes (and we could have cited a number of other papers) certainly appear, at least on the surface, as indicative of important changes in monetary thinking, we are not convinced. While there is no doubt that central banks have come a long way in repudiating some of the elements of the old model, we argue they have not successfully done so in their entirety. What is left is perhaps best described as a hybrid model. We agree with Fiebiger and Lavoie (2020, p. 78) who have argued that 'The NCM replaced money supply targeting with inflation targeting while preserving monetarist results.' This is exactly what Lavoie (2006, p. 167) meant when he wrote, almost two decades ago, that new consensus models 'simply look like old wine in a new bottle'.

Let us once again refer to the nine arguments above:

1. Central banks control the supply of high-powered money or reserves.
2. Central banks exert control over the growth of monetary aggregates, the money supply.
3. Central banks control reserve requirements.
4. The money multiplier is at the core of the transmission mechanism.
5. Debate over rules versus discretion, favouring the former.
6. The natural rate of interest is a relevant variable for policy.
7. Money and inflation are linked.
8. Central banks must be independent.
9. The long-run neutrality of money.

We can conclude that arguments 1–4 have been abandoned by many central banks, and in new consensus models as well. However, despite these advances, welcome as they are, we are still not entirely in agreement with the idea that mainstream thinking is any closer to the post-Keynesian story of endogenous money. That is, the new model of central banking certainly leaves behind a number of assumptions of the old model, but from a post-Keynesian perspective, it does not go far enough. Five elements still remain at the core of the model.

Argument 5: as regards the debate over rules versus discretion, we can summarize that it has evolved, but perhaps not by much. The old model contains a monetary rule, while the new model contains an interest rate rule. However, Taylor (1993, p. 195) defines his approach as akin to 'a responsive rule'. Indeed, Taylor (1993, p. 196) claims that 'Policymakers do not, and are not evidently about to, follow policy rules mechanically', therefore leaving some room for discretion, and warns about making Taylor rules 'too complex'. So, in many ways, central banks use fine-tuning to adjust interest rates in response to inflation shocks.

Argument 6: as regards the natural rate of interest, it is still at the heart of new consensus models. In a Wicksellian manner, it acts as an anchor to short-term benchmark rates. The purpose of the central bank is to set the rate and to move it up or down until it reaches an inflation target, corresponding presumably with the natural rate.

The question is whether we can have a theory of endogenous money while also espousing a natural rate of interest. Rochon (1999) and Smithin (1994) have always rejected the claim that a theory of endogenous money can accommodate a natural rate of interest. If post-Keynesians believe the benchmark rate is truly exogenous, then that would rule out a natural rate that acts as an anchor for central bank rates. At best, as Palley (2006, p. 80) writes, the new consensus 'is a conception of endogeneity that is fundamentally different from the Post Keynesian conception, which is rooted in the credit nature of money'. Palley names the new consensus (NC) approach as 'central bank endogeneity'. In a similar vein, we would argue that the new consensus lacked a '*theory* of endogenous money'. As Setterfield (2004, p. 41) arrives at the same conclusion: 'whereas the stock of money is endogenous in practice in NC macroeconomics, it is endogenous in principle in PK macroeconomics'.

Argument 7: in addition, inflation is still thought to be linked to monetary policy. Only central banks are equipped to regulate economic activity efficiently in order to influence inflation and achieve its target, with minimal damage to the economy. Inflation, we can say, is always and everywhere a monetary policy phenomenon.

Argument 8: central bank independence is still considered a sine qua non of mainstream monetary policy. Advocates claim that it is at the core of current monetary thinking, especially now (at the time of writing this introduction) as inflation is starting to increase around the world. According to Goodhart (2021), if inflation persists, central banks must move to swiftly increase interest rates or risk losing credibility. Central bank independence is tied to notions of credibility: 'It is important to have in place adequate mechanisms to "guard the guardians" of monetary and financial stability' (Goodhart and Lastra 2018, p. 49).

There is also a staunch defence of the long-run neutrality of money. This is particularly so in current research on the links between monetary policy and income distribution. While some central banks recognize the income distributive impact of monetary policy, it is said to be small and temporary (see Rochon 2022). For instance, Romer and Romer (2001, p. 910) claim that 'It is certainly true that expansionary policy can generate a boom and reduce poverty temporarily. But the effect is unquestionably just that: temporary.' In a recent survey,[1] Colciago et al. (2019, p. 1224) argue that 'Over the longer horizon, the distributional impact is likely to die out given the temporary nature of the effects of monetary policy shocks.' This is a required conclusion to a theory that insists on long-run neutrality.

The new model is thus not too far from Friedman (Fiebiger and Lavoie 2020), well evidenced in the following quote by Bernanke (2003, online speech): 'I am ready and willing to praise Friedman's contributions wherever and whenever anyone gives me a venue ... We can hardly overstate the influence of Friedman's monetary framework on contemporary monetary theory and practice ... both policymakers and the public owe Milton Friedman an enormous debt'.

THE POST-KEYNESIAN MODEL OF CENTRAL BANKING

While mainstream economists have had to face new realities and come to some realizations about how central bank policy operates, post-Keynesians have also made some changes in the way they perceive central banks and monetary policy. Endogenous money is still the copingstone of post-Keynesian theory, where the rate of interest is set by central banks in a total disconnect with the natural rate, which is rejected. Loans make deposits, and banks are never constrained by a lack of deposits or reserves, but only by a lack of creditworthy borrowers. While Kaldor (1970) and Moore (1988) are central to this view, the ideas were present in many of Joan Robinson's writings, especially *The Accumulation of Capital* (1956).

Post-Keynesians have pushed the boundaries of central banking by advocating against the use of fine-tuning, and by linking monetary policy to income distribution. As regards the first of these, the concept of fine-tuning consists of incrementally increasing and decreasing interest rates until the correct rate of interest is found, which delivers an inflation consistent with its target. However, a great deal is assumed here. In new consensus models, this fine-tuning is based on well-established IS and Phillips curves: central banks change interest rates in an effort to generate just the right amount of change in output, which in turn will generate just enough change in unemployment and inflation. However, these are empirical relationships that need to be tested, and thus far the empirical evidence is weak.

Both Keynes and Robinson rejected fine-tuning. Keynes is famous for having said that fine-tuning 'belongs to the species of remedy which cures the disease by killing the patient' (Keynes 1936, p. 323). In a similar vein, Robinson, in a greatly underappreciated essay, argues that 'The regulating effect of changes in the rate of interest was at best very weak' (1943, p. 26), and again in 1952, where she describes as a 'false scent' the use of counter-cyclical monetary policy, and rejects:

> the conception of an economy which is automatically held on a path of steady development by the mechanism of the rate of interest ... But it is by no means easy to see how the monetary mechanism is supposed to ensure how that the rate of interest actually assumes its full employment value ... The automatic corrective action of the rate of interest is condemned by its very nature to be always too little and too late. (Robinson 1952, pp. 73–4)

While recognizing this, post-Keynesians further argue that monetary policy is foremost about income distribution. While the mainstream is starting to recognize this, as stated previously, there is nevertheless a stark difference with post-Keynesians. While for the mainstream, monetary policy may have income distributive effects in the short run, for post-Keynesians, monetary policy is income distribution. It is for both of these reasons that Lavoie (1996, p. 537), in rejecting fine-tuning, concludes that:

> It then becomes clear that monetary policy should not so much be designed to control the level of activity, but rather to find the level of interest rates that will be proper for the economy from a distribution point of view. The aim of such a policy should be to minimize conflict over the income shares, in the hope of simultaneously keeping inflation low and activity high.

PURPOSE OF THE CENTRAL BANKING AND MONETARY POLICY SERIES

In early 2018, we decided to organize a small gathering on 'the future of central banking', and applied for a financial grant from the Social Sciences and Humanities Research Council (Canada) as they have a wonderful programme for that purpose.

The three of us had been having discussions around this topic for a few years previously, noticing what appeared to be important changes in central banking and monetary policy, from 'unconventional policies' such as quantitative easing and lower-bound policies, to discussions over income distribution, the environment and the quasi-embrace of at least some version of endogenous money by some central banks.

It was in this spirit that we gathered in Talloires (France), on the shores of Lake Annecy, over a few days on 26–28 May 2019. We invited some well-known heterodox scholars, such as Elissa Braunstein, Gary Dimsky, Juliet Johnson, Marc Lavoie, Dominique Plihon and Mario Seccareccia, but also some more mainstream scholars, such as Etienne Farvaque and Ulrich Bindseil, in an effort to encourage a dialogue of sorts on central bank-related topics. We also partnered with the Young Scholars Initiative, from the Institute for New Economic Thinking, which funded the travel and accommodation of 11 young scholars. This partnership has proven rewarding for all those involved.

By all accounts, it was a huge success and it was from this gathering that the idea of a book on the same topic was born. The ensuing book went well beyond the initial plan, as we expanded its scope and breadth. *The Future of Central Banking* is the first book of this series, and we divided it into several sections, each dealing with the relationship between central banking, monetary policy and various themes, such as the environment, gender, income distribution, macro-prudential policies, structural change and central bank independence.

While we are very proud of this book, and it remains in many ways ground-breaking, it soon became apparent that there was more to be said on each of these topics, and so we began discussions with Edward Elgar Publishing to create a series dedicated to all aspects of central banking. While we signed the contract for the book in July 2019, by November we signed a contract to create the series. That first book would then anchor the rest of the series.

From there, we felt that many of the topics from the first book needed to be developed, so we decided to do entire books on each of these themes. We agreed on the next four titles – income distribution, the environment, social responsibility and the future of money – and quickly contacted some possible contributors.

This then launched us in new directions, and new reflections, with the aim of moving forward the critical discussion over the future of central banking, and pushing the boundaries of heterodox thought. In many ways, the mainstream was 'out-researching' us on some of these topics, and heterodox economists had to return to monetary policy and push forward. This was also the rationale for creating the Monetary Policy Institute, which we all direct.

The overall goal of this new series is to contribute to a new research agenda on central banking and monetary policy. Note, the title of the series is not simply 'monetary policy' as we understand it, that is, interest rates and their impact on the economy. While there is still a great deal of work to be done in this respect, for instance, understanding the impact of incremental changes in interest rates on income distribution and social classes, on gender, on the environment, and so on, we need to go beyond a mere discussion over interest rates, and consider central banks as institutions. This remains a gravely under-developed area of research in economics, though sociologists have considered this topic with great promise. In this context, economists have much to learn from sociology, and their emphasis on power, for instance.

Sociological studies on central banking highlight that, as institutions, central banks produce rules that 'coerce' individuals and shape their lives through their policies. In that, central banks exert what Susan Strange termed 'structural power' on the economy and society. This 'structural power' is personally concentrated in central bankers' hands, whose sociological profile should be put in relation to the distributive nature of monetary policy: do central bankers really serve the people? This crucial argument demonstrates that central banks reciprocally need people's confidence in order to gain social legitimacy: central banks' power needs to be 'socially embedded'. Central banks are undoubtedly non-neutral institutions, and for that reason, economics has a lot to learn from other social sciences.

Finally, the crucial question is whether central banks serve the interests of the people (see Fontan et al. 2018). This opens up a Pandora's Box of questions and more, about central banking, monetary policy and social responsibility, democracy, gender, income distribution and structural change. One by one, these themes are covered in the books in this new series which aims to push the boundaries of how we currently analyse, reflect and write about central banks.

THE STRUCTURE OF THE BOOK

When it comes to the relationship between monetary policy and the environment, it is not entirely clear to at least one of us if that relationship is strong. Nevertheless, it deserves to be explored and discussed. What we know is that the assumed relationship is bi-directional, in the sense that monetary policy, that is the rate of interest, may affect the environment, and in return, the environment may affect monetary policy.

Yet, examples of the first relationship are largely based, we think, on the mainstream view, and the existence of a relationship between interest rates and economic activity. Yet, as some of us have shown, the empirical support for this relationship may not be that strong. In other words, what is the transmission mechanism of monetary policy and the environment? Rochon (2022) has written on 'the general ineffectiveness of monetary policy', questioning the standard relationship between changes in the rate of interest and output. Such a relationship, embedded in mainstream thinking which relies on the existence of a robust IS curve and Phillips curve, should apply to dirty or green investment alike. There is therefore work to do to show how this may impact the environment, and this book goes a long way in trying to show this relationship.

The book contains eleven chapters by leading post-Keynesian and heterodox economists.

In the opening chapter, Robert Guttmann argues that irrespective of their unique histories and specific institutional characteristics, central banks all over the world share enough in common to allow certain generalizations about them. They typically carry out three strategic roles simultaneously, acting both as the government's bank as well as the banks' bank while managing their economy's insertion into whatever international monetary system prevails at the time. The particular configuration of policy objectives in pursuit of this triple role has unfolded in distinct historic phases which most, if not all, central banks have gone through at the same time. Guttman argues that as central banks are about to enter a new phase in their evolution, this one shaped by central banks' incorporation of the climate change challenge, it is appropriate to wonder where they are right now in identifying what kind of institutional challenge they face to deal with this global systemic problem arguably located outside their purview. He reminds us that central banks all over the world are currently engaged in an exploratory effort, coordinated to some degree among themselves as grouped together in the Network for Greening the Financial System (NGFS), to define new 'rules of the game' how best to support the worldwide effort at a zero-carbon transition between now and mid-century.

Central banks are focusing in this endeavour on managing climate-specific risks as potential sources of financial instability, micro-prudential regulation of climate change (e.g. climate-related financial disclosure), macro-prudential regulation of climate change (e.g. climate stress tests), and 'greening' of monetary policy by moving beyond traditional market neutrality to a melange of 'green'-supporting and/or 'brown'-penalizing incentives.

In Chapter 2, Malcom Sawyer argues that when it comes to climate change, the arguments for an 'independent central bank' are several undermined. There is discussion of taxonomies for environmentally friendly ('green') investments. There is only a very limited contribution from 'green QE' to tackling the climate emergency. The potential use of forms of credit guidance and controls as part of monetary policy is then considered. The responsibilities of central banks for financial stability have implications for dealing with financial instability arising from revaluation of 'stranded assets'.

Considering the objectives and mandates of central banks, it is argued here that the arguments for an 'independent central bank' are severely undermined when monetary policy and the climate emergency are under the spotlight. There is discussion of taxonomies for environmentally friendly ('green') investments. Proposals for a 'green QE' (Quantitative Easing), where it is argued that there is only a very limited contribution from 'green QE' to tackling the climate emergency. The use of forms of credit guidance considered as part of monetary policy is then considered. The responsibilities of central banks for financial stability have implications for dealing with financial instability arising from revaluation of 'stranded assets'. The possible role of the central bank in the funding of 'green' investment projects is considered and it is argued that a dedicated state development bank would be preferred.

Chapter 3, by Basil Oberholzer, begins with a reminder that the mainstream approach to green finance considers private financial institutions as essential agents in enabling a smooth transformation to a sustainable economy. This narrative where money is supposed to be withdrawn from environmentally harmful assets in order to be shifted to green investment projects is implicitly based on a conception of exogenous money. However, in a world of endogenous money, a shift of funds does not per se reduce the financing of environmental pollution. This chapter criticizes the mainstream idea of green finance and considers whether the central bank is able to make a difference where private banks cannot. The author argues that while private financial institutions are ineffective in steering the green transformation due to the endogeneity of money, it is precisely endogenous money which enables monetary policy to foster ecological sustainability. In the end however, for monetary policy to be successful in driving green investment, the author believes it has to be embedded in a comprehensive framework of economic and environmental policies as well as large-scale public investment.

In Chapter 4, Romain Svartzman argues that central bankers across the world have recently acknowledged that the physical impacts of climate change, just like the sudden and disorderly transition to a low-carbon economy, could create systemic financial risks ('Green Swans'). In order to manage these climate-related risks within the remit of their price and financial stability mandates, some central banks have started to explore climate-related prudential and monetary policies. While some scholars and civil society members call for greater efforts from central banks, including actions that would go beyond their existing mandates (e.g. 'green' quantitative easing), fewer have questioned the strategy of relying almost exclusively on central banks to address climate change. In this context, for the author, insights from post-Keynesian theory will be critical to factor in the inability of monetary and financial policies to generate a structural economic change, and the need for a much larger role for fiscal policy. This chapter therefore highlights how post-Keynesian theory can help manage climate-related systemic risks, but also why mitigating climate change and other ecological risks requires considering new questions (such as the potential limits to economic growth and the need for new institutional arrangements to govern our environmental commons) which still largely escape the post-Keynesian toolbox. Indeed, as we enter the Anthropocene, post-Keynesian theory will be useful only to the extent that it can contribute to building an analytical framework tailored to the new ecological reality.

In Chapter 5, by Michel Aglietta and Étienne Espagne, the authors explore the links between environmental change and the international lender of last resort. For them, the necessary alignment of the financial system to the objectives of the Paris Agreement has been the object of an increasing number of studies since 2015, giving a new role to central banks. But the international aspects of this alignment have not been specifically addressed yet. International financial flows are nowadays a key determinant of the macro-dynamics of all types of economies. In the case of developing and emerging economies, the capacity to attract international financial flows from developed economies, or to protect themselves against sudden stops, determines not only their ability to generate growth, but also the quality of that growth. In that respect, the capacity to finance the investments required for a low-carbon transition or for adaptation strategies to climate change, or the possibility to avoid investments detrimental to the environment, depends heavily on the financial position of the country in a hierarchical international monetary system.

Aglietta and Espagne argue that as the lender of last resort in the domestic financial system, the central bank is the key actor at the country level to ensure that liquidity provision is aligned with a sustainable development path. But its own action is constrained by its need to guarantee some access to international liquidity to its domestic actors. The international lender of last resort thus holds the ultimate position in this intricate network of liquidity provision, providing the means of payments for international transactions. However, this actor does not exist as an upperhand institution. It can only proceed from arrangements between central banks and other actors. Therefore, aligning financial flows with the objectives of the Paris Agreement implies that the institutions at the heart of the function of the international lender of last resort are aligned as well.

In the following chapter, on climate change, financial instability and central banking, Giada Valsangiacomo presents the salient impacts of climate change on financial stability and discusses the role that central banks can play in addressing the resulting issues. After an overview of the commonly acknowledged features of the climate emergency, the author presents a brief illustration of climate-related risks together with transmission channels linking those risks to the financial system. The chapter will also show how the ensuing menace to financial stability, of which a new operational definition is given, provides scope for central banks to act without jeopardizing their existing mandates. To be read as a critique of mainstream analysis, the analysis also points out how radical uncertainty, as defined by Frank H. Knight a century ago, is a factor that utterly reshapes the analytical framework and thus the range of potential central bank responses. The latter should focus not only on merely upgrading macro-prudential policies, but more importantly on implementing precautionary measures, which would ultimately improve financial market resilience to climate-related risks. Most notably, this new financial stability framework would impart clear guidance to the greening of financial markets and momentum for an orderly transition to a carbon-neutral economy. Despite the valuable promise of these measures, strong evidence persists that central bank action would need to be supported by a more comprehensive set of economic policies, in order to effectively overcome both climate and financial instability.

In 'Towards an ecological market', Chapter 7, Wesley Marshall proposes the creation of a new currency, the green dollar, that would be designed to create financial incentives for environmentally helpful activities, and in the process attend to long-standing problems of wealth inequality and poverty. This author goes to some lengths to explain the nature of money and how it is currently conceptualized and utilized in order to argue for the creation of a new financial system to support an ecological agenda. Such a proposal contrasts from others in that it will need very few resources, either financial or technological, to be implemented.

In his contribution to this book, Josh Ryan-Collins, in Chapter 8, argues that the notion that climate change and the transition to a net-zero-carbon economy poses financial stability risks is now widely accepted by central banks. However, how financial authorities should measure, manage and act to ameliorate such 'climate-related financial risks' (CRFR) remains an open question. Yet, the author argues that very few regulatory interventions have been taken by central banks up until now despite the clear materiality of CRFR to their mandates. The author insists that the roots of this absence of action lie with central banks' reluctance to move beyond 'market failure' conceptualizations of policy intervention from neoclassical welfare economics focused on information asymmetries and price discovery. Policies in this vein include disclosure of perceived climate risks, climate scenario analysis and stress tests. This approach is misguided as the net-zero transition involves systemic and endogenous forms of risk which make their quantification and efficient price discovery impossible. An alternative, precautionary policy approach is developed that seeks to ameliorate catastrophic and irreversible financial and economic losses and direct markets towards more sustainable forms of credit allocation. This draws on the 'precautionary principle' and post-crisis inequality.

Eric Kemp-Benedict, in Chapter 9, entitled 'Money and the environment', argues that links between the environment and money – or, more precisely, points of contact between the monetary circuit and ecosystems – are pervasive, with the greatest environmental impact occurring through extraction of raw materials and emission of wastes. The author focuses on the point at which natural resources enter the economy through commodity markets, approaching them within a tradition that can be traced back to Kaldor. From the winding down of fossil fuel extraction to the ramping up of the 'bio-economy', links between commodity markets, financial markets, and the rest of the economy can be expected to rise in importance.

Chapter 10, on 'A green mandate: The Central Bank of Nigeria and sustainable development', by Salewa Olawoye-Mann, begins with a reminder that the United Nations Millennium Summit of 2000 suggested eight Millennium Development Goals for countries. Environmental sustainability was one of the eight goals established during this summit. By 2015, these goals were modified to 17 Sustainable Development Goals, four of which were geared towards the climate, environment and sustainability, thereby significantly increasing the urgency in addressing climate change issues. This is particularly important for an extraction economy like Nigeria, which has struggled with environmental degradation, water and sanitation issues. These environmental issues threaten human health and life expectancy. So, working towards these goals are in Nigeria's best interest, as well as, the global climate interest, argues the author. However, there are many challenges that developing countries face in ensuring environmental sustainability. Some of these challenges include policy implementation and financing. This chapter addresses the challenges of environmental sustainability, and the plans and steps taken by the Central Bank of Nigeria towards addressing these challenges.

Finally, in the last chapter by Lilit Popoyan and Giorgos Galanis, the authors argue that since the Paris Agreement, the debate among researchers and practitioners on the solid role of central banks and financial regulators in supporting a smooth transition from a high- to low-carbon economy has been levitating. Few monetary authorities took a step to incorporate the policies mitigating the climate-related financial risks to their operational radar, creating a rather heterogeneous picture of climate action. This chapter sheds light on the current state-of-the-art debate on the involvement of central banks and financial regulators in green debate and their contribution in aligning the finance sector with sustainable transition roadmaps. The authors conduct their analyses through the lenses of different governance setups of money and financial regulatory authorities, finding that policy inaction is mainly connected to the conflict the integration of climate-related policy could bring to operational mandates. We highlight that the conflict can be less pronounced in a specific policy arrangement than the others respecting Tinbergen's principle.

NOTE

1.   For a survey following a post-Keynesian perspective, see Kappes (2021).

REFERENCES

Bernanke, B.S. (2003), 'Remarks by Governor Ben S. Bernanke', at the Federal Reserve Bank of Dallas Conference on the 'Legacy of Milton and Rose Friedman's *Free to Choose*', Dallas, TX, 24 October, accessed 23 March 2022 at https://www .federalreserve.gov/boarddocs/speeches/2003/20031024/default.htm.

Bernanke, B.S. (2012), 'Five questions about the Federal Reserve and monetary policy', speech at the Economic Club of Indiana, Indianapolis, IN, 1 October, accessed 23 March 2022 at https://www.federalreserve.gov/newsevents/speech/ bernanke20121001a.htm.

Bindseil, U. and P.J. König (2013), 'Basil J. Moore's horizontalists and verticalists: an appraisal 25 years later', *Review of Keynesian Economics*, **1** (4), 383–90.

Borio, C. and P. Disyatat (2010), 'Unconventional monetary policies: an appraisal', *The Manchester School*, **78** (September), 53–89.

Colciago, A., A. Samarina and J. de Haan (2019), 'Central bank policies and income and wealth inequality: a survey', *Journal of Economic Surveys*, **33** (4), 1199–231.

Deutsche Bundesbank (2017), 'The role of banks, non-banks and the central bank in the money creation process', Monthly Report, April, accessed 23 March 2022 at https:// www.bundesbank.de/resource/blob/654284/df66c4444d065a7f519e2ab0c476df58/ mL/2017-04-money-creation-process-data.pdf.

Dodge, D. (2010), '70 years of central banking in Canada', remarks to the Canadian Economic Association, accessed 23 March 2022 at https://www.bankofcanada.ca/ wp-content/uploads/2010/06/dodge.pdf.

Fiebiger, B. and M. Lavoie (2020), 'Helicopter Ben, monetarism, the new Keynesian credit view and loanable funds', *Journal of Economic Issues*, **54** (1), 77–96.

Fontan, C., F. Claveau and P. Dietsch (2018), *Do Central Banks Serve the People?*, Cambridge: Polity Press.

Goodfriend, M. (2007), 'How the world achieved consensus on monetary policy', *Journal of Economic Perspectives*, **21** (4), 47–68.

Goodhart, C. (2011), 'The changing role of central banks', *Financial History Review*, **18** (2), 135–54.

Goodhart, C. (2021), 'What may happen when central banks wake up to more persistent inflation?', VOX EU, Centre for Economic Policy Research, London, 25 October.

Goodhart, C. and R. Lastra (2018), 'Populism and central bank independence', *Open Economies Review*, **29** (1), 49–68.

Ihrig, J., G.C. Weinback and S.A. Wolla (2021), 'Teaching the linkage between the banks and the Fed: RIP money multiplier', Economic Research, Federal Research Bank of St Louis, September, accessed 23 March 2022 at https://research.stlouisfed .org/publications/page1-econ/2021/09/17/teaching-the-linkage-between-banks-and -the-fed-r-i-p-money-multiplier.

Jakab, Z. and M. Kumhof (2018), 'Banks are not intermediaries of loanable funds: facts, theory and evidence', Bank of England Staff Working Paper No. 761, Bank of England, London.

Kaldor, N. (1970), 'The new monetarism', *Lloyds Bank Review*, July, 1–17.

Kappes, S. (2021), 'Monetary policy and personal income distribution: a survey of the empirical literature', *Review of Political Economy*, June, doi:10.1080/09538259 .2021.1943159.

Kent, C. (2018), 'Money – born of credit', remarks at the Reserve Bank's Topical Talks Event for Educators, Sydney, 19 September.

Keynes, M. (1923), *A Tract on Monetary Reform*, London: Macmillan.

Keynes, M. (1936), *The General Theory of Employment, Interest and Money*, London: Macmillan.

Lavoie, M. (1996), 'Monetary policy in an economy with endogenous credit money', in G. Deleplace and E.J. Nell (eds), *Money in Motion: The Post Keynesian and Circulation Approaches*, Basingstoke: Macmillan, pp. 532–45.

Lavoie, M. (2006), 'A post-Keynesian amendment to the new consensus on monetary policy', *Metroeconomica*, **57** (2), 165–92.

McLeay, M., A. Radia and R. Thomas (2014), 'Money creation in the modern economy', *Bank of England Quarterly Bulletin*, Q1, accessed 23 March 2022 at https://www.bankofengland.co.uk/quarterly-bulletin/2014/q1/money-creation-in -the-modern-economy.

Moore, B.J. (1988), *Horizontalists and Verticalists: The Macroeconomics of Credit Money*, Cambridge: Cambridge University Press.

Palley, T. (2006), 'A post-Keynesian framework for monetary policy: why interest rate operating procedures are not enough', in C. Gnos and L.P. Rochon (eds), *Post-Keynesian Principles of Economic Policy*, Cheltenham, UK and Northampton, MA, USA: Edward Elgar Publishing, pp. 78–98.

Robinson, J. (1943), 'The problem of full employment', Workers' Educational Association & Workers' Educational Trade Union Committee, London.

Robinson, J. (1952), *The Rate of Interest and Other Essays*, London: Macmillan.

Robinson, J. (1956), *The Accumulation of Capital*, London: Macmillan.

Rochon, L.P. (1999), *Credit, Money and Production: An Alternative Post-Keynesian Approach*, Cheltenham, UK and Northampton, MA, USA: Edward Elgar Publishing.

Rochon, L.-P. (2022), 'The general ineffectiveness of monetary policy or the weaponization of inflation', in S. Kappes, L.-P. Rochon and G. Vallet (eds), *The Future of Central Banking*, Cheltenham, UK and Northampton, MA, USA: Edward Elgar Publishing, forthcoming.

Romer, C.D. and D.H. Romer (2001), 'Monetary policy and the well-being of the poor', in J. Rabin and G.L. Stevens (eds), *Handbook of Monetary Policy*, London: Routledge, pp. 887–912.

Romer, D. (2000), 'Keynesian macroeconomics without the LM curve', *Journal of Economic Perspectives*, **12** (2), 149–69.

Rudd, J.B. (2022), 'Why do we think that inflation expectations matter for inflation? (And should we?)', *Review of Keynesian Economics*, **10** (1), 25–45.

Setterfield, M. (2004), 'Central banking, stability and macroeconomic outcomes: a comparison of new consensus and post-Keynesian monetary macroeconomics', in M. Lavoie and M. Seccareccia (eds), *Central Banking in the Modern World: Alternative Perspectives*, Cheltenham, UK and Northampton, MA, USA: Edward Elgar Publishing, pp. 35–56.

Skidelsky, R. (2009), *Keynes: The Return of the Master*, London: Allen Lane.

Smithin, J. (1994), *Controversies in Monetary Economics: Ideas, Issues and Policy*, Aldershot, UK and Brookfield, VT, USA: Edward Elgar Publishing.

Storm, S. (2019), 'Summers and the road to Damascus', Institute for New Economic Thinking, New York, 3 September, accessed 23 March 2022 at https://www .ineteconomics.org/perspectives/blog/summers-and-the-road-to-damascus.

Summers, L.H. and A. Stansbury (2019), 'Whither central banking?', Project Syndicate, 23 August, accessed 23 March 2022 at https://www.project-syndicate.org/ commentary/central-bankers-in-jackson-hole-should-admit-impotence-by-lawrence-h -summers-and-anna-stansbury-2-2019-08.

Taylor, J.B. (1993), 'Discretion versus policy rules in practice', Carnegie-Rochester Conference Series on Public Policy, Stanford University, CA, **39**, 195–214.

Taylor, J.B. (2000), 'Teaching modern macroeconomics at the principles level', *American Economic Review*, **90** (2), 90–94.

The Economist (2021), 'Does anyone actually understand inflation?', *The Economist*, 9 October, accessed 23 March 2022 at https://www.economist.com/finance-and -economics/2021/10/09/does-anyone-actually-understand-inflation.

Woodford, M. (2003), *Interest and Prices: Foundations of a Theory of Monetary Policy*, Princeton, NJ: Princeton University Press.

1. Central banks and the zero-carbon transition: an institutional challenge

Robert Guttmann

1. INTRODUCTION

Irrespective of their unique histories and specific institutional characteristics, central banks all over the world share enough in common to allow certain generalizations about them. They typically carry out three strategic roles simultaneously, acting both as the government's bank and the banks' bank while managing their economy's insertion into whatever international monetary system prevails at the time. The particular configuration of policy objectives in pursuit of this triple role has unfolded in distinct historic phases, which most, if not all, central banks have gone through at the same time. As they are about to enter a new phase in their evolution, this time shaped by central banks' incorporation of the climate change challenge, it behooves us to locate where they are right now to identify what kind of institutional challenge they face to deal with this global systemic problem arguably located outside their purview.

2. THE TRIPLE ROLE OF CENTRAL BANKS

Central banks' role as the government's bank dates back to the very origins of central banking. After all, the earliest central banks – Sweden's Sveriges Riksbank (1668), the Bank of England (1694), Banque de France (1800), and De Nederlandsche Banke (1814) – were each set up to help the monarch finance their wars and support their military alliances. In peacetime, for much of the Pax Britannica (1815–1914), this support role was constrained by the prevailing gold-exchange or bimetallic standards limiting the deficit-spending capacity of the state. The collapse of the gold standard in September 1931 opened the way for chronic budget deficits, crystallized in the Keynesian Revolution as put into practice by Roosevelt's New Deal, Hitler's rearmament program, and the social reform program of France's Front Populaire, which central banks helped to finance. Since then, central banks have normalized their institutional support for deficit spending, mostly by means of open-market operations involving purchases of government bonds, while also trying to limit government's proclivities for hidden inflation taxation.

The history of central banks becoming the banks' bank is in many respects even more complex. Many of these institutions started out as commercial banks themselves, but then were afforded exclusive note-issuing powers by the state (as happened, for example, to the Bank of England in the Bank Charter Act of 1844 or the Banque de France in 1848). The long-standing practice of fractional reserve banking had commercial banks accept deposits, set aside only a fraction of those in case depositors wanted their money back, and then loan out the rest to borrowers for interest income. Such capacity for endogenous money creation in acts of lending posited two challenges. One was the integration of private bank money and government-issued currency, most of it in the form of central bank notes, within a payments system that assured automatic convertibility between all domestic money forms. Such payments systems came to be operated by central banks, who were thus empowered to decide what counts as money (or quasi-monies) and what does not. The other was the cyclical behavior of banks, for whom the act of money creation (and credit extension) had become their principal source of income as they turned zero-yielding excess reserves into interest-earning loan assets. Given the recurrent propensity of commercial banks to overextend and thereby trigger paralyzing credit crunches, central banks emerged early on as a "lender of last resort," which saw them lend emergency funds to stricken banks in exchange for acceptable collateral so as to contain such crises.[1] Once commercial banks were no longer constrained by gold reserves, from the early 1930s on, their innately pro-cyclical money-creation activity came to be managed by central banks exercising a variety of "monetary policy" tools (e.g. reserve requirements) in counter-cyclical fashion. Government-funded bank deposit insurance mitigated effectively against bank runs.

The international responsibilities of central banks were well defined and quite limited during the various versions of the gold standard, even after the 1922 Conference of Genoa had allowed direct exchange of currencies for the first time. Freed of the gold standard in 1931, the world's leading central banks engaged in competitive devaluations on top of trade wars until they negotiated a truce in the Tripartite Agreement of 1936.[2] Under the Bretton Woods system (1945–1971), central banks collectively administered a global payments system after the return to currency convertibility in 1958, then formed the Group of Ten in 1962 under the auspices of the Bank for International Settlements (BIS) to cooperate in maintaining an increasingly wobbly system of fixed exchange rates, which fell apart in the early 1970s. Since the Jamaica Agreement of 1976, central banks have chosen the preferred regime for their currencies' exchange rates – from free float to hard peg – while also managing the rapidly evolving trans-national offshore banking system, which has made much of the regulatory framework for banking on a national scale redundant because it is so easily bypassed. Since 1988, central banks have cooperated, once again under the auspices of the BIS serving as a sort of central bank of central banks, to regulate this parallel global banking system (via the Basel Accord of 1988, the two-part Basel II agreements of 1996/2004, and Basel III of 2010–2019). Today's multi-layered monetary pyramid of currencies with different degrees of international acceptance and circulation also projects a hierarchy of central banks whose relative standing in that order will determine their respective room to maneuver with regard to exchange-rate management, accumulation of foreign-exchange reserves, space for capital controls and/or exchange controls, and domestic policy priorities. This hierarchy is changing in the face of new challenges, such as climate change, while an evolving multi-polar world order moves us away from unipolar US dominance.

3.   CENTRAL BANKING IN HISTORIC PERSPECTIVE

We can identify distinct historic chapters in the evolution of central banking, with the transition from one chapter to the next marked by crisis and chaos. I have consciously chosen the expression of "central banking" here, as opposed to "central banks," to indicate the presence of shared characteristics and practices being more determinant than whatever institutional differences may have prevailed during this or that period to set them apart. As already indicated previously (in section 1), central banking had a fairly narrow focus during the gold standard whose convertibility restrictions and specie-flow adjustment mechanisms defined most aspects of money and banking as a matter of automaticity. The collapse of the gold standard in 1931, in the midst of a global depression and wave after wave of bank failures, necessitated fundamental reform of the monetary regime, first implemented by the US at the onset of Roosevelt's New Deal (1933–1935), subsequently extended into the international realm following the Bretton Woods Conference of July 1944, and copied across the board by America's allies after the end of World War II in 1945.[3,4]

3.1   The Post-War Regime of Nationally Administered Credit-Money

The post-war monetary regime emerging from these reforms, replacing the rigid gold standard with an elastic currency whose supply responded directly to the public's funding needs, was tightly regulated. Some of these regulations concerned the financial structure, dampening competition between banks to quell risk-taking (e.g. geographic branching restrictions) and separating banks from other financial institutions such as thrifts, investment banks, and mutual funds. In some countries (e.g. the United States) commercial banks were kept at arm's length from the nation's capital markets by regulatory design, while in other countries banks repressed stock and bond markets to maintain their direct influence over industry (e.g. Germany's *Hausbank* system, Japan's *Keiretsu* system). The other regulatory thrust concerned the prices of money, committing central banks to keeping interest rates low and exchange rates fixed. They were also busy perfecting counter-cyclical monetary policy and using their daily practice of open-market operations to link their policy realm to fiscal policy for an integrated macro-stabilization "policy mix" in compliance with domestic full-employment mandates (Employment Act of 1946). Some central banks, such as the Banque de France and the Bank of Japan, were given additional means to impact credit allocation.[5] These well-regulated banking systems, which were spared incidences of instability for more than a quarter of a century, supported continuous debt financing of chronic budget deficits in support of the "welfare state," mass production technologies, and ambitious middle-class consumption norms – the key pillars of the post-war boom. Internationally, within the context of the US-led Bretton Woods system, American capital exports combined with the dollar's overvaluation to spur export-led growth in Germany, Japan, and other industrial nations.

The post-war boom gave way to a new kind of structural crisis combining slow growth and intensifying inflation of the "cost-push" kind that dominated the 1970s. There was a certain complexity to this stagflation crisis, rooted as it was in a nominal accumulation process of "paper" profits (derived from historic-cost accounting) and redistributive gains from hiking prices earlier and more aggressively than others. At the center of this process was central bank accommodation of accelerated money creation boosted by banks' access to new money-market instruments as sources of funds and the growing scale of their offshore operations in the so-called "Eurocurrency markets." Central banks were thus locked into an inflationary process, intermittently disrupted whenever the actual inflation rate shot above interest-rate ceilings to prompt pullbacks by savers and lenders facing negative "real" interest-rate losses. The stagflation crisis was thus marked by increasingly intense credit crunches (1969–1970, 1973–1975, 1979–1980, 1981–1982), compounded on a global scale by turmoil in currency and commodity markets.[6] Just as much as supposedly counter-cyclical Keynesian macro-economic policy turned into a confusing zig-zag in the face of simultaneously rising inflation and unemployment, so the post-war monetary regime came apart at the seams in the thralls of steadily worsening financial instability. Fixed exchange rates broke down in March 1973. Capital and exchange controls began to be phased out in 1974. The emergence of money-market funds in 1975 triggered massive disintermediation out of the banking system, illustrating the futility of interest-rate ceilings during a period of rising inflation rates and the obsolescence of outdated financial-structure regulations that were ultimately reformed after

1989. The Jamaica Accords of 1976 ratified the post-Bretton-Woods dollar standard, giving central banks all over the world guidance as to determining their exchange-rate regime vis-à-vis the normally freely floating US dollar as a vehicle currency. Interest rates were deregulated starting in October 1979. Ultimately it was up to the central banks, starting with America's Federal Reserve (the Fed), to squeeze inflationary pressures out of the domestic economy through sky-high interest rates, an inverted yield curve, and even selective credit controls at the expense of a steep double-dip recession during the early 1980s.

3.2   The Reign of Finance-Led Capitalism

Such systematic dismantling of all of its post-war pillars left the monetary regime open to transformation, a process moved along swiftly during the 1980s by an unprecedented wave of financial innovation and shaped by the conservative counter-revolution against Keynesianism that found its policy outlet during the Thatcher/Reagan years. Globally speaking, this shift in thinking has been referred to as "neo-liberal" for its emphasis on returning to the 19th-century ideas of economic liberalism, free-market capitalism, deregulation, and a limited role for government, albeit given a modern mantle with a series of theoretical upgrades reshaping the economics profession in the 1980s.[7] Conservatives also favored fixed rules for economic policy, such as balanced budgets or slow and steady money-supply growth, to reduce the room for discretionary policy-making by governments. A major crisis, the LDC debt crisis (1982–1987), helped spread neo-liberal policy prescriptions across the globe through the so-called "Washington Consensus" of pro-market and fiscal-austerity reforms imposed by the US Treasury–International Monetary Fund (IMF)–World Bank troika on heavily indebted governments in developing countries as a condition for bail-out assistance and eventual debt restructuring.

One great beneficiary of the emerging neo-liberal order were financial institutions and markets, as evidenced by a seemingly irresistible "financialization" process combining a rapidly growing finance sector, increasing presence of financial assets and liabilities on the balance sheets of non-financial actors, and growing shares of the national income pie going to capital income (interest, dividends, capital gains). Financial globalization, fueled by an explosion of cross-border portfolio investments and speculative activity, made it possible for now fully deregulated banks to turn themselves into the equivalent of financial supermarkets seeking a worldwide presence ("universal banks") and for financial markets or networks to become increasingly intertwined. This was the era of finance-led capitalism.[8] Its growth dynamic, global in scope and integrating scores of emerging-market economies and transition economies into the capitalist system for the first time, came to depend increasingly on chronically large US trade deficits absorbing a large portion of the rest of the world's surpluses. The US economy was supercharged by three consecutive speculative bubbles – the stock-market boom of the corporate "raiders," 1983–1987; the "dot-com" boom, 1996–2000; and the housing bubble, 2001–2007. These asset bubbles generated considerable wealth effects, which turned US households into "buyers of the last resort" for products across the globe.[9] Americans' excess spending supported the export-led growth strategies of many advanced capitalist economies (e.g. Germany, Japan) and emerging-market economies (e.g. China, Brazil), which recycled large portions of their surpluses back into the US for automatic financing of its private-, public-, and external-sector deficits so that these could continue unabated. This global growth pattern collapsed in 2007 when the US housing bubble burst and in its wake triggered the Great Financial Crisis (GFC) of 2007–2008.

One implication of this finance-driven and US-centered global growth pattern was its success in coping with a demographic and socio-economic revolution that has no precedent. During the 1980s and early 1990s, half of the world's population, about 3 billion people, entered the capitalist world economy from which they had been excluded up to that point. We are talking here not only about the transformation of communist command economies into market-based economies, following the collapse of the Soviet Union in 1991. We are also talking about other heavily state-directed single-party regimes (e.g. Mexico, Brazil, India, Malaysia, Indonesia) whose post-colonial import-substitution strategies of industrialization, initially quite successful, had atrophied into the LDC crisis of the 1980s, in the wake of which they had to undertake fundamental pro-market reforms under the direction of the aforementioned "Washington Consensus." This success, which ultimately lifted billions from poverty to middle-class status, came with a heavy price. Rapid economic growth, insatiable energy demand met by coal and oil, spectacular growth of transportation, unfettered urbanization, and intensive agriculture all added to greenhouse gas emissions, whose explosive growth has brought us to the brink of environmental disaster in a generation's time.[10]

The role of central banks during the era of finance-led capitalism was tightly circumscribed, very much in response to their ultimately counter-productive participation in the stagflation dynamic of the 1970s and shaped by the prevailing neo-liberal prescriptions dominating the discourse at the time. We can summarize the following three characteristics of central banking during that era as widely shared practice:

(i)   For one, most central bankers made price stability their over-riding policy objective, in reaction to the traumatic experience of a dozen years of accelerating inflation (1968–1980). Toward that objective, central banks all over the world, irrespective of the income level of the economies they oversee (from Ghana to the United States), have adopted inflation targeting. This practice started with the Reserve Bank of New Zealand in 1990, and most leading central banks (the Fed, the European Central Bank (ECB), the Bank of England, the Bank of Japan) have opted for a 2 percent target.

(ii)   In pursuit of such explicit inflation targets, central banks have focused on moving short-term interest rates under their control – the rate they charge for loans to reserve-deficient banks as the ceiling rate, the rate they offer banks on their reserve deposits as the floor rate, and the domestic inter-bank rate at which banks with excess reserves loan those out to banks with reserve deficiencies in the middle of the band. That inter-bank rate is targeted, and such target is maintained by open-market operations for which the actual inter-bank rate relative to the target rate serves as a signal. If, for example, the actual inter-bank rate threatens to push above the target, indicating a scarcity of reserves relative to demand, the central bank will buy securities to add reserves into the system and so push the rate back toward the target. Regular target-rate adjustments, at the heart of monetary policy conduct during that period, followed the so-called "Taylor Rule," which most central banks started paying attention to during the 1990s. This reaction function replaced targeting monetary aggregates, which used to be the monetary policy mantra following the Monetarists' Quantity Rule. The latter policy rule was rendered less practical by incessant innovation with regard to near-money and quasi-money forms since the late 1970s and more unstable velocity of money from the first half of the 1980s on.[11]

(iii)   During the heyday of finance-led capitalism, a lot of emphasis was placed on the supposed "independence" of the central bank from the rest of the government, a reaction to the rather abysmal performance of central bankers during the inflation-prone 1970s when they were often seen to succumb to pressure from politicians following a "political business cycle" to secure re-election and/or hidden inflation tax benefits. Renewed calls for independence, often followed by concrete administrative steps in that direction, were thus seen as a prerequisite for restoring central bank credibility. With unelected technocrats now given more power, central bankers stressed decision-making by consensus and also greater accountability by giving the public as well as politicians steadily more information about their choices and decisions. In the process, they came to understand that the central bank's communication strategy had a big impact on shaping the public's expectations, which made a big difference to macro-economic performance.

While these characteristics applied pretty much to most, if not all, central banks, the prevailing dollar-centered international monetary system and its global growth dynamic driven by US asset bubbles and chronic current-account deficits afforded the Fed a position of special importance. There has been an asymmetry concerning the Fed ever since the US central bank gained freedom to pursue counter-cyclical monetary policy in the Treasury-Fed Accord of 1951. On the one hand, the Fed hardly ever lets its monetary policy be shaped by considerations of the USD's dominant world-money role. Exceptions proved the rule, such as Volcker's dramatic interest-rate hike to stop a speculative attack on the dollar in October 1979, the Plaza Agreement of October 1985, or the Louvre Agreement of February 1987 for exchange-rate cooperation with other leading central banks, or offering other central banks currency swap lines in 2008–2009. On the other hand, the Fed's policy moves have often had a dramatic impact on the rest of the world, whose various transmission channels, such as commodity prices, exchange-rate fluctuations, terms-of-trade effects, interest-rate movements and spreads, securities prices, or credit conditions, are all framed institutionally by having the USD as the primary form of world money.[12]

When Alan Greenspan became Fed chair in 1987, he immediately faced a major financial crisis, the stock-market crash of October 1987, to which he responded with a massive dose of monetary policy stimulation, a policy response that he subsequently repeated whenever instances of financial instability threatened to rock the US economy. This so-called "Greenspan Put" became the trigger for the recurrent US asset bubbles driving the global growth dynamic, and whenever such a bubble burst the Fed's sustained push for low interest rates in response set the stage for the next bubble. There was an intense debate within the Fed during the 2000s concerning those bubbles, known as the "lean versus clean" debate, which was ultimately resolved by a change in Fed leadership in 2005. Greenspan, a proponent of letting bubbles run their course unimpeded and then "cleaning up" after them once they had burst, gave way to Ben Bernanke, whose life-long study of financial instability had made him more inclined to "lean" against a bubble heating up. Already during the last year of Greenspan's rule, the Fed had started pushing back against a fast-growing economy driven by rapid housing appreciation, ultimately pushing up the Federal funds (inter-bank target) rate in 17 consecutive quarter-point hikes from 1.25 percent in January 2004 to 5.25 percent in June 2006. Such sustained hiking of interest rates played a key role in setting off the "subprime" crisis in late 2006, which ultimately morphed into the GFC by September 2008, a systemic crisis whose global virulence literally broke the reign of finance-led capitalism.

3.3   Post-Crisis Adjustments

Once the US housing bubble burst during 2007, losses ricocheted through a variety of inter-connected shadow-banking networks and brought down major financial institutions, until the failure of Lehman Brothers in September 2008 triggered a global freeze of money markets from which followed the most intense credit crunch since the Great Depression of the 1930s. Like that crisis, this one too threatened to set off the kind of debt-deflation spiral typically triggered in the wake of systemic financial crises as an avalanche of spending cutbacks, forced asset sales, price declines, and defaults that, if left to run its course, pushes the economy into a depression.[13] And we have had a more recent example reminding us how devastating such deflationary spirals can be and how difficult they are to get out of. We are referring here to Japan's three decades of low growth and falling prices following the spectacular collapse of a major asset bubble in 1990–1991, which serves as a warning to others. Because the US, the European Union (EU), China and others responded to the GFC of 2008–2009, as Minsky (1986) highlighted, with both "Big Government" (i.e. deficit spending through fiscal stimulus packages) and "Big Bank" (central bank injections of liquidity), they managed to keep the debt-deflation spiral contained to a milder version of "balance sheet recession" followed by a slow-growth pattern of "secular stagnation."[14] They were just about to get globally onto a more solid growth path in the late 2010s when the world was hit by a pandemic necessitating recurrent lockdowns, a deflationary shock like no other in our lifetime. As we bring this crisis behind us in 2022, global recovery could well use a massive worldwide decade-long infrastructure investment program if we are to realize the net-zero-emission targets announced by so many governments for the middle of the century in our struggle against climate change.

Going back to the GFC of 2008–2009 and its complicated aftermath, it has had a very dramatic and lasting impact on the modus operandi of central banks. We need to take note of all the major post-crisis adjustments these institutions have gone through over the last decade in order to pinpoint more precisely where they are today as they are beginning to face the institutional challenge of figuring out their contribution to the global struggle against climate change.

When the 2008 credit crunch hit, central banks lowered interest rates under their control sharply all the way down to zero and then kept it there. Later, key central banks (the ECB in 2014, the Swiss National Bank in 2015, the Bank of Japan in 2016) even moved their floor rate, the rate on reserves banks keep in their accounts with the central bank, into negative territory, typically ranging from −0.1 percent to −0.75 percent, in order to disincentivize banks from hoarding excess reserves rather than loaning them out in support of greater levels of spending. In late 2015 the Fed began to lift its policy rates off the zero bound, pushing the Federal funds rate all the way to 2.4 percent in February 2019, before lowering them again. When the pandemic hit the US in March 2020, the Fed very swiftly moved them back to zero and has since committed to keeping them there for an extended period of time (by announcing a change in its inflation-target formula toward period averaging, which postpones any future tightening moves until inflation has accelerated beyond 2 percent). Other major central banks are similarly committed to keeping their policy rates at the zero bound until post-pandemic recovery is well underway.

A major new development in central banking following the GFC has been so-called "quantitative easing" (QE), which involves sizeable asset-purchase programs. What was initially conceived as an extraordinary cyclical policy tool, in late 2008 when the Fed started its first QE package (QE1) by buying $500 billion in mortgage-backed securities and $100 billion in other debt, has since become structural as central banks all over the world launch QE packages on a continuous basis. Between 2008 and 2015 the Fed, for example, engaged in four different QE packages, which together ballooned the size of its balance sheet fivefold from $900 billion to $4.5 trillion. Facing its own systemic eurozone crisis during the first half of the 2010s, the ECB's QE programs more than doubled its size to €4.65 trillion between 2015 and 2018. Such QE has several purposes. Pumping lots of liquidity into the banking system overcomes a liquidity trap typical in the aftermath of a systemic financial crisis, when banks keep lots of excess reserves on their books instead of loaning them out. Having central banks buy massive quantities of government bonds pushes up their prices, which relate inversely to yields, thus lowering long-term interest rates (to the point where we now have the unprecedented situation of negative market yields for about a quarter of the world's outstanding top-rated government bonds). Lower long-term rates have boosted bond as well as stock markets and, to a lesser extent, should also help sustain productive investment activity. To the extent that QE programs have gone beyond just government bonds, central banks can support other segments of their capital markets. This has become especially significant since the March 2020 lockdowns in response to which leading central banks, such as the Fed and the ECB, have extended their massive asset purchases to corporate bonds and municipal bonds (increasing the Fed's balance sheet, for example, from $4.3 trillion in March 2020 to nearly $7.2 trillion at the end of 2020).[15] Such widening and deepening of QE is of crucial significance for the upcoming zero-carbon transition, whose massive infrastructure investment spending for over a decade (i.e. "Green New Deal") depends greatly on very low long-term interest rates for the long haul, while the asset-purchase programs of central banks could also help boost important sustainable finance products such as "green" bonds in support of this transition.

These QE interventions, as "unconventional" as they may appear, can be justified by the new "financial stability" mandate central banks acquired in response to the GFC.[16] In pursuit of that new mandate, central banks have also expanded their emergency lending facilities considerably. During the GFC of 2008–2009 the Fed, for example, used its extraordinary Section 13(3) powers for the first time ever to extend credit "under unusual and exigent circumstances" to anyone in need. It set up over a dozen lending facilities in support of impaired financial institutions (e.g. money-market funds), instruments (e.g. commercial paper), and markets (e.g. mortgage-backed securities), which were highly targeted and managed to repair much of the damage in these specific niches of the financial system.[17] This crisis-induced extension of credit facilities moved central banks beyond their traditional crisis-management function of lender of last resort to become "market maker of last resort."

During the pandemic-induced lockdown of 2020, the cash-flow disruption was so massive and immediate that huge numbers of actors needed government support to sustain a modicum of cash inflows needed for day-to-day survival. While much of that income-support assistance came from fiscal relief packages, such as the $2.3 trillion CARES Act passed by US Congress in March 2020, various central banks were authorized for the first time to buy corporate bonds (e.g. the Fed, the Bank of England, the Bank of Canada, Sveriges Riksbank). Riskier lending to smaller businesses was put into the hands of specialized government agencies (e.g. small-business administration in the US) or government-sponsored development banks (e.g. Germany's KfW, the British Business Bank). The Fed, however, gained authority (and first-loss support from the US Treasury) in the CARES Act to offer direct lending facilities to small- and medium-sized businesses, municipalities, and even not-for-profit organizations (e.g. Main Street Lending Facilities) as backstops to private credit markets and commercial bank lending.[18]

It is worth noting that these massive central bank interventions, pumping literally trillions into the financial system, have helped bond and stock markets recover spectacularly from their initial lockdown-induced crash in the March to May 2020 period, which has greatly benefited financial investors, the already well-to-do, while large numbers of lower- and middle-class households have suffered significant income losses from the pandemic. Even though governments all over the world have given various types of income-support assistance to households and businesses, those have not fully compensated for the income destruction from shutting down economic activity, especially not during the subsequent waves of infection, and they were ultimately dwarfed by the benefits accruing to the wealthy from the central banks' support of financial markets. The asymmetric fiscal-monetary policy mix in place since the GFC of 2008–2009, and now rendered even more pronounced by the pandemic, barely contains deflationary pressures in the "real" economy of production and employment while feeding asset inflation in financial markets. We thus need fiscal policy to catch up with monetary policy for a better balance, including a return to more progressive taxation. Luckily, the zero-carbon transition, involving a large-scale infrastructure investment program stretching for over a decade, offers us a chance for such policy-mix correction as it focuses on a fairly massive and sustained amount of private–public spending aimed directly at energy efficiency, technological advances, productivity gains, and job creation.

4.   THE RE-REGULATION OF FINANCE

The 2008–2009 crisis also led to a significant effort of providing the financial system with a new regulatory framework. One dimension of that global effort was the decade-long implementation of the so-called "Basel III agreement" (2010), which has subjected banks to (a) much stronger minimum capitalization requirements as protection against loss-induced insolvency, (b) liquidity cushions to avoid illiquidity in the face of money-market disruptions or bank runs, and (c) leverage caps limiting the overall size of individual banks. The other thrust consisted of broader domestic regulatory reform, which followed similar principles in the United States (Dodd–Frank Wall Street Reform and Consumer Protection Act of 2010), the United Kingdom (Banking Reform Act of 2013), and the EU (various directives).[19] These focused on shadow banking, financial market resilience, resolution authority for failing banks, systemic risk management (i.e. macro-prudential regulation), and structure regulations separating commercial banks from riskier financial activities.

4.1   New Supervisory and Regulatory Responsibilities

One consequence of this re-regulation effort is that central banks have gained more responsibilities for regulating and supervising their country's banking system. While banking regulation/supervision had been typically kept separate from central banks so that those could focus on monetary policy alone during the neo-liberal period of finance-led capitalism, this institutional division of labor came apart during the GFC of 2008–2009. In the course of that crisis central banks were surprised by the wave of financial instability hitting them from a hitherto hidden corner of the financial system, the shadow-banking system. They were overwhelmed by the systemic nature of that crisis tearing apart a tightly interwoven web of inter-connected markets and institutions. They were ultimately obliged to undertake major rescue operations, spending billions to save banks threatened by failure. Under the Dodd–Frank Act of 2010 the Fed gained additional supervisory powers over large banks and non-bank financial institutions (e.g. insurance companies) deemed systemically important. The Single Supervisory Mechanism, implemented in 2013 as the first of three pillars of post-crisis regulatory reform in the eurozone known as the banking union, made the ECB the central prudential supervisor of financial institutions in the union.

That same year, the UK replaced its independent banking regulator, the Financial Services Authority, with a new regulatory agency known as the Prudential Regulation Authority (PRA), which operates under the auspices of the Bank of England as the regulator of banks and insurers. We could go on with other examples of supervisory reform involving central banks, but instead want to stress that post-crisis reforms have more generally also imposed many more information disclosure requirements beyond banks across the finance sector, including hedge funds, broker-dealers, credit rating agencies, asset managers, money-market mutual funds, and special-purpose vehicles to which central banks have access. It can be assumed, as we shall discuss further below, that climate-related financial disclosure standards being prepared worldwide for imminent implementation, probably by 2023, will therefore also fall under the domain of central banks.[20]

Among their newly gained supervisory and regulatory powers, central banks were charged with paying special attention to the "too-big-to-fail" banks and non-bank financial institutions, which they are asked to classify as such in terms of "systemically important financial institution" (SIFI), "systemically important bank" (SIB), or "global systemically important bank" (G-SIB). Those G-SIBs, SIBs, and SIFIs are subject to higher capital requirements under Basel III. They are also subject to more intense supervision and more frequent as well as stringent examinations. They have to follow special crisis-management procedures, such as preparing "living wills" (US) or issuing a certain amount of "contingent convertibles" debt, which converts automatically into equity under predetermined conditions of crisis. Most importantly, these systemically important banks are regularly subjected to so-called "stress tests," which were put in place following the 2008 crisis when many banks were found to have been severely undercapitalized relative to the risks they were carrying on their balance sheets. Such stress tests involve hypothetical crisis scenarios, specified by their central bank in question in terms of various types of shocks (e.g. financial market crash, deep economic recession, natural disaster), to see whether the bank concerned would have enough capital on hand to absorb the losses arising from such a scenario without going under. The stress test analysis is usually conducted by both the banks' risk-management team and the central bank, the findings are published, and any deficiencies identified must be corrected in accordance with central bank recommendations. Central banks are currently preparing so-called "climate stress tests," which would examine bank resilience in the face of climate change shocks and losses, an innovation we will discuss further below.

4.2   Systemic Risks and Macro-Prudential Regulation

The elevated focus on systemically important financial institutions is part of a broader mission rooted in the new "financial stability" mandate that central banks assumed after the GFC of 2008–2009 – the timely identification and containment of systemic risks prone to destabilize the entire system. Systemic risk, as the GFC proved in dramatic fashion, is more than the "sum of its parts"; in other words, it is more than the summation of the individual idiosyncratic risks in the system. It has its own cumulative dynamic thanks to interconnections and panic reactions, which can bring down the entire system or at least an entire market. There is typically a disruptive trigger event with strong contagion potential, such as the failure of "too-big-to-fail" institutions, which then spreads instability through the entire system. System-wide desta-bilizers following the trigger event may involve bank panics, banking crises due to falling asset prices, flaws in the system's financial architecture (e.g. the special-purpose vehicles at the heart of the pre-2008 shadow-banking system in the United States), foreign-exchange mismatches in the banking system (the "original sin"), behavioral effects from so-called "Knightian uncertainty" indicating completely unexpected events (e.g. Brexit), or "fat-tail" events indi-cating an irregularly high probability of catastrophic events (a characterization quite applicable to climate change). Over the last decade there has been a con-centrated effort by financial economists to model systemic risk in a variety of ways, bringing forth such measures or models as SRISK and CoVaR. These are proxies for major trouble brewing to leave banks seriously undercapital-ized and as such better than nothing, but they do not capture the uniqueness and complexity of the kinds of zig-zag sequences of ruptures and negative feedback loops typifying once-in-a-lifetime systemic crises. The conceptual limits and predictive quality of these systemic-risk models and measures are bound to become a matter of far more reflection when facing systemic crisis brought about by climate change.[21]

The renewed concern with systemic risk, at the heart of their post-crisis commitment to safeguarding financial stability, has generally involved giving central banks a whole new institutional infrastructure for that purpose. Some examples are worth mentioning here:

Dodd–Frank set up the Financial Stability Oversight Council (FSOC), which combines all the major US financial regulators under one umbrella (the Fed, Federal Deposit Insurance Corporation, Comptroller of Currency, Securities Exchange Commission, Commodity Futures Trading Commission, and Consumer Financial Protection Bureau) and meets quarterly under the auspices of the US Treasury to identify risks to financial stability, respond to emerging threats, and promote market discipline. FSOC has the power to require extensive reporting from banks and non-bank financial institutions about their financial condition, threat perceptions, risk-management controls, and third-party interactions. Dodd–Frank also set up the Office of Financial Research (OFR, financialresearch.gov) to help FSOC identify emerging systemic risks.

From 2009 onwards the Bank of England has published biannual Systemic Risk Surveys to examine how risk managers and market participants view risks and financial stability. In 2010 the Bank of England gained a new body, the Financial Policy Committee (FPC), to identify sources of systemic risk and then carry out macro-prudential policy for its containment. In that endeavor it is helped by various Bank of England teams, notably its Financial Market Infrastructure (FMI) and Financial Stability Strategy and Risk (FSSR).

In 2010 the European Systemic Risk Board (ESRB) was set up very much with the same mission as the UK's FPC, namely to identify systemic risks and carry out macro-prudential policy, and also with a similar structure to the US's FSOC, as an umbrella organization combining central banks (in this case the ECB and national central banks of the entire EU), the European Banking Authority (EBA), the European Insurance and Occupational Pensions Authority (EIOPA), and the European Securities Markets Authority (ESMA).

These institutional adjustments, coupled with the focus on systemic risks, aim to provide central banks with the toolkit for macro-prudential regulation. That relatively recent dimension of central bank activity focuses on containing the build-up of systemic risks and reducing the macro-economic costs of financial instability. When systemic financial crises hit, they impose enormous costs in terms of lost output and income not just during the crisis-induced downturn but also subsequently because of typically slow and uneven recoveries following such a crisis. Better, then, to avoid such crises from arising in the first place. The GFC of 2008–2009 has been a watershed event in this regard, fostering a global commitment to macro-prudential intervention capacity for central banks, which had already begun to be built in countries hit earlier by major financial crises such as the Asian crisis of 1997–1998 (e.g. the Bank of Korea, the Bank of Thailand).[22]

At the heart of macro-prudential regulation or policy are the measures forming the core of Basel III, notably counter-cyclical capital buffers, liquidity cushions for crisis periods characterized by flight-to-safety cash outflows as well as stable long-term funding structures matching liquid liabilities with appropriately liquid assets, and leverage caps limiting the amount of debt relative to capital. In a similar vein, central banks, such as the Bank of England, have also already used loan-to-value ratio limitations to slow down the use of debt feeding potential asset bubbles. Other counter-cyclical restraints, such as reserve requirements, margin requirements restricting the use of debt in financial markets, and haircuts applied to collateral in repurchasing agreements or other funding arrangements, are also conceivably effective. Central banks are thinking of going beyond individual stress tests to system-wide stress tests to identify vulnerable linkages and points of pressure. We can also imagine the use of selective credit controls applied to certain types of funding and/or limiting credit access for certain sectors of the economy. While largely unspecified, the powers of central banks when it comes to implementing macro-prudential regulation are potentially enormous.[23] Given its scope, this policy tool may emerge as crucially important when applied to the zero-carbon transition and its massive reallocation of capital.

5.   CENTRAL BANKING AND CLIMATE CHANGE

We have made repeated reference to post-crisis changes in the modus operandi of central banks bearing a certain relevance for addressing the challenge of climate change. While we still have a few climate change deniers in our midst (especially in the United States), worrisome meteorological trends, extreme-weather events, and indications of high-cost environmental damage from the already accumulated stock of greenhouse gases (GHGs) in the atmosphere in terms of melting sea ice, disappearing glaciers, dying coral reefs, shrinking fish stocks, rising sea levels, devastating wildfires, accelerating desertification, and so much more are finally creating a certain sense of urgency that the problem must be addressed forthwith.

Dealing with this issue requires an industrial revolution, generally referred to as zero-carbon transition, which reduces GHG emissions to a low-enough ("net-zero") level that they can be absorbed by natural carbon sinks (e.g. rainforests) or carbon capture and storage technology yet to be developed. This can be achieved by phasing out fossil fuels (coal, oil, natural gas) as an energy source in favor of renewables (e.g. solar, wind, hydro), improving energy efficiency, installing smart electricity grids, replacing gasoline cars with electric cars, transforming transportation (e.g. trucks, shipping, aviation), promoting climate-friendly agriculture, expanding recycling, improving waste management, retrofitting buildings, altering industrial processes, and focusing on Scope 3 emissions accruing beyond the emitter's boundaries.

Those objectives necessitate a large-scale private–public infrastructure investment program stretching at least over a decade to de-carbonize the economy. There is also the challenge of putting an adequate price on carbon, whether by imposing a carbon tax on high-emission products and processes or by setting up cap-and-trade markets for tradeable emissions permits, in order to provide appropriate market signals for the needed redeployment from high-emissions "brown" assets (e.g. oil and gas) to low- or zero-emissions "green" assets (e.g. solar panels, wind turbines). Climate change, a global phenomenon, represents a distributional challenge as well, inasmuch as many of the most severely affected areas are poorer and less responsible for the GHG emissions stock in the atmosphere. Those countries need, and deserve, help from lesser-affected, richer regions, which have contributed disproportionately to the problem. Finally, we also need to launch a massive global research and development effort to advance technologies that may help us fight climate change, with results widely shared in knowledge commons or open-source arrangements of shared access and use.[24]

None of this seems at first sight to have much to do with finance, let alone central banks. Most of these objectives defining the low-carbon transition will in effect involve all kinds of other government institutions in tandem with corporations and non-profit non-governmental institutions. However, a closer look at the challenge ahead will reveal a considerable role for finance, which central banks can help move along decisively. The Paris Climate Agreement of December 2015, which set up an institutional framework for dealing with the problem on a global scale to keep the cumulative temperature increase to below 2°C, and preferably closer to 1.5°C, above pre-industrial levels, prescribes an explicit role for finance. Its Article 2.1c included a commitment to "making finance flows consistent with a pathway towards low greenhouse gas emissions and climate-resilient development." In the years since passing this path-breaking international accord, we have seen the emergence of several tracks along which finance may help address the challenge of climate change, some of which will have direct implications for the practices of central banks.

5.1 Climate Change as a Source of Risk

In September 2015, in the run-up to the Paris COP21 conference passing the global climate deal, Bank of England governor Mark Carney addressed British insurers at Lloyd's of London in what came to be known as his "tragedy of the horizon" speech, widely considered the opening shot calling for creating a new specialization in finance linking it to climate change and sustainability. It should be noted here that Carney at that point also headed the Financial Stability Board (FSB), an international body monitoring and making recommendations about the global financial system set up by the G-20 in 2009. Among its responsibilities, and very much thanks to Carney's leadership, the FSB has since then focused intensely on climate finance, setting up a Task Force on Climate-Related Financial Disclosures that reported its recommendations in June 2017 and also publishing a report on the implications of climate change for financial stability published in November 2020.[25]

Mark Carney's September 2015 speech to Britain's insurers emphasized three different climate-related sources of risk to financial stability. Physical risks arise primarily from extreme-weather events, such as storms, flooding, droughts, and wildfires, whose frequency and severity are certain to increase exponentially in the not-too-distant future. We are already seeing this trend take off in frightening fashion. Just looking at 2020, there were 22 billion-dollar weather and climate disaster events in the United States alone, compared to an average of only seven such events per year during the 1980–2020 period and shattering the previous record of 16 such events in 2011 and 2017. Global weather-related economic losses totaled an estimated $232 billion in 2019, which is 17 percent above the 21st-century average.[26] Only a fraction of these are insured, and yet such climate-related losses are already putting a serious strain on property and casualty insurers.

Liability risks refer to the possibility that those suffering climate change losses seek compensation from those they hold responsible. There have already been close to 1,000 climate change-related class action lawsuits filed in 25 countries. The widespread lack of adequate mitigation action so far leaves many climate change culprits deeply exposed to later liability claims from those having been provably hurt by such inaction.

The move to a fully de-carbonized economy, which sooner or later will be an inevitable necessity in the face of an existential threat to the survivability of our species, is itself the source of transition risks. Most of those crystallize around losses from the revaluation of hitherto highly valued assets that become much less valuable all the way to possibly worthless in the transition to a low-carbon economy. Having to write off such "stranded" assets (e.g. oil reserves that can no longer be used) is going to trigger large losses for companies obliged to do so.

All three types of climate-related risks have no precedence, thus come with a lack of data from the past. None follow a Gaussian probability distribution, but instead carry fat-tail risks, which have a potentially devastating impact at low, yet tangibly present probabilities. Worse, these probabilities are likely to rise exponentially as time passes without adequate mitigation action being taken. Carney's emphasis on the "tragedy of the horizon" pointed to this time consistency problem inherent in climate change. It is a very long-run problem with exponentially cumulative impact over decades, far beyond the usual short- to medium-term planning horizons of financial markets (one to two years at most) and banks (three to five years as the norm). These features of the climate change problem – the lack of past data, the unbalanced probability distribution, the long time horizon – make traditional risk modeling techniques less than useful. Yet at the same time, the risks associated with climate change and the urgency of doing something about those are both bound to grip every single business or financial institution in a rather existential way, and we are rapidly approaching the threshold of that era descending upon the globe.

5.2   Micro-Prudential Regulation of Climate Change

For individual actors, climate change represents a more or less impactful, if not altogether transformative, change in their operating environment within which the conditions of their daily existence are embedded. While micro-prudential regulation involves typically both firm-level oversight and regulation of financial institutions to make sure their balance sheets can withstand specific shocks, the nature of climate change is such that it threatens greater exposure to qualitatively unprecedented shocks within a steadily degrading operating environment, while requiring in the coming years a series of difficult trade-offs about how best to minimize individual-actor exposure to such long-term deterioration. This triple challenge, going beyond what we have faced so far in terms of individual shocks, requires an appropriately expanded framework of climate-related micro-prudential regulation that many governments are just beginning to put into place.

One crucial effort in this regard concerns implementing the recommendations of the FSB's Task Force on Climate-Related Financial Disclosures (TCFD) with regard to governance, strategy, and risk management, as well as metrics and targets. Including both risks and opportunities (e.g. new markets), the TCFD recommendations cover all sectors, with additional sector-specific guidance for emissions-intense sectors such as energy, transportation, materials, and buildings, as well as agriculture. The proposed disclosure rules focus on financial impact measures for income, cash flows, and balance sheets. Businesses are expected to describe management oversight of climate-related (transition and physical) risks and set out their risk-management processes. They will have to evaluate how their strategy would work in different temperature-rise scenarios. Finally, they would have to assess their progress as measured against targets. The TCFD initiative also provides specific guidelines for financial institutions to account for their exposure to climate-related risks, with particular emphasis on banks, insurance companies, and asset managers (such as mutual funds or pension funds). So far, adoption of TCFD recommendations has been strictly voluntary, with businesses totaling $135 trillion in assets committing to them. Both the Bank of England and the ECB pushed for mandatory adoption of TCFD disclosure rules at the COP26 in Glasgow in November 2021.[27]

Putting climate-related financial disclosure rules in place is just one aspect of a broader effort at business adaptation to the challenge of global warming. Most producers look only at their direct emissions from their own operations and electricity consumption, yet need to go beyond that and also take account of emissions outside their boundaries along the entire corporate value chain of suppliers and customers and the life cycle of their products. These so-called "Scope 3 emissions," much harder to measure, will eventually have to be incorporated in uniform fashion, as put forth in the "Scope 3 Calculation Guidance" of the Greenhouse Gas Protocol (ghgprotocol.org). The Sustainability Accounting Standards Board (SASB), trying to connect businesses and investors on the financial impacts of sustainability, is working on setting international standards for different sectors on how to identify material sustainability-related impacts and the metrics for reporting them.

Companies are expected to announce, if they have not already done so, how they intend to contribute to the zero-carbon transition by specifying ambitious, science-based emission reduction targets (sciencebasedtargets.com). A rapidly growing number of businesses in advanced capitalist economies have in recent years adopted Environmental Social Governance (ESG) criteria combining environmental considerations (e.g. use of renewable energy, waste management, pollution controls), social relationships applying predominantly to the firm's employees (e.g. pay, benefits, workplace policies, training), and good governance practices (e.g. executive compensation, independence of board of directors, stakeholder interests). There is mounting evidence that firms adopting ESG criteria and committing to their full implementation, rather than just pretending to do so as in many examples of "greenwashing," are in the long run more profitable than firms just concerned with their quarter-to-quarter bottom line, which has been standard practice since the mid-1980s. This has not gone unnoticed by institutional investors and asset managers. A rapidly growing number of those have begun to express consistently stronger preferences for ESG-centered firms, starting in the process a possible revolution in corporate governance that will greatly aid the transition to a zero-carbon economy as it approaches take-off.[28]

Central banks, together with other financial regulators, can push for adoption of these climate-related changes in corporate practice and coordinate their "best-practice" standardization across the globe. They can also bear down on banks and non-bank financial institutions (e.g. insurance companies, investment funds) to insist on proper implementation of these practices and develop their own standards of evaluating and managing climate-related impacts. The idea is to give investors, insurers, and lenders appropriate signals based on dependable information on how to price climate-related risks, assess mitigation efforts and their progress, and reallocate capital appropriately, and so put pressure on laggards. In December 2017 a small group of central banks and financial regulators set up the Network for Greening the Financial System (NGFS), under the auspices of the Banque de France, to advance climate finance and determine best-practice standards for its various aspects. In just a little over three years that network has expanded from eight members to 82 members, with even the Fed joining right after the November 2020 election. It is now up to the NGFS to move the various components of climate finance, especially the TCFD's recommendations for climate-related disclosure and the use of ESG criteria, beyond the current birth phase of experimentation and discussion to the point of implementation. It is high time to have a system where every financial decision takes climate change into account.

5.3 Macro-Prudential Regulation of Climate Change

Over the last couple of years there has been a debate within the EU about whether and how best to use bank capital requirements as a regulatory mechanism to encourage speeding up the needed zero-carbon transition. To the extent that climate change represents tangible risks to financial stability, an argument can be made in favor of factoring those climate-related risks into determination of bank capitalization requirements that, after all, have been made proportional to the riskiness of the banks' assets. There seems to be growing sentiment, as recently voiced by Banque de France governor François Villeroy de Galhau and also amply discussed in the Bank of England, in favor of instituting a so-called "brown-penalizing factor." That provision would impose a higher capital requirement on banks for their carbon-intense ("brown") assets, since those carry high sustainability risks as they contribute disproportionately to the problem and are also likely to have to be phased out eventually. The problem is that we do not yet have reliable data about the kinds of risks these brown assets pose over a sufficiently long time horizon. Less obvious is the opposite, namely a "green-supporting factor" instituting lower bank capital requirements for low-carbon ("green") assets such as for loans that are effectively contributing to acceleration of the zero-carbon transition. We have had a bad experience in the past, under Basel II, when allowing banks to lower capital requirements for presumed risk reductions, which are easily abused. It is also not clear to what extent the movement toward green assets comes with lower, rather than greater, risks at this rather early stage in the transition. Both of these objections can be addressed by the planned EU classification system for environmentally sustainable economic activities known as the EU Taxonomy Regulation of June 2020.[29]

Introducing a second macro-prudential policy mechanism in the fight against climate change, both the ECB and the Bank of England have recently, in late 2020, laid out guidelines for climate stress test procedures, which they will initiate over the next year or two. At first conceived as a primarily supervisory exercise, such climate stress tests will be designed to discuss with banks how they are taking account of their exposure to potential physical and transition risks buried in their balance sheets and what they are doing to protect themselves against possible losses associated with eventual actualization of such risks. The exercise aims to force banks now to accelerate their efforts concerning climate risk management and reallocation of their funding supplies. In comparison to the standard bank stress tests that have become widespread practice over the last decade, climate stress tests promise to be much more complex as they posit several uniquely daunting challenges. For one, such climate stress tests cover a very long time horizon, as some of the most important risk sources associated with climate change, such as the transition to a zero-carbon economy or rising sea levels, will surely take decades to unfold. Banks have never before had to think about evolving risks over such a long period. Banks will have to make difficult predictions about how climate change will affect different clients in their asset portfolio, depending on which scenario is to be played out. They will have to figure out how different sectors will adapt to rising temperatures. They will also have to make certain assumptions about climate policies being put into effect in coming years. Given the complexity and high degree of uncertainty involved in climate stress tests, it remains to be seen what kind of regulatory consequences should follow from those tests. Even then, they are bound to have already at this stage potentially valuable information-enriching value, especially as they force serious collective consideration of climate change scenarios and discussion thereof.

But central banks will also want to go beyond the micro-level dimensions of these stress tests focusing on the readiness of individual banks and build a macro-level analytical framework of systemic climate risk triggers affecting the whole financial system, as part of their macro-prudential policy approach in pursuit of their financial stability mandate. This is bound to be a complex and time-consuming exercise, which the NGFS umbrella of central banks and financial regulators has also placed high on its agenda of priorities. In June 2020 the NGFS published stress testing guidance for its members, focusing on different climate stress testing scenarios ranging from an "orderly transition" scenario to a "hot house world" scenario of unmitigated global warming triggering severe to catastrophic climate impacts.[30]

There is still time to pursue an "orderly transition" scenario, which would have relatively limited negative effects on either physical or transition risks. But that window of opportunity is closing rapidly, since we have already seen average temperatures rise by a bit more than 1°C above pre-industrial levels while having barely started the phase-out of fossil fuels. At the same time, it is also reasonable to assume that the worst-case "hot house world" scenario of temperature hikes ≥ 3°C may be avoided to the extent that the world community is finally realizing it will soon have to act in decisive fashion. We are already beginning to understand with growing clarity that prevention of the worst-case "hot house world" scenario by means of mitigation, pushing forward a concerted zero-carbon transition effort, is far more preferable than *ex post* adaptation to a disastrously hot planet. Most likely is therefore some kind of "disorderly" transition scenario where we do not act adequately for quite some time and then scramble to catch up once we realize that our inaction so far will soon have irreversibly disastrous consequences.

In the NGFS's "disorderly transition" scenario, such a shift toward accelerated catching-up action is scheduled to arrive around 2030. It may be far too
late then. We are rapidly approaching various tipping points whereupon the
cumulative emissions pathway shifts into higher gear, whether the melting of
ice caps on both poles pushing up sea levels, the disappearance of glaciers, the
thawing of the tundra's permafrost releasing huge quantities of methane gas,
or the destruction of the rainforest as a carbon sink. As those various environmental catastrophes kick in, they will each trigger serious macro-economic and
financial instability effects, such as unprecedented extreme-weather events
leaving much high-risk property uninsurable, collapsing agricultural yields or
fish stocks pushing up food inflation while hitting the foodstuffs sector, and the
devaluation of "brown" assets imposing large losses on asset-holders such as
pension funds or banks. Central banks, while not principal actors in our global
struggle against climate change, will play an important crisis-management role
in this context. At that point they should have developed climate stress tests
sufficiently to project them onto a system-wide level of crisis scenarios, aided
by new environmental macro-economic modeling such as stock-flow consistent models factoring in different shock scenarios with agent-based modeling of
heterogenous individual actors as their micro-foundations. Central banks tend
to have large resources for pushing this kind of research and modeling work.[31]

As we leave the global pandemic of 2020–2021 behind us and commit to
"building back better," we have an unprecedented opportunity to put in place
ambitious "Green New Deal" infrastructure investment programs. If we miss
this opportunity as our last chance for an "orderly transition" scenario, then
central banks may well be obliged to carry out more far-reaching interventions to direct funds away from "brown" assets and toward "green" assets.
Their considerable macro-prudential policy powers in defense of financial
stability and to contain systemic risks can then be mobilized for that purpose
on a whole new level. The People's Bank of China (PBoC) has already begun
a concerted effort in that direction as part of China's recent commitment to
become a global leader in climate policy, including what the PBoC refers
to as "green finance." Apart from introducing climate policy criteria into its
monetary policy operations, the PBoC has also introduced incentives for banks
to finance "green" activities such as accepting green bank loans as collateral
for refinancings.[32] As the matter of climate policy gains in urgency, central
banks can adopt stronger macro-prudential measures. For example, they could
impose variable asset-based reserve requirements on different types of assets,
higher ones for funding or holding of "brown" assets representing growing
climate-related risks and lower ones when investing in "green" assets primed
to be the growth engines of a more sustainable economy being created in the
wake of the zero-carbon transition these assets help to shape.[33]

5.4   "Greening" Monetary Policy

The most immediate monetary policy support for the zero-carbon transition about to be launched is to have all the leading central banks maintain their current policy stance of keeping interest rates very low, as close as possible to zero, across the entire term structure – including long-term interest rates of 10 years and beyond. Governments and businesses will spend trillions on that transition over more than a decade. Ultra-cheap debt will make this gigantic spending program financially feasible, especially when considering its anticipated productive consequences of job creation, energy efficiency gains, useful new technologies, damage control, and a more sustainable environment. Let us also remember that such ultra-low interest rates will boost corporate investment decisions in favor of climate change mitigation projects with very long time horizons. Regulatory agencies dealing with climate change, such as the US Environmental Protection Agency, are already prescribing so-called "social discount rates" at low levels of, say, 1 or 2 percent (compared to normal market-determined rates usually around 5 to 7 percent) with which to assess "green" investments in order to assure society it is spending enough on zero-carbon transition projects. Bringing the (currently very low) market rate into closer alignment with that regulatory social discount rate will make it easier to "normalize" such projects, even from a financial investor's perspective.

In that regard, it is also helpful that central banks, in the wake of the pandemic-induced double-dip recession of 2020–2021, have committed to keeping interest rates at very low levels for a long period of time, at least for a couple of years into recovery. For example, in August 2020 the Fed announced that going forward, (a) it would tolerate a considerably lower unemployment rate than in the past before tightening, as long as such a rapid pace of job creation shows no sign of heating up inflation, and (b) it would conceive of its long-run 2 percent inflation target over the entire cycle, which implies higher than 2 percent inflation rates for a few years if and when recovery will have accelerated to the point of above-average growth rates.[34] This dovish shift, much in line with the Fed's dual mandate of "price stability" and "maximum employment," means in effect that the Fed will not raise interest rates from their currently very low levels for years to come. Even the ECB, long focused in excessively hawkish fashion on price stability as its supposedly over-riding if not sole mandate, has recently under its current leader Christine Lagarde recognized that its original constitution gives it a much broader range of policy objectives to pursue, as long as those do not enter into conflict with its primary goal of price stability. The ECB has a legal obligation, as laid out in Article 3 of the 1992 Treaty of European Union ("Maastricht Treaty"), to "support the (European Union's) general economic policies," which Article 3 also clarifies as including, among various goals, full employment, economic and social cohesion, and improvements to the quality of the environment. That also implies ECB support for the EU's December 2019 commitment to "zero net emissions" by 2050 and the launch of a "European Green Deal" to that effect. In February 2020 Christine Lagarde declared climate change a central issue for the ECB to tackle – it is "mission critical," as she put it – and promised a policy review of how best to approach this institutional challenge.[35]

More recently, in January 2021, the ECB's review concerning its incorporation of climate change as a policy objective has led it to consider a crucial change, namely the abandonment of its long-standing commitment to "market neutrality," which almost all the world's leading central banks, with the exception of the PBoC and perhaps also Sveriges Riksbank, still abide by – at least in their formal declarations. This principle requires central banks to conduct their open-market operations or asset-purchase programs in the wake of QE in such a way as not to distort financial markets by favoring some assets over others and thereby affecting the market price discovery mechanism. A majority of central banks adopted that stance of "market neutrality" during the neo-liberal era as one dimension of their purported "independence" legitimating the supposedly apolitical, purely technocratic nature of their policy-making (see section 3.2).

In effect, central banks have moved away from strict market neutrality ever since they began engaging in unconventional monetary policy a decade ago in post-crisis pursuit of the financial instability mandate. The Bank of Japan, for example, began in 2010 to buy Japanese equities, in the form of equity exchange-traded funds linked to the Nikkei 225 index, which has clearly boosted the market valuation of the firms comprising that index. When the Fed started buying mortgage-backed securities in November 2008, it committed to directing liquidity to the (by then severely damaged) US housing sector. Its Operation Twist of late 2011 and throughout 2012 discriminated between Treasury bills (which it sold) and Treasury bonds (which it bought) to flatten the yield curve. Now central banks, such as the Fed and the ECB, are buying up massive amounts of corporate bonds. Since large firms in carbon-intense sectors, such as the energy giants, utilities, and airlines, issue disproportionate amounts of corporate bonds, they tend to be substantially overrepresented in any "market-neutral" portfolio of asset-purchase programs of any central bank. Moreover, financial markets have failed so far to measure environmental risks properly and factor those into the securities prices correctly. Both biases make "market neutrality" effectively non-neutral when applied to corporate bonds.[36]

By mid-2021, following conclusion of its policy review, the ECB may well join Sveriges Riksbank, the Bank of England, the PBoC, and a few other central banks ready to advance the zero-carbon transition with a monetary policy stance benefiting "green" assets in contradistinction to "brown" assets.

Such explicitly discriminatory policy differentiation will be greatly helped by completion of the EU's aforementioned "taxonomy," which classifies assets according to their respective degrees of climate-friendliness. There are several ways to play out this alignment of monetary policy with climate policy. Asset-purchase programs, especially those involving corporate bonds, can make portfolio adjustments favoring securities issued by firms playing a strategic role in the zero-carbon transition, which would lower their market yield and so make them easier to issue. The opposite may be achieved by cutting back purchases of the bonds of carbon-heavy firms, raising thereby their market yields and rendering them less attractive. Such adjustment will create a significant interest-rate differential between low-carbon and high-carbon assets, the so-called "green spread." Central banks can also help augment the green spread by redirecting bank lending, favoring lending to "green" firms at the expense of "brown" firms. Third, central banks can adjust collateral levels, so-called "haircuts," when conducting their refinancing operations or their reverse repurchasing agreements. They can require higher collateral levels for "brown" assets compared to "green" assets. One advantage of pushing central banks in the direction of pushing the "green spread" gradually toward higher target levels is to signal to financial markets the need for revaluing "brown" assets downward gradually rather than having that carbon bubble burst in one violent and systemically destabilizing shift.[37]

As the zero-carbon transition gathers strength and urgency, we can expect central banks all over the world to get more deeply involved in using their considerable macro-prudential powers and monetary policy tools in support of their countries' climate policies. Of central concern will be facilitating the financing of the socio-economic transformation implied by this transition. Soon enough, we can expect central banks to extend their asset-purchase programs also to so-called "green bonds" issued to finance environmentally friendly projects and certified as such in order to boost that kind of climate-related debt. Governments will launch public development banks, like the EU's European Investment Bank, France's Caisse des Dépôts et Consignations, or Germany's KfW, to play a central role in the zero-carbon transition, and central banks can buy "agency" securities issued by these institutions to make them as "good" as government bonds. The leading central banks, from the Fed (which under the Biden Administration will upgrade its climate policy) to the ECB and PBoC, can expand their bilateral swap facilities with other central banks so that those can help their governments and domestic economic actors access the global sustainable finance platforms, networks, and markets in support of their local de-carbonization programs. Perhaps they will even consider multi-lateral arrangements, as for instance in support of IMF issues of Special Drawing Rights or the Green Climate Fund. No matter the specifics, it is obvious that we are at the threshold of a new era in central banking aligning with the global effort to combat climate change.

NOTES

1. See, in this regard, W. Bagehot (1873) as an early and widely read classic discussing the central bank's role as "lender of last resort" in managing banking crises.
2. The Tripartite Agreement of 1936 has been most recently discussed meaningfully by M. Harris (2021).
3. I have used the notion of "monetary regime" (see R. Guttmann 1997) to denote a specific configuration of monetary policy tools, financial regulations, lender-of-last-resort mechanisms, and international monetary arrangements dominating a particular chapter in the historic evolution of capitalism.
4. Roosevelt's reforms of money, banking, and financial markets included the Emergency Banking Act of 1933, the Glass–Steagall Act of 1933, the Securities Act of 1933, the Securities Exchange Act of 1934, the Gold Reserves Act of 1934, and the Bank Act of 1935.
5. Also argued by G. Epstein (2009), this credit allocation power has been even more pronounced among so-called "developmental central banks" of newly industrializing countries in pursuit of accelerated "catching-up" growth, as was the case in South Korea, China, Thailand, India, Mexico, and Brazil.
6. See A. Wojnilower (1980) and M. Wolfson (1986) for good analyses of those credit crunches. A broader analytical framework for the role of money and banking in the stagflation dynamic is presented in R. Guttmann (1994).
7. Monetarism, supply-side economics, rational expectations, "real" business cycle theory, and dynamic stochastic general equilibrium models come to mind here, on top of major advances in financial economics.
8. The notion of "financialization" had been elaborated at length in G. Krippner (2005), G. Epstein (2005) and E. Hein and T. Van Treeck (2008). For analyses of finance-led capitalism, see E. Hein (2012) and R. Guttmann (2016).
9. It should be noted that Alan Greenspan, former Chair of the Federal Reserve during most of the period of finance-led capitalism, was very interested in the wealth effect(s) arising from asset bubbles, dedicating the only publication he wrote while at the Fed to this topic. See A. Greenspan and J. Kennedy (2007).
10. Annual total global CO_2 emissions from fossil fuels and cement production rose, according to data collected by the Global Carbon Project (see https://ourworldindata.org/co2-and-other-greenhouse-gas-emissions), from 19 billion tons in 1980 to 22.88 billion tons in 1990, 25.17 billion tons in 2000, 33.17 billion tons in 2010, and 36.58 billion tons in 2018.
11. This new central bank reaction function, making interest-rate targeting a positive function of the inflation gap and a negative function of the output gap, was first formulated by J. Taylor (1993). The Quantity Rule, which pushed for steady and slow money-supply growth in line with the economy's natural growth rate, derived from I. Fisher's (1911) Equation of Exchange and was reformulated by the "father" of monetarism, M. Friedman (1956).
12. S. Schulmeister (2000) has demonstrated this asymmetry convincingly in a wonderfully argued chronology of Fed policy impact on the rest of the world during

Bretton Woods, the stagflation turmoil of the 1970s, and the dollar standard of the 1980s and 1990s.

13. The debt-deflation spiral has been powerfully described in detail by I. Fisher (1933) and more recently elaborated in H. Minsky (1982). When it comes to the analysis of financial crisis, H. Minsky's (1986, 1992) "financial instability hypothesis" is still the best point of reference. I would also recommend an earlier and lesser-known contribution, H. Minsky (1964), to help us understand bigger, systemic financial crises like the GFC of 2008–2009.

14. The notion of "balance sheet recession," analyzed by R. Koo (2011), involves lasting cutbacks in spending by consumers and businesses as they try to pay down debts after having suffered sharp declines in asset prices. L. Summers's (2020) "secular stagnation" refers to a situation where inadequate levels of private investment fail to absorb significantly higher levels of private savings to yield persistently insufficient levels of aggregate demand.

15. The Bank of Japan, the only central bank in the world with that capacity, is empowered to buy even equity shares of domestic firms, having in the process acquired a $434 billion portfolio.

16. See C. Goodhart (2011) and B. Bernanke (2012) on the post-crisis inclusion of the financial stability mandate.

17. See R. Guttmann (2012) for more detail on these targeted credit facilities of the Fed and their impact.

18. See P. Mosser (2020) for more detail on these direct lending facilities and other central bank responses to the pandemic's simultaneous demand and supply shocks.

19. Among the key EU directives re-regulating finance is the Alternative Investment Fund Managers Directive (2011), Capital Requirements Directive IV (2013), European Markets Infrastructure Regulation (2014), and Markets in Financial Instruments Directive II (2018).

20. For a good summary of increased regulatory and supervisory powers afforded central banks all over the world, see World Bank (2020). I also recommend Bank for International Settlements (2018) for a broader discussion of post-crisis regulatory and structural changes affecting banks and non-bank financial institutions.

21. F. Allen and E. Carletti (2013) have done a good job trying to define systemic risk. For more on the SRISK measure, see C. Brownlees and R. Engle (2016). The CoVaR model has been presented well by T. Adrian and M. Brunnermeier (2016). A good summary of the decade-long evolution of systemic-risk models and measures can be found in R. Engle (2018).

22. See J.-H. Hahm et al. (2012) and R. Maino and S. Barnett (2013).

23. For general discussions of scope, toolkit, theoretical considerations, and objectives of macro-prudential regulation, see C. Borio (2009).

24. Among the many reports discussing the zero-carbon transition in detail, I recommend in particular Organisation of Economic Co-operation and Development (2017) and D. Victor, F. Geels, and S. Sharpe (2019).

25. See M. Carney (2015) for his "tragedy of the horizon" speech. The two FSB reports on climate finance are TCFD (2017) and Financial Stability Board (2020).

26. See NOAA National Centers for Environmental Information (2021).

27. See L. Hook and M. Arnold (2020).

28. See G. Giese et al. (2019) or K. Spellman and D. Nicholas (2020) for empirical studies confirming that ESG-centered firms perform better than those managed

with traditional shareholder value maximization focus. ESG criteria are also at the heart of the United Nations' Principles for Responsible Investment (unpri. org) to which investors can sign up as explicit commitment.

29. For more on the debate over "green-supporting" and "brown-penalizing" factors for bank capital requirement regulation, see European Commission (2018). Details on the EU taxonomy for sustainable activities can be found in European Commission (2020).

30. For details on the central bank initiatives regarding supervisory climate stress testing, see European Central Bank (2020), Bank of England (2020), and Network for Greening the Financial System (2020).

31. See E. Campiglio et al. (2018) or A. Tooze (2019) on the role of central banks in the shift toward accelerated climate-change mitigation action. S. Battiston et al. (2017) have offered methodologies for system-wide climate stress tests. For more on ongoing efforts in environmental macro-economic modeling, see T. Jackson, P. Victor, and A. Asjad Naqvi (2015), L. Hardt and D. O'Neill (2017), or Y. Dafermos, M. Nikolaidi, and G. Galanis (2018).

32. See SIPA Center on Global Energy Policy (2019) for details on China's and the PBoC's push into "green finance."

33. See T. Palley (2007) for more detail on how asset-based reserve requirements would work.

34. See J. Powell (2020), the Fed chair's speech announcing this dual change in policy stance.

35. European Commission (2019) lays out the European Green Deal. In C. Lagarde (2020), the ECB president announced the central bank's new focus on climate change.

36. S. Jourdan and W. Kalinowski (2019) critically assess the ECB's corporate-bond purchase program and the misalignment of financial markets with the EU's climate policy objectives. See M. Arnold (2020) for the ECB's recent recognition of this challenge.

37. In an important speech, ECB Executive Board member I. Schnabel (2020) presented the central bank's strongest argument so far to abandon its long-standing "market neutrality" as a flawed principle and instead adopt a more aggressive stance in favor of supporting the EU's climate policy. M. Sandbu (2020) explains the implications of such a policy shift in terms of targeting the so-called "green spread."

REFERENCES

Adrian, T. and M. Brunnermeier (2016), "CoVaR," *American Economic Review*, **106**(7), pp. 1705–1741. (DOI: 10.1257/aer.20120555).

Allen, F. and E. Carletti (2013), "What is systemic risk?" *Journal of Money, Credit and Banking*, **45**(1), pp. 121–127. (DOI: 10.1111/jmcb.12038).

Arnold, M. (2020), "ECB to consider using climate risk to steer bond purchases, says Lagarde," *Financial Times*, October 14. (https://www.ft.com/content/f5f34021-795f -47a2-aade-72eb5f455e09?desktop=true&segmentId=d8d3e364-5197-20eb-17cf -2437841d178a#myft:notification:instant-email:content).

Bagehot, W. (1873), *Lombard Street: A Description of the Money Market*, London: Henry King.

Bank for International Settlements (2018), "III. The financial sector: post-crisis adjustment and pressure points," *BIS Annual Economic Report*. (https://www.bis.org/publ/arpdf/ar2018e3.pdf).

Bank of England (2020), *The 2021 Biannual Exploratory Scenario on the Financial Risks from Climate Change*. December. (https://www.bankofengland.co.uk/paper/2019/biennial-exploratory-scenario-climate-change-discussion-paper).

Battiston, S. et al. (2017), "A climate stress test of the financial system," *Nature Climate Change*, **7**(4), pp. 283–288. (https://www.nature.com/articles/nclimate3255#article-info).

Bernanke, B. (2012), "The effects of the Great Recession on central bank doctrine and practice," *The B.E. Journal of Macroeconomics*, **12**(3). (DOI: 10.1515/1935-1690.120).

Borio, C. (2009), "Implementing the macroprudential approach to financial regulation and supervision," Banque de France *Financial Stability Review*, no. 13, pp. 31–41. (https://ideas.repec.org/a/bfr/fisrev/2009134.html).

Brownlees, C. and R. Engle (2016), "SRISK: a conditional capital shortfall measure of systemic risk," *Review of Financial Studies*, **30**(1), pp. 48–79. (DOI: 10.1093/rfs/hhw060).

Campiglio, E. et al. (2018), "Climate change challenges for central banks and financial regulators," *Nature Climate Change*, **8**(6), pp. 462–468. (https://www.nature.com/articles/s41558-018-0175-0).

Carney, M. (2015), "Breaking the tragedy of the horizon: climate change and financial stability," speech at Lloyd's of London, September 29. (https://www.bis.org/review/r151009a.htm).

Dafermos, Y., M. Nikolaidi, and G. Galanis (2018), "Climate change, financial stability and monetary policy," *Ecological Economics*, **153**, pp. 219–234. (DOI: 10.1016/j.ecolecon.2018.05.011).

Engle, R. (2018), "Systemic risk 10 years later," *Annual Review of Financial Economics*, **10**, pp. 125–152. (DOI: 10.1146/annurev-financial-110217-023056).

Epstein, G. (2005), *Financialization and the World Economy*, Cheltenham: Edward Elgar.

Epstein, G. (2009), "Post-war experiences with developmental central banks: the good, the bad and the hopeful," United Nations Conference on Trade and Development *G-24 Discussion Paper Series*, no. 54. (https://unctad.org/system/files/official-document/gdsmdpg2420091_en.pdf).

European Central Bank (2020), *Guide on Climate-Related and Environmental Risks*, November. (https://www.bankingsupervision.europa.eu/ecb/pub/pdf/ssm.202011finalguideonclimate-relatedandenvironmentalrisks~58213f6564.en.pdf).

European Commission (2018), *Final Report 2018 by the High-Level Expert Group on Sustainable Finance: Financing a Sustainable European Economy*. Brussels, January. (https://ec.europa.eu/info/sites/info/files/180131-sustainable-finance-final-report_en.pdf).

European Commission (2019), *A European Green Deal*. Brussels, December. (https://ec.europa.eu/info/strategy/priorities-2019-2024/european-green-deal_en).

European Commission (2020), *EU Taxonomy for Sustainable Activities*. Brussels, June. (https://ec.europa.eu/info/business-economy-euro/banking-and-finance/sustainable-finance/eu-taxonomy-sustainable-activities_en).

Financial Stability Board (2020), *The Implications of Climate Change for Financial Stability*. (https://www.fsb.org/wp-content/uploads/P231120.pdf).

Fisher, I. (1911), *The Purchasing Power of Money*, New York: Macmillan.

Fisher, I. (1933), "The debt-deflation theory of great depressions," *Econometrica*, **1**(4), pp. 337–357.

Friedman, M. (1956), "The quantity theory of money: a restatement," in M. Friedman (ed.), *Studies in the Quantity Theory of Money*, Chicago, IL: University of Chicago Press, pp. 3–21.

Giese, G., L.E. Lee, D. Melas, Z. Nagy, and L. Nishikawa (2019), "Foundations of ESG investing: how ESG affects equity valuation, risk, and performance," *The Journal of Portfolio Management*, **45**(5), pp. 69–83. (DOI: 10.3905/jpm.2019.45.5.069).

Goodhart, C. (2011), "The changing role of central banks," *Financial History Review*, **18**(2), pp. 135–154. (DOI: 10.1017/S0968565011000096).

Greenspan, A. and J. Kennedy (2007), "Sources and uses of equity extracted from homes," Federal Reserve Board *Finance and Economics Discussion Series*, no. 20. (https://www.federalreserve.gov/pubs/feds/2007/200720/200720pap.pdf).

Guttmann, R. (1994), *How Credit-Money Shapes the Economy: The United States in a Global Context*, Armonk, NY: M. E. Sharpe.

Guttmann, R. (1997), *Reforming Money and Finance: Toward a New Monetary Regime*, Armonk, NY: M. E. Sharpe.

Guttmann, R. (2012), "Central banking in a systemic crisis: the Federal Reserve's 'credit-easing'," in L.-P. Rochon and S. Olawoye (eds.), *Monetary Policy and Central Banking: New Directions in Post-Keynesian Theory*, Cheltenham: Edward Elgar, pp. 130–165.

Guttmann, R. (2016), *Finance-Led Capitalism: Shadow Banking, Re-Regulation and the Future of Global Markets*, New York: Palgrave Macmillan.

Hahm, J.-H., F. Mishkin, H.S. Shin, and K. Shin (2012), "Macroprudential policies in open emerging economies," *NBER Working Paper*, no. 17780. (https://www.nber .org/system/files/working_papers/w17780/w17780.pdf).

Hardt, L. and D. O'Neill (2017), "Ecological macroeconomic models: assessing current developments," *Ecological Economics*, **134**, pp. 198–211. (DOI: 10.1016/j. ecolecon.2016.12.027).

Harris, M. (2021), *Monetary War and Peace: London, Washington, Paris and the Tripartite Agreement of 1936*, Cambridge: Cambridge University Press.

Hein, E. (2012), *The Macroeconomics of Finance-Dominated Capitalism – and Its Crisis*, Cheltenham: Edward Elgar.

Hein, E. and T. Van Treeck (2008), "'Financialization' in post-Keynesian models of distribution and growth," *IMK Working Paper*, no. 10.

Hook, L. and M. Arnold (2020), "Carney and Lagarde press for business action on climate change," *Financial Times*, February 27. (https://www.ft.com/content/ b39cf39e-58d3-11ea-abe5-8e03987b7b20).

Jackson, T., P. Victor, and A. Asjad Naqvi (2015), "Towards a stock-flow consistent ecological macroeconomics," *PASSAGE Working Paper*, 15-02. University of Surrey. (https://www.prosperitas.org.uk/assets/passage-wp-15-02.pdf).

Jourdan, S. and W. Kalinowski (2019), "Aligning monetary policy with the EU's climate targets," Veblen Institute *Policy Brief*, April. (https://www.veblen-institute .org/Aligning-Monetary-Policy-with-EU-s-Climate-Targets.html).

Koo, R. (2011), "The world in balance sheet recession: causes, cure, and politics," *Real-World Economic Review*, no. 58. (http://www.paecon.net/PAEReview/issue58/ Koo58.pdf).

Krippner, G. (2005), "The financialization of the American economy," *Socio-Economic Review*, **3**(2), pp. 173–208.

Lagarde, C. (2020), "Climate change and the financial sector," speech at the launch of the COP26 Private Finance Agenda, London, February 27. (https://www.ecb.europa.eu/press/key/date/2020/html/ecb.sp200227_1~5eac0ce39a.en.html).

Maino, R. and S. Barnett (2013), *Macroprudential Frameworks in Asia*. IMF Asia and Pacific Department. (https://www.elibrary.imf.org/doc/IMF087/20143-9781475517194/20143-9781475517194/Other_formats/Source_PDF/20143-9781475572148.pdf).

Minsky, H. (1964), "Longer waves in financial relations: financial factors in the more severe depressions," *American Economic Review*, **54**(3), pp. 324–335.

Minsky, H. (1982), "Debt deflation processes in today's institutional environment," *Banca Nazionale del Lavoro Quarterly Review*, **35**(143), pp. 375–395. (https://digitalcommons.bard.edu/cgi/viewcontent.cgi?article=1228&context=hm_archive).

Minsky, H. (1986), *Stabilizing an Unstable Economy*, New Haven, CT: Yale University Press.

Minsky, H. (1992), "The financial instability hypothesis," The Jerome Levy Economics Institute *Working Paper*, no. 74. (www.levyinstitute.org/pubs/wp74.pdf).

Mosser, P. (2020), "Central bank responses to COVID-19," *Business Economics*, **55**, pp. 191–201. (DOI: 10.1057/s11369-020-00189-x).

Network for Greening the Financial System (2020), *Guide to Climate Scenario Analysis for Central Banks and Supervisors*. June. (https://www.ngfs.net/sites/default/files/medias/documents/ngfs_guide_scenario_analysis_final.pdf).

NOAA National Centers for Environmental Information (2021), U.S. billion-dollar weather and climate disasters. (DOI: 10.25921/stkw-7w73).

Organisation of Economic Co-operation and Development (2017), *Investing in Climate, Investing in Growth*, OECD: Paris. (DOI: 10.1787/9789264273528-en).

Palley, T. (2007), "Asset-based reserve requirements: a response," *Review of Political Economy*, **19**(4), pp. 575–578. (DOI: 10.1080/09538250701622568).

Powell, J. (2020), "New economic challenges and the Fed's monetary policy review," speech at the annual FRB Kansas City symposium, Jackson Hole, Wyoming, August 27. (https://www.federalreserve.gov/newsevents/speech/powell20200827a.htm).

Sandbu, M. (2020), "ECB gets ready to target the 'green spread'," *Financial Times*, October 1. (https://www.ft.com/content/7f73b22c-fded-4be3-a92e-220f443df223?desktop=true&segmentId=d8d3e364-5197-20eb-17cf-2437841d178a#myft:notification:instant-email:content).

Schnabel, I. (2020), "When markets fail – the need for collective action in tackling climate change," speech at the European Sustainable Finance Summit, Frankfurt, September 28. (https://www.ecb.europa.eu/press/key/date/2020/html/ecb.sp200928_1~268b0b672f.en.html).

Schulmeister, S. (2000), "Globalization without global money: the double role of the dollar as national currency and as world currency," *Journal of Post Keynesian Economics*, **22**(3), pp. 365–395.

SIPA Center on Global Energy Policy (2019), *Guide to Chinese Climate Policy: Green Finance*. (https://chineseclimatepolicy.energypolicy.columbia.edu/en/green-finance).

Spellman, K. and D. Nicholas (2020), *ESG Matters*, Institutional Shareholder Services. (https://www.issgovernance.com/library/esg-matters).

Summers, L. (2020), "Accepting the reality of secular stagnation," *Finance and Development*, **57**(1), pp. 17–20. (https://www.imf.org/external/pubs/ft/fandd/2020/03/pdf/larry-summers-on-secular-stagnation.pdf).

Taylor, J. (1993), "Discretion versus policy rules in practice," *Carnegie-Rochester Conference Series on Public Policy*, **39**, pp. 195–214.

TCFD (2017), *Final Report: Recommendations of the Task Force on Climate-Related Financial Disclosures*. (https://www.fsb-tcfd.org).

Tooze, A. (2019), "Why central banks need to step up on global warming," *Foreign Policy*, **233**, pp. 16–23. (https://foreignpolicy.com/2019/07/20/why-central-banks -need-to-step-up-on-global-warming).

Victor, D., F. Geels, and S. Sharpe (2019), *Accelerating the Low Carbon Transition: The Case for Stronger, More Targeted and Coordinated International Action*. Brookings Institution. (https://www.brookings.edu/wp-content/uploads/2019/12/ Coordinatedactionreport.pdf).

Wojnilower, A. (1980), "The central role of credit crunches in recent financial history," *Brookings Papers on Economic Activity*, **2**, pp. 277–339. (https://www.brookings .edu/wp-content/uploads/1980/06/1980b_bpea_wojnilower_friedman_modigliani .pdf).

Wolfson, M. (1986), *Financial Crises: Understanding the Postwar U.S. Experience*, Armonk, NY: M. E. Sharpe.

World Bank (2020), *Global Financial Development Report 2019/2020: Bank Regulation and Supervision a Decade after the Global Financial Crisis*. Washington, DC: World Bank. (https://openknowledge.worldbank.org/handle/10986/32595).

2. Monetary policy, environmental sustainability and the climate emergency

Malcolm Sawyer

1. INTRODUCTION

This chapter focuses on the roles of monetary policy broadly interpreted as policies on interest rates, credit conditions and so on (potentially or actually) conducted by the central bank, which could be related to addressing the climate emergency, environmental degradation, damage to nature and the loss of bio-diversity. The policies considered include those on financial stability, even if in some jurisdictions those policies are in the hands of a separate regulatory agency.

Addressing the climate emergency and achieving environmental sustainability requires, inter alia, major shifts in the structures of economic activity with transitions to a low-carbon economy, including, but not limited to, developments of renewable energy and reductions in energy-intensive activities. Structural transformation requires major shifts between sectors with the decline of some sectors (notably those that are carbon-intensive) and the funding of investments in environmentally friendly production activities. There are, of course, many other policies required for structural transformation, including those that ensure the redeployment of labour and the provision of the relevant skills. The assets of the declining carbon-intensive sectors decline in valuation, producing the phenomenon of 'stranded assets'.

Section 2 briefly reviews the objectives, mandates and policy instruments of central banks to set the background for the discussion of central bank policies in the face of the climate emergency, and the ways in which the objectives and concerns of the central bank would need to be changed. The arguments for an independent central bank are severely undermined when monetary policy and the climate emergency are under the spotlight, and there is a need for co-ordination between monetary policy and fiscal policy; the central banks' operations have to be consistent with the environmental policies of the government. Section 3 addresses issues of taxonomies for environmentally friendly ('green') investments. Section 4 discusses proposals for a 'green' quantitative easing (QE), where it is argued that there is only a very limited contribution from 'green QE' to tackling the climate emergency.

Section 5 moves on to the possibilities of central bank policies in the form of credit controls and guidance. Such policies would seek to encourage and favour provision of funds by banks and financial institutions for environmentally friendly activities.

Central banks have responsibilities with regard to financial stability. Policies designed to reduce carbon-intensive production would tend to reduce the financial value of such production. Many have pointed to the possibilities of financial instability arising from revaluation of 'stranded assets'; that is, assets that lose usefulness and value through transitional shifts. A major concern of central banks and the monetary authorities is financial stability. Section 6 discusses the issues involved, and Section 7 offers some concluding comments.

2. OBJECTIVES AND INSTRUMENTS OF MONETARY POLICY

Monetary policy has often been closely identified with the setting of the key policy interest rate by the central bank, though there have always been other dimensions to monetary policy. The dominant approach to monetary policy in the past three decades or so has been inflation targeting (IT). Under IT, there is a single policy objective set for the 'independent' central bank, namely to achieve an inflation target (sometimes described as price stability). A single policy instrument of the policy interest rate set by the central bank is to be used in pursuit of the single objective. This represented a downgrading or disappearance of other concerns such as the level of employment and exchange rate, which had hitherto featured in the conduct of monetary policy.

Central bank independence means decision-making and implementation by central banks without direct instructions from the government. It also means that monetary policy cannot be co-ordinated with other economic policies pursued by central government. In that context, the main focus of discussion has been around the absence of any co-ordination of monetary and fiscal policies.

The full thrust of IT is often modified in practice. For example, the mandate of the European Central Bank (ECB) is to support the general economic policies in the European Union with a view to contributing to the achievement of its objectives. The Federal Reserve in the USA is given the dual mandate of price stability and maximum sustainable employment.

There are two basic notions underlying IT. First, interest-rate variations along with commitment to an inflation target were viewed as the appropriate and effective way of controlling inflation. Expectations on inflation are argued to be aligned with the inflation target provided that the IT policy is viewed as credible by the public. Second, there is a strong linkage from the policy interest rate to interest rates on borrowing and lending to the level of demand to price inflation.

Within the IT framework, the arguments for 'independence' rested on the idea that an independent central bank would have to make interest-rate decisions based on the economic circumstances and forecasts (on expected inflation) in order to target the inflation rate, and would not take short-term political considerations into effect. The 'conservative' central bank argument viewed the central bank as more focused on inflation than on unemployment, as compared with a democratically elected government. Expectations on inflation would be anchored to the inflation target on the basis that there was a credible commitment by the central bank and government to achieve the inflation target. The significance of this line of argument is that it is closely tied to the control of inflation, the role of credibility and inflationary expectations.

There were significant changes in monetary policy in the decade after the global financial crisis of 2007/09. There have been ultra-low interest rates, negative in some cases, and a tacit dropping of IT. Many central banks have pursued 'unconventional' policies with forms of QE foremost among them. The key feature of QE is that a target is set in terms of the extent of purchases of financial assets by the central bank by agreement between government and central bank.

There have also been shifts towards issues of financial stability, at the macro- and micro-levels, and some responsibilities for financial stability moved to the central bank. In the case of the UK, for example, the mandate of the Bank of England has been extended to cover financial stability, and the Financial Policy Committee was established in 2013, which "identifies, monitors and takes action to remove or reduce systemic risks with a view to protecting and enhancing the resilience of the UK financial system. The FPC also has a secondary objective to support the economic policy of the Government" (https://www.bankofengland.co.uk/financial-stability).

The climate crisis and the transition to a low-carbon economy have implications for financial stability, as discussed below. A remit for the central bank to pursue policies to address financial instability means that the climate crisis has implications for the decision-making of the central bank. The UK Chancellor of the Exchequer set out the 'remit and recommendations for the Financial Policy Committee' in his letter of 3 March 2021 to the Governor of the Bank of England. He wrote of "delivering a financial system which supports and enables the transition to an environmentally sustainable net zero economy by expanding the supply of green finance, and that is resilient to the physical and transition risks that climate change presents". Hence,

> consistent with its objectives the [Financial Policy] Committee should continue to act with a view to building the resilience of the UK financial system to the risks from climate change and support the government's ambition of a greener industry, using innovation and finance to protect our environment and tackle climate change. (Sunak, 2021, p. 2)

Central banks have a role to play in support of strategies on addressing climate emergence and the transition to a low-carbon economy. Campiglio et al. (2018) indicate four types of interventions that central banks (and financial regulators) could adopt to help deal with climate-related risks. The first would be development of "methodologies and tools that would promote a better understanding of these risks and their economic and financial implications". Second, "investors can be encouraged or required to disclose their exposure to climate-related risks". Third, "these risks can be explicitly taken into account in setting financial regulations". And fourth, "central banks can take into account climate-related risks in their policy toolkit (for example, through monetary policy)" (p. 463). However, at present, as Dikau and Volz (2021) report, only 12% of the 135 central banks they consider have explicit sustainability mandates. However, 40% of those central banks are mandated to support the government's policy priorities, which often include sustainability goals.

Climate change and transition policies have clear implications for the IT framework. The first, and most general, is the need to extend central bank mandates well beyond IT, and to incorporate concerns over financial stability and over climate change into their decision-making. The second relates to the need for central bank actions to be co-ordinated with government policies; as such, there is removal of the independence of the central bank (even if interest-rate decisions remain largely in the hands of the central bank). The stated mandate of the central bank needs to be changed and elements of its independence ended (if that independence has not already de facto ended), as co-ordination with government policies more generally is required. The third relates to transmission mechanisms of monetary policy. The ECB, for example, argued that "macroeconomic and financial markets disruptions linked to climate change and transition policies could affect the conduct of monetary policy and the ability of the ECB to deliver on its price stability mandate through various channels" (2021, p. 11). The ECB mentions that "climate risks may affect the transmission of monetary policy through financial markets and the banking sector, notably via the stranding of assets and sudden repricing of climate-related financial risks" (p. 104). The ECB also considers that "the policy rate could hit the effective lower bound (ELB) more often, limiting the monetary policy space for conventional tools", derived from the assumption that the so-called 'natural rate of interest' may be lower (p. 104). The uncertainties of the nature and magnitude of the effects of climate change and the identification of changes and shocks arising from climate change and policy responses make decision-making much more complex. And in a similar vein, "climate change can undermine the effectiveness of the IT framework, which is at the core of central banks' operations", as "physical and transition risks can affect asset prices, exchange rates, expectations and bank lending, which constitute significant channels by which changes in policy rates influence price developments" (Dafermos, 2021, p. 1).

3.   DEFINING GREEN

A range of central bank policy options are discussed below which are intended to support and favour environmentally friendly investments, and the financing and funding of such investments require definitions of what constitutes environmentally friendly 'green' investments and by default what constitutes environmentally unfriendly ('dirty') investments (and perhaps a range of investments which are deemed neither particularly environmentally friendly or unfriendly). In the context of monetary policies, and as further discussed below, the policy instruments can include the purchase of financial assets and selective credit policies.

A simple definition comes from the World Bank (2015) that "a green bond is a debt security that is issued to raise capital specifically to support climate-related or environmental projects". With bonds issued by private companies, supranational institutions and government (municipal, state, federal), "Green bonds allow issuers to reach different investors and promote their environmental credentials". The Green Bond Principles (GBP), a set of voluntary guidelines framing the issuance of green bonds, recognise several broad categories of potential eligible projects, which include but are not limited to the following: renewable energy, energy efficient, sustainable waste management, sustainable land use, bio-diversity conservation, clean transportation, sustainable water management and climate change adaptation (based on World Bank, 2015).

EU (2020) provides an example of seeking to draw up a taxonomy of 'green investments'. The taxonomy sets performance thresholds for economic activities that make a substantive contribution to one of seven environmental objectives of climate change mitigation, climate change adaptation, sustainable protection of water and marine resources, transition to a circular economy, pollution prevention and control, protection and restoration of bio-diversity and ecosystems, and meeting minimum safeguards such as the UN Guiding Principles on Business and Human Rights. A green bond would need to meet a range of requirements, including that the proceeds "shall be exclusively used to finance or re-finance in part or in full new and/or existing Green Projects".

In a similar vein, the Green Loan Principles (GLP) seek to create a framework of market standards and guidelines to support the development of green loans. For a loan to be considered 'green', "the selection of green projects should be done using the EU Taxonomy", and "the borrowers of the green loans should clearly inform the lenders about the environmental sustainability objectives ... the evaluation process and the assessments to identify and manage potentially significant environmental risks" (EU, 2020, p. 42).

There are numerous issues surrounding delimiting green financial instruments. There are concerns as to how funds can be hypothecated to a specific project rather than contributing to a company's ability to fund investment in general. There are well-known issues of 'greenwashing'; that is, the process of conveying a false impression or providing misleading information about how a company's production and products are more environmentally sound and downplaying those activities that are not environmentally friendly. Indeed, the ECB found that

> firms that issue green bonds do not behave significantly differently from firms that do not issue such securities. This result likely arises from the prevailing uncertainty surrounding what qualifies as a green activity, the lack of granular information on activities and the lack of *ex post* verification and accountability. In other words, what is known as greenwashing appears to remain prevalent. (ECB, 2021, p. 90)

"Because green labels apply to standalone projects rather than to the firm's overall activities, projects promising carbon-reductions could be offset by carbon increases of the same firm elsewhere" (Ehlers et al., 2020, p. 34). Those authors then find that "green bond labels are not associated with falling or even comparatively low carbon emissions at the firm level" (p. 32).

A highly significant question arises here: who should be responsible for setting out which investment and activities are to be considered 'green' and which 'dirty'? The responsibilities for environmentally friendly policies lie firmly with the government, and the central bank (and other institutions) should undertake policy decisions that support the policies of the government. In this context, the government should be responsible for setting out what is deemed environmentally friendly and what is not to enable support for the former to be provided.

4.   QUANTITATIVE EASING AND CLIMATE EMERGENCY

Under programmes of QE, central banks have purchased financial assets, predominantly but not exclusively government bonds, in the secondary markets, and did so to a pre-set amount and generally in support of a low-interest-rate policy. To date, since QE policies were first introduced in 2009, those policies in terms of increasing the amount of financial assets held by the central bank have operated infrequently, being extended in a major way during the COVID-19 pandemic. While the asset purchases were intended to be temporary, there has been very limited reversal in terms of reduction in the scale of assets held by central banks.

Policies of QE conducted by central banks over the past decade have further implications. First, since QE appears to provide money to the banking system through purchase of financial assets from them, then money created by the central bank could not be supplied to others. Second, the central bank decides which financial assets to purchase and which not, and the quantity of financial assets to be held. The purchase of financial assets by central banks has now often extended to corporate bonds.

Drawing on the experiences of QE, there have been two quite distinct, though often conflated, sets of policies that are placed under headings such as 'green QE'. One set of proposals focuses on money creation by the central bank being used to directly finance 'green investment', while the other focuses on the 'greenness' of the financial assets acquired by the central bank within a programme of QE.

An early example of the first type of proposal comes from Murphy and Hines (2010), who wrote that the objectives of Green QE2 include financing a Green New Deal, refinancing existing government-related loans at low cost. Further, "A second round of quantitative easing should involve *direct* expenditure on new infrastructure projects in the UK" (p. 12, emphasis added). Coppola (2019) develops a general case for "people's quantitative easing", and as part of that considers its use to address the climate emergency. She argues that "central bank financing of green initiatives, low-carbon technologies and renewable energy projects undertaken by governments and public investment banks around the world may be the only realistic way of funding what will be the world's largest ever development project" (p. 133). It is recognised that this would require the co-operation of government and central banks, with the central bank enabling the expenditure to be financed. However, this leaves open the scale of the expenditure, and, more significantly in the case of monetary policy, the degree to which any rise in the budget deficit (after allowance for multiplier effects and enhanced tax payments) would be monetised and how much covered by increased government debt.

A central bank has to provide initial finance (to use the circuitist terminology[1]) for any form of government expenditure – that is, allow the government's balance with the central bank to diminish, whether through agreement that the existing balance can be so used or through overdraft facilities; the existing balance may be reinforced by acquisition by the central bank of government bonds. Government expenditure cannot take place unless the central bank provides initial finance: in practice, the initial finance is (nearly) always provided. It is often suggested that the 'green' government expenditure is funded by the central bank money (final finance in circuitist terminology) and in effect any additional budget deficit is monetised.

Insofar as the volume and structure of the expenditures that come under the ambit of green QE are decided by the central bank, there is a rather strong undemocratic element with decisions made by unelected central bankers. If, on the other hand, the volume and structure of the expenditures are determined by the government, then there is nothing unique here in that the central bank provides (initial) finance to enable the expenditures to occur, and there are further decisions as to the degree to which any resulting budget deficit is monetised.

Meanwhile, government expenditure, whatever the nature of that expenditure, has to be initially financed by the central bank. Some of the suggestions in respect of 'green QE' spill over into the provision of funds for 'green' investment. I would argue that central banks do not have the capacity to assess and monitor the allocation of funds for 'green' investment, and a more appropriate vehicle would be state development/green banks: "PDBs [public development banks] should do more to combine their resources with those of the private sector, and help to mobilize commercial financing for projects that the market alone often will not fund. These include mitigating climate change, promoting innovation, building infrastructure, financing small businesses, and providing affordable housing" (Griffith-Jones et al., 2020). PDBs "are both providers of public funding and enablers to leverage private finance. PDBs need to acquire 'sustainable development tools' to select operations on the basis of criteria other than purely financial ones" (Marodon, 2022).[2]

Proposals along the lines of 'green QE' run into (at least) two difficulties. First, the extent of QE is linked with the macroeconomic conditions and balance sheets, and the extent to which funds are supplied for 'green investment' should not be judged by the macroeconomic conditions but rather by the needs for 'green investment'. Second, such proposals place decisions on the forms and level of public expenditure in the hands of unelected central bankers rather than in the hands of elected politicians.

Through QE programmes, central banks have been involved with the purchase of existing financial assets rather than the financing of new investment, which was largely the purchase of government bonds, though extended to corporate bonds. There have been a range of proposals which would focus on the purchase by the central bank of environmentally friendly bonds and non-purchase of 'dirty' bonds (however defined). In doing so, the central bank would move away from market neutrality and favour some forms of bonds ('green') over others. In Dafermos et al.'s (2018) model, for example, "purchase of corporate green bonds by central banks reduces the interest rate on these bonds compared to the interest rate on conventional bonds. As a result, firms become more willing to invest in projects related to the renewables and energy efficiency". They conclude that "the effects of a green corporate QE programme are not very substantial in quantitative terms: even if we adopt very optimistic assumptions about the responsiveness of green investment to changes in the interest rates, the difference in 2100 temperature compared to a scenario without a green QE is not higher than 0.5°C" (p. 5).

Ferrari and Landi (2020) study the effects of a temporary green QE, a policy which "tilts the central bank's balance sheet towards green bonds, i.e. bonds issued by firms in non-polluting sectors", in a model based on a dynamic stochastic general equilibrium (DSGE) framework with environmental issues added on. They find

> that the imperfect substitutability between green and brown bonds is a necessary condition for the effectiveness of Green QE … A temporary green QE is an effective tool in mitigating detrimental emissions. However, Green QE has limited effects in reducing the stock of pollution, if pollutants are slow-moving variables such as atmospheric carbon. (p. 1)

A number of studies have concluded that the current QE programme does not support 'green' bonds. Dafermos, Pawloff et al. (2020), for example, argue that the ECB's purchase of corporate bonds is biased towards carbon-intensive sectors. "An important consequence of the carbon bias is that it may lower the cost of borrowing (an implicit subsidy) and encourage more debt issuance by the most carbon intensive firms relative to low-carbon firms" (p. 3). The authors argue that the ECB "should abandon its market neutrality approach, the key driver of this carbon bias, and adopt alternative low-carbon strategies" (p. 3).

In early 2021 the Bank of England held around £20 billion in its Corporate Bond Purchase Scheme (CBPS), which amounted to 6.5% of the sterling corporate bond market. The CBPS had been introduced in 2016 as part of the QE programme. Their approach to the assets purchased was "to minimise the impact of the CBPS on relative borrowing costs across sectors: the so-called 'market neutrality'" (Bank of England, 2021, p. 1). Dafermos, Gabor et al. (2020) argue that the CBPS "is mis-aligned with the government's climate goals and implicitly creates better financing conditions for carbon-intensive economic activities. The CBPS biases the allocation of capital towards carbon-intensive sectors, while at the same time failing to reflect climate-related financial risks" (p. 4).

The Bank of England (2021) argued that "there is increasingly persuasive evidence that market prices materially under-estimate the risks and opportunities associated with the transition to net zero" (p. 1). They put forward suggestions for the 'greening' of CBPS which include setting a target path for the emissions properties of the CBPS, placing tight restrictions on involvement in activities which are inconsistent with the transition to net zero and rebalancing bond purchases towards issuers with stronger climate performance.

Specifically with regard to coal (though it could be extended to others), van Lerven (2020) proposed "excluding coal-exposed assets from central bank collateral frameworks and asset purchases"; "accounting for coal risks in setting microprudential capital requirements"; "introducing macroprudential capital buffers for coal exposures"; and "ensuring that the risks of coal asset stranding are adequately reflected in stress tests".

Oil Change International (2021) focus on fossil fuel usage, and study a range of central bank policies which could be adopted to reduce fossil fuel usage. Among the policies are the exclusion of fossil fuel assets from the central bank's financial asset portfolio. Oil Change International (2021) evaluate whether fossil fuel assets are excluded from asset purchases in relation to the central banks' management of funds (that they control). For COVID-19-related asset purchases, all of the six central banks (out of 12) involved in such purchases were deemed grossly insufficient. For other asset purchases, nine central banks were grossly insufficient, two insufficient and the test was not applicable to the remaining one.

These types of QE policies through favouring 'green' financial assets over 'dirty ones' clearly represent a departure from the notion of 'market neutrality'.

5.   CREDIT GUIDANCE AND CREDIT CONTROLS

There is a long history of policies, often implemented by the central bank, which seek to influence or direct credit and loans into favoured activities and away from others. These types of policy have generally fallen out of favour under pressures of financial liberalisation. There have been suggestions for policy instruments which would favour funds for 'green' investment. Credit guidance and controls would clearly be designed to lead to finance being cheaper and/or more readily available for 'green' investment than for 'dirty' investments. As with the QE policies discussed in the last section, these policies would mean a move away from any form of 'market neutrality'.

Bezemer et al. (2018) reviews policies known variously as 'credit guidance', 'credit controls', 'credit ceilings', 'directed credit, 'window guidance' and 'moral suasion'. As Bezemer et al. note,

> in advanced economies credit guidance policies were largely abandoned in the 1980s. This was part of a widen liberalisation of the financial sector that followed the collapse of the Bretton Woods system of fixed exchange rate controls. Such policies were viewed as distorting or 'repressing' the efficient allocation of capital and undermining domestic and global competition in the banking sector, leading to lower levels of productive investment than would otherwise have been available. (2018, p. 3)

In their empirical work covering the period 1973 to 2005, they find that "the relaxation of credit controls, financial account restrictions and the privatisation of state-owned banks are all significantly associated with a lower share of credit extended to non-financial firms, but interest rate controls are not" (2018, p. 21).

Bezemer et al. (2018, their Table 1) provide a comprehensive list of policies which can be included under the heading of credit guidance. On the supply side this includes credit ceilings and quotas, interest-rate ceilings, reserve requirements leverage ratios (exemptions), capital (risk-weight) requirements, supervisory pressure and moral suasion, loan-to-deposit ratios, sectoral discount rates, collateral requirements, funding for lending and targeted longer-term refinancing operations, proportional lending ratios, central bank asset purchase programmes, state investment banks, and specialised public credit intermediaries.

Credit guidance was treated as causing a mispricing of capital/finance, distorting the efficient allocation of funds and resources and leading to lower levels of productive investment (than would have been the case). It was generally then taken that interventions in credit markets would lead to interest rates below some notion of market equilibrium levels. The rationale for forms of credit guidance in the context of climate change is to foster the allocation of funds towards environmentally friendly activities and away from environmentally damaging ones. It echoes the arguments which were formerly deployed to encourage investment to promote industrial development. The climate emergency can be viewed in terms of a massive market failure, and as such corrective action includes favouring those activities which are environmentally friendly.

Bezemer et al. (2018) argue that "some of the contemporary macroprudential measures are in fact – if not in name – forms of credit guidance. This includes higher risks for mortgages, the Basel III lower risk weights for SMEs and infrastructure projects, and countercyclical capital buffers with sectoral differentiation" (p. 14). Campiglio (2016), for example, proposed that "a dif-

ferentiation of reserve requirements according to the destination of lending …
may fruitfully expand credit creation towards low-carbon sectors" (p. 220).

Lamperti et al. (2021) test what they term 'green' finance policies which
address the risks to the banking sector arising from the climate emergency
and which foster climate change mitigation. These are, first, green Basel-type
capital requirements, which would exclude loans to green firms from banks'
capital requirements regulation. The macroprudential framework leads to
credit being allocated to both green and brown firms on a pecking-order basis,
and expands credit allocated to green firms. Second, there are green public
guarantees with government providing a guarantee to the bank on the full
amount of the loan by a 'green' firm. Government-backed green loans have
the same default risk as sovereign bonds. Third, there is carbon-risk adjustment
in credit ratings with firms having to disclose their level of emission intensity
with their balance sheet information, which is observed by banks and used in
their credit ranking. These types of policies would combine elements of credit
guidance policies along with measures seeking to reduce financial instabilities
coming from climate change. They deploy a macro-financial agent-based
model to explore the interaction between climate change, credit and economic
dynamics, and test a mix of policy interventions. Their results "point to the
need to complement financial policies cooling down climate-related risks
with mitigation policies curbing emissions from real economic activities"
(Lamperti et al., 2021, p. 1).

There are proposals for differentiated capital requirements. One formulation
is in terms of 'green supporting factor' (GSF), by which banks need to hold less
capital for loans provided to support activities that can lead to reduced carbon
emissions; and 'dirty penalising factor' (DPF), whereby banks are required
to hold more capital for loans that fund high-carbon activities. Dafermos
and Nikolaidi (2021) examine such proposals in the context of an ecological
macro-financial model. They find, among other things, that green differentiated capital requirements can affect credit provision and loan spreads, and can
reduce the pace of global warming and thereby the physical financial risks.[3]

6.   STRANDED ASSETS AND FINANCIAL INSTABILITY

Two categories of climate-related risks – physical risks and transition risks
– are identified which have consequences for the financial sector and its stability, and thereby implications for the central bank and its policy operations.
Physical risks cover, for example, gradual global warming and its associated
physical changes, natural disasters such as hurricanes, floods and heatwaves,
and the lasting environmental damages. Transition risks are posed by the
policy and technological changes necessary to achieve a greener economy. As

the ECB argues, "climate change affects macroeconomic outcomes, financial markets and institutions primarily through two channels: physical risk and transition risk" (ECB, 2021, p. 6). Further, "climate change is a systemic risk to the financial sector ... In the financial system, systemic risks are risks that have the potential to destabilize the normal functioning of the system and lead to serious negative consequences for the real economy" (Gelzinis and Steele, 2019, n.p.).

The issues of climate emergency and needs for a structural transformation raise concerns for a central bank from the connections with financial instability. Particularly in regard to the transition to a low-carbon economy, a number of people have argued that such a transition, if not well managed, could have destabilising effects on the financial system. The Financial Stability Board (2020, p. 1), for example, suggest that "a disorderly transition to a low carbon economy could also have a destabilising effect on the financial system". Sudden and unanticipated changes in public policy, changes in household behaviour and increased materialisation of physical risks could bring changes in market valuations. "[P]hysical and transition risks might combine, amplifying their overall effect on financial stability. Central estimates of the impact on asset prices of a well-anticipated transition to a low carbon economy are relatively contained, although there are many measurement uncertainties" (Financial Stability Board, 2020, p. 1). "Climate-related risks may also affect how the global financial system responds to shocks. They may give rise to abrupt increases in risk premia across a wide range of assets. ... This may in turn affect financial system resilience and lead to a self-reinforcing reduction in bank lending and insurance provision" (Financial Stability Board, 2020, p. 2).

The severity and frequency of climate-related events can affect the ability of households and firms to repay debt. The prices of bonds and stocks issued by companies that are particularly impacted by these physical changes are likely to decline. The financial position of carbon-intensive companies may be adversely affected, though the financial position of environmentally friendly companies may be strengthened. The idea of 'stranded assets' raises possibilities of financial instability of companies which own the 'stranded assets' and for financial institutions which have provided funds to those companies. A key example would be a large fraction of existing reserves of oil, gas and coal remaining in the ground and their value written down in the balance sheets of the companies which own them. The shifts away from these non-renewable energy sources can involve unemployment in those sectors, though a transition would involve employment rises in, for example, renewable energy sectors (and in the sectors producing the investment goods for those sectors). The changes in asset values (assumed to be downwards, though the valuation of carbon non-intensive assets could well rise) have implications for the range of financial institutions and households who own the corresponding assets. This may well be another example of financial markets mispricing financial assets – why have the risks involved not been incorporated into the financial asset prices? The asset stranding could affect the market valuation of the companies which own those assets, with potential cascade effects in an interconnected financial system. As central banks have been assigned responsibility for protecting the stability of the financial system and guarding against financial instability, it is now widely accepted that central banks should be analysing these risks and taking action to help cope with those risks.

Mercure et al. (2018) analyse the macroeconomic impact of stranded fossil fuel assets. They estimate the magnitude of the discounted global wealth loss from stranded fossil fuel assets at $1 trillion to $4 trillion, depending on the range of new climate policies adopted and how far low-cost producers maintain levels of production. While it may be relevant for the central banks and others to warn about the likely shifts in asset prices, it is not obvious what actions would follow for monetary policy.

Although the language used is that of 'risk', it is rather a situation of fundamental uncertainty. As Bolton et al. (2020) argue, "In this context of deep uncertainty, traditional backward-looking risk assessment models that merely extrapolate historical trends prevent full appreciation of the future systemic risk posed by climate change" (p. 1).

Chenet et al. (2021, p. 1) note that while climate-related financial risks (CRFR) are recognised by central banks as significant to their financial stability mandates, the emerging policy framework for dealing with those financial risks "has largely focused on market-based solutions that seek to reduce perceived information gaps that prevent the accurate pricing of CRFR. These include disclosure, transparency, scenario analysis and stress testing". This approach is limited, however, as CRFR are characterised by radical uncertainty and so-called 'efficient' price discovery would not be possible. Further, the authors argue that "this approach tends to bias financial policy toward concern around avoiding short-term market disruption at the expense of longer-term, potentially catastrophic and irreversible climate risks" (p. 1).

One line of proposal is prudential measures targeted at banks with assets at risk of being stranded and that contribute to climate-related macroprudential risk (Philipponnat, 2020). This would involve applying higher risk weights to existing exposures to fossil fuel assets at risk of stranding assets. Added to this, additional risk weights can be added for exposures associated with risks that are particularly high or difficult to assess.

Bolton et al. (2020, p. iii) discuss 'green swan' risks which are "potentially extremely financially disruptive events that could be behind the next systemic financial crisis". They view "climate-related physical and transition risks involv[ing] interacting, non-linear and fundamentally unpredictable environmental, social, economic and geopolitical dynamics that are irreversibly transformed by the growing concentration of greenhouse gases in the atmosphere". They further argue that

> integrating climate-related risk analysis into financial stability monitoring and prudential supervision is particularly challenging because of the distinctive features of climate change impacts and mitigation strategies. ... Exceeding climate tipping points could lead to catastrophic and irreversible impacts that would make quantifying financial damages impossible. Avoiding this requires immediate and ambitious action towards a structural transformation of our economies, involving technological innovations that can be scaled but also major changes in regulations and social norms.

Bolton et al. (2020, p. 1) also state that "Climate-related risks will remain largely unhedgeable as long as system-wide action is not undertaken". 'Green swan' events, rather like the 'black swan' event involved with the global financial crises of 2007–09, may well threaten the stability of the whole financial system. Then "Green swan events may force central banks to intervene as 'climate rescuers of last resort' and buy large sets of devalued assets, to save the financial system once more" (Bolton et al., 2020, p. 1).

Lamperti et al. (2019) use an agent-based climate-macroeconomic model and their results indicate that climate change will increase the frequency of banking crises by between 26% and 28%. The rescue of insolvent banks is estimated to cause an additional fiscal burden equivalent to around 5% to 15% of gross domestic product per year. They "estimate that around 20% of such effects are caused by the deterioration of banks' balance sheets induced by climate change" (p. 829).

7.   CONCLUDING COMMENTS

The policies of central banks should be supportive of and consistent with government policies on environmentally sustainability and climate change. The concern from central banks over climate change requires co-ordination between central bank and government, and at least in that dimension an end to the independence of central banks. This co-ordination should include the financing and funding of government expenditure by the central bank and the use of a common taxonomy on environmentally friendly investment and activities. The central bank purchase of financial assets under schemes such as QE should involve acceptance of 'green' financial assets only in a departure from 'market neutrality'. 'Green' financial assets are thereby favoured over 'dirty' financial assets.

Climate change and responses to it can have implications for the operations of the central bank. The changes in the structure of the economy can make

IT more complex (even though there may be doubts on the effectiveness of interest-rate variations in the control of inflation). Financial stability, a key concern for many central banks, may be threatened by 'stranded assets', with possibilities of sharp price adjustments and threats to loan repayments. Financial stability policies may be designed to alleviate the impacts which could arise rather than be able to address the underlying causes of instability. However, systemic risks from the climate emergency cannot be effectively addressed through monetary policy and financial regulation. There is a role for the revival of selective credit controls and guidance to encourage lending for 'green' activities and firms.

NOTES

1. See, for example, Graziani (2003).
2. See also Riaño et al. (2022) and Griffith-Jones et al. (2022).
3. See also Dunz et al. (2021) for a stock-flow consistent model analysis of revision of the microprudential banking framework via a Green Supporting Factor (GSF).

REFERENCES

Bank of England (2021), "Options for greening the Bank of England's Corporate Bond Purchase Scheme, Discussion Paper, May 2021". Available at: https://www.bankofengland.co.uk/paper/2021/options-for-greening-the-bank-of-englands-corporate-bond-purchase-scheme.

Bezemer, D., Ryan-Collins, J., van Lerven, F. and Zhang, L. (2018), "Credit where it's due: A historical, theoretical and empirical review of credit guidance policies in the 20th century", *UCL Institute for Innovation and Public Purpose Working Paper Series* (IIPP WP 2018-11).

Bolton, P., Després, M., Pereira da Silva, L., Samama, F. and Svartzman, R. (2020), *The green swan: Central banking and financial stability in the age of climate change*. Bank for International Settlements. Available at: https://www.bis.org/publ/othp31.pdf.

Campiglio, E. (2016), "Beyond carbon pricing: The role of banking and monetary policy in financing the transition to a low-carbon economy", *Ecological Economics*, 121, 220–230.

Campiglio, E., Dafermos, Y., Monnin, P., Ryan-Collins, J., Schotten, G. and Tanaka, M. (2018), "Climate change challenges for central banks and financial regulators", *Nature Climate Change*, 8, 462–468.

Chenet, H., Ryan-Collins, J. and van Lerven, F. (2021), "Finance, climate-change and radical uncertainty: Towards a precautionary approach to financial policy", *Ecological Economics*, 183, 106157.

Coppola, F. (2019), *The case for people's quantitative easing*, New York: Wiley.

Dafermos, Y. (2021), "Climate change, central banking and financial supervision: Beyond the risk exposure approach" in S. Kappes, L.-P. Rochon and G. Vallet (eds), *The future of central banking*, Cheltenham: Edward Elgar Publishing.

Dafermos, Y., and Nikolaidi, M. (2021), "How can green differentiated capital requirements affect climate risks? A dynamic macrofinancial analysis", *Journal of Financial Stability*, 54, 100871.

Dafermos, Y., Nikolaidi, M. and Galanis, G. (2018), "Can green quantitative easing (QE) reduce global warming?", FEPS *Policy Brief*, July 2018.

Dafermos, Y., Gabor, D., Nikolaidi, M. and van Lerven, F. (2020), "Decarbonising the Bank of England pandemic QE: Perfectly sensible?", *Policy Briefing*, New Economics Foundation, June 2020.

Dafermos, Y., Pawloff, A., Gabor, D., Nikolaidi, M. and van Lerven, F. (2020), "Decarboninising is easy: Beyond market neutrality in the ECB's corporate QE", London: New Economics Foundation.

Dikau, S., and Volz, U. (2021), "Central bank mandates, sustainability objectives and the promotion of green finance", *Ecological Economics*, 184, 107022.

Dunz, N., Naqvi, A. and Monasterolo, I. (2021), "Climate sentiments, transition risk, and financial stability in a stock-flow consistent model", *Journal of Financial Stability*, 54, e100872.

Ehlers, T., Mojon, B. and Packer, F. (2020), "Green bonds and carbon emissions: Exploring the case for a rating system at the firm level", *BIS Quarterly Review*, September, Bank for International Settlements, pp. 31–48.

EU Technical Expert Group on Sustainable Finance (2020), *Financing a sustainable European economy: taxonomy*, Brussels: European Union.

European Central Bank (ECB) (2021), "Climate change and monetary policy in the euro area", ECB Occasional Paper Series, No. 271.

Ferrari, A. and Landi, V. N. (2020), "Whatever it takes to save the planet? Central banks and unconventional green policy", *European Central Bank Working Paper* no. 2500.

Financial Stability Board (2020), "The implications of climate change for financial stability". Available at: https://www.fsb.org/2020/11/the-implications-of-climate -change-for-financial-stability.

Gelzinis, G., and Steele, G. (2019), "Climate change threatens the stability of the financial system", Center for American Progress, 21 November 2019.

Graziani, A. (2003), *The monetary theory of production*, Cambridge: Cambridge University Press.

Griffith-Jones, S., Marodon, R., Ocampo, J. A. and Xu, J. (2020), "The age of public development banks has arrived", *Project Syndicate*, 6 November 2020.

Griffith-Jones, S., Spiegel, S., Xu, J., Carreras, M. and Naqvi, N. (2022), "Matching risks with instrument in development banks", *Review of Political Economy*, 34, 197–223.

Lamperti, F., Bosetti, V., Roventini, A. and Tavoni, M. (2019), "The public costs of climate induced financial instability", *Nature Climate Change*, 9, 829–833.

Lamperti, F., Bosetti, V., Roventini, A., Tavoni, M. and Treibich, T. (2021), "Three green financial policies to address climate risks", *Journal of Financial Stability*, 54, 100875.

Marodon, R. (2022), "Can development banks step up to the challenge of sustainable development?", *Review of Political Economy,* 34(2), 268–285.

Mercure, J.-F., Pollitt, H., Vinuales, J. E., Edwards, N. R., Holden, P. B., Chewpreecha, U., Salas, P., Sognnaes, I., Lam, A. and Knobloch, F. (2018), "Macroeconomic impact of stranded fossil fuel assets", *Nature Climate Change*, 8, 588–593.

Murphy, R., and Hines, C. (2010), *Green quantitative easing: Paying for the economy we need*, Norfolk, VA: Finance for the Future.

Oil Change International (2021), "Unused tools: How central banks are fueling the climate crisis". Available at: https://priceofoil.org/2021/08/24/unused-tools-central -banks.

Philipponnat, T. (2020), "Breaking the climate-finance doom loop", *Finance Watch*, June.

Riaño, M. A., Boutaybi, J., Barchiche, D. and Treyer, S. (2022), "Scaling up public development banks' transformative alignment with the 2030 agenda for sustainable development", *Review of Political Economy*, 34, 286–317.

Sunak, R. (2021), "Remit and recommendations for the Financial Policy Committee", Letter to Governor of Bank of England, 3 March 2021. Available at: https://www.bankofengland .co.uk/-/media/boe/files/letter/2021/march/fpc-remit-and-recommendations-letter-2021 .pdf.

van Lerven, F. (2020), "Banking on coal: How central banks can address the financial risks and support a capital shift from coal", London: New Economics Foundation.

World Bank (2015), "What are green bonds?", Washington, DC: World Bank.

3. Endogenous money, green finance and central bank power

Basil Oberholzer

1.   INTRODUCTION

With the emergence of climate change and other pressing environmental problems in the wider public and policy debates, the financial system and its relevance for the environment have also attracted growing attention. In some political movements as well as general common sense, money is considered as a hidden lever to enable economic and political change. In times of climate emergency, there is a tendency to screen policies in various areas regarding their environmental impact. The focus has also turned to monetary policy, particularly on the specific measures after the financial crisis such as quantitative easing. The coronavirus crisis of 2020 has further widened the view of what monetary policy is supposed to deliver in terms of crisis management, implying that those extraordinary measures may become the subject of environmental policy considerations, too.

The intense and expanding debate on sustainable, or green, finance reveals the ideas considering money and the financial system as very powerful mechanisms to enable ecological transition. Money is needed to finance the achievement of environmental goals such as the goal of zero-carbon emissions. Therefore, the debate concerns how money can be shifted from the bad to the good; that is, out of fossil fuel production and into the renewable energy sector, sustainable transport technologies, energy efficiency and more. Banks and other institutional investors, also facing increasing demand for sustainable investment from their clients, make promises to do clean business by gradually turning their conventional assets into sustainable ones. Sustainable finance is attractive for commercial banks and mainstream economics because it promises a transition accomplished by the market that does not require heavy policy interventions.

As will be discussed in this chapter, the sustainable finance narrative is implicitly based on an exogenous money conception, even though an explicit theory of money is missing. Moreover, sustainable investment is assumed to be a profitable business case, implying that there is nothing that stops money from flowing in the right direction. However, if these assumptions are wrong – that is, if the profitability of sustainable investment is not a given and if economic analysis is done on grounds of endogenous rather than exogenous money – the sustainable finance story gets into trouble fulfilling its promise.

If commercial banks are not able to enable ecological transition, the next question is if things are different for the central bank and whether monetary policy is a specific case where the sustainable finance story can make a difference. This chapter argues that while endogenous money makes sustainable finance by private agents a powerless approach, it is an essential mechanism for monetary policy to have an impact on the ecological transition. However, this does not imply that greening quantitative easing is sufficient since it is by no means clear that purchasing green assets affects real investment. Monetary policy is most effective when it is able to channel finance toward real green investment as an element of a comprehensive industrial policy strategy.

The chapter is structured as follows: section 2 introduces the general idea of sustainable finance as portrayed by the proponents of this approach. Section 3 criticizes this mainstream view from a heterodox macroeconomic perspective. In section 4, we will examine whether there are differences for central banks compared to private banking and what the requirements are for green monetary policy to become effective. Section 5 concludes.

2.   THE MAINSTREAM IDEA OF GREEN FINANCE

Relating investment decisions to the environment, known under the terms 'sustainable finance' or 'green finance', has become a cornerstone in the debate on the green economy and transition to a more sustainable way of living. The mainstream debate focuses on the private sector while attributing only a minor role, if at all, to the government. In particular, the state's financing capacity is argued to be tightly restricted, which is why the private sector needs to step in in order to close the investment gap preventing the achievement of environmental goals such as the Sustainable Development Goals (SDGs; UNEP FI, 2018, p. 9). The issue of green finance includes two different perspectives, which are connected but should nonetheless be separated. The risk perspective considers how the financial sector *depends* on the environment, while the impact perspective emphasizes the *influence* of investment decisions *on* the environment.

The risk perspective usually distinguishes between several risk categories in varying ways (Bank of England, 2020a; Battiston et al., 2017): physical risks describe the probability of physical destruction of real assets due to environmental disasters such as droughts and floods but also long-term damages arising from climate change. Liability risks occur when polluters or their insurers have to pay for the damages suffered by other individuals or companies. The third risk category includes reputational risks to which companies are exposed if they do not act in a way responsible to the environment and society. Then there are transition risks, which arise from the possibility of stricter environmental regulation in the future. In the context of the latter risk category, there is a discussion about 'stranded assets', describing real and financial assets directly or indirectly related to fossil fuels (Carney, 2015, p. 8; Mercure et al., 2018). Since the major share of existing fossil fuel reserves must not be consumed if the goals of the Paris Climate Agreement are to be achieved, the corresponding assets inevitably have to lose most of their value and thus may push their owners into financial trouble. All those risks turn into financial risks arising from the repercussions of such harmful events showing in financial assets and hence on financial institutions' balance sheets. This also involves second-round effects (see Battiston et al., 2017, pp. 286–287) and indirect impacts on sectors upstream or downstream a supply chain.

Green finance thus has an eye on environmental risks and argues that financial institutions need to consider these risks and reduce them. Otherwise, they risk financial losses because environmental risks are financial risks (see Grippa et al., 2019). Moreover, those risks jeopardize financial stability at a systemic level. While evidence on the systemic impact of these risks is certainly there but often difficult to measure, it is often also not clear whether the initiatives that aim at making those risks transparent consider a healthy environment as a first priority or whether their main interest is in business performance and financial stability (see, for instance, TCFD, 2017).

The impact perspective wants to align financial flows with sustainability benchmarks such as the environmental goals agreed in international conferences, for example the SDGs. The idea is simple: money should be used for environmentally beneficial investment projects and withdrawn from harmful assets. This may take place via regulation or voluntarily thanks to convinced investors, sometimes called 'impact investors' (see Agrawal and Hockerts, 2019; Bugg-Levine and Emerson, 2011). Industries such as fossil fuel producers thus will run short of capital and have to cut down their production plans. Since providers are withdrawing from those sectors, environmentally harmful companies have to compete for a shrinking fund of finance, which gives rise to increasing rates on loans and bonds. The most prominent strand in this regard is the divestment movement (see, for example, Fossil Free, 2019). It has convinced municipalities, pension funds, sovereign wealth funds, churches and other organizations to withdraw their wealth from fossil fuels. As a second consequence of this shift, sustainable projects such as renewable energy but also biodiversity protection have improved access to finance.

There is a connection between the impact and the risk perspective that proponents of green finance make use of to develop their argument: it says that investment in sustainable projects pays off. Since green finance is able to reduce corporate risk via some or even all the risk categories mentioned above, there is a favorable shift in the risk–return curve, thus raising expected profits. The stranded-asset argument is an example of this. Indeed, there is evidence that returns on sustainable investments do not significantly deviate from conventional investments (Boermans and Galema, 2019, pp. 58–59; Friede et al., 2015; Kaiser, 2020). This means that there is no reason not to invest in green assets because there is no fine in terms of reduced returns. To the extent that they avoid risks that conventional assets have not noticed yet, performance may even be better. Overall, the connection is twofold: green investment has a positive impact on the environment by reducing environmental damages and hence economic risks and costs. At the same time, lower risks make green investment a business case.

3.   A CRITICAL VIEW OF GREEN FINANCE

There are quite a few shortcomings in this mainstream green finance narrative. It is not always clear whether proponents consider sustainable finance a way to reduce risk or to achieve positive impact. This needs to be disentangled.

3.1   Do Environmental Risks Affect Investment Decisions?

The motivation for green finance from the risk perspective usually is that when transparency is established, markets provide the best mechanism to ensure ecological sustainability because they are able to allocate resources efficiently; that is, in a risk-minimizing way (see, for instance, TCFD, 2017, p. ii). The efficient market hypothesis provides the implicit underpinning to argue that by disclosing environmental risks, agents adjust their decisions and make investments in line with sustainable development. This point of view is paradoxical as it assumes that markets are efficient in accounting for risks in the most efficient way but are unable to detect the existence of those risks themselves.

Moreover, neither markets nor any sophisticated methodologies are able to foresee ecological tipping points in areas such as climate change or biodiversity loss. Those tipping points describe a moment when environmental damages reach a level where they not only are irreversible but start self-enforcing themselves (Lenton et al., 2019). This would lead to the final collapse of ecosystems and make certain world regions or even the planet uninhabitable (ibid.). Tipping points including the uncertainty of their moment of occurrence and the extent of their impact may make risk calculation not only impossible but even entirely useless.

Finally, the argument that environmental risks are financial risks can only have an effect on companies' or investors' behavior if the risks they create are relevant at their level. Hence, companies and investors only consider measures to reduce their harmful environmental impact if the risks arising from it have a direct influence on their cash flows. However, in reality, risks often emerge for other agents and regions than those who caused them. For an individual company, reducing carbon emissions usually involves costs, while most of the benefits arise to the whole society or even other regions in the world. Making environmental risks transparent thus is unlikely to be a major instrument in the transition to a more sustainable economy as long as the relevant agents consider those risks to be low. Transition risks, signifying the probability of stricter environmental regulations in the future, may be a particular case in this regard: the issue is most likely not the ignorance of this risk. The main challenge is ambitious environmental policies to actually make those risks not only a vague possibility but a reality, meaning that investors get the signal that regulation is actually implemented.

3.2   The Assumptions Needed to Make Green Finance Impactful

The impact perspective is based on a macroeconomic framework that is never made explicit such that its flaws go unnoticed. Namely, the argument that sustainable finance as autonomous action by the private sector is effective in steering an ecological transition ignores two important macroeconomic aspects, which are the endogeneity of money and the meaning of profitability. Regarding the first aspect, the sustainable finance narrative implicitly assumes that money is exogenous; that is, exogenously determined by the central bank in line with the quantity theory of money. For the argument of withdrawing money away from environmentally harmful sectors in order to dry them up financially to be meaningful, the quantity of money has to be limited. For example, oil companies only face financing constraints if they do not have alternatives to the funds that financial institutions withdraw from them. Likewise, the limitation of money makes it necessary to remove it from polluting sectors such that it can be made available for sustainable investments.

Yet, money is not exogenous. The endogeneity of money is based on the view that money comes into existence via the issuance of loans and thus can be provided upon demand (see Moore, 1988; Rochon and Rossi, 2017). According to the different theories of endogenous money, supply accommodates any demand for money with partially differing assumptions on the role of the interest rate (see, for instance, Dow, 2006; Lavoie, 2006). The loanable funds idea of sustainable finance is wrong because loans create deposits, which means that supply of finance does not depend on the existence of loanable funds but, eventually, on the lender's decision whether or not to provide a loan. This decision is not determined by the availability of deposits but by due diligence assessing the borrower's creditworthiness. The decision of one or several banks to withdraw investments from certain sectors thus does not make the supply of finance tighter as long as there are other investors and financial institutions interested in those sectors. Likewise, financing of more sustainable sectors is not constrained by money being invested in damaging sectors.

Whereas endogenous money concerns the mechanism via which finance is provided, the profitability principle determines whether investment actually takes place. The simple principle mostly emphasized by classical economics (Shaikh, 2016, p. 616), but also by Keynes (1936/1997, pp. 135–137) in his reference to the marginal efficiency of capital, and other authors, makes a sufficient profit rate a precondition for investment to take place at both the microeconomic and macroeconomic levels. Neoclassical theory approaches the issue in a paradoxical way because profits are maximized by agents but end up being zero in a general equilibrium with conventional properties (Bénicourt and Guerrien, 2008, pp. 185–186). However, hardly anyone in the green finance community denies the importance of sufficient returns for any business activity. Nevertheless, private sector sustainable finance proponents usually fail to connect the two principles of profitability and endogenous money. When the banking system and other investors consider the profitability of an investment project sufficient, they are willing to make the investment. If required, a new loan provides the additional monetary units. A profitable company in a sector from which certain investors have withdrawn their investments thus does not face any financing constraints and can still access finance at general market rates.

We can make certain qualifications depending on the type of investment, even though they confirm the general argument. Investment is *income-neutral* when it only consists in the purchase of existing financial or real assets. For example, an investor may sell shares in fossil fuel companies and purchase assets with a positive contribution to environmental quality. No company gains or loses any financial capital and hence no change is made in the real economy. Trading in financial assets may have an influence on asset prices that may favor the green sectors over the brown sectors. However, as long as the profitability of polluting assets generates sufficient cash flows, those assets will find a new buyer who even gets an extra benefit by getting hold of those cash flows at a reduced price. Arbitrage thus will reincrease asset prices and prevent significant punishment of the respective sectors via a drop in asset prices (see Ansar et al., 2013, p. 30). Green assets, on the other hand, may potentially experience a rally of price increases when financial investment keeps flowing based on speculative expectations of further price growth. However, to the extent that such a development is not based on sufficient asset returns, a green bubble builds up that is unlikely to last long and may harm rather than support ecological transition. So far, any preference for green assets does not substantially show in a structural favorable premium, as can be seen from the infinitesimal differential between the rates of green and non-green bonds (see Zerbib, 2019).

To the extent that investment involves the creation of new production capacity, it has a real impact and is *income-creating*, which means that a new loan is required to provide the monetary units corresponding to this additional income (see Bailly, 2008). Divestment in this context means that a financial institution or another investor denies the issuance of a loan or purchase of newly issued bonds or, respectively, the renewal of hitherto existing debt. In a world of endogenous money, the borrower will find an alternative source of finance as long as the investment project generates a sufficient profit rate. New investment in a green sector, on the other hand, is financed via a new loan if profitability is high enough, as has just been explained.

The entire argument about the importance of profitability excludes possible deviating situations when there is an explicit or implicit subsidy to invest- ments. For instance, a philanthropist may be willing to invest in a project even if it provides below-average returns and divests from highly profitable but polluting assets. This includes depositors who shift deposits to a bank, which is dedicated to green investments, and accept lower interest rates on those savings. Apart from this niche, shifting savings between banks is of limited importance when there is liquid exchange of reserves in the interbank market because savings are not the source but the product of investment.

To sum up, the principles of endogenous money and profitability imply that, first, every investment project with sufficient (expected) profitability will be financed. Second, any project that is not profitable enough will not be financed. The first conclusion reveals the relevance of endogenous money, whereas the first and second combined explain profitability as a necessary and sufficient condition.

The notion of profitability includes adjustments of expected profits for per- ceived risks. The evidence that returns on sustainable assets are equal to those on conventional assets (see, for instance, Friede et al., 2015) is less a confirma- tion that solving environmental problems is a business case than a confirma- tion of the importance of the profitability requirement. Green investment must yield average market returns as otherwise it would not take place. The exist- ence of those green assets and their returns in line with conventional markets is almost a tautology. On the other hand, the fact that green investment is still far from sufficient, as unsolved environmental problems testify, indicates that investment in the respective sectors to solve those problems is not profitable enough. The observation of equal returns on sustainable and conventional assets thus reveals the limits of the sustainable finance approach rather than supporting it.

3.3   Green Finance as a Result Rather Than a Cause

From a heterodox macroeconomic perspective, money is the expression of real output in numerical terms stemming from the fact that the issuance of loans to finance production associates money with output (see Rochon, 1999, pp. 5–9). The financial side and the real side of an asset thus eventually are identical, even if things are often more complicated because securitization of assets in financial markets and their trading involves fluctuations in market prices. Changes in the real economy thus are inevitably reflected in the financial assets that a financial institution, a company or a household have on their balance sheets. Regarding green finance, this means that companies and assets in general may become cleaner over time, which shows up in the greener and greener balance sheets of financial institutions but does not say anything about the origin of change and its causal direction.

To provide an example of this, let us assume that environmental policies impose stricter regulations on buildings to replace their oil- and gas-driven heating systems with a renewable and more efficient system including improved insulation. This will make buildings more sustainable in a period of, say, twenty years. After twenty years, investors find that their mortgage portfolios have become sustainable and thus claim that their efforts to foster green investment are effective. In fact, however, causality goes from the real economy to the financial sector, meaning that the latter has not made a relevant contribution.

While ecological transition obviously requires a shift from brown to green investment, it is doubtful whether the current sustainable finance debate can make a significant contribution. It is simply correct that if all investors followed the pioneers and started divesting from environmentally harmful assets, the latter would eventually be left without finance. Yet, first, there is no incentive entailing such positive herding dynamics. Second, completely drying up finance sources for, say, fossil fuel industries is tantamount to a ban on fossil fuels. But this is, in fact, a policy decision. Forbidding the production of fossil fuels does not depend on the financial sector to drive impact.

To actually trigger a shift in investment, there must be a significant profitability differential between green and conventional assets favoring the former. This may take place via subsidies such as financial contributions to renewable energy or protected habitats by the government or higher taxes on polluting sectors (see Monasterolo and Raberto, 2019). As mentioned above, it also involves raising the perceived risks for investors such as transition risks, which actually stem from measures such as subsidies, taxation, bans and other rules. Yet, again, this is a matter of setting regulations right and, therefore, a task of environmental and economic policies. The financial sector is not able to move autonomously but will follow the regulations and adjust investment decisions accordingly. Additionally, simply setting the prices right by internalizing the external costs of environmental damages may not be enough due to uncertainty regarding climate change and other ecological problems as well as future demand and price patterns. Agents may not adjust their decisions fast enough. As will be argued below, for economic and environmental policies to be successful, they should take measures to reduce uncertainty and stabilize expectations (Chang and Andreoni, 2020, p. 328).

4.   CAN MONETARY POLICY MAKE A DIFFERENCE?

Central banks, being not general but very specific agents in financial markets and the monetary system, may potentially be better able than private investors to support the transition to a sustainable economy. The chance for this to happen depends on their ability to avoid the shortcomings of the private sector's activity. It remains to be seen whether frequent propositions for the greening of monetary policy are effective in this regard.

4.1   Green Quantitative Easing and More

A growing number of proposals provide ideas about how central banks may contribute to a shift from brown to green investment. Some of those follow a perception of central banks as entities with many common characteristics with commercial banks. There is the proposal of the integration of ESG ('environment, social, governance') criteria into the central bank's investment portfolio, meaning that it has to screen its assets with respect to environmental and social performance so that companies within the same sector may also be rated differently according to their engagement, while some may be excluded altogether (see Schoenmaker, 2019, pp. 8–12). With these different strategies of sustainable investment and divestment, the central bank's impact thus is argued to be exerted via the individual assets' performance in the real economy, much like in the case of commercial banks.

Other propositions may not exclude ESG integration and divestment explicitly but approach the issue from a different perspective. Rather than focusing on the management and composition of portfolios, they consider the impact of monetary policy's power in financial markets via the volume of its investment, as well as via the setting of new market conditions. Hence, the focus is on how monetary policy has a leverage effect by affecting financial markets such that agents change their behavior, which then impacts the real economy.

One of these proposals suggests that central banks may adjust their requirements for collaterals in repo operations with commercial banks (Campiglio et al., 2018, p. 466). Green assets may be favored over brown assets, whether because the former is argued to include a higher default risk than the former or as an impact-driven policy decision. Collaterals based on environmentally damaging assets then have a 'haircut' imposed and have less purchasing power to buy central bank reserves. Banks thus have an incentive to have sustainable rather than unsustainable assets in their books. Such collateral requirements might trigger a demand shift between assets, giving way to increasing prices of green assets and falling prices of brown assets.

The most prominent ideas concern a different way of divestment from unsustainable assets by the central bank by referring to the so-called green quantitative easing (see, for instance, Dafermos et al., 2018, 2020; Honohan, 2019; Schoenmaker, 2019). Quantitative easing as part of what mainstream economics calls 'unconventional monetary policy' has altered central banks' position and importance since the outbreak of the global financial crisis in 2007/2008. Central banks in advanced economies have become major asset owners and investors since they started purchasing assets in the secondary market to raise their price and press down market interest rates. Instead of just taking the assets' conventional risk rating as the only criterion on which to decide on a purchase, monetary policy may also start favoring green over brown assets. This applies to the sections of the purchases that concern assets of private companies rather than sovereign bonds such as the European Central Bank's Corporate Sector Purchase Programme (CSPP; see Dafermos et al., 2020). Again, this would create a price differential between green and environmentally damaging assets. Green bonds can be issued at lower financing costs, while issuers of sustainable stocks also enjoy a green premium showing in an improved Tobin's q (Tobin, 1969).

Opponents of green quantitative easing, among them many central bankers, argue that monetary policy should have a market-neutral investment portfolio in order to prevent any market distortions (see, for example, van 't Klooster and Fontan, 2020). The rationale behind this argument is motivated by the efficient market hypothesis and monetarism, namely that monetary policy is supposed to be in line with the market equilibrium that is able to detect optimal outcomes on its own (see, for example, Goodfriend, 2007, p. 29). However, empirical evidence shows that a central bank is not able to guarantee this neutrality by simply purchasing assets in financial markets because a significant share of companies is not listed and hence is not financed via issuance of financial assets. With regard to climate concerns, for instance, it can be shown that listed companies are more carbon-intensive than non-listed ones, implying that current quantitative easing structurally favors climate-harming over climate-saving assets (Dafermos et al., 2020; Matikainen et al., 2017).

Another bottleneck for green quantitative easing may arise from concerns that a more limited focus on green assets, which also have to fulfill the general risk rating requirements, may leave central banks with too few purchasing options, thus jeopardizing the overall effectiveness of quantitative easing (Campiglio et al., 2018, p. 465). Finally, quantitative easing, designed as a cyclical tool, may end up being permanent because it has to fulfill environmental policy goals in addition to its traditional objectives that are limited to short-term stabilization and therefore compromise those. However, some proponents take up this argument by explicitly making the point that green quantitative easing is not merely a cyclical market intervention but part of an industrial policy strategy (Dafermos et al., 2018, p. 226).

Green quantitative easing may potentially be effective for the following reason: the central bank does not purchase assets primarily in search of return but in order to influence market conditions; that is, to bring the general level of market interest rates to an acceptable level. Dropping the profitability principle but making use of the endogenous money principle allows the market to be pushed in the desired direction. Divestment then becomes the back side of green quantitative easing, with the additional qualification that the central bank not only excludes them from its balance sheet (or does not add them anymore) as private banks do but also disadvantages them structurally in financial markets via financing conditions.

4.2   The Tight Limits of Green Quantitative Easing

By creating a price differential between green and brown assets, monetary policy affects the profitability of different types of assets and therefore has an influence on the decisions of private investors. However, interest rates, or refinancing costs in general, are just one variable in the profit equation of companies as well as their profit expectations (Keynes, 1936/1997, pp. 147–149). The impact of green quantitative easing on actually greening the economy thus faces certain limits a priori. It brings us back to the debate on the general effectiveness of monetary policy in spurring economic activity where post-Keynesian economists have been particularly critical (see, for example, Rochon and Setterfield, 2011). Moreover, given that the profitability of sustainable assets relative to conventional assets is largely driven by highly volatile prices of commodities such as crude oil, gas and coal, interest-rate differentials can obviously only have a minor impact.

As long as the profitability of green investment is generally low, a change in the interest rate and improved financing conditions will change little, meaning that companies classified as sustainable will hardly expand production. The impact of green monetary policy in this case is analogous to what happens with income-neutral investment by private investors: assets change hands in the sense that the central bank acquires green assets and sells brown assets. This act alone, however, does not affect the real economy. In the case of private investment, we argued that there is also hardly a significant change in asset prices following green investment and divestment from damaging assets because as long as brown assets are profitable, capital flows will find their way there, while the green sector is unlikely to constantly absorb more capital in the middle term because of unaltered returns. While, in contrast, green quantitative easing is supposedly able to at least create a price and interest-rate differential between the green and brown assets, it will still not necessarily deteriorate financing conditions for the environmentally harmful sectors substantially. As long as returns in those sectors are sufficient, financial flows will be secured and will compensate for the central bank's withdrawal. Moreover, there might be a spillover caused by green quantitative easing when central bank purchases focused on green sectors also raise the asset prices of the brown sectors because private investors rebalance their portfolios in search of higher yields. In that case, the brown sectors still reap some of the quantitative easing's benefits.

If green quantitative easing is not able to significantly alter the profitability of companies' real-world activities for the reasons mentioned above, its effects are limited to those within financial markets. Asset purchases by central banks drive up asset prices, implying that the central bank's high spending volumes are more due to high prices than newly emitted assets. Quantitative easing, even if it is green, contributes to bubble-building in financial markets with the well-known side effects such as more leveraged investments by private investors and financial instability once purchasing programs are supposed to fade out. Moreover, the high prices of financial assets favor wealthy households such that green quantitative easing contributes to inequality (see, for example, Montecino and Epstein, 2015). In the end, even if we assume that green quantitative easing has a certain impact on companies' real investments, the channel is rather inefficient since a large share of the central bank's asset purchases turns into extra returns for private financial investors who own those assets.

4.3   Ensuring Impact on Real Green Investment

Monetary policy can circumvent the side effects of green quantitative easing and other measures involving price effects of tradable assets and still influence companies' financing conditions by adjusting its more conventional policy instruments. For example, environmental sustainability may come in as a new weighting factor for the assessment of commercial banks' reserve and capital requirements. Thus the fewer brown assets and the more green assets a bank has on its balance sheet, the lower minimum reserves and equity would have to be (Campiglio, 2016). The weighting factor can represent the suggested higher risk of assets such as those based on fossil fuels or may potentially even discriminate stronger in order to be in line with specific environmental goals. Banks are incentivized to lend more to sustainable economic activities and to refuse finance to polluting companies.

Similarly, the central bank may discriminate environmentally harmful financing activities by setting a higher discount rate for its repo operations. As van 't Klooster and van Tilburg (2020) argue, this instrument would be particularly effective in the current circumstances when very long-term tenders are provided by central banks such as in the case of the European Central Bank. In a larger sense, this can be considered as a kind of selective credit allocation (Chang and Andreoni, 2020, p. 333).

All these measures – green quantitative easing, adjustment of requirements regarding collateral and minimum reserves, and differing discount rates for repo operations – are able to create a wedge that affects asset valuation by financial investors. Generally speaking, they are each a kind of subsidy of green assets or tax on brown assets, respectively, and as such they can be effective in greening investment activities. This is what makes green central banking more effective than the private sector sustainable finance approach.

While differentials in reserve requirements and lending rates may be more efficient because they do not contribute to general asset price inflation such as green quantitative easing, their success is still uncertain. These measures, too, affect only one variable in companies' profit equation and therefore are limited in their impact.

4.4   Embedding Monetary Policy into Environmental and Economic Policies

As long as investment decisions are made by private agents, profitability will pose a limit to real green investment and hence the transition toward sustainability. Monetary policy, jointly with environmental and economic policies, can overcome this bottleneck by setting up or expanding the activities of public banks. Public banks, in their traditions as development banks, can put environmental and societal goals to the fore while profitability is not the first priority (see, for example, Macfarlane and Mazzucato, 2018). The European Investment Bank (EIB) has already committed to not financing any new coal projects and by 2025 making at least 50 percent of its investment in projects dedicated to fighting climate change (EIB, 2020). This is relevant because unlike commercial banks, public banks such as the EIB finance projects, which would not necessarily find other investors in the private sector.

A particular type of monetary policy and lending activity that does not rely on profitability was established in advanced economies when the COVID-19 pandemic broke out in spring 2020. While the asset purchasing programs were expanded to unseen volumes, several central banks such as the US Federal Reserve (2020) and the Bank of England (2020b) even started providing loans directly to non-financial companies. The commercial banks were circumvented in order to provide finance to firms at the best possible conditions. The central banks thus took the role of public lending banks.

In a more general setting, the central bank and the public banks would be separate institutions. The central bank can support such a public green bank by applying the instruments discussed here, implying that green investment enjoys lower reserve requirements, better capability to serve as collateral and lower costs for central bank reserves. Endogenous money provides the power to finance all the green investment that is necessary while the public bank applies it the best way by maximizing the contribution to environmental goals rather than maximizing profits. By not adding a profit margin to its loans, the public bank, in contrast to commercial banks, makes green investment more competitive. Together with the subsidy instruments offered by the central bank, this makes public finance a powerful tool to finance the ecological transition.

Some proponents still label such a financing structure as green quantitative easing, for example when the ECB accommodates any financing activities of the EIB by purchasing all green bonds the latter issues (Batsaikhan and Laurentjoye, 2020). While this may be a matter of perspective, it is perhaps worth noting that in such a framework, the investment impulse is given by the public green bank with monetary policy merely having the role of accommodating these investments either via the purchase of bonds or the provision of reserves. In proper green quantitative easing, in contrast, the impulse is suggested to come from the central bank itself as it aims to push green finance by creating a green wedge in asset prices.

Bringing down borrowing costs is not the only barrier that needs to be removed for green investment to take off. The very high investment volume is an obstacle in itself. Many private households and firms do not feel able to borrow the high amounts of capital required, even though green investments are competitive in the long term because they have low, or zero, operation costs. High initial fixed investments for solar power plants, sustainable heating systems, insulation of buildings and so on represent a bottleneck. A public bank can remove this bottleneck by not only minimizing borrowing costs but also providing very long-term loans. Moreover, the public bank may be combined with public green agencies, which make the investment on behalf of the private firms and households such that the latter do not bear any investment risks and merely pay as clients for the use of the investments (Oberholzer, 2019). Such a setting would scale up and speed up the achievement of climate and other environmental goals.

Setting up a public bank, which makes decisions on real green investment, gives rise to an additional benefit. Subsidizing green investment while penalizing polluting investment is certainly an important cornerstone of any ambitious environmental policies. However, even if monetary policy is successful in ensuring the internalization of external environmental costs, an obstacle that private investors are not able to overcome, it is hardly enough to tackle fundamentally uncertain environmental problems such as climate change and biodiversity loss. Public banks allow for a macroeconomic strategy in line with green industrial policies, which enable economies of scale, guarantee demand and reduce uncertainty (see also Chang and Andreoni, 2020). Expanding this framework could potentially also involve monetary and fiscal policy intervention in commodity markets in order to increase and stabilize the prices of fossil fuels such that sustainable modes of production definitely become competitive in the long term compared to carbon-intensive activities (see Oberholzer, 2017, ch. 6). Unlike the 'market-fixing' approaches that merely focus on price adjustments in order to restore the otherwise efficient market equilibria, such a 'market-shaping' approach is able to overcome the fundamental obstacles to green transition (see Kattel et al., 2018, p. 21).

5.   CONCLUSION

Sustainable finance has become an influential narrative in the sense that it has definitely arrived in the political establishment in industrial countries. Part of its attractiveness may be explained by the fact that it promises change while not affecting any political economy questions; that is, without requiring any larger structural change. However, endogenous money reveals that the idea of shifting scarce money from bad to good investment is useless. In capitalism where finance follows profitability, unprofitable investments are not made at all, while endogenous money allows for the financing of any asset that is deemed profitable. Hence, with the profitability of green assets either high or low, the sustainable finance idea is either not necessary or not sufficient.

The central bank may be considered as a special case of the general green finance approach. Taking environmental considerations into account in the application of monetary policy instruments and strategies such as quantitative easing may have an influence, but its substance and efficiency are doubtful. The more green monetary policy is embedded in a comprehensive green industrial policy strategy, the more its benefits can be reaped. Discrimination in discount rates and support of selective credit policies via accommodating reserve requirements of public banks in a preferential way are most effective to guide investment. Public investment will guarantee the direction of sufficient financial flows to green assets, thereby reducing uncertainty while creating economies of scale, stable demand and crowding-in effects.

REFERENCES

Agrawal, A. and Hockerts, K. 2019. Impact investing: review and research agenda. *Journal of Small Business and Entrepreneurship, 33*(2): 153–181.

Ansar, A., Caldecott, B. and Tilbury, J. 2013. Stranded assets and the fossil fuel divestment campaign: what does divestment mean for the valuation of fossil fuel assets? *Smith School of Enterprise and the Environment and University of Oxford*, Stranded Assets Programme.

Bailly, J.-L. 2008. Consumption, investment and the investment multiplier. In C. Gnos and L.-P. Rochon (eds.), *The Keynesian Multiplier*. New York: Routledge (127–149).

Bank of England. 2020a. Climate change: what are the risks to financial stability? Available at https://www.bankofengland.co.uk/knowledgebank/climate-change -what-are-the-risks-to-financial-stability.

Bank of England. 2020b. Our response to coronavirus (Covid). Available at https://www.bankofengland.co.uk/coronavirus.

Batsaikhan, U. and Laurentjoye, T. 2020. A real European safe asset: the purchase of EIB bonds by the Eurosystem. Available at https://www.positivemoney.eu/2020/11/real-safe-asset-eib-bonds.

Battiston, S., Mandel, A., Monasterolo, I., Schütze, F. and Visentin, G. 2017. A climate stress-test of the financial system. *Nature Climate Change, 7*(Mar): 283–288.

Bénicourt, E. and Guerrien, B. 2008. *La théorie économique néoclassique: microéconomie, macroéconomie et théorie des jeux* (3rd ed.). Paris: La Découverte.

Boermans, M.A. and Galema, R. 2019. Are pension funds actively decarbonizing their portfolios? *Ecological Economics, 161*: 50–60.

Bugg-Levine, A. and Emerson, J. 2011. *Impact Investing: Transforming How We Make Money While Making a Difference* (1st ed.). San Francisco, CA: Jossey-Bass.

Campiglio, E. 2016. Beyond carbon pricing: the role of banking and monetary policy in financing the transition to a low-carbon economy. *Ecological Economics, 121*: 220–230.

Campiglio, E., Dafermos, Y., Monnin, P., Ryan-Collins, J., Schotten, G. and Tanaka, M. 2018. Climate change challenges for central banks and financial regulators. *Nature Climate Change, 8*: 462–468.

Carney, M. 2015. Breaking the tragedy of the horizon: climate change and financial stability. Speech at Lloyd's of London, London, September 29, 2015.

Chang, H.-J. and Andreoni, A. 2020. Industrial policy in the 21st century. *Development and Change, 51*(2): 324–351.

Dafermos, Y., Nikolaidi, M. and Galanis, G. 2018. Climate change, financial stability and monetary policy. *Ecological Economics, 152*: 219–234.

Dafermos, Y., Gabor, D., Nikolaidi, M., Pawloff, A. and van Lerven, F. 2020. Decarbonising is easy: beyond market neutrality in the ECB's corporate QE. New Economics Foundation. Available at https://neweconomics.org/2020/10/decarbonising-is-easy.

Dow, S.C. 2006. Endogenous money: structuralist. In P. Arestis and M. Sawyer (eds.), *Handbook of Alternative Monetary Economics*. Cheltenham: Edward Elgar Publishing (35–51).

European Investment Bank (EIB). 2020. Climate bank roadmap 2021–2025. Available at https://www.eib.org/en/videos/the-eib-group-climate-bank-roadmap.

Federal Reserve. 2020. Federal Reserve announces extensive new measures to support the economy. Press Release (March 23). Available at https://www.federalreserve.gov/newsevents/pressreleases/monetary20200323b.htm.

Fossil Free. 2019. Not a penny more for fossil fuels. Available at https://gofossilfree.org/not-a-penny-more.

Friede, G., Busch, T. and Bassen, A. 2015. ESG and financial performance: aggregated evidence from more than 2000 empirical studies. *Journal of Sustainable Finance and Investment*, *5*(4): 210–233.

Goodfriend, M. (2007). How the world achieved consensus on monetary policy. *National Bureau of Economic Research*, Working Paper No. 13580.

Grippa, P., Schmittmann, J. and Suntheim, F. 2019. Climate change and financial risk. International Monetary Fund: Finance and Development, December: 26–29.

Honohan, P. 2019. Should monetary policy take inequality and climate change into account? Peterson Institute for International Economics, Working Paper 19-18.

Kaiser, L. 2020. ESG integration: value, growth and momentum. *Journal of Asset Management*, *21*: 32–51.

Kattel, R., Mazzucato, M., Ryan-Collins, J. and Sharpe, S. 2018. The economics of change: policy appraisal for missions, market shaping and public purpose. UCL Institute for Innovation and Public Purpose, Working Paper Series, IIPP WP 2018-06. Available at: https://www.ucl.ac.uk/bartlett/public-purpose/wp2018-06.

Keynes, J.M. 1936/1997. *The General Theory of Employment, Interest, and Money*. New York: Prometheus Books.

Lavoie, M. 2006. Endogenous money: accommodationist. In P. Arestis and M. Sawyer (eds.), *Handbook of Alternative Monetary Economics*. Cheltenham: Edward Elgar Publishing (17–34).

Lenton, T.M., Rockström, J., Gaffney, O., Rahmstorf, S., Richardson, K., Steffen, W. and Schellnhuber, H.J. 2019. Climate tipping points: too risky to bet against. *Nature*, *575*: 592–595.

Macfarlane, L. and Mazzucato, M. 2018. State investment banks and patient finance: an international comparison. Institute for Innovation and Public Purpose, Working Paper IIPP WP 2018-01.

Matikainen, S., Campiglio, E. and Zenghelis, D. 2017. The climate impact of quantitative easing. Grantham Research Institute on Climate Change and the Environment. Available at https://www.lse.ac.uk/granthaminstitute/publication/the-climate-impact-of-quantitative-easing.

Mercure, J.-F., Pollitt, H., Viñuales, J.E., Edwards, N.R., Holden, P.B., Chewpreecha, U., Salas, P., Sognnaes, I., Lam, A. and Knobloch, F. 2018. Macroeconomic impact of stranded fossil fuel assets. *Nature Climate Change*, *8*: 588–593.

Monasterolo, I. and Raberto, M. 2019. The impact of phasing out fossil fuel subsidies on the low-carbon transition. *Energy Policy*, *124*: 355–370.

Montecino, J.A. and Epstein, G. 2015. Did quantitative easing increase income inequality? Institute for New Economic Thinking, Working Paper No. 28.

Moore, B.J. 1988. *Horizontalists and Verticalists: The Macroeconomics of Credit Money*. Cambridge: Cambridge University Press.

Oberholzer, B. 2017. *Monetary Policy and Crude Oil: Prices, Production and Consumption*. Cheltenham: Edward Elgar Publishing.

Oberholzer, B. 2019. Klimabank und Klima-Agenturen: Die massive Beschleunigung des ökologischen Umbaus. Denknetz Working Paper. Available at https://www.denknetz.ch/wp-content/uploads/2020/03/Klimabank_Oberholzer.pdf.

Rochon, L.-P. 1999. The creation and circulation of endogenous money: a circuit dynamique approach. *Journal of Economic Issues, 33*(1): 1–21.

Rochon, L.-P. and Rossi, S. (eds.). 2017. *Advances in Endogenous Money Analysis.* Cheltenham: Edward Elgar Publishing.

Rochon, L.-P. and Setterfield, M. 2011. Post-Keynesian interest rate rules and macro-economic performance: a comparative evaluation. In C. Gnos and L.-P. Rochon (eds.), *Credit, Money and Macroeconomic Policy: A Post-Keynesian Approach.* Cheltenham: Edward Elgar Publishing (116–141).

Schoenmaker, D. 2019. Greening monetary policy. Working Paper, 2019-02. Brussels: Bruegel. Available at https://www.bruegel.org/2019/02/greening-monetary-policy.

Shaikh, A. 2016. *Capitalism: Competition, Conflict, Crises.* New York: Oxford University Press.

Task Force on Climate-Related Financial Disclosures (TCFD). 2017. Final report: recommendations of the Task Force on Climate-Related Financial Disclosures (June 2017). Available at https://www.fsb-tcfd.org/publications/final-recommendations -report.

Tobin, J. 1969. A general equilibrium approach to monetary theory. *Journal of Money, Credit, and Banking, 1*(1): 15–29.

UNEP Finance Initiative (UNEP FI). 2018. Rethinking impact to finance the SDGs: a position paper and call to action prepared by the Positive Impact Initiative. Available at https://www.unepfi.org/positive-impact/rethinking-impact.

van 't Klooster, J. and Fontan, C. 2020. The myth of market neutrality: a comparative study of the European Central Bank's and the Swiss National Bank's corporate security purchases. *New Political Economy, 25*(6): 865–879.

van 't Klooster, J. and van Tilburg, R. 2020. Targeting a sustainable recovery with green TLTROs: green, targeted and long-term refinancing operations. Positive Money Europe and Sustainable Finance Lab. Available at www.positivemoney.eu.

Zerbib, O.D. 2019. The effect of pro-environmental preferences on bond prices: evidence from green bonds. *Journal of Banking and Finance, 98*: 39–60.

4. Monetary and financial policies for an ecological transition: An overview of central banks' actions and some reflections on post-Keynesian insights

Romain Svartzman[1]

1. INTRODUCTION

Until a few years ago, central bankers had barely (if at all) considered the potentially catastrophic impacts of climate change emphasized by the scientific community (IPCC, 2018), as if those were far remote from their mandates and practical concerns. However, the situation rapidly changed as of 2015 with Mark Carney's (then Governor of the Bank of England) seminal speech, "Breaking the Tragedy of the Horizon" (Carney, 2015), in which he argued that climate change could pose systemic and irreversible threats to financial stability. Indeed, the risks posed by climate change are such that they could take the form of a "climate Minsky moment" (Carney, 2015) or "Green Swans" (Bolton et al., 2020a): climate-related events (such as an increase in natural catastrophes or fire sales related to a sudden disorderly low-carbon transition) could generate systemic and in some cases irreversible impacts for the financial system.

In the face of this reality, central bankers' and financial supervisors' interest in climate change has grown rapidly over the past few years. In 2017, the NGFS (Network for Greening the Financial System) was created, after which its membership grew from eight central banks and financial supervisory authorities at its inception to 72[2] of them (as of the end of September 2020). NGFS members consider that climate change is "a source of financial risk. It is therefore within the mandates of central banks and supervisors to ensure the financial system is resilient to these risks" (NGFS, 2018, p. 3). Some central banks have started to explore (and in some cases implement) climate-related micro- and macroprudential regulations (see D'Orazio and Popoyan, 2019), including by conducting "climate stress tests" (e.g. Allen et al., 2020). More recently, they have also started to explore how climate change could affect the nature and transmission channels of monetary policy (NGFS, 2020a). In short, central banks increasingly acknowledge that climate change can affect their mandates of price or financial stability,[3] and many of them have already started to act.

In this context, many tend to think that central banks could be the "game changer" that the world needs to radically decarbonize our socioeconomic systems. Others consider that the current risk-based approach of central banks (which consists in considering that central banks should act on climate change only insofar as they can precisely measure how climate-related impacts affects their mandates) will be insufficient because of the radical uncertainty (Chenet et al., 2019) at stake. As such, bolder initiatives would be needed from central banks. For instance, several proposals have emerged calling for a "green" quantitative easing (e.g. Dafermos et al., 2018) and for financial regulations that would strongly penalize all financial institutions that are involved in carbon-intensive activities (Finance Watch, 2020; Chenet et al., 2019). Hence, the main source of contention in this rapidly growing literature seems to be about whether central banks can solve climate change while operating within the remit of their existing mandates, or whether they need to go beyond their mandate to do so.

However, fewer studies examine whether the quasi-exclusive reliance on monetary policy and prudential regulation as the solutions to climate change is a good strategy. In other words, ongoing debates rarely explore how far monetary and financial policies can go in triggering the structural change needed to address climate change. In fact, many scholars, in particular within the field of post-Keynesian economics, have long argued (although not in relation to climate change) that the impact of monetary policy is strongly limited, especially when interest rates are low and effective demand lacking (Lavoie, 2016; Rochon and Vallet, 2019). Put bluntly, no level of monetary policy can make up for a lack of fiscal policy. Such claims carry even more weight when one accepts that mitigating climate change demands a structural change that will require massive and long-term investments in "green" infrastructure and technologies, with uncertain returns. Market forces alone cannot implement such changes, even if nudged by monetary and financial policies, meaning that a much larger role is needed for fiscal policy. The challenge on hand, then, is to find which policy mixes are needed to tackle climate change and other ecological issues.

What should be the role of monetary and financial policies in this new policy mix fit for an ecological transition? In order to bring some insights into this question, this chapter first summarizes how and why the question of climate change (in particular) and ecological breakdown (to a larger extent) have become a topic of concern to central banks. It then explores the limitations to the dominant risk-based approach to the problem, given the radical uncertainty at stake and the need for a structural change (Aglietta and Espagne, 2016). The third section highlights how post-Keynesian theory sheds light on these limitations, but also why solving climate change and other ecological issues requires exploring new avenues and addressing new questions that escape traditional economic theories and debates (e.g. that neither neoclassical nor post-Keynesian theory can fully resolve). The fourth section concludes by calling for a renewed analytical framework that can fully account for the dreadful ecological reality we currently live in – that of the Anthropocene.

2. CENTRAL BANKS' MANDATES OF PRICE AND FINANCIAL STABILITY ARE THREATENED BY CLIMATE CHANGE

Earth's atmospheric concentration of carbon dioxide (CO_2) is higher than ever in human history, far above the levels that had prevailed for millennia up to the Industrial Revolution. These levels of atmospheric CO_2 concentration, which are caused by human activity and have been increasing particularly rapidly over the past decades (IPCC, 2018), hinder the Earth's natural cooling cycle. As a result, the global mean temperature has already increased by more than 1°C since the mid-19th century, and is now increasing at an ever-faster pace.

These trends, if persisting, can put humanity on track to a "hothouse Earth" pathway (Steffen et al., 2018), filled with systemic disruptions such as a greater frequency and intensity of storms, increasing droughts, and rising sea levels (IPCC, 2018). These events could lead to a massive extinction of wildlife (Ripple et al., 2017) but also severely impact human populations. For instance, saltwater intrusion due to sea-level rises and soil erosion could lead to major agricultural losses, thereby decreasing food security and biodiversity (IPCC, 2019); a two-metre sea-level rise (which could occur sooner than expected if ice sheets melt) could displace hundreds of million people by 2100 (Bamber et al., 2019); and entire regions in South America, Africa, India, Southern Asia, and Australia could become so hot and humid that they may become uninhabitable, potentially leading to massive migrations and conflicts (Im et al., 2017; Mora et al., 2018). The effects of climate change could then wipe out the progress achieved in terms of poverty reduction (Human Rights Council, 2019) and lead to "untold suffering" for future generations, according to more than 11,000 scientists (Ripple et al., 2020).

While these trends have been acknowledged for quite a long time by policy-makers (for instance, the Intergovernmental Panel on Climate Change (IPCC) was established in 1988) and some economists (e.g. Stern, 2006; Weitzman, 2011), although clearly not all of them,[4] it is only recently that central bankers have started to pay attention to them. In particular, following the 2015 speech by Mark Carney mentioned above, a group of central banks and financial supervisors came together to create the NGFS in 2017. The network rapidly grew and now gathers more than 70 members across the world.

The rationale behind the NGFS' interest in climate change is grounded in the realization that the latter could represent a significant threat to the two main mandates of central banks, those of safeguarding price stability and financial stability, as discussed below.

2.1   Climate Change as a Threat to Financial Stability

Shortly after its creation the NGFS acknowledged that "climate-related risks are a source of financial risk. It is therefore within the mandates of central banks and supervisors to ensure the financial system is resilient to these risks" (NGFS, 2018, p. 3). That is, the first and main reason why central banks should be concerned about climate change is because it may hinder their ability to safeguard financial stability.

The two main types of climate-related financial risks usually identified are the so-called physical and transition risks. Physical risks correspond to the financial losses caused by increasing frequency and severity of climate-related weather events (e.g. storms and floods) and long-term changes in climate patterns (e.g. ocean acidification and rising sea levels). For instance, the credit-worthiness of firms and sovereigns could be impacted by an increase in natural catastrophes, while banks and insurance companies could have insufficient capital to absorb the losses caused by such events (Cleary et al., 2019).

A rapid and successful shift to a low-carbon economy could avoid most of these physical risks but would remain subject to the second type of risks: transition risks. Indeed, avoiding the worst impacts of climate change amounts to an unprecedented challenge: human activities are currently emitting close to 40 gigatonnes (Gt) of CO_2 per year when we need to reduce these emissions to almost zero by 2050 in order to comply with the UN Paris Agreement of 2015 (UNFCCC, 2015), which set the goal of keeping global warming well below 2°C and as close as possible to 1.5°C above pre-industrial levels.

As a result of this urgency and the scale of the necessary action, the transition to a low-carbon economy could involve abrupt and disordered measures, including sudden shifts in fiscal and regulatory policies aimed at mitigating climate change (e.g. taxation on carbon or a ban of certain activities). Transition risks could arise from such events. In particular, limiting global warming to less than 1.5°C or 2°C requires keeping a large proportion of existing fossil fuel reserves in the ground. These "stranded assets" (McGlade and Ekins, 2015; Mercure et al., 2018) could lead to abrupt shifts in their prices and to a "climate Minsky moment" (Carney, 2015); that is, to a systemic crisis triggered by the fire sales of devalued fossil fuel assets.

Figure 4.1 presents these risks, their potential interactions, and their contagion channels. All agents (sovereigns, firms, households), assets (loans, bonds, equity), and channels of contagion (such as credit, market, and liquidity risks) are concerned with climate-related risks, which could worsen because of second-round or feedback loops.

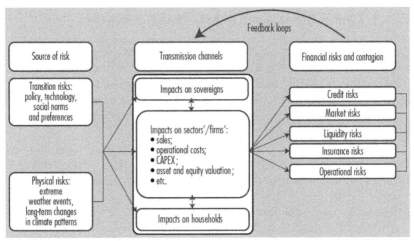

Source: Bolton et al. (2020b).

Figure 4.1   *Channels and spillovers for the materialization of physical and transition risks*

2.2   Climate Change as a Threat to Price Stability

More recently and to a more limited extent, central banks have also explored how their "core" mandate of price stability could be impacted by climate change (see NGFS, 2020a). Climate-related shocks could affect monetary policy through both supply-side and demand-side shocks. For instance, the increase in extreme climate events could exert pressures on the supply of agricultural products (McKibbin et al., 2017), while generating so much uncertainty that it could reduce household wealth and consumption (Batten, 2018). Climate-related shocks could therefore pull inflation (up) and output (down) in opposite directions, bringing central banks to operate difficult trade-offs between stabilizing inflation and stabilizing output fluctuations (Debelle, 2019). If they are severe, physical risks could even lead to prolonged situations of stagflation that monetary policy may be unable to easily reverse (Villeroy de Galhau, 2019).

In addition to these supply-side and demand-side shocks, climate change can affect the balance sheets of financial institutions (as discussed above), which can in turn impair the transmission channels of monetary policy (NGFS, 2020a). Moreover, if climate-related risks end up affecting productivity and growth, this may have implications for the long-run level of the real interest rate (Brainard, 2019). In an economy in which interest rates are already low, more frequent and severe physical risks "could imply, all else being equal, that the central bank is more likely to hit the zero – or effective – lower bound on policy interest rates. This would reduce policy space for conventional tools" (NGFS, 2020a, p. 6).

The trends and impacts described above could create three major challenges for the future of monetary policy, according to central bankers themselves: (i) monetary policy could become ineffective as it is designed for the short to medium term, whereas climate change is expected to maintain its trajectory for long periods of time (Cœuré, 2018); (ii) climate change is a global problem, whereas monetary policy remains largely designed at the scale of the nation-state. As a result, actions taken by a single central bank may be useless to revert price dynamics generated by climate-related impacts (Pereira da Silva, 2019); (iii) even if central banks were able to react to some climate-related inflationary shocks, it remains unclear whether they could take pre-emptive measures to hedge *ex ante* against these shocks, given the difficulty of anticipating climate-related shocks (Cœuré, 2018).

2.3   From Climate-related Risks to Climate Uncertainty: The Need to Revisit Central Banking in the Age of "Green Swans"

2.3.1   The limitations of a risk-based approach and the development of scenario analysis

The approach of central bankers to both financial and price stability in the age of climate change has been similar so far: it is necessary to better measure climate-related risks so as to manage them. In other words, the impacts of climate change should be managed according to the "old adage [...] that which is measured can be managed" (Carney, 2015).

With regard to financial stability, this approach implies that climate-related risks could become factored in micro- and macroprudential regulation. The first recommendation of the NGFS precisely aims at "integrating climate-related risks into financial stability monitoring and micro-supervision" (NGFS, 2019, p. 3). With regard to monetary policy, the NGFS "recommends that central banks assess the implications [of climate change] for risk management practices, as climate-related shocks may affect the riskiness of their financial portfolios and market operations" (NGFS, 2020a, p. 7) and further argues that a better understanding of such risks could provide insights into the future "design of monetary regimes, including the choice of (i) the central bank's target, (ii) the horizon over which a central bank is expected to meet its target, and (iii) the degree of flexibility embedded in monetary strategy" (NGFS, 2020a, p. 9).

However, this integration of climate-related risks into financial stability supervision and monetary policy faces a significant challenge: traditional approaches to financial risk will not be able to capture the nature of climate-related risks. Indeed, whereas risk management models are based on historical data and normal distribution assumptions, climate-related risks have barely started to materialize (physical risks are increasing and transition risks are virtually inexistent given the lack of ambitious policies) and they are likely to follow extreme values rather than normal ones (Weitzman, 2011). As a result, traditional regulatory tools such as those used to determine banks' capital requirements, which are typically calculated on a one-year horizon and based on credit ratings that largely rely on historical track records, will be unable to measure climate-related risks.

In order to overcome this limitation, a consensus is emerging among central banks: to capture climate-related risks, it is necessary to rely on forward-looking, scenario-based analyses (NGFS, 2020b). Unlike backward-looking risk management approaches, scenario analyses seek to set up plausible hypotheses for the future without attributing them a probability of occurrence. In particular, by building on the stress tests conducted to assess the resilience of banking institutions in an adverse macro-financial scenario (Borio et al., 2014), several central banks have started to develop "climate stress tests" (e.g. Allen et al., 2020; Vermeulen et al., 2019). For instance, Banque de France (Allen et al., 2020) proposed an analytical framework to quantify the potential impacts of different low-carbon transition narratives on specific macroeconomic and financial variables. Focusing on transition risks, the scenarios developed include unexpected increases in carbon prices and productivity shocks that could affect financial institutions' balance sheets.

More recently, work has also started to integrate climate-related risks into monetary policy. For instance, Oustry et al. (2020) build on existing scenarios to explore how climate-related risks could be systematically integrated into the collateral framework of a central bank. Such work is likely to develop rapidly as the integration of climate-related risks into monetary policy was a prominent topic of the Eurosystem's Strategy Review (Schnabel, 2020) conducted in 2021.

Some central banks and financial regulators, particularly in emerging economies (Dikau and Ryan-Collins, 2017), have already started to implement climate-orientated policies. For instance, financial institutions in Bangladesh are required to allocate 5% of their total loan portfolio to "green" sectors; China and Lebanon have started differentiating reserve requirements in proportion to local banks' lending to "green" sectors (D'Orazio and Popoyan, 2019); and Brazil's central bank requires commercial banks to incorporate environmental risks into their governance framework (FEBRABAN, 2014).

Have central banks, then, found the solution to ensure that the financial system and the transmission of monetary policy are resilient to climate-related risks? Unfortunately not, given the nature of the risks at stake.

2.3.2 Radical uncertainty and "Green Swans": new challenges for central banks

Climate-related risks are so peculiar that they can be characterized as "Green Swans" (see Figure 4.2). The Green Swan concept finds its inspiration in the concept of "Black Swans" (Taleb, 2007) and shares its three defining characteristics; that is, it refers to risks that: (i) are unexpected in light of past events; (ii) have wide-ranging or even extreme impacts; and (iii) are rationalized by conceptual frameworks developed *ex post*. But in addition to these features, Green Swans are also characterized by the fact that: (i) it is nearly certain that climate-related risks will materialize, even though there is profound uncertainty as to where, when, and how they will emerge; and (ii) they can carry irreversible and potentially civilizational impacts (Ripple et al., 2020), and thus require a systemic response. In other words, Green Swans will remain *unhedgeable* until a system-wide transition is undertaken.

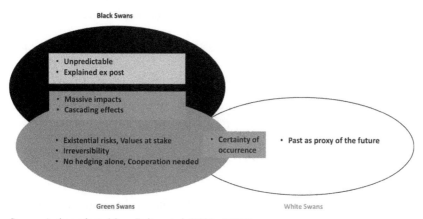

Source: Author, adapted from Bolton et al. (2020a, 2020b).

Figure 4.2   *Black, White, and Green Swans*

This suggests that managing climate-related risks demands a structural economic and social change; that is, a radical shift in the way we produce and consume but also how we eat, commute, and live (Geels et al., 2004). Indeed, mitigating climate change will bring major socioeconomic and even geopolitical changes. For instance, the history of energy and social systems shows that the evolution of primary energy uses is deeply connected to profound transformations of existing socioeconomic systems (Pearson and Foxon, 2012). Similarly, an ambitious low-carbon transition could reshuffle trade flows and global value chains (e.g. because of the shift from fossil fuels to new materials needed to power renewable technologies), possibly generating new tensions regarding access to certain minerals (IRENA, 2019).

As a result, aiming to anticipate such patterns with precision and to tackle them through a risk-based approach becomes impossible. While scenario analyses are an essential tool that can enable financial institutions and supervisors to envision different futures, they will be insufficient to handle the radical uncertainty and the complexity associated with climate change impacts (physical risks) and mitigation (transition risks), as well as the need for a structural change (Aglietta and Espagne, 2016).

This new ecological reality creates a dilemma for central banks (Svartzman, Bolton et al., 2020). They cannot simply develop scenarios while waiting for government agencies to take action: this could expose them to the real risk of not being able to deliver on their mandates of price and financial stability, given the systemic nature of the physical risks and the impossibility of hedging from them through a risk-based approach. However, central banks cannot substitute for public policies (fiscal, industrial, spatial planning, etc.) in order to trigger the structural change required.

How, then, should we envision monetary and financial policies in the age of Green Swans? In what follows, we explore how post-Keynesian theory provides critical insights to overcome this dilemma.

3.   INSIGHTS AND POTENTIAL LIMITATIONS OF POST-KEYNESIAN ECONOMICS

3.1   New Policy Mixes and Central Bank Mandates Towards a Green New Deal?

Post-Keynesian scholars have long emphasized the inherent limits to monetary policy, especially when interest rates are already low and effective demand lacking (Lavoie, 2016; Rochon and Vallet, 2019), as well as the need for coordinating monetary and financial policies with fiscal policies. In fact, in the face of prevailing low interest rates, many non-post-Keynesian economists have recently raised similar concerns and called for stronger fiscal policies, given the low prevailing interest rates in advanced economies (e.g. Borio and Shin, 2019; McCulley and Pozsar, 2013). In that sense, the limitations of monetary and financial policies are not specific to climate change but they become even more palatable when it comes to handling climate change, given the need for a structural socioeconomic shift.

In this context, it is promising to observe that the quest for new policy mixes that can serve climate purposes (see Krogstrup and Oman, 2019) has gathered momentum around the concept of a Green New Deal (e.g. Macquarie, 2019; Pettifor, 2020), which seeks to revive Roosevelt's response to the Great Depression while putting it at the service of a low-carbon transition. In this approach, monetary and financial policies have a critical role to play but only insofar as they are connected to fiscal and industrial policies. For instance, the fact that central banks in advanced economies are setting interest rates near or even below zero at a time when massive "green" investments are needed is probably the greatest contribution that central banks can provide to help combat climate change.

Some have even gone further by aiming to integrate insights from post-Keynesian thought into those of ecological economics, through the development of a relatively new field of "ecological macroeconomics" (Holt et al., 2009; Fontana and Sawyer, 2016; Røpke, 2016). At the very core of this emerging discipline lies a reliance on the concept of radical uncertainty, which is critical to approach both economic and ecological dynamics. Ecological macroeconomics also strongly relies on an endogenous approach to money as an essential component to appreciate how financial instability and ecological degradations may interact with one another (Svartzman et al., 2019). An example of this collaboration between post-Keynesian and ecological economics lies in the use of the stock-flow consistent (SFC) approach, developed originally within the post-Keynesian school of thought, to explore ecological questions such as resource depletion or climate damages (Dafermos et al., 2017). Some authors (e.g. Forstater, 2003; Lawn, 2010; Godin, 2013) have also built on the post-Keynesian concept of government as "employer of last resort" to suggest that it be used for "green" full employment mechanisms "including monitoring, clean up, recycling, education, and more" (Forstater, 2003, p. 385).

It is noteworthy that under this approach, government action would not seek to manage climate-related risks optimally but rather to steer markets "in broadly the right direction" (Ryan-Collins, 2019). That is, the goal would no longer be to manage what gets measured but rather to use the power of coordinated fiscal, monetary, and prudential regulation to steer markets away from carbon-intensive to cleaner activities. Such a proactive shift in policy-making could then lead market players to reassess the risks related to climate change. According to some, such a new policy mix could trigger a new era of "greener" and more dynamic growth than what prevailed in the past decades of financialized capitalism. For instance, public investments in the low-carbon transition could "become the next big technological and market opportunity, stimulating and leading private and public investment" (Mazzucato and Perez, 2015, p. 230).

Emphasizing the role of fiscal policy does not mean that monetary and financial policies no longer have a role to play. Quite the contrary: building on post-Keynesian scholarship advocating for central banks' multi-goals mandates that would include a stronger commitment to questions such as full employment (e.g. Seccareccia and Khan, 2019) and gender (Vallet, 2019), several propositions were recently articulated to better include climate considerations in central banks' mandates and/or practices. For instance, Chenet et al. (2019) suggest a precautionary approach through which central banks and financial supervisors would take bold measures to steer markets in a low-carbon direction. Such measures could include: sharp increases in capital requirements for banks exposed to fossil fuels, as also suggested by Finance Watch (2020); credit controls and guidance, as already applied in several countries such as China (Campiglio et al., 2018; D'Orazio and Popoyan, 2019); climate-related unconventional monetary policy such as an exclusion of carbon-intensive assets from quantitative easing purchases of corporate bonds (Jourdan and Kalinowski, 2019), and even direct green monetary financing of governments (Dafermos et al., 2018).

In short, the post-Keynesian perspective calls for a major institutional shift not only with regard to the mandate of central banks, which may include overcoming the principle of central bank independence and the exclusive focus on inflation targeting (two notions that post-Keynesians consider hallmarks of the ongoing era of financialized capitalism (Seccareccia and Khan, 2019)), but also a more balanced distribution of responsibilities between monetary policy and democratically grounded fiscal policies.

3.2   Limitations to a "Green" Post-Keynesian Agenda?

Despite the important insights provided by post-Keynesian theory, it seems that significant obstacles could emerge on the way to their implementation. Without aiming for exhaustivity, we mention three of them: (i) the potential limitations to a green growth agenda; (ii) the need to account for ecological crises other than climate change; and (iii) the fact that the structural change needed to face climate and ecological crises brings new questions (such as an ecological reform of the international monetary system) that have not yet been considered by post-Keynesian scholars.

First, regarding the ability of a post-Keynesian agenda to engage the global economy in the path of green growth: most of the literature calling for stronger fiscal policies assumes more or less explicitly that they will have a positive impact on economic growth, employment, and the environment. This "win–

win–win" perspective, however, tends to ignore the potential limitations and trade-offs that may emerge between those goals. For instance, if, as many ecological economists argue, a low-carbon economy needed to rely more strongly on labour-intensive activities (e.g. Jackson, 2017), the latter could reinforce the "Baumol's cost disease" effect; that is, accelerating the ongoing slowdown in productivity and economic growth (Jackson, 2017). More broadly, a large literature calls into question the very feasibility of decoupling economic growth from environmental harm (e.g. Hickel and Kallis, 2020; Jackson, 2017; Parrique et al., 2019).

While this chapter cannot delve in depth into such questions, it is noteworthy that post-Keynesian scholarship has barely started to address them. For instance, one can wonder what would happen to the "fair" rate of interest (Lavoie and Seccareccia, 1999) in an ecological system where the growth of productivity would remain low, either because priority would be given to labour-intensive sectors with low productivity growth (as suggested by Jackson, 2017) or because existing gains in productivity would be used to reduce working time, as advocated by many ecological economists and by Keynes himself (1930). Similarly, assuming that the transition will take place through massive green investments with positive investment multipliers may be overly optimistic. For instance, drastically improving energy efficiency and reducing absolute energy use through more simple or "sober" (NégaWatt, 2018) lifestyles, which are key conditions to meet ambitious climate targets, could reduce the amount of investment needed for the transition (Grubler et al., 2018). Moreover, some investments in energy efficiency could paradoxically lead to a decrease in GDP or at least to some level of crowding out, especially if energy is assessed through ecological economics models (see Keen et al., 2019). For instance, successful investments in railroad transportation should lead to reducing the number of individual cars.

Second, the limitations discussed above become even more constraining when one zooms out of climate change and accounts for the broader set of ecological risks we currently face. Indeed, climate change is only the "tip of the iceberg" (Steffen et al., 2011): other biogeochemical cycles that are as essential for life on Earth as a stable climate are also being severely affected by human activity. Rockström et al. (2009) have identified and quantified nine of these cycles or "planetary boundaries" which define the "safe operating space for humanity" (ibid.): if specific thresholds are crossed for each of them, some Earth (sub)systems could shift into a new state, with "deleterious or potentially even disastrous consequences for humans" (Rockström et al., 2009, p. 472). For instance, the massive loss of biodiversity[5] generated by human activity (IPBES, 2019) seems to have already crossed a tipping point, which could make the occurrence of Green Swans such as pandemics more likely. In fact, many scholars have pointed out that the COVID-19 pandemic may have been caused, like many previous infectious diseases, by increased human contact with wildlife (Wolfe et al., 2007) resulting from the destruction of their natural habitat (Grandcolas and Justine, 2020).

The problem for post-Keynesian theory is that the "solutions" to climate change can hardly be applied to other ecological risks such as biodiversity. Indeed, unlike low-carbon investments, environmental restoration often requires minimizing human claims upon nature, which implies a reduction of economic activity rather than an increase in investments (Kedward et al., 2020). For instance, decreasing pressures on biodiversity in a country such as France includes halting the degradation of soils that is caused, among other things, by the construction of residential and commercial activities in previously rural areas (Ministère de l'écologie, 2010). In other words, not investing is the best investment in natural capital in such a case. This does not suggest that investments are not needed to preserve biodiversity (e.g. to hire staff in charge of natural reserves, to promote agroecological practices, and so on), but rather that addressing our biodiversity crisis can hardly rely solely on "green" investments.

Third, and as a result of the first two points, it becomes obvious that an ecological transition entails deeper social changes than those envisioned by both (neoclassical) risk-based and (post-Keynesian) uncertainty-based approaches. Put differently, several areas of socioeconomic transformations not envisioned by either orthodox or heterodox perspectives may be essential to a successful transition. For instance, protecting the environmental commons that enable all economic and human activity may require new governance schemes that go beyond traditional understandings of both private and public property (Dron et al., 2020; Ostrom, 2010) and a better understanding of the different types of relationship that can be developed by human systems and their natural environment across the world, including in indigenous communities that are often marginalized from economic theory (Levrel, 2020; Muradian et al., 2013).

Yet another avenue for transformation pertains to the necessary transformation of the international monetary system (IMS) so as to account for climate stability as a global public good. While calls for reforms of the IMS are emerging, including through International Monetary Fund issuances of "green" Special Drawing Rights (SDRs) to finance "green" funds (Aglietta and Coudert, 2019; Bredenkamp and Pattillo, 2010; Ocampo, 2019), the dwindling stock of carbon that can be used while limiting global warming to less than 1.5°C or 2°C may be so constraining[6] that tensions could rapidly emerge with regard to its use: the wealthiest countries may not only need to enable the funding of the transition in poorer countries (as advocated so far) but first and foremost drastically reduce their own emissions (the wealthiest 10% currently emit 50% of the CO_2), thereby intentionally reducing their own growth rates or even degrowing their economy in order to give poorer countries a chance to achieve sustainable development on a habitable planet (Althouse et al., 2020; Svartzman and Althouse, 2020). If this was necessary, the quest for a global and fair transition would pose unprecedented challenges of international social and environmental justice. However, such discussions still largely escape the economic discipline at large or often remain limited to sterile debates between supposedly optimistic advocates of green growth versus supposedly pessimistic proponents of degrowth.

While it is impossible to discuss all the implications for central banks of these three potential limitations to a post-Keynesian green growth agenda (ecological constraints, the multiplicity of ecological crises, and the need for deeper reforms than those traditionally envisioned), it can be safely argued that the future of central banking will likely consist not simply in returning to the practices and institutional arrangements that prevailed during the post-World War II Golden Age (which seems to be what most post-Keynesians have in mind as a desirable future). Indeed, the material and ecological reality of the world has become so different that an evolutionary perspective on the role of central banks and monetary institutional arrangements (à la Aglietta, 2018) suggests that deeper questions need to be asked about the institution of money for a finite planet (e.g. Svartzman, Ament et al., 2020).

4. CONCLUSION: WHICH FRAMEWORK TO THINK ABOUT MONETARY AND FINANCIAL POLICIES IN THE AGE OF GREEN SWANS?

The severity of the ecological crises the world currently faces (including but not limited to climate change) has led many to argue that we have already entered the Anthropocene, an epoch in which "human impacts on essential planetary processes have become so profound that they have driven the Earth out of the Holocene epoch in which agriculture, sedentary communities, and eventually, socially and technologically complex human societies developed" (Steffen et al., 2018, p. 8252). The COVID-19 pandemic may even be considered as "the first economic crisis of the Anthropocene" (Tooze, 2020); that is, as the first Green Swan of a new era (Bolton et al., 2020c).

In turn, avoiding the unhedgeable Green Swans that may arise if we keep crossing different planetary boundaries requires nothing less than creating a stabilized Earth pathway, which "can only be achieved and maintained by a coordinated, deliberate effort by human societies to manage our relationship with the rest of the Earth System, recognising that humanity is an integral, interacting component of the system" (Steffen et al., 2018, p. 8257). This requires finding an "environmentally safe and socially just space in which humanity can thrive", between social foundations and ecological ceilings

(Raworth, 2017, p. E48). In other words, nothing less than a structural transformation of our global socioeconomic system is needed.

Envisioning the future of central banking (both in terms of monetary and financial policies) in such a context is particularly challenging. Such a task will certainly entail revisiting the dominance of monetary policy over fiscal policy and fully embracing the concept of radical uncertainty; post-Keynesian theory can undoubtedly help towards these two ends. In addition, monetary and financial policies will need to account for a broader scope of concerns, including ecological issues, as discussed in this chapter.

However, other issues such as the governance of our global ecological commons and of our finite resources escape the traditional debates that have animated the field of economics to date. That is, they demand addressing questions (such as the potential limitations to a green growth agenda and the need to account for many ecological crises that cannot be solved solely through "green" investments, as discussed above) that neither neoclassical nor post-Keynesian theories are yet equipped to handle. In the face of these new challenges, it seems that new conceptual frameworks will be needed. While this chapter barely touched upon some possible areas of transformation such as that of an ecological reform of the international monetary system, its main goal was to lay the groundwork for further work on such questions.

NOTES

1. The views expressed in this chapter are those of the author and do not necessarily represent the views of the Banque de France.
2. All members are central banks or financial supervisory authorities. The NGFS also counts 13 observers including the Bank for International Settlement (BIS), the International Monetary Fund (IMF), and the World Bank.
3. The mandates of central banks vary throughout the world, but they typically include responsibility for both price stability and financial stability. The financial stability mandate is often more "de facto" than legally grounded.
4. See Keen (2020) for an assessment of the misrepresentation of climate science by some neoclassical economists.
5. For example, the biomass of wild mammals has fallen by 82% since the pre-industrialization era; about a third of reef-building corals is threatened with extinction (IPBES, 2019).
6. If we are to remain within a 50% probability of achieving the 1.5°C target, the carbon budget from 2020 onwards is of 495 gigatonnes of CO_2 ($GtCO_2$), corresponding to about 10 years of current emissions and much less if we factor in recent trends of annual increases in emissions.

REFERENCES

Aglietta, M. (2018). *Money: 5,000 Years of Debt and Power*. Verso Books.

Aglietta, M., and Coudert, V. (2019). The dollar and the transition from key currency to multilateralism. *CEPII Working Paper*, 2019-26.

Aglietta, M., and Espagne, E. (2016). Climate and finance systemic risks, more than an analogy? The climate fragility hypothesis. *CEPII Working Paper*, 2016-10.

Allen, T., Dees, S., Boissinot, J., Caicedo Graciano, C., Chouard, V., Clerc, L., De Gaye, A., Devulder, A., Diot, S., Lisack, N., Pegoraro, S., Rabate, M., Svartzman, R., and Vernet, L. (2020). Climate-related scenarios for financial stability assessment: An application to France. *Banque de France Working Paper*, 774.

Althouse, J., Guarini, G., and Porcile, J.G. (2020). Ecological macroeconomics in the open economy: Sustainability, unequal exchange and policy coordination in a center-periphery model. *Ecological Economics*, 172, 106628.

Bamber, J. L., Oppenheimer, M., Kopp, R. E., Aspinall, W. P., and Cooke, R. M. (2019). Ice sheet contributions to future sea-level rise from structured expert judgment. *Proceedings of the National Academy of Sciences of the United States of America*, 166(23), 11195–200.

Batten, S. (2018). Climate change and the macro-economy: A critical review. *Bank of England Working Paper*, 706.

Bolton, P., Després, M., Pereira da Silva, L., Samama, F., and Svartzman, R. (2020a). The Green Swan, central banking and financial stability in the age of climate change. Bank for International Settlements and Banque de France.

Bolton, P., Després, M., Pereira da Silva, L., Samama, F., and Svartzman, R. (2020b). "Green Swans": Central banks in the age of climate-related risks. *Banque de France Bulletin*, 229(8).

Bolton, P., Després, M., Pereira da Silva, L., Samama, F., and Svartzman, R. (2020c). Penser la stabilité financière à l'ère des risques écologiques globaux: Vers de nouveaux arbitrages entre efficience et résilience des systèmes complexes. *Revue d'Economie Financière*, 138, 41–54. https://doi.org/10.3917/ecofi.138.0041.

Borio, C., and Shin, H. S. (2019). BIS quarterly review, September 2019 – media briefing. Bank for International Settlements.

Borio, C., Drehmann, M., and Tsatsaronis, K. (2014). Stress-testing macro stress testing: Does it live up to expectations? *Journal of Financial Stability*, 12(1), 3–15.

Brainard, L. (2019). Why climate change matters for monetary policy and financial stability. Speech delivered at "The Economics of Climate Change", a research conference sponsored by the Federal Reserve Bank of San Francisco, San Francisco, California, 8 November 2019.

Bredenkamp, H., and Pattillo, C. (2010). Financing the response to climate change. *IMF Staff Position Note*.

Campiglio, E., Dafermos, Y., Monnin, P., Ryan-Collins, J., Schotten, G., and Tanaka, M. (2018). Climate change challenges for central banks and financial regulators. *Nature Climate Change*, 8(6), 462–8.

Carney, M. (2015). Breaking the tragedy at the horizon: Climate change and financial stability. Speech at Lloyd's of London.

Chenet, H., Ryan-Collins, J., and Van Lerven, F. (2019). Climate-related financial policy in a world of radical uncertainty: Towards a precautionary approach. *UCL Institute for Innovation and Public Purpose*, 2019-13.

Cleary, P., Harding, W., McDaniels, J., Svoronos, J. P., and Yong, J. (2019). FSI insights on policy implementation turning up the heat: Climate risk assessment in the insurance sector. Bank for International Settlements.

Cœuré, B. (2018). Monetary policy and climate change. Speech at a conference on "Scaling Up Green Finance: The Role of Central Banks", organized by the Network for Greening the Financial System, the Deutsche Bundesbank, and the Council on Economic Policies, Berlin, 8 November 2018.

Dafermos, Y., Nikolaidi, M., and Galanis, G. (2017). A stock-flow-fund ecological macroeconomic model. *Ecological Economics*, 131, 191–207.

Dafermos, Y., Nikolaidi, M., and Galanis, G. (2018). Climate change, financial stability and monetary policy. *Ecological Economics*, 152, 219–34.

Debelle, G. (2019). Climate change and the economy. Speech at the Public Forum hosted by the Centre for Policy Development, Sydney, 12 March 2019.

Dikau, S., and Ryan-Collins, J. (2017). Green central banking in emerging market and developing country economies. New Economics Foundation.

D'Orazio, P., and Popoyan, L. (2019). Fostering green investments and tackling climate-related financial risks: Which role for macroprudential policies? *Ecological Economics*, 160, 25–37.

Dron, D. Espagne, E., and Svartzman, R. (2020). Une monnaie au service des communs? *Esprit*, March.

FEBRABAN (2014). The Brazilian financial system and the green economy: Alignment with sustainable development. UNEP.

Finance Watch (2020). Breaking the climate-finance doom loop. *Finance Watch*, June.

Fontana, G., and Sawyer, M. (2016). Towards post-Keynesian ecological macroeconomics. *Ecological Economics*, 121, 186–95.

Forstater, M. (2003). Public employment and environmental sustainability. *Journal of Post Keynesian Economics*, 25(3), 385–406.

Geels, F. W., Boelie, E., and Green, K. (2004). General introduction: System innovations and transitions to sustainability. In B. Elzen, F. W. Geels, and K. Green (Eds.). *System Innovation and the Transition to Sustainability: Theory, Evidence and Policy* (pp. 19–47). Edward Elgar Publishing.

Godin, A. (2013). Green jobs for full employment, a stock flow consistent analysis. In M. J. Murray and M. Forstater (Eds.). *Employment Guarantee Schemes* (pp. 7–46). Palgrave Macmillan.

Grandcolas, P., and Justine, J.-L. (2020). Covid-19 or the pandemic of mistreated biodiversity. *The Conversation*, 29 April.

Grubler, A., Wilson, C., Bento, N., Boza-Kiss, B., Krey, V., McCollum, D. L., Rao, N. D. et al. (2018). A low energy demand scenario for meeting the 1.5 °C target and sustainable development goals without negative emission technologies. *Nature Energy*, 3(6), 515–27.

Hickel, J., and Kallis, G. (2020). Is green growth possible? *New Political Economy*, 25(4), 469–86.

Holt, R. P. F., Pressman, S., and Spash, C. L. (2009). *Post Keynesian and Ecological Economics*. Edward Elgar Publishing.

Human Rights Council (2019). Climate change and poverty: Report of the Special Rapporteur on Extreme Poverty and Human Rights. UN Human Rights – Office of the High Commissioner.

Im, E. S., Pal, J. S., and Eltahir, E. A. B. (2017). Deadly heat waves projected in the densely populated agricultural regions of South Asia. *Science Advances*, 3(8).

IPBES (2019). Summary for policymakers of the global assessment report on biodiversity and ecosystem services of the intergovernmental science: Policy platform on biodiversity and ecosystem services. *IPBES Secretariat*.

IPCC (2018). Summary for policymakers. In *Global warming of 1.5°C: An IPCC Special Report on the impacts of global warming of 1.5°C above pre-industrial levels and related global greenhouse gas emission pathways, in the context of strengthening the global response to the threat of climate change.* IPCC.

IPCC (2019). Climate change and land: An IPCC Special Report on climate change, desertification, land degradation, sustainable land management, food security, and greenhouse gas fluxes in terrestrial ecosystems. IPCC.

IRENA (2019). A new world: The geopolitics of the energy transformation. International Renewable Energy Agency (IRENA).

Jackson, T. (2017). *Prosperity Without Growth.* 2nd edition. Routledge.

Jourdan, S., and Kalinowski, W. (2019). Aligning monetary policy with the EU's climate targets. Veblen Institute for Economic Reforms and Positive Money Europe.

Kedward, K., Ryan-Collins, J., and Chenet, H. (2020). Managing nature-related financial risks: A precautionary policy approach for central banks and financial supervisors. UCL Institute for Innovation and Public Purpose, Working Paper Series (IIPP WP 2020-09).

Keen, S. (2020). The appallingly bad neoclassical economics of climate change. *Globalizations*, 18(7), 1149–77.

Keen, S., Ayres, R. U., and Standish, R. (2019). A note on the role of energy in production. *Ecological Economics*, 157, 40–6.

Keynes, J. M. (1930/1980). *The Collected Writings of John Maynard Keynes. 1940–1944, Shaping the Post-War World: The Clearing Union* (vol. 15). Cambridge University Press.

Krogstrup, S., and Oman, W. (2019). Macroeconomic and financial policies for climate change mitigation: A review of the literature. *IMF Working Paper*, 19 (185).

Lavoie, M. (2016). Rethinking macroeconomic theory before the next crisis. Institute for New Economic Thinking (INET), 23 September.

Lavoie, M., and Seccareccia, M. (1999). Fair interest rates. In P. A. O'Hara (Ed.). *Encyclopedia of political economy*, vol. 1. London: Routledge.

Lawn, P. (2010). Facilitating the transition to a steady-state economy: Some macroeconomic fundamentals. *Ecological Economics*, 69, 931–6.

Levrel, H. (2020). D'une économie de la biodiversité à une économie de la conservation de la biodiversité. Fondation pour la recherche sur la biodiversité.

Macquarie, R. (2019). Of course we can pay for a green new deal, but we can't escape hard choices. *Open Democracy*, 13 March.

Mazzucato, M., and Perez, C. (2015). Innovation as growth policy: The challenge for Europe. In J. Fagerberg, S. Laestadius and B. Martin (Eds.). *The Triple Challenge for Europe: Economic Development, Climate Change and Governance* (pp. 229–64). Oxford University Press.

McCulley, P., and Pozsar, Z. (2013). Helicopter money: Or how I stopped worrying and love fiscal-monetary cooperation. Global Society of Fellows.

McGlade, C., and Ekins, P. (2015). The geographical distribution of fossil fuels unused when limiting global warming to 2°C. *Nature*, 517(7533), 187–90.

McKibbin, W., Morris, A., Panton, A. J., and Wilcoxen, P. J. (2017). Climate change and monetary policy: Dealing with disruption. *CAMA Working Paper*.

Mercure, J. F., Pollitt, H., Viñuales, J. E., Edwards, N. R., Holden, P. B., Chewpreecha, U., Salas, P., Sognnaes, I., Lam, A., and Knobloch, F. (2018). Macroeconomic impact of stranded fossil fuel assets. *Nature Climate Change*, 8(7), 588–93.

Ministère de l'écologie (2010). Stratégie Nationale pour la Biodiversité 2011–2020. https://www.ecologie.gouv.fr/sites/default/files/Strat%C3%A9gie%20nationale%20pour%20la%20biodiversit%C3%A9%202011-2020.pdf.

Mora, C., Spirandelli, D., Franklin, E. C., Lynham, J., Kantar, M. B., Miles, W., Smith, C. Z. et al. (2018). Broad threat to humanity from cumulative climate hazards intensified by greenhouse gas emissions. *Nature Climate Change*, 8(12), 1062–71.

Muradian, R., Arsel, M., Pellegrini, L., Adaman, F., Aguilar, B., Agarwal, B., Corbera, E. et al. (2013). Payments for ecosystem services and the fatal attraction of win–win solutions. *Conservation Letters*, 6(4), 274–9.

NégaWatt (2018) Scénario négaWatt 2017–2050. *négaWatt*, Hypothèses et résultats.

NGFS (2018). NGFS First Progress Report. Network for Greening the Financial System.

NGFS (2019). NGFS First Comprehensive Report. A call for action – Climate change as a source of financial risk. Network for Greening the Financial System.

NGFS (2020a). Climate change and monetary policy: Initial takeaways. Network for Greening the Financial System.

NGFS (2020b). Guide to climate scenario analysis for central banks and supervisors. Network for Greening the Financial System.

Ocampo, J. A. (2019). The SDR's time has come. *Finance and Development*, 56(4), 62–3.

Ostrom, E. (2010). Beyond markets and states: Polycentric governance of complex economic systems. *American Economic Review*, 100, 641–72.

Oustry, A., Bunyamin, A., Svartzman, R., and Weber, P. F. (2020). Climate-related risks and central banks' collateral policy: A methodological experiment. *Banque de France Working Paper*, 790.

Parrique, T., Barth, J., Briens, F., Spangenberg, J. H., and Kraus-Polk, A. W. (2019). *Decoupling debunked: Evidence and arguments against green growth as a sole strategy for sustainability*. European Environmental Bureau.

Pearson, P., and Foxon, T. (2012) A low carbon industrial revolution? Insights and challenges from past technological and economic transformations. *Energy Policy*, 50, 117–27.

Pereira da Silva, L. A. (2019). Research on climate-related risks and financial stability: An epistemological break? Based on remarks at the Conference of the Central Banks and Supervisors Network for Greening the Financial System (NGFS), Paris, 17 April.

Pettifor, A. (2020). *The Case for the Green New Deal*. Verso Books.

Raworth, K. (2017). A doughnut for the Anthropocene: Humanity's compass in the 21st century. *The Lancet Planetary Health*, 1(2), E48–E49.

Ripple, W. J., Wolf, C., Newsome, T. M., Galetti, M., Alamgir, M., Crist, E., Mahmoud, M. I., and Laurance, W. F. (2017). World scientists' warning to humanity: A second notice. *BioScience*, 67(12), 1026–8.

Ripple, W., Wolf, C., Newsome, T., Barnard, P., Moomaw, W., and Gutiérrez Cárdenas, P. D. A. (2020). World scientists' warning on climate emergency. *BioScience*, 70, 8–12.

Rochon, L. P., and Vallet, G. (2019). Economía del Ave María: El modelo teórico detrás de las políticas monetarias no convencionales. *Revista Ola Financiera*, 12(34), 1–24.

Rockström, J., Steffen, W., Noone, K., Persson, A., Chapin, F. S., Lambin, E. F., Lenton, T. M. et al. (2009). A safe operating space for humanity. *Nature*, 461(7263), 472–5.

Røpke, I. (2016). Complementary system perspectives in ecological macroeconomics: The example of transition investments during the crisis. *Ecological Economics*, 121, 237–45.

Ryan-Collins, J. (2019). Beyond voluntary disclosure: Why a "market-shaping" approach to financial regulation is needed to meet the challenge of climate change. *SUERF Policy Note*, 61.

Schnabel, I. (2020). Never waste a crisis: COVID-19, climate change and monetary policy. Speech by Isabel Schnabel, Member of the Executive Board of the ECB, at a virtual roundtable on "Sustainable Crisis Responses in Europe" organized by the INSPIRE research network, 17 July.

Seccareccia, M., and Khan, N. (2019). The illusion of inflation targeting: Have central banks figured out what they are actually doing since the global financial crisis? An alternative to the mainstream perspective. *International Journal of Political Economy*, 48(4), 364–80.

Steffen, W., Grinevald, J., Crutzen, P., and Mcneill, J. (2011). The Anthropocene: Conceptual and historical perspectives. *Philosophical Transactions of the Royal Society A: Mathematical, Physical and Engineering Sciences*, 369(1938), 842–67.

Steffen, W., Rockström, J., Richardson, K., Lenton, T. M., Folke, C., Liverman, D., Summerhayes, C. P. et al. (2018). Trajectories of the Earth system in the Anthropocene. *Proceedings of the National Academy of Sciences of the United States of America*, 115(33), 8252–9.

Stern, N. (2006). The economics of climate change: The Stern review. http://mudancasclimaticas.cptec.inpe.br/~rmclima/pdfs/destaques/sternreview_report_complete.pdf.

Svartzman, R., and Althouse, J. (2020). Greening the international monetary system? Not without addressing the political ecology of global imbalances. *Review of International Political Economy*. https://doi.org/10.1080/09692290.2020.1854326.

Svartzman, R., Dron, D., and Espagne, E. (2019). From ecological macroeconomics to a theory of endogenous money for a finite planet. *Ecological Economics*, 162, 108–20.

Svartzman, R., Bolton, R., Despres, M., Pereira Da Silva, L., and Samama, F. (2020). Central banks, financial stability and policy coordination in the age of climate uncertainty: A three-layered analytical and operational framework. *Climate Policy*, 21(4), 563–80. https://doi.org/10.1080/14693062.2020.1862743.

Svartzman, R., Ament, J., Barmes, D., Erickson, J. D., Farley, J., Guay-Boutet, C., and Kosoy, N. (2020). Money, interest rates and accumulation on a finite planet: Revisiting the "monetary growth imperative" through institutionalist approaches. In R. Costanza, J. Erickson, J. Farley, and I. Kubiszewski (Eds.). *Sustainable Wellbeing Futures: A Research and Action Agenda for Ecological Economics* (pp. 266–83). Edward Elgar Publishing.

Taleb, N. (2007). *The Black Swan*. Penguin Random House.

Tooze, A. (2020). We are living through the first economic crisis of the Anthropocene. *The Guardian*, 7 May.

UNFCCC. (2015). *Paris Agreement*. United Nations.

Vallet, G. (2019). This is a man's world: autorité et pouvoir genrés dans le milieu des banques centrales. *Revue de la régulation. Capitalisme, institutions, pouvoirs* (25).

Vermeulen, R., Schets, E., Lohuis, M., Kölbl, B., Jansen, D. J., and Heeringa, W. (2019). The heat is on: A framework measuring financial stress under disruptive energy transition scenarios. *De Nederlandsche Bank Working Paper*, 625.

Villeroy de Galhau, F. (2019). Climate change: Central banks are taking action. *Banque de France Financial Stability Review*, 23, 7–16.

Weitzman, M. L. (2011). Fat-tailed uncertainty in the economics of catastrophic climate change. *Review of Environmental Economics and Policy*, 5 (2), 275–92.

Wolfe, N., Panosian, C., and Diamond, J. (2007). Origins of major human infectious diseases. *Nature*, 447, 279–83.

5. Environmental change and the international lender of last resort

Michel Aglietta and Étienne Espagne

1. INTRODUCTION

1.1 The Missing Transboundary Climate Risks

The new macroeconomic consensus around the low-carbon transition under-lines that the financial sphere should be de facto very proactively involved (NGFS, 2019). Although carbon pricing mechanisms remain central compo-nents of low-carbon strategies (Gollier, 2019), aligning financial flows with the mitigation and adaptation objectives of the Paris Agreement (article 2) requires a much broader approach, whereby climate policies fully incorporate the financial side as an enabler of required investments and an area of acute distribution issues in the transition (Svartzman et al., 2019).

In order to break the now famous tragedy of the horizon (Carney, 2015), new tools have already been developed to better assess transition and phys-ical risks kept inside the financial system (Battiston, 2019). The progress is ongoing, notably as central banks and regulators organize themselves into the Network for Greening the Financial System (NGFS, 2019) to share and diffuse these methodologies, and more and more figure out how to apply them in their daily mandate (Oustry et al., 2020).

An accounting of the amount of "climate finance" all over the world is also regularly updated, while financial actors try to settle around shared principles on green bond issuance (TCFD, 2016). If the methodologies to incorporate climate policies in financial and monetary decisions are still only emerging (Espagne, 2018), it is now clear that the financial world now considers it a mandate to mobilize and transform itself to support the objectives of the Paris Agreement and avoid the occurrence of a climate systemic risk (Aglietta and Espagne, 2016). But few of these debates grasp the international scale of the climate/finance nexus.

Climate change is for the financial world not only a new type of risk but also a radical uncertainty with transformative implications on a global scale

(Bolton et al., 2020). As a biophysical phenomenon, climate change naturally deploys itself on the global scale. Furthermore, the functioning of the financial system itself relies heavily on a hierarchical network of national and international institutions, which build a set of macroeconomic constraints for national policies. The twin combination generates transboundary risks that have not yet been fully grasped, but nonetheless determine the climate policy space at the national level. The goal of this chapter is to highlight the transboundary nature of the climate issue for the alignment of the financial system.

1.2   Defining the Lender of Last Resort

In most countries, the central bank plays the role of lender of last resort and market-maker of last resort for its own financial and banking institutions (Le Maux and Scialom, 2013). It means that in a crisis involving vanishing market liquidity or funding liquidity, blurring the line between illiquidity and insolvency, central banks are tempted to provide specific liquidity vehicles to financial institutions in order to restore the value of investment projects and counteract the negative effect of the liquidity shortage on asset prices. They may have very different types of constraints, which will determine the effectiveness of their interventions; however, they share the specificity of using exorbitant financial means, which are not directly determined by market rules, even if they can be constrained in their impact.

In the current monetary and financial system, cross-border bonds, equities and loans holdings especially affect the vulnerability of countries to financial shocks. On the one hand, they reflect the relative trade positions of countries and the associated vulnerabilities to external shocks along the value chain (Dellink et al., 2017). On the other hand, they reflect the relatively autonomous momentum of capital flows, shaping financial cycles, which depend on the monetary policy decisions of a few developed economies with international reserve currencies (Rey, 2015). In this context, central banks of developing and emerging economies, which do not directly manage a reserve currency, find themselves facing the quasi-impossibility of running independent monetary policies, unless they directly manage their capital account in resorting to quantitative restrictions to reduce their exposure to cross-border financial flows, which in turn could be detrimental to their short-term growth prospect and their access to reserve currencies. In that sense, the national lender of last resort has its exorbitant power of money issuance constrained by its own position in the international monetary system (IMS).

Indeed, the coordination of central banks and international financial institutions, such as the International Monetary Fund (IMF), the World Bank or the Bank for International Settlements (BIS), as well as systemic private financial actors, becomes essential in order to avoid contagion effects on the international scale in the case of a major crisis. This complex and moving network of institutions delineates what might be called the international lender of last resort. The IMF was the official lender of last resort of the Bretton Woods system instituted in 1944. Even if the Bretton Woods system itself officially disappeared in 1971, the IMF still provides financial assistance for countries in liquidity needs and macro-financial surveillance for all parties. It thus remains a central actor of this international lender of last resort system. The BIS is a ninety-year-old financial institution, created to ensure the settlement of World War I reparations against Germany. It was soon transformed into an institution fostering active cooperation between central banks, the Basel Committee of central banks, with a self-given mandate moving toward the surveillance of global financial stability after the official end of the Bretton Woods system. The G20 is a political gathering of the chiefs of state, assisted by a preparatory committee of ministers of finance and central bankers, who played a key coordination role in the response to the 2008 financial crisis.

The international lender of last resort is thus essentially the result of power relations between key reserve currency countries, which varies depending on their own relative financial, economic and geopolitical dynamics, while being stabilized by multilateral formal or informal arrangements. The dollar has had the role of the global key currency since the end of World War II, managing to keep its position in very different geopolitical and financial circumstances (Tooze, 2021). Regional lenders of last resort can also arise in the form of more or less formal monetary cooperation as a consequence of a crisis (the currency swap arrangement of the Chiang Mai Initiative and the macro-surveillance framework of the ASEAN+3 Macroeconomic Research Office for South-East Asia and Asia after the Asian financial crisis of 1997) or of historical ties (the Franc CFA and the sterling systems after the colonial era), or as a consequence of deeper political integration dynamics (the Eurosystem).

At first glance, these technical macro-financial issues seem very far from the more long-term concerns of climate change and climate policies. And, indeed, little has been said so far on the management of international liquidities and international financial flows in a low-carbon transition context, both as an additional risk for countries in their transition dynamics of coping strategies and as an opportunity under the condition of potential reforms. The IMF very recently engaged in evaluating climate risks for financial markets (Krogstrup and Oman, 2019), in order to assess to what extent climate change is priced, but without specifically addressing its own role as part of the international lender of last resort in relation to the climate issue. However, BIS has recently recognized that the management of foreign reserves by central banks may be profoundly changed by incorporating climate-related risks (Fender et al., 2019). The same institution only slightly touched on the topic of the international lender of last resort at the end of its landmark report on the "Green

Swan" (Bolton et al., 2020), suggesting a potential new role for special drawing rights, the foreign exchange reserve asset of the IMF, in the ramp-up of the transition, derived from Aglietta and Espagne (2018). The institutional arrangement that we call the lender of last resort has been under-investigated in the climate finance debate, while it may well also be a key lever in the process of aligning financial flows with sustainable development paths.

1.3   The International Monetary Side of the Anthropocene

In times of crisis, it is often said that some structural properties of money can be revealed (Théret, 2007). The current pandemic crisis is certainly no exception. Its particular ecological origins, at a time of crucial international choices in terms of environmental policies, shed new light on the role of the lender of last resort in the IMS with regard to political ecology dynamics.

In this crisis, all related monetary policy decisions, voluntary or not, are equivalent to a crucial choice in political ecology. The new carbon-neutrality horizon adopted by most major economies (with reserve currencies) in 2020 could sound as a positive response to the concern about a recovery that would only lead us further away from the planetary boundaries. But it also opens the question of the international monetary coordination, so that the climate target is not eventually trespassed, or simply reached at the expense of the legitimate development of developing and emerging economies. It can also be argued that the 2020 crisis is itself endogenous to the system, as it has been generated by the huge ecological transformations of the previous four decades of deep financialized globalization. The ecological endogeneity of the crisis brings with it an even deeper assessment of the ecological consequences of the lender of last resort.

Whether central banks acted quickly and massively to avoid what they feared would be the potentially dramatic consequences of a sudden shutdown of a large number of Western and Asian economies, their reaction was very much driven by their institutional memory of the previous Great Financial Crisis (GFC) of 2008 and its aftermath, while essentially ignoring their longer-term impacts on the climate policy agenda. Embedded in the unequal structure of the international lender of last resort, central banks are also not equal in their ability to cope with such crisis or to take the climate issue into account in their response. The macroeconomic space to increase low-carbon investments or to develop adaptation strategies is scarce when the primary macroeconomic goal becomes to develop export-oriented activities that allow the accumulation of international reserves in order to face the potential consequences of a downturn in the financial cycle. Therefore, the governance of the international lender of last resort becomes a core climate policy issue in order to progressively build a global financial safety net that includes the consideration of the planetary boundaries (Aglietta and Espagne, 2018).

The carbon-neutrality horizon adopted in 2020 by major powers has its flip side in the direct or indirect control over the necessary mineral resources for the necessary surge in low-carbon investments, the new transmission lines for a much more electricity-based economy and the disruptive technologies of electricity uses. It is tempting, as recently emphasized in Svartzman and Althouse (2020), to cut through the institutional complexities and historical contingencies of the lender of last resort and generalize the idea that some sort of implicit political ecology consideration drives the structure of the IMS. This seems true when looking at the history of IMSs, starting from the Italian merchant cities and their financial innovations to harness precious material from the first silk road to the dawn of the oil-based Bretton Woods system, all the way through the coal-powered expansion of the British gold standard. It is even more true in an extremely globalized financial world, facing the climate and environmental threats it has generated. In that sense, a global path toward carbon neutrality, which requires key mineral resources for its realization, may then give birth to a specific lender of last resort that reflects the strategic control of these resources in the transition process. But one should also be careful not to over-emphasize the importance of this deterministic link between ecologies and economies. The stunning variety of institutional settings in historical international monetary arrangements opens the door to multiple institutional settings in the Anthropocene as well.

1.4   Announcement of the Plan

Section 2 will briefly review the historical elements in favor of a political ecology approach to the lender of last resort, while also presenting the limitations of this approach. Section 3 will emphasize the specificities of the current globalized financial system as embedded in a set of hierarchically dependent ecologies. Section 4 will concentrate on the COVID crisis and the carbon-neutrality horizons as two critical aspects of the first crisis of the Anthropocene era for the international lender of last resort. Section 5 will adopt a prospective view on the different possible paths forward for a lender of last resort in the Anthropocene, and conclude.

2.   WHICH POLITICAL ECOLOGY OF INTERNATIONAL MONETARY SYSTEMS?

2.1   The Standard Political Economy of Key Currency Regimes

According to Boswell et al. (2020),

> four key elements are usually proposed in determining reserve currency status: the economic size/dominance of reserve issuers (role in international trade and financial networks), the credibility of reserve issuers (stable store of value over time, the reserve issuers' policy credibility and their financial markets' depth and liquidity), the transactional demand of reserve holders for trade and finance-related payments or foreign exchange market interventions, the inertia of the system.

This traditional line of argument in IMS thinking addresses the determinants of currency hegemony in essentially purely economic terms. At best, it only implicitly incorporates the question of the control over key resources via concepts such as the geopolitical situation or power relations (Cohen, 2018). But power in this sense is restricted to economic size, financial development, foreign policy ties and military reach.

2.2   The Monetary Role of Material Resources

This entire strand of literature tends to ignore more recent arguments from the ecological macroeconomic domain or the environmental history literature, which emphasize the strong link between the key currency issuer and direct or indirect control over key resources, and the specific political arrangement that led to a certain type of control over the resource. A seminal work in this direction is certainly Timothy Mitchell's (2011) book *Carbon Democracy*, which digs into the social and financial history of oil and makes visible the multiple institutional arrangements built upon the social relations that the oil industry has woven. Mitchell shows how the access to cheap oil made the Keynesian era (and the underlying Bretton Woods arrangement) possible and how bankers, oil companies and US policymakers used the 1973–4 oil crisis to allow the world's largest debtor nation to gain hegemony over other states, creating what is now called the neoliberal area. Soon after, the history of the coal transition was revisited in the same institutionalist vein by Andreas Malm (2013), giving a determining role to social conflicts both within the British labor class and the broader British empire in the choice of the steam engine technology. Sager (2016) later generalized the idea that the global energy and monetary systems appeared to be deeply linked. He argued that considering energy and finance as linked systems allows us to understand more clearly the contemporary global economic and climate impasse, while also including China's monetary role in the new century as part of a larger solution. In that framework, China appears to be the putative new monetary hegemon, having built its power through the use of cheap coal and becoming the new chimney of the world (Malm, 2012). Scheidler (2020) goes so far as to consider mining activities as the original matrix of subsequent characteristics of capitalism, mainly property rights and trade money.

2.3   Monetary and Ecological Hierarchies

The analysis of the monetary history of colonial powers has also provided insights into the resource/international monetary relations nexus (Servet et al., 2020). Later on, postcolonial monetary arrangements gave rise to a new moment of these hierarchical regimes. In that respect, the CFA franc was established in French African colonies after World War II; it was initially pegged against the French Franc and subsequently against the euro, guaranteeing France against the need for foreign reserves for much of its key resource imports. Furthermore, countries using the CFA franc have been obliged to keep half of their reserves at the French Treasury and to have a French representative on the currency union board in exchange for French guarantees on their balance-of-payments needs. Recent moves have been made, however, to loosen such historical obligations – which may have implications not only for the allocation of reserves but also for their composition.

In the same vein, historical (political and economic) ties continued to support the sterling area and the international role of the British pound, despite the declining role of the United Kingdom in the global economy. More specifically, after the United Kingdom left the gold standard in 1931, it created the sterling zone, encouraging key trading partners and colonies to peg their currencies against the pound to facilitate trade and keep their foreign reserves in sterling. Following World War II, the sterling area was formalized into a legally defined group with pegged exchange rates to sterling, common exchange controls against the rest of the world and the maintenance of national reserves in sterling (Iancu et al., 2020). Despite episodes of sterling devaluation, in 1970 the sterling area still comprised the United Kingdom and thirty-five other countries, together with all British dominions, protectorates, protected states and trust territories, except Canada and Zimbabwe. The sterling area effectively dissolved with the demise of the Bretton Woods system in 1972. These kinds of institutional monetary arrangements have allowed former colonial powers to maintain some of their former dominance over newly independent countries, and especially to orient their policies in a direction that would favor the economy of the core country, notably by providing cheap or guaranteed prices of raw materials.

2.4   Transitioning Resources and Key Currencies

The question of the transition from a regime to another has also been linked to shifts in the modes of key resource control. As Boswell et al. (2020) underline, the transition from one dominant currency to another has taken anywhere from several years to many decades. After the Westphalian Treaty of 1648, nations asserted themselves, driven by the development of manufacturing. However, the seventeenth century was an era of persistent wars and revolutions. Despite its rise as an industrial and commercial power, the British financial system was weakened by the financing of wars in Europe and domestic revolutions. The turnaround arose with the establishment of the Orange House on the throne of England, following the "glorious revolution" of 1688, and the creation of the Bank of England in 1694. The year after, the philosopher John Locke introduced a new concept in the political sphere: the natural monetary order. Monetary disorders were interpreted as imbalances owing to bad coinage. The Recoinage Act of 1695 transformed radically monetary sovereignty in demon-etizing silver and anchoring the British pound on the gold standard (Aglietta, 2018). This supported the concurrent rise of London as the dominant financial center and the pound sterling as the international reserve currency (Aglietta, 2018).

In the twentieth century, the US dollar replaced sterling as the dominant international currency only many decades after the United States overtook Great Britain economically. The great deflation of the 1930s led to chaos, fol-lowed by segmentation in the IMS until the Popular Front in France devalued the franc in 1936. Then a tripartite monetary accord was concluded between the US, the UK and France for the purpose of containing competitive deval-uations (Aglietta, 2018). In the end, there was no more sterling dominance, and no dominance of any currency from September 1931 to July 1944 and the Bretton Woods agreement. It took World War II and the complete spread of oil-dependent technologies to stabilize the new dollar dominance. Later, Smith-Nonini (2016) examined the relationship between the United States' rapid loss of energy sovereignty in the 1970s and the rise of speculative finance and neoliberal ideology that reshaped global trade relationships.

2.5   Toward a Political Ecology of International Monetary Systems

In view of these symmetric developments of both IMSs and ecological imbal-ances, it is tempting to develop a political ecology of international monetary relations, or as Svartzman and Althouse (2020) emphasize, "to understand how monetary hegemony permits and depends upon the continuous and uneven flow of resources from Peripheral to Core countries". Indeed, mon-etary hegemonies tend to be based on the direct access to the key resources of the dominant mode of development of the period and might change when this mode of development shifts to other key resources. This view tends to support a political ecology of the gold standard (through the dominance on coal production), of the dollar dominance in the Bretton Woods system and beyond (through the core role of oil domination) and even the prospective future hegemonic role of China in view of its control over key resources of the transition.

This political ecology of the international monetary system does not only relate the control over resources to the hegemonic power. Indeed, access to key resources induced by a certain mode of development is not necessarily the direct cause of a hegemonic position in the international monetary structure. The determination also goes in the reverse direction where the dominant power and especially specific groups within this dominant power can impose a certain mode of development because it gives them an advantage, which is only then reflected in a certain resource arrangement. It has indeed been argued that the choice of oil as the dominant energy source was heavily driven by the choice to get rid of the organized power of the working class of the coal age. In this sense, monetary hegemony dynamics can be viewed as the prolongation of the national social tensions over ways of living and distribution, but at the international level. It is not so much the access to key resources of a supposedly homogenous national actor as the competition between social groups by means of their influence over the national monetary power that has an important feedback effect on ecological hierarchies.

Introducing social groups as specific actors in the dynamics of the international monetary relations offers a more complex but also more subtle political ecology of the international lender of last resort. The organized power of the working class of the coal age had a structural effect on the wage dynamics in Western economies after World War II, the cost of which was passed to peripheral countries and their environment, with the active collaboration of an elite for some of these countries. The maintenance (or even the reinforcement) of the dollar as the key currency after the end of Bretton Woods can also be understood through specific social tensions whereby a group of oil-producing countries willing to negotiate better terms on their rent met with financial and business interests to tame wage inflation in Western economies. The dollar is reinforced as the key currency as the best available recycling option for the new so-called petro-dollars. We will now try to apply this political ecology framework to the pandemic crisis, while also considering the specificities of the international lender of last resort that emerged out of the GFC of 2008.

3.   FINANCIAL LIQUIDITY AND THE INTERNATIONAL LENDER OF LAST RESORT

3.1   On the Use of Foreign Exchange Reserves

Countries hold foreign exchange reserves to finance balance-of-payments needs, intervene in foreign exchange markets and provide foreign exchange liquidity to domestic economic agents, and for other related purposes, such as maintaining confidence in the domestic currency and facilitating foreign borrowing. As such, reserves are generally denominated in currencies widely used for international payments and widely traded in global foreign exchange markets. The accumulation of foreign exchange reserves by the official sector is but one of many examples of the international use of currencies. Other countries' currencies can also be used by the private sector for external trade and cross-border investment, and as a vehicle for financial transactions. Different international uses are complementary and tend to reinforce each other. For instance, widespread use by the private sector for trade and financial transactions often goes hand in hand with official sector use as exchange rate anchor and reserve currency, which, in turn, can bolster credibility and reinforce private sector use.

In addition, non-bank financial intermediaries (hedge funds, mutual funds, asset managers, private equity) have been the vectors in their "search for yield" of the international expansion of bond markets, supported by the US Federal Reserve (Fed) after the GFC of 2008 with the long decline in interest rates. This is why the financial markets have been building an unusual and particularly dangerous situation: the equity and bond markets are jointly overvalued, making the usual benchmark for institutional asset allocations particularly fragile because they are entirely dependent on the continuation of core interest rates at zero, or below zero in the eurozone and Japan. Ten years after the GFC, the peak of the financial cycle has become global.

3.2   A Dollar System in Transition

Despite trends toward greater reserve diversification following the GFC, and China's efforts to boost the internationalization of the renminbi and promote its reserve currency status over the last decade, the dollar stands out as the currency most traded on the foreign exchange market (44 percent of turnover), and most used for trade invoicing (54 percent of global trade) and financial claim denomination (51 percent of cross-border bank claims) (Boswell et al., 2020). From the GFC of 2008 to the 2020 pandemic COVID-19 crisis, financial vulnerabilities have shifted significantly from banks in the US and

Europe (more strongly regulated since 2010) to financial markets worldwide. The international bond markets, both in dollars and national currencies, inter-mediated by unregulated non-bank financial intermediaries in search of yield, have been fueled permanently by accommodative US monetary policy and have become globalized. In the meantime, corporate and sovereign debts in emerging market and developing economies (EMDEs) have become hugely leveraged.

The COVID crisis has caused this dynamic of market finance to get out of control, with obviously the greatest vulnerabilities in emerging countries (excluding China) and especially in the so-called frontier developing countries. Over the year 2020, developing countries faced a protean crisis: a massive capital flight to developed countries, leading, according to the Organisation for Economic Co-operation and Development (OECD), to a 211 billion (−80 percent compared to 2019) drop in portfolio flows; a reduction in foreign direct investment of 217 billion (−35 percent compared to 2019); a drop in remit-tances from nationals abroad of 105 billion (−20 percent compared to 2019); a lasting slowdown in world trade (−17.7 percent in May 2020); and a drop in energy raw material prices of more than 30 percent compared to January 2019 (−60 percent in April), slightly offset by a rise in agricultural raw materials (currently +6 percent) and metals (currently +12 percent). The resulting drop in the exchange rates of developing countries (5 to 25 percent against the dollar) makes imports or loan repayments in these currencies more expensive, increasing the risk of default.

3.3   Beyond the COVID Shock, Without Taking Stock of the Lessons of the Pandemic

The need for liquidity in strong currencies jeopardizes the recovery. Faced with the reversal of capital flows out of developing and emerging countries, many of which found themselves in a foreign exchange crisis and in urgent need of liquidity, the Fed had to respond to a sudden demand for dollars and treasury bills. To do so, it has been setting up currency swap lines with a small number of countries and a sales and repurchase agreement for treasury bills for countries considered to be of lower political priority. In addition, the Fed has deployed an unprecedented battery of quantitative easing tools to stabilize domestic financial markets. At the same time, the European Central Bank (ECB) has launched its unconventional monetary policy program linked to the Pandemic Emergency Purchase Program. Quantitative easing, using asset pur-chase programs (APPs), has been for the first time extended to central banks in a number of EMDEs with the ability to do so. In some respect, APPs succeeded in mitigating market stress and signaling that EMDE central banks were ready to stand as bond buyers of last resort, as well as advanced economies. This means that more countries have resorted to the portfolio balance channel of monetary policy.

Therefore, the unconventional monetary policies following the 2008 financial crisis became largely conventional in 2020. This channel pertains to a de facto change in monetary doctrine whereby fiscal, monetary and prudential policies keep their own responsibilities, but interact and are coordinated. The coordination has so far been mainly informal or loosely organized via specific forums of discussion, and strictly focused on economic and monetary policy topics. For the countries that were not able to activate this portfolio balance channel, in order to cope with urgent foreign exchange needs, many countries have asked for IMF financing facilities. Without conditionality for countries with a debt situation deemed sustainable, these emergency facilities are limited in volume (100 billion dollars in total). The larger IMF loan programs imply heavy macroeconomic conditionalities on key macroeconomic variables (such as reserve to GDP ratio and tax but also trade liberalization and privatization), while increasing the debt burden of countries. This restricts their fiscal and monetary space to develop public policies in the long run, such as climate change or broader biodiversity-enhancing policies (Munevar, 2020).

4.   THE INTERNATIONAL MONETARY SYSTEM REVEALED BY THE COVID CRISIS

4.1   An Endogenous Crisis of the International Monetary System

A key line of argument during the COVID crisis has been its purely exogenous property with respect to the financial system. In fact, the coordination between fiscal, economic and financial actors has largely ignored the natural origins and human dissemination of the COVID crisis. The endogeneity of the crisis is a key line of argument, which would be valid for any future climate change-related crisis. As has been emphasized repeatedly in the past, crises in the international monetary and financial system often have some resource conflict origin. For the time being, the origin of the crisis is the consequence of anterior over-exploitation of resources.

While contact with pathologies that existed in wildlife has always tended to generate epidemics or even pandemics in history, the number of species involved in the passage of pathogens between humans and animals has been constantly increasing. The problem is not the species carrying the pathogens, but the impoverishment of ecosystems due to the pressure on natural resources that reduce the dilution of opportunities for passage to humans (Lugassy et al., 2019). Imbalances in an ecosystem, in turn, can lead to the emergence of viruses or pathogens that proliferate. For example, the depletion of their predators allows mosquitoes to proliferate and propagate the diseases, as can be observed near hydroelectric dams.

The increase in human–animal promiscuity, linked to the trade in domestic animals and above all to factory farming, creates incubators for the production of pandemics by selecting productive, genetically homogenous breeds that are not very resistant to disease but are highly secured by closed buildings or the preventive use of anti-parasite products or antibiotics. The spread of an emerging virus is then very rapid because of the number and susceptibility of infected animals. Finally, the emergence of future pandemics might be caused by climate change in the future. On the one hand, climate change involves the increase in vector-borne diseases; that is, animals (migratory birds, insects) that transmit diseases to other animals or from one human to another, and which are shifting their areas of propagation because of climate change. On the other hand, the accelerated melting of permafrost poses a risk of reawakening viruses that have been frozen for a very long time, beyond human history, and against which human populations have no immunity.

The second aspect of this crisis is the speed with which it has spread across the planet, becoming a global pandemic in just two months. The densification of human populations and the acceleration of trade is one of the major characteristics of the latest globalization. More than half of the world's population lives in cities. This proportion could rise to 70 percent by 2050, while 90 percent of the world's urban growth is taking place in Asia and Africa. African cities, which today are home to 472 million inhabitants, would be home to more than 1.2 billion city dwellers by 2050. Coupled with an acceleration in the movement of people, animals and products, the opportunities for the spread of emerging diseases associated with this major global shift are immense.

As an inevitable consequence of these negative externalities, induced by the extreme spatial concentration of economic activities and the mobility of people and goods, the intensity of pollution in megacities is very high, and sometimes even fatally dangerous, as was observed in autumn 2020 in cities such as Delhi. In the case of coronavirus, this intense pollution may have created co-morbid conditions for city dwellers.

The two phenomena of the climate and the COVID crisis may be different in their relationship to time. The virus is brutal; it attacks everyone, even if it reveals and increases certain inequalities. It is temporary, while climatic disturbances that await us are of a very long duration. The brutality of the arrival of the virus makes it possible to implement a "shock doctrine", as Naomi Klein (2007) calls them, for better or worse. On the contrary, the climate emergency, strongly emphasized by climate experts, has only been recognized by political leaders in public speeches, with very little effect on their political orientations. The relay to the population (and vice versa from the population to the political leaders) is still too marginal or focuses on indirect topics such as access to networks and transport. The coronavirus pandemic and climate change are, however, part of the same objective reality: a general disruption of our relationship with nature. It is by highlighting this common cause that solutions to end the COVID crisis could contribute to the implementation of a true political ecology.

4.2   Indispensable Coordination and the Change in Central Banks' Strategies

The creation of the Network for Greening the Financial System (NGFS) in 2017 marks a tentative coordination of central banks on climate (and environmental) issues. Some (see Bolton et.al., 2020) have argued that climate-related systemic risks proceed from non-linear dynamics with tipping points, resulting from the interaction of multiple mutually reinforcing destructive forces. Like the COVID crisis we are suffering from, financial risks of climate origin can have a large amplitude and a strong intensity, as they propagate across economic sectors and countries. In the same vein, the transition toward a low-carbon path can interact in a non-linear way with financial systems and create "transition risk" that goes beyond the country level.

As early as its first report in 2018, the NGFS recognized that weather-related financial risks were not adequately reflected in asset valuations by financial markets. In its second report in October 2019, the NGFS stated that central banks should lead by example in introducing environmental sustainability considerations into the management of their securities portfolios, without prejudice to their mandate, in order to demonstrate the sustainable and responsible investment approach to other investors. In its 2020 technical papers, the NGFS observed that central banks need to strengthen their range of analytical tools to incorporate climate risks into their macroeconomic models and forecasting instruments, as climate change is likely to alter the transmission channels of monetary policy. They must therefore revise the operational framework and the guideline of their monetary strategy.

Consequently, the NGFS suggests that central banks use the analysis of the scenarios recommended by the Taskforce on Climate-Related Financial Disclosure (TCFD) to extend their domains in taking account of the balance-sheet constraints of private actors, in a stock-flow approach to capture the hysteresis of supply constraints on macroeconomic situations. Long-term scenarios are built from the indicators most sensitive to transition risk. The recommendations for companies are to connect to the macroeconomic scenarios, structuring their governance on four themes that meet the purpose of the environmental, social and governance (ESG) criteria: participative governance, strategy, risk management, implementation of metrics when available and targets derived from the TCFD recommendations.

The limited impact the NGFS has had so far in actually shifting the practices of financial actors or the forms of central banking with regards to climate change reflects the difficulty of transforming the national and international lender of last resort without a proper political ecology coalition. The technocratic achievements of the NGFS may only lead to real results when they resonate with a powerful enough coalition of interests in the transition and control over its underlying resources and technologies. This political ecology moment of the lender of last resort may have happened in 2020 with the new carbon-neutrality horizons adopted by all major economies.

4.3   The New Power Factor: Carbon-Neutrality Diplomacy

In September 2020, President Xi Jinping announced the commitment to carbon neutrality by 2060 and a peak in greenhouse gas emissions to be reached by 2030. This commitment was confirmed by the official approbation of the fourteenth five-year plan by the National Assembly of the People in March 2021. Admittedly, it is still insufficient in relation to an international objective of compliance with the commitments of the Paris Agreement. The revised intentions of the countries were formalized at the COP26 in Glasgow in the last quarter of 2021. A study by the *New York Times* considers that compliance with the Paris Agreement would require a peak in emissions reached in 2025 and a complete phase-out of coal by 2040. Nevertheless, the announcement appears as a surprise in the landscape of the year 2020, and could revive the Paris Agreement, which was based on the bold (and so far unsuccessful) wager of an international dynamic of mutually reinforcing virtuous circles between nations (Tooze, 2020).

The geopolitical effect of this announcement is already beginning to be felt. Japan, through the voice of Japanese Prime Minister Yoshihide Sugade, announced in October 2020 that his country, the world's third largest economy and sixth largest emitter, would aim for carbon neutrality by 2050. Soon after, it was Korea, the eleventh largest economy in the world and sixth largest exporter, that followed with a statement by President Moon Jae-In, speaking to his country's National Assembly, committing to neutrality by 2050. In a country that still produces 40 percent of its electricity from coal, the objective implies a reduction in emissions of 10 percent per year and massive investments in renewables that are like a Green New Deal.

The European Union, which in 2019 set itself the goal of becoming the world's first carbon-neutral continent by 2050, an objective confirmed in September by the Commission and then in October by the Parliament, is thus joined by an Asian bloc based on very different modes of development. The United States rejoined the Paris Agreement at the beginning of 2021 with the election of Joseph Biden. It then announced a horizon of carbon neutrality by 2050, as well as a series of measures that would cancel the environmental deregulation during the Trump presidency. Biden's plan, announced during the electoral campaign, involves $2 trillion in investments in renewable energy. Therefore, the political picture of carbon neutrality potentially included, by 2021, virtually all of the world's most developed and emissions-intensive economies. In this respect, the Paris Agreement could indeed seem to be back on track and the diplomatic drive of these economies should increase the pressure to raise the climate ambitions of emerging powers such as India, Indonesia, Brazil and even Russia.

The political ecology of carbon neutrality seems to have penetrated the realm of high geopolitics. By announcing its intention to achieve carbon neutrality two months before the American presidential election and just before the European Parliament's validation of the Green Deal project, China has made climate policy a subject of power rivalry between hegemonic blocs. China's importance in international relations allows it to potentially define the playing field for future rivalries. In this respect, Xi Jinping's declaration is indeed a realistic turning point in political ecology, as Pierre Charbonnier (2020) was able to point out. Ecology is no longer (only) the language of minority and fanciful bands of satiated Western societies; still less that of the desperate social struggles of developing populations who are the victims of globalization. It is becoming the very object of the politics of power between nations and social groups within nations.

Nevertheless, such a turning point (still to be verified) comes up against major obstacles. Its success would mean a driving force on the rest of the world. Apart from the unspoken aspects of the trajectories envisaged for carbon neutrality, there are still major difficulties to be overcome in order to achieve the momentum of this driving force. Indeed, the objectives most often focus on the emissions produced, and not on the carbon footprint (i.e. the emissions consumed and produced). While undeniable efforts to transform sectors and consumption patterns are planned most of the time, the biggest worry remains the exporting of emissions outside carbon-neutral regions. This is made all the easier by the many free trade agreements signed in recent years that do not provide for alignment with the Paris Agreement. The ambitious European Green Deal is thus still based on very high levels of imported deforestation of Brazilian or Indonesian tropical forests (Fuchs et al., 2020).

Therefore, the dependency of developed countries on emissions imported from southern countries appears to be the key obstacle against a possible global Green New Deal that is the only way to guarantee a stabilized climate with a 2°C increase in temperature compared to pre-industrial times. The (very) persistent tension with GDP as the ultimate objective of economic policies through the still recurrent discourse on green growth is likely to transform the ecological ambition into a game of Mistigri in which each party tries to offload its obligations on the other to keep only the most "carbon-neutral" activities.

Even more fundamentally, the international financial flows that underpin trade, while developing their own dynamics, are particularly poorly aligned to date with these long horizons of carbon neutrality. While the disclosure of information on the carbon content of portfolios should certainly soon extend to the US financial sector, the reform of the international monetary and financial system remains at the heart of a complete realistic shift in political ecology.

5. PROSPECTIVE VIEWS FOR AN ECOLOGICAL INTERNATIONAL LENDER OF LAST RESORT

5.1　The Legacy of the GFC

In the 2008 financial crisis turmoil, the former governor of the People's Bank of China, Dr. Zhou Xiaochuan, delivered a much-noticed speech on the reform of the IMS. He quoted the Triffin dilemma, stating that it is impossible to meet adequately the global demand for ultimate liquidity if the issuer of the key currency is pursuing exclusively domestic objectives. He asserted,

> reforming the IMS should be based on the creation of an international reserve currency, which is not the debt of any individual nation, thus, removing the inherent deficiencies caused by using credit-based national currencies. The reform should be guided by a grand vision. It should be a gradual process that yields win–win results for all (Zhou, 2009).

He spoke out for the special drawing rights (SDRs) as the ultimate reserve currency.

The GFC has left severe deficiencies and some accomplishments in global finance. On the positive side, financial stability has become an objective of central banks all over the world. On the negative side, governance in finance has failed dramatically beyond banking regulation. The G20 has already been an achievement in its own existence, since it makes feasible an embryo of world governance. It would be improved if it were endowed with a permanent secretariat. Nonetheless, the very existence of the G20 is potentially strengthening two international institutions whose collaboration is essential in the detection and understanding of global systemic risk: the IMF and the Financial Stability Board. However, up to now, the G20 has left aside international monetary matters.

The long-standing disparity in views about currencies haunts the Triffin dilemma. US political leaders consider the dollar a "natural hegemon" and have the veto power in the IMF to oppose any reform. In China, an off-market solution grounded on the SDRs is viewed as preferable. In Europe, there is an inner political problem because political sovereignty is separated between nations, while the currency is common. No unified view exists about the role of the euro as an international reserve currency. Globally, political dissensions between the main powers prevent any reform of the IMS in the near term. Indeed, a cardinal theorem in international macroeconomics stipulates the following: a stable financial system based upon fixed exchange rates, a deep global financial integration and the prevalence of national preferences in economic policy are incompatible without a supranational ultimate liquidity. One of the three must yield. The one that has yielded so far is the exchange rate. Even if progress has been made nationally lately under the impact of the COVID crisis, shortcomings and dissents in international monetary matters still prevail.

5.2   The SDR Option and the Multilateralization of the Lender of Last Resort

Since the beginning of the COVID crisis, there have been a growing number of proposals for the use of a new SDR issued by the IMF. Public statements have also highlighted this possibility, including by IMF Managing Director Kristalina Georgieva, IMF Executive Director for China Zhongxia Jin and UN Secretary-General António Guterres. However, an initial discussion on the subject was put aside in the G20 at the April 2020 meeting. The opportunity for a new SDR issue resurfaced with the American election of November 2020. Proposals for new issues currently under discussion range from 500 billion to 4,000 billion, with a consensus around 1,000 billion. An issue of 1,000 billion SDRs corresponds to less than 10 percent of current global reserves or a little more than one point of global GDP in 2019. Such a 1,000-billion SDR issue would lead to an increase of 330 billion in reserves for low- and middle-income countries.

From the point of view of developing and emerging countries, a new SDR issue creates immediate access to hard currencies under better conditions, while markets are dysfunctional. In Africa, government bond spreads remain 100 to 300 basis points higher than their pre-crisis level, even though estimates of default risk have returned to pre-crisis levels. Once SDRs are allocated to member countries, countries can decide to keep these SDRs as a reserve or lend or sell them to other member countries, accredited institutions such as the World Bank and regional development banks or international institutions such as the ECB and BIS. Those SDR reserves are desperately needed in countries that have been disproportionately affected by disruptions in world trade, by capital outflows and by the sharp fall in commodity prices. Thus, poorer developing countries need urgently to cover financing gap and essential imports. According to the IMF, more than 100 countries have asked the IMF for help. The IMF did not have, by far, the financial capacity in spring 2020 to allow distressed countries in sub-Saharan Africa and South-East Asia to purchase agricultural, protective and medical equipment. This is why an SDR allocation is vital.

At the same time, three economic zones are emerging, covering most of three continents – America, Europe and Asia. They can support a principle of subsidiarity in managing financial market disequilibria. In Europe, the ECB is doing whatever it takes on interest-rate spreads within the eurozone. In committing to keeping spreads between bond yields at a low level with its asset purchase policy, the ECB is pursuing de facto a policy of yield curve control. It can be expanded, if necessary, in organizing regional swap lines with other currencies beyond the European Union, for example Switzerland, Norway and the UK. As long as investors see the ECB's asset purchases as a tool to keep a lid on spreads, they feel safe.

In Asia, the Bank of Japan has been following a monetary policy of flattening the yield curve for a long time. The People's Bank of China is eager not to derail the economic recovery that is ahead of all other large countries. The conclusion of the Regional Comprehensive Economic Partnership (RCEP) is likely to reinforce the network of swap lines developed by the Chiang Mai Initiative created after the Asian financial crisis of 1997 and made operational in 2000. Therefore, the development of regional ties will limit the use of the dollar, compared to the huge flood of dollar bonds worldwide in the decade following the GFC.

The dollar swap network has been extended to fourteen central banks. Going further, the Fed has created a direct credit line for allowing foreign central banks to borrow directly dollar liquidity against the treasury bonds they hold, accepted as collateral. Nonetheless, those facilities are far from being the means of an international lender of last resort. They depend on the acceptance of the US Treasury, hence of the political discriminations established by the US government, which are only erratically aligned with long-term climate mitigation goals.

There are thus now three large currency areas in America, Europe and Asia, leading to an IMS evolving progressively into a multilateral, multi-currency system. The question of the ultimate reserve asset to manage global liquidity as a global public good will become inescapable. The now shared horizon of carbon neutrality only strengthens this imperative, as it amounts to a complete redistribution of powers along very different lines than in the oil age.

5.3   Managing Global Liquidity as a Global Public Good in the Anthropocene

More than ten years after the GFC, after the inundation of dollar liquidity bridging GFC and COVID crises, while the IMF financial capacity makes less than 1 percent of global external liabilities, a working party of the Robert Triffin International think tank (2019) has revisited the question of global liquidity. In the current context, an asset is liquid if any investor expects that others will have the same view. The rise in global liquidity through bond markets entails opaque risks under uncertainty, highly sensitive to reversals in market sentiment. The dynamics of financial markets under uncertainty is called a momentum. It rises through speculative stages of euphoria, fueled by borrowing, that turn around in crises as soon as there is a perception of a liquidity shortage, followed by panic and balance-sheet recession under the imperative of debt reduction that propagates through financial markets. The dominance of the financial cycle can have dire macroeconomic consequences. Instead of an optimal growth regime, only temporarily disturbed by benign external shocks, multiple equilibria exist, including secular stagnation. It is why potential interventions by a surrogate of an international lender of last resort to anchor confidence in reserve assets are indispensable to mitigate international financial cycles. The Nakaso Report (BIS, 2017) identified issues that remain unsolved, while liquidity shortages straddle national borders and affect several jurisdictions simultaneously.

Meanwhile, the UNEP "emission gap" report (Olhoff and Christensen, 2020) established in December 2020 that the concentration of greenhouse gas emissions is off track vis-à-vis the Paris Agreement top-down objectives, but also vis-à-vis the less ambitious determined contributions of countries. If G20 countries, responsible for 75 percent of global emissions, go on following the present track, it will lead the world to between 3.4 and 3.9°C warming, compared to less than 2°C committed to in 2015. Therefore, the revision of intentions must be tripled to keep the 2°C warming target. To do so, there is no other solution than an entirely green recovery from the COVID pandemic.

In the longer term, a possible path of reform of the IMS could thus institute the SDR as the ultimate reserve asset. In its latest restating of the dilemma induced by the key currency system, Robert Triffin (2014) observed that it was independent of the exchange rate regime. As long as the key currency is the liability of the issuer toward the reserve-holding users, the latter invest the reserves into financial assets issued by the reserve currency country. This automatic capital inflow creates the "exorbitant privilege", since the liquidity created abroad by countries holding external reserves is not offset by a contrary reduction in the monetary base of the issuer. The consequence is a worldwide "built-in destabilizer", because the finality of payment is violated on a global scale. After the GFC and up to 2020, the over-accumulation of liquidity and correlative disequilibria in the balance of payments had reached an extravagant level. The dilemma was seriously aggravated by the Trump government, who rejected the principle of the global world order for a transactional view of international politics, making the dollar an instrument of neomercantilism.

Whatever the approach to the question, there cannot be any solution to the Triffin dilemma without the issuance of an ultimate reserve asset that is not the debt of any country. Such a reserve asset would be able to solve two intertwined problems: more symmetrical adjustments in the balance of payments of national economies and an international lender of last resort. The reform can only be progressive, starting from the evidence that SDRs already exist as the basis for an effective management of global liquidity. Indeed, the SDR has several advantages as a multilateral standard: its issuance as a pure fiduciary asset, which already has an agreed existence in the IMF; and its definition as a basket of currencies, making it largely immune to the impact of floating exchange rates and thus useful for invoicing international contracts related to commodities. However, to use the SDR as an international lender of last resort in financial crises, it needs expansion, because its share in official reserves is still insignificant. Therefore, enhancing the role of official SDRs to make it the principal reserve asset between central banks and international public institutions would be significant if the IMF converted all its operations to an SDR basis.

According to existing rules, general allocations are made in proportion to quotas that do not align with the weights of non-Western countries in the twenty-first-century world economy. A revision of quotas in multiple steps along with an agreed schedule would alleviate and then correct the misdistribution of new SDRs. Obviously, this means changing the balance of powers within the IMF. Three principles can guide this institutional overhaul. First, no single country should enjoy a blocking minority vote for qualified-majority decisions. Second, countries of the eurozone must merge their quotas in sympathy with the greater integration of the eurozone agreed in July 2020, so as to get a unique political representation in the IMF that will give more power than the scattered representation of individual countries. Third, the IMF executive committee must be upgraded with the participation of high-ranking government officials to speed up the approval of key decisions, thus strengthening the power of the IMF executive director.

To enhance the procedures through which central banks could acquire SDRs against excess dollar reserves, a substitution account in the IMF will do the trick without undergoing the fluctuations in exchange rates triggered by a conversion in the foreign exchange markets. In addition, to make SDR assets attractive to international financial investors, the way interest rates are computed should be based on long-term bonds, while the basket of currencies making the SDR should be progressively enlarged. This is a further step since it involves the transition to privately owned SDRs to develop a competitive SDR market in SDR-denominated bonds. For that to happen, an interbank market between commercial banks will emerge for SDR liquidity that would require a clearing house able to attract non-bank intermediaries like mutual funds and exchange-traded funds. Interbank clearing arrangements will be able to connect public and private SDRs.

At that point, the IMS will swing to an SDR-based multi-currency system that could replace SDR allocation by an issuance rule managed by the IMF that would become de facto the central bank of central banks. It would define the international unit of account upon which national currencies link according to their monetary policy regimes. It would fulfill the criteria of a concerted institutionalized IMS. It would support the development of policies of EMDEs in providing a universal collective insurance against systemic risks, including the climate risk. Hopefully, before 2030, the IMS would be able to service the environmental common goods.

REFERENCES

Aglietta, M. (2018). *Money: 5,000 Years of Debt and Power*. Verso Trade.
Aglietta, M., and Espagne, E. (2016). *Climate and Finance Systemic Risks: More Than an Analogy? The Climate Fragility Hypothesis*. CEPII, Centre d'etudes prospectives et d'informations internationales.
Aglietta, M., and Espagne, É. (2018). Le Système Monétaire International Face aux Cycles Biogéochimiques. In *Annales des Mines-Responsabilite et environnement* (No. 4, pp. 64–68). FFE.
Bank for International Settlements (BIS) (2017). Designing frameworks for central bank liquidity assistance: Addressing new challenges. A report of a central bank group chaired by H Nakaso. CGFS Papers no. 58, April.
Battiston, S. (2019). The importance of being forward-looking: Managing financial stability in the face of climate risk. *Financial Stability Review*, *23*, 39–48.
Bolton, P., Despres, M., Da Silva, L. A. P., Samama, F., and Svartzman, R. (2020). *The Green Swan*. BIS Books.
Boswell, E., Gamba, A., Hakobyan, S., Lusinyan, L., Meads, N., and Wu, Y. (2020). *Reserve Currencies in an Evolving International Monetary System*. https://www.imf.org/en/Publications/Departmental-Papers-Policy-Papers/Issues/2020/11/17/Reserve-Currencies-in-an-Evolving-International-Monetary-System-49864.
Carney, M. (2015). Breaking the tragedy of the horizon: Climate change and financial stability. Speech given at Lloyd's of London.
Charbonnier, P. (2020). Le tournant réaliste de l'écologie politique. *Le Grand Continent.* https://legrandcontinent.eu/fr/2020/09/30/le-tournant-realiste-de-lecologie-politique.
Cohen, B. J. (2018). *Currency Power: Understanding Monetary Rivalry*. Princeton University Press.
Dellink, R., Hwang, H., Lanzi, E., and Chateau, J. (2017). International trade consequences of climate change. OECD Trade and Environment Working Papers, 2017/01, OECD Publishing.

Espagne, E. (2018). Money, finance and climate: The elusive quest for a truly integrated assessment model. *Comparative Economic Studies*, *60*(1), 131–143.

Fender, I., McMorrow, M., Sahakyan, V., and Zulaica, O. (2019). Green bonds: The reserve management perspective. BIS Quarterly Review, September.

Fuchs, R., Brown, C., and Rounsevell, M. (2020). Europe's Green Deal offshores environmental damage to other nations. *Nature*. https://www.nature.com/articles/d41586-020-02991-1.

Gollier, C. (2019). Le prix du risque climatique et le prix du carbone. *Revue d'économie financière*, *1*, 171–182.

Iancu, A., Anderson, G., Ando, S., Boswell, E., Gamba, A., Hakobyan, S., ... Wu, Y. (2020). Reserve currencies in an evolving international monetary system. Departmental Papers, 2020(002).

Klein, N. (2007). *The Shock Doctrine: The Rise of Disaster Capitalism*. Knopf.

Krogstrup, S., and Oman, W. (2019). Macroeconomic and financial policies for climate change mitigation: A review of the literature. IMF. https://www.imf.org/en/Publications/WP/Issues/2019/09/04/Macroeconomic-and-Financial-Policies-for-Climate-Change-Mitigation-A-Review-of-the-Literature-48612.

Le Maux, L., and Scialom, L. (2013). Central banks and financial stability: Rediscovering the lender-of-last-resort practice in a finance economy. *Cambridge Journal of Economics*, *37*(1), 1–16.

Lugassy, L., Amdouni-Boursier, L., Alout, H., Berrebi, R., Boëte, C., Boué, F., ... Livoreil, B. (2019). What is the evidence that ecosystem components or functions have an impact on infectious diseases? A systematic review protocol. *Environmental Evidence*, *8*(1), 1–11.

Malm, A. (2012). China as chimney of the world: The fossil capital hypothesis. *Organization and Environment*, *25*(2), 146–177.

Malm, A. (2013). The origins of fossil capital: From water to steam in the British cotton industry. *Historical Materialism*, *21*(1), 15–68.

Mitchell, T. (2011). *Carbon Democracy: Political Power in the Age of Oil*. Verso.

Munevar, D. (2020). Arrested development: International Monetary Fund lending and austerity post Covid-19. Eurodad. https://www.eurodad.org/arrested_development.

NGFS (2019). Premier rapport complet. https://www.ngfs.net/en/premier-rapport-complet-un-appel-laction.

Olhoff, A., and Christensen, J. M. (2020). Emissions gap report 2020. UNEP DTU. https://backend.orbit.dtu.dk/ws/files/237967179/EGR_2020_Web.pdf.

Oustry, A., Erkan, B., and Svartzman, R. (2020). Climate-related risks and central banks' collateral policy: A methodological experiment. Banque de France. https://www.banque-france.fr/sites/default/files/wp790.pdf.

Rey, H. (2015). Dilemma not trilemma: The global financial cycle and monetary policy independence (No. w21162). National Bureau of Economic Research.

Sager, J. (2016). The crown joules: Resource peaks and monetary hegemony. *Economic Anthropology*, *3*(1), 31–42.

Scheidler, F. (2020). *The End of the Megamachine: A Brief History of a Failing Civilization*. John Hunt Publishing.

Servet, J. M., Théret, B., and Yildirim, Z. (2020). Universality of the monetary phenomenon and plurality of moneys: From colonial confrontation to confluence of the social sciences. In Pierre Alary, Jérôme Blanc, Ludovic Desmedt and Bruno Théret (Eds), *Institutionalist Theories of Money* (pp. 157–197). Palgrave Macmillan.

Smith-Nonini, S. (2016). The role of corporate oil and energy debt in creating the neoliberal era. *Economic Anthropology*, *3*(1), 57–67.

Svartzman, R., and Althouse, J. (2020). Greening the international monetary system? Not without addressing the political ecology of global imbalances. *Review of International Political Economy*, 1–26.

Svartzman, R., Dron, D., and Espagne, E. (2019). From ecological macroeconomics to a theory of endogenous money for a finite planet. *Ecological Economics*, *162*, 108–120.

TCFD (2016). Recommendations of the Task Force on Climate-Related Financial Disclosures. https://www.fsb-tcfd.org/wp-content/uploads/2017/06/FINAL-TCFD-Report-062817.pdf.

Théret, B. (2007). La monnaie dévoilée par ses crises. *Crises monétaires d'hier et d'aujourd'hui, 2*.

Tooze, A. (2020). China takes the climate stage. https://adamtooze.com/2020/10/19/china-takes-the-climate-stage.

Tooze, A. (2021). The rise and fall and rise (and fall) of the U.S. financial empire. *Foreign Policy*. https://foreignpolicy.com/2021/01/15/rise-fall-united-states-financial-empire-dollar-global-currency.

Triffin International Foundation (2014). *Using the special drawing rights as a lever to reform the international monetary system* (No. 1267).

Triffin International Foundation (2019). *Managing global liquidity as a global public good: A report of an RTI working party* (No. 1293).

Zhou, X. (2009). Reform the international monetary system. People's Bank of China, Beijing. http://www.pbc.gov.cn/english//detail.asp?col=6500&ID=178.

6. Climate change, financial instability and central banking

Giada Valsangiacomo

1. INTRODUCTION

The climate emergency is one of the most daunting challenges facing the world today. This menace originated more than a century ago, around the same time as the birth of modern industrial capitalism. Since then, continuous economic and population growth has been the main driver of the increase in carbon dioxide (CO_2) emissions (IPCC, 2014, p. 5). At 408.52 parts per million (ppm), the concentration of CO_2 in 2018 was the highest ever seen, far above the stable values inferred from the previous 70,000 years (Figure 6.1).

Global average long-term atmospheric concentration of carbon dioxide (CO_2), measured in parts per million (ppm)

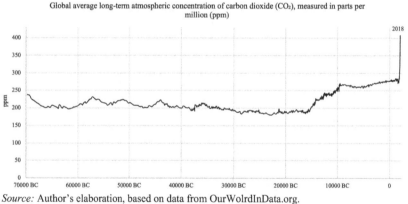

Source: Author's elaboration, based on data from OurWolrdInData.org.

Figure 6.1   Atmospheric CO_2 concentration since 70,000 BC

Although a direct and unambiguous causality is quite difficult to prove, the concentration of CO_2, along with methane and nitrous oxide, is extremely likely to have been the primary cause of the observed 0.87°C increase in the global mean surface temperature for the decade 2006–15 (IPCC, 2014, p. 4; IPCC, 2018, p. 4). Indeed, these gases irreversibly trap part of the sun's heat that would normally radiate from the Earth back into space, thereby triggering a global warming that disrupts the terrestrial climatic stability (Reichle, 2020, pp. 214–15). This perilous instability, better known as climate change, could entail not only rising average temperatures but also extreme weather events, changes in precipitation patterns, rising seas, habitat destruction and population displacement (IPCC, 2018, pp. 5–7 and 212–71). As a matter of fact, according to an eminent group of scientists, this current pathway is leading the Earth system out of the glacial and interglacial cycles characterizing the past 1.2 million years by activating important tipping points (Steffen et al., 2018, pp. 8253 and 8257).[1] More specifically, Fischer et al. (2018, p. 476) argue that sustained warming can be seen as a potential trigger of the long-term melting of ice in Greenland and Antarctica, which could cause the sea level to rise by 6–9 metres, thus endangering a large part of the population and infrastructure situated along coasts and on small islands. These projections bear out, most notably, that although the effects of climate change may affect every macro-agent in the economy (NGFS, 2019a, p. 12), the former are not evenly distributed. By and large, it is expected that the poorest countries and populations will suffer first and most (Stern, 2007, p. vii).

While the scientific community is providing formal proof that anthropogenic climate change is a far-reaching, irreversible and disruptive phenomenon (Anderegg et al., 2010, pp. 12107–9; IPCC, 2018, pp. 4–9), and that inaction could prove lethal to humanity (Lenton et al., 2019, p. 595), it is only with a certain degree of tardiness and wariness that society is finally taking up this thorny challenge, not least because the effects of climate change are expected to be felt far beyond the business and political cycle, but also beyond the horizon of technocratic authorities, such as central banks (Carney, 2015, p. 3).

Among the first to experience a salutary wake-up call, we count the insurance and financial community (Carney, 2015, p. 2), which now forthrightly recognizes that not only the physical impacts of climate change but also those associated with mitigating it are likely to have profound implications for the future functioning of the macro-financial system (NGFS, 2019a, p. 12). By developing new approaches (NGFS, 2020c, p. 5) to grasping and assessing the economic and financial implications of this full-blown global crisis (NGFS, 2020c, pp. 26–30), they have identified a promising way forward in a rapid but orderly transition to a sustainable zero-emission economy (NGFS, 2019a, p. 6), investing large amounts of economic resources in the greening of current production processes and the development of new technologies, industries and green sectors (NGFS, 2020c, pp. 14–18). Under pressure, central banks and financial regulators are also increasingly acknowledging the risks to the financial system posed by climate change (Carney, 2016, p. 1).

In the next section, after clearly categorizing climate-related risks and the transmission channels linking the latter to the financial realm, we will briefly ascertain whether central banks should respond to the issues that climate change entails. We readily appreciate that it is precisely the looming threat of climate change to financial stability – of which we provide an unambiguous and workable definition in the third section – that is the linchpin for legitimizing central bank responses. While avoiding getting involved in a fine-grained analysis of ongoing policy instruments, we define a new financial stability framework – compliant with the current legal remit of the major central banks. Embedding two fundamental bedrocks, this framework is intended to make the financial system more resilient to external shocks, notably those of climate change, though not exclusively. The first keystone – presented in the third section – encompasses the development of an enhanced macroprudential policy. Based both on the improvement of Basel III Agreements and on the application of financial stability assessment methods, it mainly addresses climate-related risks but neglects the hazy effects related to uncertainty. To overcome this shortcoming, the third section provides a new prudential framework that can be combined with it. Preventative reinforcement of macroprudential measures and regulatory action against financial actors that pose a potentially high systemic risk to the financial sector are its two main-stays. However, it appears that only by integrating these off-the-shelf central bank measures into a broader set of policies can financial stability finally be ensured, while at the same time steering the economy on the path to better environmental sustainability. Drawing on this last argument, the fourth section details our main conclusions and recommendations.

2.   CLIMATE-RELATED RISKS AND TRANSMISSION CHANNELS

As of today, it is widely recognized that climate-related risks fall into two main categories; to wit, physical risks and transition risks. In this respect, physical risks can be defined as "those risks that arise from the interaction of climate-related hazards (including hazardous events and trends) with the vulnerability of exposure of human and natural systems, including their ability to adapt" (Batten, 2018, p. 4). Two main sources of physical risks are identified: gradual global warming and increase in extreme weather events, such as droughts, floods or storms (NGFS, 2020b, p. 10). Transition risks, on the other hand, are defined as "those risks that might arise from the transition to a low-carbon economy" (Batten, 2018, p. 4).

Going a step further, a growing body of literature thoroughly unveils the channels linking climate risks to the economy and the financial system. It is accepted that physical risks materialize as economic shocks affecting the demand and supply side of the economy (Batten, 2018, p. 4; Bolton et al., 2020, p. 14), and with them the pattern of fundamentals driving asset prices. By way of example, transition risks may lead to financial risks by altering both the profitability of business and the wealth of households, or by challenging the broader macro-economy via investment reduction. Conversely, acute impacts from extreme events can trigger business disruption and damage to property, thereby affecting asset prices and increasing the risks for insurers (NGFS, 2020b, p. 12). More generally, physical and transition risk channels manifest themselves through a series of existing financial risk types, including credit, market, liquidity, underwriting, strategic, operational and reputational risks (NGFS, 2020b, p. 39). The awareness that the accretion of those risks could potentially create a backlash on both individual investors, as well as the financial system as a whole, has spurred the emergence of cutting-edge, scenario-based and forward-looking modelling approaches (Bolton et al., 2020, pp. 21–2). Alongside climate risk management that aims to evaluate the severity of the impacts on firms, banks and insurance companies, stress-testing is also coming into the spotlight as part of the assessment of the strategic resilience of the financial system (Carney, 2019, pp. 4 and 7). While not sticking to Value at Risk (VaR) calculation – a very poor tool since climate-related risks fit fat-tailed distribution and thus concentrate in the 1 per cent not considered by the VaR (Bolton et al., 2020, p. 21) – these new methods are also released from the analysis of historical trends, the latter blatantly leading to a mispricing of climate-related risks (Bolton et al., 2020, p. 21). Not least, they partly acknowledge the importance of feedback loops[2] between the financial system and the economy (NGFS, 2019b, p. 13) and avoid bonding to probabilistic calculations as the basis of their forecasts (Chesney et al., 2017; Battiston, 2019, p. 42).

These undeniable advances are countervailed by the ubiquitous quest to measure and forecast not only the magnitudes of climate-induced losses but first and foremost those of climate-related risks (see, for instance, Battiston et al., 2017), hence perpetuating the illusion that the latter can be accurately identified.

Now, this beguiling illusion can be easily outsmarted. As a first point, it is worthwhile noticing that the peculiar characteristics of climate change – such as tipping points and the dependence on the awakening of humanity – are already a first factor that muddies the waters in forecasting the future path of physical and economic impacts. In this sense, climate change can be seen as a phenomenon entailing radical uncertainty. The latter concept was already explained a century ago by Knight (1921, pp. 201–2) and refers mainly to future situations involving human actions. Since human responses have no scientific basis, no calculable probability can be applied. Intuitively, this rationale applies as much to the fight against anthropogenic global warming as it does to climate-related macroeconomic and financial effects, since the latter entail human perception and reaction.

Let us take the example of risks arising from the gradual shift of climate patterns.[3] It can be expected that they will be largely underestimated, since they are not clearly visible until the extremely perilous approach of a tipping point. The collective and immediate awakening of *Homo Sapiens*, who is *de facto* not endowed with perfect rationality and foresight, could create unpredictable and perhaps panic-driven reactions. Moreover, when our species realizes that it can no longer rely on the past to predict the future, it will change its way of making decisions.

Indeed, in accordance with Kalecki's investment equation (see Kalecki, 1971, pp. 110–23) reworked by Setterfield (2016, p. 223), climate change can, on the one hand, directly affect the main driver of aggregate demand – that is, investment (I) – through fluctuations in output (Y) and profits (πY):

$$LI = \alpha + \beta Y + \gamma \pi Y \tag{1}$$

but, on the other hand, physical risks could also trigger a change via the parameter α, which captures the reaction of firms facing uncertainty about the future, thereby further reducing investments well beyond deterministic output-related forecasts.

Yet, according to Larson (2002, pp. 242–57), at a macroeconomic level uncertainty affects not only investment but also other components of aggregate demand, such as private and public consumption. As any effort to reduce uncertainty through the acquisition of empirical information from individual past trends is bound to fail, economic agents – households, firms and governments – in a desperate attempt to boost their confidence seek additional information by looking at the current savings and investment decisions of other agents. In this framework, the premises for a decision are created by the whole set of interdependent agents, and the climate-related uncertainty underlying their behaviour is supposed to shape multiple components of aggregate demand, further undermining the endemic instability of our current economic system (Guttmann, 2016, pp. 342–4).

This reasoning applies as much to financial markets and their actors. Indeed, investors have expectations about future asset prices of carbon-intensive resources and industries (NGFS, 2019b, p. 16), listed start-ups promising revolutionary CO_2 recycling technology or insurance companies incurring colossal losses due to extreme weather events (Carney, 2015, p. 5). However, being unable to predict the future and to rely on past and present trends, investors are condemned to build their beliefs on what other market participants believe, and since the latter do exactly the same, they all create such dynamic interdependencies that they can shift financial market variables in principle anywhere, well beyond the pattern of fundamentals (Oberholzer, 2017, p. 42). It is also in this environment of uncertainty that speculation arises. Indeed, the behaviour of imperfectly foresighted investors involuntarily influences the prices of financial assets, thereby causing fluctuations that go beyond changes in demand or supply conditions (Kaldor, 1939, p. 1). Any attempts to quantify this climate-related uncertainty in financial markets will be in vain, including those undertaken by the Network for Greening the Financial System[4] in its own studies (NGFS, 2020c, p. 32).

Against the background of all these critical considerations, Figure 6.2 depicts the transmission channels connecting climate change to the financial system, thereby providing the basis for the elaboration of our dual central bank policy framework. Whereas the latter will be dealt with in detail in the following sections, it is already beneficial to point out that it is only by considering both transmission channels that climate-related effects on the financial system may be properly assessed and possibly kept at bay.

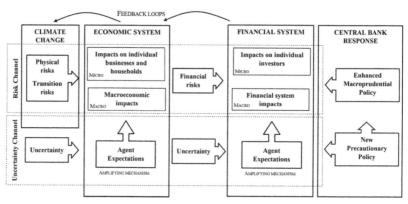

Source: Author's elaboration.

Figure 6.2   *Transmission channels, feedback loops and central bank responses*

3. CLIMATE-RELATED FINANCIAL INSTABILITY AND CENTRAL BANK RESPONSES

In light of our investigation hitherto – apart from the impacts on the real economy – climate-related risks and uncertainty, as well as the possible feedback loops to the economic system, are a matter of concern for the financial system and its own stability. Now, financial stability is an explicit objective mentioned in the mandates of several central banks (Jeanneau, 2014, p. 51; Barkawi and Monnin, 2015, pp. 164–5; Campiglio et al., 2017, p. 7), even if the increasing importance of price stability has gone along with the tendency to delegate financial supervisory functions from central banks to dedicated financial regulators (Goodhart, 2010, pp. 1–2). Thus, although 82 per cent of the 114 central bank mandates recently investigated by the Bank for International Settlements (BIS) have some form of explicit financial stability objective, for just over half the latter is secondary to price stability (Jeanneau, 2014, p. 50). Notwithstanding the Global Financial Crisis (GFC) of 2007–8 and the ensuing political pressure, at least 21 central banks have experienced a revision of their financial stability mandate, yet one that neither makes significant changes to its articles nor specifically mentions a potential link to climate change. This creates a legal loophole that has so far been used by central bankers as a smokescreen for declining to respond to the threat that climate change poses to the economic and financial spheres. However, there is a silver lining to this shortcoming. Indeed, as long as the instruments of monetary policy and the bulwark of the price stability mandate are not disrupted and the Tinbergen rule[5] violated, central banks have some leeway in their monitoring and responding to climate-related financial instability concerns.

The first step in developing operational solutions consists in knowing exactly what central banks need to monitor and protect. According to our definition of financial stability,[6] a financial system is deemed stable if it is in a position to ensure these four *sine qua non* conditions, to wit:

1. ensure its primary role of financial intermediation;
2. withstand its endogenous disequilibrating dynamics;
3. withstand the exogenous shocks resulting from significant disruptive events;
4. avoid adverse effects to the economic system.

Ensuring that the primary role of the financial system reverts back to financial intermediation, while resisting and perhaps thwarting the intrinsic self-balancing dynamics and the adverse effects on the real economy, requires fundamental change. As a consequence, not only the structure of the banking system and financial markets but also the role of governments and the legal mandate of central banks must be radically rethought. Instead, the dual-policy framework we propose aims at immediately helping central banks to monitor and hopefully reduce the negative consequences of exogenous climate-related shocks across financial markets – while minimizing feedback loops to the economy. Although specific to the fight against climate change, this dual framework can serve as inspiration to combat external shocks from diverse sources and transmission channels. For the sake of clarity, it is worth repeating that focussing only on these two proposals will not fully guarantee financial stability, as they improve the resilience of the financial system mainly with regard to only one of the four necessary stability conditions listed above.

3.1   Bedrock 1: Enhanced Macroprudential Framework

In recognition that transitional impacts and mitigation strategies can lead to financial risks that affect both individual wealth and profitability as well as the macroeconomic situation at large, the central bank should foster the embedding of such risks in both its financial stability monitoring and prudential supervision (Bolton et al., 2020, p. 50). Yet, the question may arise whether isolated and scattered national central banks can have an adequate impact in addressing system-wide financial risks. In order to increase their effectiveness, central banks' policy responses should be given through coordinated action within a global policy framework. In this regard, Basel III – featuring its well-known three-pillar structure – comes across as the perfect conduit for the enforcement of such policies in whichever eligible and favourable jurisdiction. In this respect, not only the 28 jurisdictions participating in the Basel Committee (BCBS, 2020, p. 9) but also the 60 non-BCBS member countries that have already partially integrated Basel III into their prudential regime (Hohl et al., 2018, p. 29) might tailor this framework to their domestic specificities. Indeed, even though the Basel regulatory standards are designed only for internationally active banks, in practice national authorities have already voluntarily extended the regulatory requirements for non-international banks operating in their jurisdictions (Hohl et al., 2018, p. 1). In the same way, national central banks (and microprudential supervisory authorities) could broaden the implementation of the requirements of Pillars 2 and 3 to other national financial institutions.

According to the Basel Committee on Banking Supervision (2019, p. 2), Pillar 2 is intended not only to ensure that banks hold adequate capital to support risks beyond the minimum requirements but also to encourage them to develop and implement finer risk management techniques. In one fell swoop, climate-related risk assessment could be included into Pillar 2 through the forward-looking and holistic scenario analyses (BCBS, 2019, p. 25) previously discussed, which can easily become an integral part of the supervisory framework and considered within the revisions of the assessment methodology, as they likewise include both specific climate-related stress tests and individual climate risk management (Carney, 2019, pp. 4 and 7). While the former could be fully integrated into the normal stress-testing process, the latter – with the objective of assessing the severity of climate change impacts for banks and other institutions – goes hand in hand with the supervisory review process embedded in Pillar 2.

Along similar lines, it is worth noticing that an unambiguous distinction between micro- and macroprudential frameworks offers an invaluable advantage in establishing the responsibilities of each supervisory body. Review processes and guidelines, as well as corrective and remedial actions to address specific deficiencies or weaknesses at individual levels, could be implemented by the established microprudential supervisory authority. On the other hand, climate-related stress-testing could become a clear macroprudential competence of central banks, while sticking within the remit of their mandate. In this regard, Basel III could also be the ideal means to legally enforce the recommendations of the NGFS. Accordingly, the bridging of data gaps and the sharing of knowledge within the banking and financial systems (NGFS, 2019a, pp. 20–32) could be gathered into the central bankers' hands. Since this deficit has been identified as a major impediment in the development of precise green stress tests (NGFS, 2020a, pp. 4 and 10), the current voluntary disclosure of climate-related risks by the private sector (implemented through the TCFD guidelines[7]) ought to be replaced by mandatory requirements.

These requirements might be enforced through Pillar 3 of Basel III, the latter pillar currently resembling enhanced disclosure with a view to making use of the disciplinary forces of markets (Blundell-Wignall and Atkinson, 2010, p. 7). Although blatantly rooted in the flawed conceptual framework of the Efficient Market Hypothesis, which fruitlessly strives to salvage the association between disclosure and efficient repricing by financial markets, the importance of the former must not be underestimated. Indeed, as a welcome consequence of this reporting, not only central banks but also the whole set of participants in the financial system would enjoy greater visibility and transparency with respect to financial market activities. As already reiterated time and again, since climate change brings uncertainty, financial agents are pushed to gather additional information on the current behaviour and decisions of other actors so as to offset the ineffectiveness of empirical information on past trends. From this standpoint, the transparent and up-to-date disclosure by other financial agents, as well as the potential progressive greening of their activities, entails an ulterior benefit. Indeed, as soon as the brownness of any financial institution is unmasked, the latter might be prompted to take climate-friendly investments (especially if other financial agents do the same) and avoid being identified as the ugly duckling of its relative financial market and jurisdiction, a judgement that may lead to great reputational damage. To get closer to this goal, the development and implementation of a formal and shared taxonomy allowing the identification of green and brown activities and related assets is likewise an essential step.

As of yet, we have not addressed any greening proposals pertaining to Pillar 1 of Basel III, even though some researchers (see, for instance, Campiglio, 2016; Volz, 2017; D'Orazio and Popoyan, 2018; Macquarie, 2018) perceive a green potential of prudential capital and liquidity measures. The strongest cases emerge in favour of strengthening the Countercyclical Capital Buffer (CCB), the Liquidity Coverage Ratio (LCR), the Stable Funding Ratio (NSFR) and the Brown Penalizing Factor (BPF).

BPF would imply the build-up of prudential capital for non-green and brown assets (D'Orazio and Popoyan, 2018), pushing banks towards a risk-sensitive attitude and rendering them more resilient when confronted with the emergence of a possible carbon bubble or repricing owing to the materialization of climate-related risks. Yet, the subjectivity of the assessment for risk inputs remains unaddressed. These can be manipulated by banks to arbitrarily reduce capital requirements, including those intended to cover brown assets and sectors, thereby undermining the regulators' efforts.

Another tool factored in, featuring more prominent macroprudential properties, is the CCB, designed to strengthen the resilience of banking institutions in the face of accumulated systemic vulnerabilities (D'Orazio and Popoyan, 2018). While creating a buffer of capital above the regulatory minimum in periods of excessive credit growth to non-green sectors, it implicitly recognizes the increasing *ex ante* risks of such activity (D'Orazio and Popoyan, 2018). These buffers could then be released to absorb potential *ex post* shocks related to the transition to low-carbon loans and thus to the materialization of transition risks. However, the practical implementation of CCB so far has proven to have no statistically significant impact on curbing growth in credit and asset prices, one of the reasons being the lack of proper risk identification, which is instrumental for the effective activation and calibration of the cushion (Borio, 2018, p. 5).

With regard to liquidity proposals, the standards implemented by Basel III through the LCR and the NSFR aim at protecting banks against short-term liquidity crises as well as matching long-term assets with stable funding (D'Orazio and Popoyan, 2018). Since the mechanism behind these two instruments is expected to discourage long-term green investments (D'Orazio and Popoyan, 2018), the European Banking Federation (EBF) proposes that any loan linked to green finance would be exempt from LCR and NSFR calculations. They also suggest the introduction of a specific incentive for the LCR and NSFR treatment of green finance, to be directly provided by banks, in order to bridge the environmentally specific long-term goals and the limits to maturity transformation of the prudential rules (EBF, 2017, pp. 34–5). Despite good intentions, these proposals could prove to be harmful in at least two respects. First, given their innate quest for profit (Minsky, 1992, p. 6), banks are expected to embrace riskier green investments that promise higher returns and are excluded from liquidity regulations, especially in a world where negative interest-rate structures compress their profit margins. These forms of behaviour can also easily become "business as usual" for firms and individuals, which would then create a potential risk for a green bubble that compromises the safety and soundness of the banking and financial systems. Second, owing to the capacity of the financial system to overcome regulation through innovations (Minsky, 2008, p. 281), banks could be propelled into a race towards "green securitization", by acquiring long-term green assets, not subject to liquidity regulations, in order to transform them into securities that are tradable. While this procedure can provide additional financing capacity for green projects, most of these operations are carried out through off-balance-sheet entities, such as Special Purpose Vehicles (SPVs), and often lack transparency, thereby exacerbating the difficulties underlying the risk assessment needed to calibrate most of the aforementioned instruments.

Yet, apart from all our theoretical criticisms tabled along with those tools, Campiglio (2016, p. 225) and Borio (2018, pp. 5–7) have already keenly pointed out that the current macroprudential framework under Pillar 1 seems to be a regulation in name only, insofar as it has not had the desired effect on the behaviour of commercial banks. In this regard, all reform proposals for greening liquidity and capital requirements might sound hollow and somewhat counterproductive, although a positive effect can be triggered through the prudential policy we will discuss in the next section.

3.2   Bedrock 2: A New Precautionary Policy

The future is uncertain. However, we should not use this as an excuse for not stepping in. As already explained, in the framework of the fight against climate change, uncertainty about future outcomes is tied not only to the lack of ability to predict them but also to the fact that the very existence of humankind is being defined: the decisions that we take today will radically change the course of our future. As soon as we accept that the world we live in is surrounded by radical uncertainty, merely paying attention to the measurement of quantifiable values, following a deterministic and probabilistic logic, clearly appears to be a misleading operational framework. As pointed out by Barmes (2019), this recognition paves the way for a precautionary principle (and approach) to be applied to the financial system.

Over the past few years, the precautionary principle has become an increasingly accepted concept in environmental policy, particularly in the fight against climate change. In broad terms, this principle posits that a lack of knowledge or scientific certainty about the potential repercussions of an action should not be used as an excuse to postpone it, when there is a threat of serious or irreversible harm (Wiesmeth, 2012, p. 36). On the contrary, if there is a suspected risk that an action could cause irreversible damage, the burden of the proof that it is harmless lies with those seeking to implement it (Barmes, 2019). Through the inclusion in Article 3.3 of the United Nations Framework

Convention on Climate Change (1992), signed by 165 countries and communities, the precautionary principle has received wide international attention (Chenet et al., 2021, p. 6). This article states that:

> The Parties should take precautionary measures to anticipate, prevent, or minimize the causes of climate change and mitigate its adverse effects. Where there are threats of serious or irreversible damage, lack of full scientific certainty should not be used as a reason for postponing such measures. (UNFCCC, 1992, Art. 3.3)

The precautionary principle is not new in economics either, particularly within the framework of an alternative view to the orthodox one. For example, Lavoie (2005) has developed a post-Keynesian theory of consumer choice based on precautionary principles such as, *inter alia*, procedural rationality, satiable needs, separability and subordination of needs (Holt, 2016, p. 369). Lavoie (2005, p. 69) also clearly states that the precautionary principle is tied to fundamental uncertainty. According to his findings, it is widely acknowledged that the precautionary approach is already spontaneously being applied at an individual level in a framework of Knightian uncertainty. As a matter of fact, when information is lacking, financial agents act with caution by postponing decisions that could increase the probability of their institution's bankruptcy. As a general rule, when private agents make decisions that affect them directly, fundamental uncertainty leads them to adopt a course of action that generates safety. From a theoretical point of view, it makes sense to apply the same principle to the environment, first and foremost in light of its nature as a public good (Wiesmeth, 2012, p. 170). Accordingly, when in doubt, no decision should be taken that increases the likelihood of an environmental catastrophe (Lavoie, 2005, p. 78), which would hit not only the natural system but also the human one. Alas, it is commonly acknowledged that there is a lack of spontaneous incentives when it comes to public goods. Consequently, to implement the rationale of the precautionary approach, coercive guidelines are needed.

Going a step further, one could argue that the same logic could be applied to financial stability: the blatant absence of spontaneous incentives to safeguard it would finally find a logical explanation. Thus, as a fundamental first move, central banks ought to recognize that financial stability has the character and function of a public good. In this respect, let us recall that the foundations of the theory of public goods were laid down in 1954 by Paul Samuelson. In his famous paper on "The Pure Theory of Public Expenditure", he defined the two main criteria for distinguishing public goods, namely their non-rivalry and non-excludability. A few years later, Musgrave (1959, p. 44) added an important trait to the classic notion of public good. Indeed, he defined it as a good "the inherent quality of which requires public production". To put it another way, a public good cannot be produced privately; that is, by individuals. Along the same lines, financial stability cannot be guaranteed through safety mechanisms at an individual level only. This is tantamount to saying that separate private individuals' optimization plans alone are insufficient for addressing the stability of the financial system as a whole (Ülgen, 2018, p. 103).

Returning to our main train of thought, as a precautionary measure, central banks (and microprudential supervisors) are allowed to act preventatively to protect financial stability – which fulfils a public-good function – against the destabilizing financial activities of single agents who do not consider public welfare but only their pursuit of profits. This amounts to saying that central banks could propose regulatory actions when a financial activity presents a potentially high risk of disrupting financial stability. In line with the precautionary principle, institutions undertaking such activities must provide regulators with proof of their safety (Ülgen, 2016, p. 13). Needless to say, this tool is very effective when combined with our enhanced macroprudential framework: armed with the results of mandatory disclosure and green stress tests, central banks are able to accurately identify which assets and activities pose higher risks to financial stability. The financial institutions at stake can be sanctioned by the central bank without the latter having to rely on factual and consensual evidence: the burden of proof is on the parties carrying the danger. In this respect, sanctions could take the form of stricter capital and reserve requirements under Pillar 1 of Basel III – although they are not particularly effective, as already argued – or an interest-rate penalty on reserves at the central bank. Stricter disclosure and risk assessment requirements (Pillars 2 and 3) could also be enforced for institutions defined as "brown": the administrative burden of such practices should prompt them to green their activities. At this juncture, Too Big To Fail (TBTF) banks would automatically be the most affected. Indeed, even though they have a portfolio with the same proportion of brown assets as smaller entities, their systemic importance mechanically amplifies the related risks to the financial system. As a welcome consequence, therefore, this new policy can act both as an incentive for the greening of TBTF banks and, perhaps, for the reduction of their size.

In addition, following the precautionary approach, all macroprudential measures can be automatically strengthened for all financial market participants and not only for those that have to face sanctions. As a matter of fact, a key feature of macroprudential policy is that it empowers central banks and supervisors to increase the resilience of financial stability while taking *ex ante* measures rather than relying on *ex post* actions. Under the precautionary approach, therefore, regulators have the necessary room for manoeuvre to act in a more robust and proactive manner to protect the public good that is financial stability. When applied to Basel III, the new precautionary policy would give central banks a green light to raise capital and reserve requirements beyond normal provisions. Hence, the enhanced green macroprudential tools of Pillar 1 can also be upgraded. For instance, by means of the BPF, a greater build-up of prudential capital for brown assets in periods of excessive credit growth to non-green sectors can be activated. In addition, the capital cushion of CCB might be further increased. Although we have questioned the effects of these instruments, we do believe that, in such a framework, the mere fact of disclosing their enhancement could give banks the incentive to move towards green assets.

Stress-testing and the supervision of risk analysis under Pillar 2 of Basel III can also be reshaped along the same lines. In this respect, it is worth noting that thanks to the guidance of the NGFS, some central banks are *de facto* embracing a forward-looking and scenario-based stress-testing approach (NGFS, 2020c, p. 5). However, the underlying assumptions are often based on subjective and arbitrary criteria. Moreover, as already highlighted, climate change entails a fundamental and non-measurable uncertainty: whether the scenarios will really materialize, and how and when policymakers will choose to react (NGFS, 2019a, p. 20), are a matter of speculation and not of certainty. As a solution to this problem, the whole set of hypothetical transition scenarios is currently being considered in assessing and comparing the future resilience of the financial market. All eventualities are contemplated, including the rosiest ones: this may lead to a certain optimism and inaction. By way of contrast, the precautionary approach would entail central banks basing their assessment of financial market resilience and subsequent macroprudential measures exclusively on worst-case scenarios (Chenet et al., 2021, p. 7) – regardless of their probability – so as to require an immediate but not hasty move towards greening the financial system. To the extent that central banks launch an impulse for that movement in a timely and orderly manner, and if the latter is accompanied by the enhanced measures to monitor and strengthen financial stability, we can hope to move towards the best of (worst-case) scenarios as far as financial and climate instability are concerned.

By way of conclusion, Table 6.1 summarizes the suggested measures to be implemented in the proposed new financial stability framework, as well as the division of tasks among central banks and other players at stake.

4.   CONCLUSION

Provided that the new financial stability framework hereby described is proactively pursued, compliant central banks would already take an essential and prompt leap forward in protecting financial stability against the looming menace of climate change, and this within the remit of their mandate. While dodging clashes with the intricate monetary policy that has been conducted in recent years, these policies also foster the values of sustainable finance and long-termism.

Table 6.1   Proposal for a new financial stability framework

Main measures to be taken by central banks		Complementary measures to be implemented by supervised institutions	
Enhanced macroprudential policy	*Precautionary policy*	*Enhanced macroprudential policy*	*Precautionary policy*
Financial stability monitoring through stress tests integrating climate-related risks	**Focus on worst-case scenarios**	**Mandatory disclosure*** of climate-related risks	**Higher requirements** for activities/ assets causing greater risk to financial stability
Prudential regulation* based on enhanced Basel III	**Precautionary reinforcement** of relevant requirements	**Adoption of taxonomy*** on green and brown activities and assets	

* To be remitted to or conducted in strong coordination with the microprudential supervisory authority.

Source: Author's elaboration.

However, the above-proposed macroprudential and precautionary policy responses should not be considered as an end in themselves. Indeed, from the outset it appears clear that improving financial stability in all its facets would require addressing the whole set of *sine qua non* conditions that underpin it. Moreover, it seems a pipe dream to assume that the implementation of a large-scale and orderly transition to a carbon-neutral economy – identified as the most effective means of preserving the human, natural, economic and financial systems – can be propelled by financial markets alone, albeit backed by central bank nudges.

Rather, this should be seen as a first step towards a broad epistemological breakthrough, whereby governments, the banking system and the private sector are likewise seen as key to responding to current and future challenges posed by climate change (Bolton et al., 2020, p. 49). In this respect, research that explores both theoretically and practically the roles of the aforementioned actors in this current dual struggle against climate and financial instability, and that identifies coordinated and more inclusive green policy actions, should be regarded as a much-needed addition to the field and therefore actively nurtured.

NOTES

1. A tipping point may be described as a threshold that, when exceeded, can lead to a reorganization in the state of the climate system and that could, in turn, cause another spate of cascading events (IPCC, 2014, p. 128).
2. According to the Network for Greening the Financial System (2019b, p. 13), "feedback loops characterize the pattern through which climate-related risks reach the financial system and swing back to the macro economy".
3. Basically, transition risks are expected to operate through channels similar to those presented so far; that is, by directly affecting the components of aggregate supply and demand, or through uncertainty.
4. The Network for Greening the Financial System (NGFS) is the global central bank coalition-of-the-willing that aims to support more sustainable financial systems.
5. The Tinbergen rule states that at least *n* independent policy instruments are required to successfully achieve *n* independent policy targets (Volz, 2017, p. 7). This is tantamount to saying that financial stability should be left to prudential policy while monetary stability should be assigned to monetary policy.
6. According to Schinasi (2004, p. 8), "a financial system is in a range of stability whenever it is capable of facilitating (rather than impeding) the performance of an economy, and of dissipating financial imbalances that arise endogenously or as a result of significant adverse and unanticipated events". Instead, we define financial stability as follows: "A condition in which the financial system is capable of ensuring its primary role of financial intermediation, and of withstanding its endogenous disequilibrating dynamics as well as exogenous shocks resulting from significant disruptive events, without creating adverse effects to the economic system".

7. The Financial Stability Board (FSB) recently established the Task Force on Climate-Related Financial Disclosures (TCFD) to improve and enhance the reporting of climate-related financial disclosures (Carney, 2019, p. 2), particularly through specific guidelines and recommendations.

REFERENCES

Anderegg, W.R.L., Prall, J.W., Harold, J. and S.H. Schneider (2010), "Expert credibility in climate change", *Proceedings of the National Academy of Sciences*, 107 (27), pp. 12107–9.

Barkawi, A. and P. Monnin (2015), "Monetary policy and green finance: exploring the links", *Greening China's financial system*, available at https://www.iisd.org/sites/default/files/publications/greening-chinas-financial-system.pdf.

Barmes, D. (2019), "Climate 'risk' vs 'uncertainty' in financial policymaking", *Positive Money*, available at https://positivemoney.org/2019/10/climate-risk-vs-uncertainty-in-financial-policymaking.

Basel Committee on Banking Supervision [BCBS] (2019), "Overview of Pillar 2 supervisory review practices and approaches", *BIS Published Documents*, available at https://www.bis.org/bcbs/publ/d465.pdf.

Basel Committee on Banking Supervision [BCBS] (2020), "Climate-related financial risks: a survey on current initiatives", *BIS Published Documents*, available at https://www.bis.org/bcbs/publ/d502.pdf.

Batten, S. (2018), "Climate change and the macro-economy: a critical review", *Bank of England Working Paper*, 706, available at https://www.bankofengland.co.uk/working-paper/2018/climate-change-and-the-macro-economy-a-critical-review.

Battiston, S. (2019), "The importance of being forward-looking: managing financial stability in the face of climate risk", *Banque de France Financial Stability Review*, 23, pp. 39–48.

Battiston, S., Mandel, A., Monasterolo, I., Schütze, F. and G. Visentin (2017), "A climate stress-test of the financial system", *Nature Climate Change*, 7 (4), pp. 283–8.

Blundell-Wignall, A. and P. Atkinson (2010) "Thinking beyond Basel III: necessary solutions for capital and liquidity", *OECD Journal: Financial Market Trends*, 2010 (1), pp. 9–33.

Bolton, P., Després, M., Pereira da Silva, L.A., Samama, F. and R. Svartzman (2020), "The Green Swan: central banking and financial stability in the age of climate change", *BIS Publications*, available at https://www.bis.org/publ/othp31.pdf.

Borio, C. (2018), "Macroprudential frameworks: experience, prospects and a way forward", in: Bank for International Settlements [BIS] (ed.), *Are Post-Crisis Statistical Initiatives Completed?*, 49, available at https://www.bis.org/speeches/sp180624a.pdf.

Campiglio, E. (2016), "Beyond carbon pricing: the role of banking and monetary policy in financing the transition to a low-carbon economy", *Ecological Economics*, 121, pp. 220–30.

Campiglio, E., Matikainen, S. and D. Zenghelis (2017), "The climate impact of quantitative easing", *Grantham Research Institute on Climate Change and the Environment Policy Brief*, available at http://www.lse.ac.uk/GranthamInstitute/wp-content/uploads/2017/05/ClimateImpactQuantEasing_Matikainen-et-al-1.pdf.

Carney, M. (2015), "Breaking the tragedy of the horizon: climate change and financial stability", Speech at Lloyd's of London, 29 September.

Carney, M. (2016), "Resolving the climate paradox", Speech at Arthur Burns Memorial Lecture, Berlin, 22 September.

Carney, M. (2019), "A new horizon", Speech at European Commission Conference to Sustainable Finance, Brussels, 21 March.

Chenet, H., Ryan-Collins, J. and F. van Lerven (2021), "Finance, climate-change and radical uncertainty: towards a precautionary approach to financial policy", *Ecological Economics*, 183, pp. 1–14.

Chesney, M., Lasserre, P. and B. Troja (2017), "Mitigating global warming: a real options approach", *Annals of Operations Research*, 255 (1–2), pp. 465–506.

D'Orazio, P. and L. Popoyan (2018), "Fostering green investments and tackling climate-related financial risks: which role for macroprudential policies?", *Ecological Economics*, 160, pp. 25–37.

European Banking Federation [EBF] (2017), "Towards a green finance framework", *EBF Reports*, available at https://www.ebf.eu/wp-content/uploads/2017/09/Geen -finance-complete.pdf.

Fischer, H., Meissner, K., Mix, A., Abram, N., Austermann, J. et al. (2018), "Paleoclimate constraints on the impact of 2°C anthropogenic warming and beyond", *Nature Geoscience*, 11 (7), pp. 474–85.

Goodhart, C.A.E. (2010), "The changing role of central banks", *BIS Working Papers*, 326, available at https://www.bis.org/publ/work326.pdf.

Guttmann, R. (2016), "Imbalances and crises", in: Rochon, L.-P. and S. Rossi (eds), *An Introduction to Macroeconomics*, Cheltenham, UK and Northampton, USA: Edward Elgar Publishing, pp. 336–58.

Hohl, S., Sison, M.C., Stastny, T. and R. Zamil (2018), "The Basel framework in 100 jurisdictions: implementation status and proportionality practices", *FSI Insights on Policy Implementation*, 11, pp. 1–39.

Holt, R.P.F. (2016), "Sustainable development", in: Rochon, L.-P. and S. Rossi (eds), *An Introduction to Macroeconomics*, Cheltenham, UK and Northampton, USA: Edward Elgar Publishing, pp. 359–80.

Intergovernmental Panel on Climate Change [IPCC] (2014), *Climate Change 2014: Synthesis Report. Contribution of Working Groups I, II and III to the Fifth Assessment Report of the Intergovernmental Panel on Climate Change*, Geneva: IPCC.

Intergovernmental Panel on Climate Change [IPCC] (2018), *Global Warming of 1.5°C. An IPCC Special Report on the Impacts of Global Warming of 1.5°C Above Pre-Industrial Levels and Related Global Greenhouse Gas Emission Pathways, in the Context of Strengthening the Global Response to the Threat of Climate Change*, Geneva: IPCC.

Jeanneau, S. (2014), "Financial stability objectives and arrangements – what's new?", *BIS Paper*, 76, available at https://www.bis.org/publ/bppdf/bispap76e_rh.pdf.

Kaldor, N. (1939), "Speculation and economic stability", *The Review of Economic Studies*, 7 (1), pp. 1–27.

Kalecki, M. (1971), *Selected Essays on the Dynamics of the Capitalist Economy*, Cambridge: Cambridge University Press.

Knight, F.H. (1921), *Risk, Uncertainty and Profits*, Boston and New York: The Riverside Press Cambridge.

Larson, S. (2002), "Uncertainty and consumption in Keynes's theory of effective demand", *Review of Political Economy*, 14 (2), pp. 241–58.

Lavoie, M. (2005), "Post-Keynesian consumer choice theory for the economics of sustainable forest management", in: Kant, S. and R.A. Berry (eds), *Economics, Natural Resources and Sustainability: Economics of Sustainable Forest Management*, Dordrecht: Kluwer, pp. 67–90.

Lenton, T.M., Rockström, J., Gaffney, O., Rahmstorf, S., Richardson, K., Steffen, W. and H.J. Schellnhuber (2019), "Climate tipping points – too risky to bet against", *Nature*, 575, pp. 592–5.

Macquarie, B. (2018), "A green Bank of England: central banking for a low-carbon economy", *Positive Money*, available at https://positivemoney.org/greenbankofengland.

Minsky, H.P. (1992), "The financial instability hypothesis", *The Jerome Levy Economics Institute Working Paper*, 74, available at http://www.levyinstitute.org/pubs/wp/74.pdf.

Minsky, H.P. (2008), *Stabilizing an Unstable Economy*, Columbus, OH: McGraw-Hill Professional.

Musgrave, R.A. (1959), *The Theory of Public Finance: A Study in Public Economy*, New York: McGraw-Hill.

Network for Greening the Financial System [NGFS] (2019a), "NGFS first comprehensive report. A call for action – climate change as a source of financial risk", available at https://www.ngfs.net/en/first-comprehensive-report-call-action.

Network for Greening the Financial System [NGFS] (2019b), "Macroeconomic and financial stability: implications of climate change – NGFS technical supplement to the first comprehensive", available at https://www.ngfs.net/en/technical-supplement-first-ngfs-comprehensive-report.

Network for Greening the Financial System [NGFS] (2020a), "A status report on financial institutions' experiences from working with green, non green and brown financial assets and a potential risk differential", available at https://www.ngfs.net/sites/default/files/medias/documents/ngfs_status_report.pdf.

Network for Greening the Financial System [NGFS] (2020b), "Guide for supervisors. Integrating climate-related and environmental risks into prudential supervision", available at https://www.ngfs.net/sites/default/files/medias/documents/ngfs_guide_for_supervisors.pdf.

Network for Greening the Financial System [NGFS] (2020c), "NGFS Climate Scenarios for central banks and supervisors", available at https://www.ngfs.net/sites/default/files/medias/documents/820184_ngfs_scenarios_final_version_v6.pdf.

Oberholzer, B. (2017), *Monetary Policy and Crude Oil: Prices, Production and Consumption*, Cheltenham, UK and Northampton, USA: Edward Elgar Publishing.

Reichle, D.E. (2020), *The Global Carbon Cycle and Climate Change*, Amsterdam: Elsevier.

Schinasi, G.J. (2004), "Defining financial stability", *International Monetary Fund Working Paper*, WP/04/187.

Setterfield, M. (2016), "Economic growth and development", in: Rochon, L.-P. and S. Rossi (eds), *An Introduction to Macroeconomics*, Cheltenham, UK and Northampton, USA: Edward Elgar Publishing, pp. 211–32.

Steffen, W., Rockström, J., Richardson, K., Lenton, T.M., Folke, C., Liverman, C. et al. (2018), "Trajectories of the Earth system in the Anthropocene", *Proceedings of the National Academy of Sciences of the United States of America*, 115 (33), pp. 8252–9.

Stern, N. (2007), *The Economics of Climate Change: The Stern Review*, Cambridge: Cambridge University Press.

Ülgen, F. (2016), "The precautionary principle and financial stability: an alternative institutional design of market organisation and regulation", *Paper for the 28th Annual EAEPE Conference,* Manchester, 3–5 November.

Ülgen, F. (2018), "Financial stability as a global public good and relevant systemic regulation as a problem of collective action", in: Bance, P. (ed.), *Providing Public Goods and Commons. Towards Coproduction and New Forms of Governance for a Revival of Public Action*, Liège: CIRIEC, pp. 95–112.

United Nations Framework Convention on Climate Change [UNFCCC] (1992), "Principles", available at https://unfccc.int/resource/ccsites/zimbab/conven/text/art03.htm.

Volz, U. (2017), "On the role of central banks in enhancing green finance", *UN Environment Inquiry Working Paper 17 (1)*.

Wiesmeth, H. (2012), *Environmental Economics: Theory and Policy in Equilibrium*, Dresden: Springer Verlag.

7. Towards an ecological market

Wesley C. Marshall

1. INTRODUCTION

In his study of the history of money, John Kenneth Galbraith relates how when faced with falling prices and monetary scarcity, the American colonies turned to monetary innovation, both in terms of new banks but also, most notably, in terms of new monetary issues: "if the history of commercial banking belongs to the Italians and of central banking to the British, that of paper money issued by a government belongs indubitably to the Americans" (Galbraith, 1975: 45). This chapter will make the case for a new monetary issue in order to achieve ecological goals. Both in the diagnosis of the shortcomings of the current carbon markets and in the outline of institutional change geared towards ecological goals, this chapter will use as a guide Robert Guttmann's *Eco-Capitalism* (2018).

Guttmann emphasizes the crucial role of finance (2018: 169) in combatting ecological breakdown, stating that "we will thus have to create, step by step, a climate-specific system of financial institutions, instruments, and markets – a climate finance" (2018: 171). This chapter offers a proposal for an alternative financial system along these lines. The basic idea would be to create a green financial market that creates an opposite set of incentives from those of the current financial market, in which the degradation and destruction of nature is profitable, while that which helps and protects nature is not.

This proposal is not to change the current system but rather to introduce a new financial market, and to open a new financial space, replete with a new green currency, a green central bank (GCB), and a green treasury (GT), that would exist alongside the current system. In financial terms, it would not be a competitor, and indeed it could be an important complement to the current system, while in the terms of the real world it would be directed towards populations that are often unattended to in – or most gravely exploited by – the current system: those of the vast urban slums of the global periphery. As such areas exist at the margin of national states, the proposal is to create private markets underpinned by a global green financial system, with the goal of establishing incentives to generate new private markets that would work with money and markets just as exist today – even with the money motive intact – but under a transformed mission, which would provide financial incentives for cleaning the planet and reducing the consumption of hydrocarbons. The proposal would aim to confer value and give a price to two things that until now have neither value nor price: human excrement and other waste. While this new green market would promote ecological ends, it would also address other human problems, such as unemployment and poverty.

The rest of the chapter is divided into two themes. The first is mainly theoretical, and examines recent research into the nature of money, and turns a historical eye to the control of money and the Keynesian revolution and counter-revolution, to then update Keynes's critiques of sound finance to today's circumstances. The second theme lays out the proposal for a green monetary space of production. After offering some context regarding the short-comings of the current carbon market, a general outline of the institutional structure of the green financial system is introduced, as well as the private market that is intended to grow around it. Focus is then turned to the monetary characteristics and features of the proposed financial system, and several scenarios are presented, from the most effective green financial system to the most limited, stripped down to the bare elements necessary to maintain a financial space capable of incentivizing ecological goals.

2.   THE UNDERLYING THEORETICAL DEBATE

At the end of 2019, Andy Newman published an article entitled "Where Rent Is $13,500, She Lives Off What's Left at the Curb" in the *New York Times*:

> In recent years, an entire economic ecosystem has sprouted from the artificial turf of a 5-cent deposit. It includes fleets of trucks, clashes between canners uptown and between truckers at an open-air canning market downtown, price wars and middle-men and coordinated handoffs. (Newman, 2019: n.p.)

Newman describes the price of 5 cents per can as "artificial". This message has been conveyed by agents of conventional thought for centuries. If anything (in this example the cans) were worth anything – if they were of any use – the market would assign them a price. "Natural" prices are governed by supply and demand in the capitalist market, and driven by the money motive – a logic accepted by most today. An "artificial" price, on the other hand, is that which is established by the state, as in the price of recycled cans mentioned in the quote. Academic economics has for centuries aligned "natural" with intrinsic value mandated by the market, while "artificial" prices set or supported by the state are deemed misaligned with intrinsic value.

As a ubiquitous part of our lives, money is rarely questioned. There is a parable of two young fish swimming in the river. An older fish swimming the other way asks, "Morning, boys. How's the water?" And the two young fish swim on for a bit, and then eventually one of them looks over at the other and asks, "What the hell is water?" (Wallace, 2005). Money is as socially present as air and water are in nature, and therefore is largely considered as natural, and there is a very strong interest in maintaining this perception:

> The production of money is accompanied by an attempt ideologically to naturalize the social relation of money. Social institutions and conventions based on no more than either an equilibrium of competing interests or a consensual agreement are fragile; they require a stronger foundation (Douglas, 1986). "There needs to be an analogy by which the formal structure of a crucial set of social relations is found in the physical world, or in the super natural world, or in eternity, anywhere, so long as it is not seen as a socially contrived arrangement" (Douglas, 1986: 48). Until the twentieth century, the ideological naturalization of money was achieved, and its social construction concealed, by the commodity form of money in the gold standard and the commodity-exchange theory of orthodox economics. With the abandonment of gold, however, the fiction of universal, immutable, natural money became increasingly difficult to sustain. (Ingham, 2004: 79–80)

John Kenneth Galbraith offered similar sentiments decades before: "The process by which banks create money is so simple that the mind is repelled. Where something so important is involved, a deeper mystery seems only decent" (Galbraith, 1975: 18–19). From even further in the past, the explicit meaning of Adam Smith's "invisible hand" is often lost today: it is the hand of God. Money is the ultimate fetish, as throughout the centuries human beings have created money and attributed it to the gods, and then allow their earthly creation to be their metaphysical master.

Appeals to respect the "nature" of the economy are often little less than a call for society to maintain its ignorance about money and not to recognize it as a mere "socially contrived arrangement". Galbraith states that "the study of money, above all other fields in economics, is the one in which complexity is used to disguise truth or to evade truth, not to reveal it" (1975: 5). It is indeed curious how most cases of human innovation triumphing over the forces of nature are celebrated, but money must be kept as God intended. Dying out of refusal to take antibiotics for religious reasons is often ridiculed, but societies must not employ human creativity to dominate money towards social ends, so as not to contravene "nature".

In the case of ecological finance, arguments based on false conceptions of money lead to an amusing logical contradiction: saving nature contravenes nature. However, if it is accepted that money is neither natural nor comes from God, logic can maintain its integrity: saving nature does not defy nature. The social creation of money can be used for purposes that societies see fit. For example, the "artificial grass" of the cans may serve to create a market and all that it entails – employment, production, and profits – from a price that would not exist without the support of the state.

Ingham speaks of several failed attempts to capture the power of money for the general interest, and states that "it is thought that 'community money' or 'social credit' can unlock the 'real' human and social capital of the people that is rendered impotent by the lack of money-income from the formal capitalist economy and its banking system" (2004: 183). However, in the history of failed projects of monetary innovation – such as the one proposed here – Ingham omits the monetary project closest to the present green money proposal, and the monetary project that has most served the general interest of humanity: the Bretton Woods monetary system.

3.   THE KEYNESIAN REVOLUTION AND THE CONTROL OF MONEY, FROM A POLANYIAN LENS

Guttmann states that "what we need is a new social contract" (2018: 52). The most recent social pact in the realm of global finance – the Keynesian revolution – is instructive. For the general public, this revolution is mostly unknown. It was a "mandarin revolution", brought about at the highest levels of the social pyramid, but rightly described as a revolution as there was a change in the groups at the helm of global money and international finance: "the sound-money men lost power" (Galbraith, 1975: 201).

The Keynesian revolution was partial both in theory and in practice. The change at the helm occurred as an armistice between gentlemen: the great bankers stayed close to the steering wheel and ensured that, although they no longer steered the ship, the secret of how the ship operated was never made too publicly evident. Thus, instead of disappearing, high finance was only subordinated and its largest markets (government bonds and foreign exchange, by stock and flow, respectively) were occupied for a few brief decades by the national state under the aegis of the Bretton Woods institutions. In the realm of theory, as Davidson (2008) narrates, the Keynesian revolution was bastardized as soon as it reached American shores.

As a partial one, the Keynesian revolution was susceptible to counter-revolution, in this case the monetarist (Kaldor, 1982) or neoliberal one, in both the academic and public policy fields. Keynesianism was purged from American universities (Lee, 2009; Davidson, 2008) and private banks were able to wrest control of the major markets from the nation states and transform the Bretton Woods institutions – the World Bank and the International Monetary Fund (Volcker, 1978) – into servants of the interests of high finance.

During the monetary counter-revolution, the mystery of money remained relatively intact. It was only in the last two decades that global financial events opened Pandora's box of money like no theory ever could. Fortunately, in recent years, great advances have also been made in the theory of money by better understanding the history and anthropology of money. Ingham's (and others') advances are not minor: "I would argue that a satisfactory answer to the question of what money was actually anchored in – if not the 'real' economy, or precious metal – required a decisive break with (neo) classical economics. Keynes and other establishment economists were ultimately unable to make it" (2004: 50).[1] Acknowledging that Keynes was unable to decipher the mystery of money does not imply any criticism on Ingham's part. Keynes himself, throughout *The General Theory*, describes his attempts to "escape" from the mental limits of neoclassical economics, and never declares victory.

Galbraith states that "attitudes toward money proceed in long cyclical swings. When money is bad, people want it to be better. When it is good, they think of other things" (Galbraith, 1975: 3). When money turned "bad" in the 1930s, many critical eyes turned to money. Keynes and Polanyi were no exceptions, and it is no coincidence that Keynes, as an economist, sought the nature of money in anthropology, and that Polanyi, as an anthropologist, provided a clear answer to economics. Finding the nature of money in anthropology is eminently logical, as only by observing and analysing a great diversity of monetary practices can the researcher arrive at its most distilled form: the essence or nature of money. Today, the task of verifying the nature of money as a "socially contrived arrangement" has been much further advanced in academia by various authors such as Henry (2003, 2017), Hudson (2018), and Graeber (2014).

The classical–neoclassical–neoliberal axiom of the scarcity of money was the ultimate limit of "economistic" thought that Keynes could not surpass at the theoretical level. Polanyi's theory of the three false commodities is useful for clearing this hurdle, and opens considerations of both theory and public policy. Polanyi claims that the idea that humans, money, and nature should be considered as commodities – and that the whole of society must be explained from the perspective of an idealized free market that gives value to these commodities – constitutes the birth defect of classical economics and the seeds of human destruction: "the fiction of their being so produced became the organizing principle of society" (Polanyi, 1944: 78).

When the market is able to control humans, nature, and money as if they were any type of real commodity – something made by people to be sold to people – the three false commodities become ruined or degraded. For example, if societies allow whaling as a market activity, all incentives go towards hunting whales until there are no more. When society decided that it did not want whales to become extinct, it turned to the government to enact laws to remove them from the market and protect them. Likewise, if a country decides that a part of its territory has more value in its natural state than in its commercial exploitation, it procures its protection from the government in the form of a national park. The sale of people for commercial purposes (slavery or child labour, for example) was prohibited by society through legislation. In order not to destroy the three false commodities, they have to be removed from the control of the market and returned to their social control.

Under the theory of the three false commodities, money is the least intuitive. Polanyi argues that money is a social convention (1944, 1950). Like language, all peoples develop their own money, and both in the absence of any authority. The creation of new money or a new word is a curious moment. The innovation belongs to an individual, but what gives it life is its social acceptance. Words or money invented but not accepted and circulated by society never come to life, like an unfertilized egg. Language and money are by nature creations of society, not of the individual or the market. In reality, they can be controlled by small groups in positions of power, but when the market disembeds them from the wider society in their creation, use, and circulation, they become ruined or degraded.

In Keynes's time, when money was still relatively embedded in society, the evident manifestations of the non-scarcity of money were relatively few, and only the sharpest minds could detect it. In recent decades, money has been thoroughly disembedded from society by the capitalist market, showing with resounding clarity that monetary creation has no limits.

The market crash in 2007–2008 was the result of a shadow banking system capable of generating new credit *ex nihilo* and *ad infinitum*, but socially conceived on a pact of fraud. Public supervision and regulation of money and credit in the US was stripped away (Black, 2010), and the financial market effectively disembedded money from society. After putting together an elaborate system in which bankers could create new financial products to sell to each other, they themselves defrauded each other and all trust within high finance was shattered: money, left to the control of the market, ruined itself. Under the Polanyian approach, the idea of "saving the banks from the bankers" makes perfect sense.

Much as private finance tested the limits of private debt creation in order to eschew all public regulation and supervision, quantitative easing (QE) programmes have tested the limits of public debt creation in order to partially fill the expanding black hole of debt deflation, and in the process have verified without theoretical escape the lack of technical limits on state debt.

We return to the concept of the artificial price of cans on the streets of New York. Conventional academic wisdom holds that money is scarce, and that the "natural" way to earn money is by working. Any state assistance is "artificial", and by relying solely on artificial prices and payments, the market cannot function as it should, inhibiting the production of a surplus. If the state of any country were directly in charge of material or financial production, the country would run out of money or suffer runaway inflation. Yet the many QE programmes around the world are the most baroquely artificial of any state programme. And while they have arguably contributed less to humanity than the much humbler can-recycling projects, they did not bankrupt countries or produce hyperinflation or inflation as they would if money were scarce. However, as reality has had such a minimal impact on conventional thinking, both in academia and public policy circles, Keynes's critiques of sound finance almost a century ago are just as relevant, if not more so, today.

Keynes states in *The General Theory* that "the ideas of economists and political philosophers, both when they are right and when they are wrong, are more powerful than is commonly understood. Indeed the world is ruled by little else" (Keynes, 1936: 383). As Keynes argued, slavery to defunct ideas was a constant hamstring to human betterment:

> we are so sensible, have schooled ourselves to so close a semblance of prudent financiers, taking careful thought before we add to the "financial" burdens of posterity by building them houses to live in, that we have no such easy escape from the sufferings of unemployment. (Keynes, 1936: 68)

In his article on recycled cans in New York, Newman does not mention Keynes, but does conjure his spirit: "to understand the business of redemption on the street, it helps to think of empty cans and bottles as very large coins that prowl the sidewalks and sewers of the city. They are there to take, but their size (their volume, more than their weight) and their relatively low value make them difficult to handle" (Newman, 2019: n.p.). For his part, while not speaking to recycling, Keynes does conjure its (financial) spirit:

> If the Treasury were to fill old bottles with banknotes, bury them at suitable depths in disused coalmines which are then filled up to the surface with town rubbish, and leave it to private enterprise on well-tried principles of *laissez-faire to* dig the notes up again (the right to do so being obtained, of course, by tendering for leases of the note-bearing territory), there need be no more unemployment and, with the help of the repercussions, the real income of the community, and its capital wealth also, would probably become a good deal greater than it actually is. It would, indeed, be more sensible to build houses and the like; but if there are political and practical difficulties in the way of this, the above would be better than nothing. (Keynes, 1936: 68)

For Newman, garbage has value because the state sets its "artificial" price; furthermore, we can see the can as a coin, since it is what it represents, and it is the state that confers this value and sets the price. In Keynes's proposal, the bottle, covered by garbage, only has value because it contains another representation of value, which is also established by the state: the banknote.

Keynes further ridicules the great gap between the nature of money as a social agreement and the way it is manifested in the reality of the moment, with another form of monetary creation: "the form of digging holes in the ground known as gold-mining, which not only adds nothing whatever to the real wealth of the world but involves the disutility of labour, is the most acceptable of all solutions" (1936: 67). If gold has the same value as a bank-note buried in a bottle in the trash, and if society's interests were to eradicate poverty and have jobs for everyone, the way of digging holes would be different, both now and in Keynes's time: "Just as wars have been the only form of large-scale loan expenditure which statesmen have thought justifiable, so gold-mining is the only pretext for digging holes in the ground which has recommended itself to bankers as sound finance" (1936: 68).

On the mental plane, sound finance meant that "The whole conduct of life was made into a sort of parody of an accountant's nightmare" (Keynes, 1933). When applied to economic systems, Polanyi stated what should be obvious: far from being the best form of social organization to assign prices, the private market is the worst, particularly in the case of the most important prices (Polanyi, 1945). By letting the private market sell what society makes (money), one can only expect the destruction of financial markets, and when the private market sells what nature makes, it can only invite its destruction. As seen time and again in financial crises, price signals lead entire markets off the cliff. Today, price signals lead to ecological destruction.

4.   A PROPOSAL FOR A GREEN MONETARY SPACE OF PRODUCTION

4.1   From the Carbon Market to a Green Financial System

In theory, the carbon market which was created under the Kyoto Protocol was established in order to counteract the market incentives for pollution and specifically the emission of greenhouse gasses. In practice, as Guttmann argues at great length and convincingly, the carbon market has not alleviated the problem, and was not designed to do so. Having now existed for decades, the reasons why this market has done more to appear to be combatting the problem than actually doing so are various. Guttmann mentions the most important: taxes on emissions would be much more effective than vouchers (Guttmann, 2018: 209), and the vouchers themselves were issued at such a high rate and low cost that there has been very little financial impact on the world's largest polluters (Guttmann, 2018: 153), with the end result that the monetary cost of pollution has not increased, and the incentives for destroying nature remain intact. If the explicit objectives of reducing carbon emissions are to be met, enforced taxation for pollution would be necessary.

However, if a truly green market were to be established, it would need a financial system that establishes negative and positive monetary incentives for both polluting and anti-polluting activities; it would not only punish pollution. Guttmann states that "what would really push climate finance forward would be to connect it with money creation" (2018: 209). In this chapter's proposal, several fundamental aspects of green money are considered, including the lifecycle of the new money, its characteristics, the reaches of its circuits, the motivation of the participants in the monetary space, and where the money would come from. Guttmann calls for a "change of mentality and system", and this proposal is one that seeks precisely that.

The change of mentality required for this proposal for green money is only in the monetary sphere, and is assisted by Alain Parguez's ideas, and the concept of the lifecycle of money. In the current system, money is born in the loan of the private bank or in fiscal expenditure, and dies when the loan or taxes are paid. Our green proposal would add a step in money's lifecycle: its conception, and it is here that the change in mentality is most needed. For centuries, alchemy has existed as an attempt to turn lead into gold, but few if any ever thought about human excrement, which does contain gold (Wald, 2017). But that's the fun of a social construct. After all, both gold and banknotes are only physical units of account, representatives of the value of a "socially contrived arrangement". In this same spirit, a social arrangement could be reached so that waste is equal to a certain amount of green money. Thus, the bill in the bottle would not be the object that would be equivalent to money, as in Keynes's example, but the bottle itself. The proposal of green money would be for its physical manifestation to be human excrement or a certain type of garbage; it would simply be valuing things differently:

> Above all, money is also a social institution through which we express and measure value, thus subjecting goods and services we produce as "commodities" for sale to a process of valuation (giving it a price) and validation (selling it for profit). The social validation is one of the crucial aspects of our economic system. (Guttmann, 2018: 210)

To reiterate, the conception of green money is the hard part: if waste could be conceived of as something of value, and given a sufficiently high price, then a system could be constructed to give it monetary validation, as suggested above. This could take many forms, and this chapter offers only one. But once the mental hurdles of monetary value are overcome, many more can be imagined.

In terms of institutions, an ideal "change of mentality and system" would not imply building a new system on top of an old one, but rather introducing a new system that could open up a new monetary space that could be complementary to already existing ones. The new institutions in our proposal would be both physical and financial. On the physical side, new collection and processing centres and trucks would be needed, along with a new network of green banks. Buildings would also be needed to house the new financial institutions: the GCB and the GT. No more is needed, and even physical banks could be dispensed with. As for green money, it wouldn't even exist physically; it would merely be a unit of account to exist in legislation and ledgers. On the financial side, the operational logic would follow that of national treasuries and central banks in the recent past. By allowing money to assume a new form (green), and having institutions to control its emission, transformation, and destruction, our proposed system would on the surface operate much like an idealized capitalist market. There would be production and employment, organized markets and banks, and employees would work for money. However, by solely changing a few key prices, the pursuit of money and production would fall in line with ecological objectives.

As for the physical market space, what one sees today would not be so different from what it would look like under our proposal. In most of the world, those who recycle materials are people of scant resources. Collecting cans in New York ranks among the best jobs in this existing market. The worst recycling jobs exist in the global periphery. For example, there are cargo ship junkyards in Bangladesh and large computer junkyards in Africa, where working materials are lethal. The same can be said of the 800,000 people in India – and many others in Africa and various other places – who collect human excrement (Black and Fawcett, 2008: 169–170). In Latin America, the garbage scavenger that lives near the landfill is a culturally well-known figure. For places with drainage and sanitation problems without recycling programmes, the goal would be to establish them to address those problems. For places with existing markets for collecting and processing waste, the idea would be to make them more hygienic and beneficial for nature and society. The lesser visibility of a human waste recycling market would represent its greater success.

The most suitable analogy for our proposal would be the artificial reef. In recent decades, people have purposely sunk school buses, ships, and other large human-made structures to which corals attach themselves and later a whole ecosystem with fish and other animals appears. Nothing more is needed than an artificial basic structure to anchor the system and everything else is generated naturally. But not every artificial reef has been successful. For example, in several places piles of used tyres were thrown into the sea, and the brilliant idea yielded unsurprising results: the coral did not adhere, and the fish were poisoned with heavy metals.

As with the successful artificial reef, the structure of the green market should be almost invisible, and the visible part would be the private market. By establishing a system that can sustain a high enough price for human and other waste – plastic in particular – it will create the monetary incentives for the emergence of a new industry and sources of work to capture and process human and other waste. Thus, the new recycling market will look like it does in the globe's urban peripheries today: poor people collecting plastic, trucks and workers collecting waste, and collection and processing centres transforming the waste. The big difference would be almost invisible: people would be paid (or paid more) for their waste.

Paying to collect human waste is nothing new, even while many projects for its transformation are. Our green proposal would be to create a financial system to support those who support ecological efforts with more resources. As Wald argues, there are many active human excrement recycling projects, and neither technology nor interest is lacking. Faced with its great promise, the big problem is "making a profit due to low market prices" (Wald, 2017).

In the current conditions of the large expanses of urban poverty where around one in seven humans live, human waste is a curse for the health, the economy, and the general well-being of the inhabitants, and it is a testament to the importance given to the poor in the current system that this curse has not been turned into a benefit or at least minimized. But both the current problem and its potential solution have important impacts far away from those cities.

Animal excrement serve as an excellent fertilizer, yet most of the world's agriculture today does not use natural fertilizers but rather petroleum-based ones. By using human waste and not oil, there would be several advantages both economically (oil costs) and ecologically: human excrement does not degrade the earth; rather, it becomes part of it. Less natural ingredients that do not integrate as well into the soil are washed off by rain, creating maritime "dead zones" around the great freshwater runoffs of the planet, where the water does not contain enough oxygen to sustain most marine life. The only reason for artificial fertilizer use is that it is currently cheaper and more available than the little-developed ecological alternative.

Once an appropriate price is established for the human waste recycling business, there would be several ways to collect it: from canals of untreated sewage; from collective septic systems; or from green toilets for individual dwellings. The encapsulation and processing of sewage would be the best option, but the scale of the investment would imply state action, the absence of which is being addressed in this proposal. Under the option of green toilets for individual dwellings, the recycling company could install green toilets and come every so often to collect the waste that has already been processed and stored inside them. In this case, the household would be paid in exchange for allowing the inconvenience of the toilet installation, and then for the collection. Ecologically, this would seem like the best option, capturing the worst element of blackwater canals at its point of creation. In economic terms, its advantage would be that it could start immediately, on a small scale, with little initial expenditure and production, and expand at the pace of social acceptance.

Just as green toilets capture waste at its source, this can also be done with a large percentage of marine litter. Without sanitation systems, the world's slums emit a large amount of garbage that could be captured before reaching the world's oceans, and under the same waste payment proposal. The collection of green toilets and (pre-)marine litter could even happen in the same place and time, and with a single transaction. When the waste truck passes, the workers collect waste and hand over money, or credit a digital account.

As seen from the participants in this monetary space, the flow of money would go from the processing centre to truckers, and then to individuals. Such centres would be the physical structure that supports the market. As with the successful artificial reef that invites all animals, the centre would pay all companies for the delivery of waste. The money in the area would increase both by hiring local workers and by paying for the residents' waste. Under the motive of money, but with a transformed system, the area could be enriched by alleviating the problem of waste drainage and garbage. Thus, the success of the programme would be an invisible (for most) transformation of the recycling market, and a very visible transformation in the living conditions of the slums.

5. THE MONETARY CHARACTERISTICS AND FEATURES OF THE GREEN SYSTEM

As argued, while the physical aspect of the green financial system would require little imagination to conceive of, the non-physical side of money would require a change in conventional thinking. However, this would only be at the top of the system, where the system architects must occupy themselves with the creation and distribution of money. For users of the system, who earn money but do not create money, green money would function just like any other money; indeed, it would be any other money.

The institutions of the new green financial circuit would mirror current ones. The treasury would receive taxes, ideally paid by the companies that pollute, and the central bank would issue currency as it does today. There would also be green banks, which, like today's commercial banks, would serve as links between local production and global finance.

The overarching goal of the green financial system would be to promote productive activities that care for the environment, and under a correctly designed system the money motive could be harnessed and directed towards the same goal. Just as the current system is designed for some – but not all – productive activity to pay, not all economic activity would earn green money.

The green banking system would confer value upon green money by only paying for green activities.

Under the green financial system, therefore, both the scarcity of money and the money motive would be used to drive economic activity; money would be earned (*ex ante*) just like today. The transformation of the system would not and should not abolish these characteristics so correctly criticized in the current system. Without scarcity it is difficult to maintain monetary value, and without a money motivation it would be difficult to set and maintain prices, and to pursue green goals. But once the final goal of economic activity changes from the generation of financial rent to the care of the planet and our societies, and once this change is reflected in prices that encourage that which is ecologically friendly, the motivation of money can converge with ecological and social motivation, and monetary scarcity no longer must be maintained as a veil for the social choice of giving money to some groups but not all. Just as not every activity (or actor) deserves to earn money today, not all productive activity would earn money under the green system; however, the call to participate would be a wide one, and one would simply have to agree to sell one's own waste in order to be incorporated into the green monetary space.

From the point of view of the architects of the system, the three main goals would be to attract as many participants as possible, to maintain the relevant prices, and to have as much funding as possible. This question of funding the system is where greater monetary creativity and a greater distancing from the precepts of sound finance are most relevant, and where recent developments in finance lead the debate.

As the green financial system described here is meant to operate alongside the current financial system, it can either fund itself or can be completely funded from the "outside" world, or a mix of the two.[2] There are at least four basic ways of financing the green financial market, which do not have to be mutually exclusive. The mechanism most aligned with the spirit of complementing and improving upon the current system would be the transformation of tax proceeds from a functioning carbon market into green currency. The second would be a toxic waste swap: to have the world's largest private and central banks transfer their worst on- and off-balance-sheet assets – at their current valuation – to the GT, which could use it as the founding capital upon which to issue the currency. The third would be to have the GT offer zero-rate bonds, and have Japanese and European financial regulators allow their largest banks and insurers to buy green bonds instead of realizing losses on the negative rates currently mandated in those countries. The fourth would be to simply finance it all from within and execute a green QE.

From the perspective of achieving ecological goals, the procurement of funding would likely be more determinant of success than the judiciousness of the mix of the above mechanisms. But both aspects fall squarely in the realm of political decisions, and in what follows, several scenarios are drawn out in general terms.

6.   GREEN MONEY: LIFECYCLE AND CIRCUIT

Under a more ideal scenario in which the green financial system is connected to the global carbon market, there would be a distinct monetary circuit, both in its spatial dimensions and in its lifecycle. Once green money is conceived, it would enter the world like an egg, with many scattered around the world in the form of garbage or human excrement, as in the example of Keynes's bottles. When the workers take the waste to the collection centres, it would be akin to taking the egg to the incubator. There, two physical transformations would occur: one when waste is transformed into useful products, and another when green money hatches from its egg in the form of payment in local currency and, like a bird, takes flight and leaves the nest.

Under the green financial system, the birds would return to their birthplace upon death. If basically all human activity degrades the earth under our current system, every dollar spent is almost by definition polluting, and therefore every new emission of green money by the GCB would return to the GT in the form of polluting companies paying their green taxes. If the green monetary system is connected to the carbon market, the circuit would be wide – the whole planet – but it would be relatively closed, and the lifecycle relatively simple. Green money is born in the form of waste, is first transformed into local currency once it is brought to the green market, and eventually is converted into a strong currency, whose monetary circuit includes the world's most polluting companies and from which the pollution taxes will be drawn.

The GCB would therefore issue its own currency and be funded in foreign currency. This wouldn't be so different from the financial system currently operating in places with large-scale waste problems in urban peripheries. For example, the Mexican peso, when born in the Bank of Mexico, can circulate or enter the financial system or it can be converted into a dollar. Unlike the Mexican peso, the dollar is accepted almost everywhere on the planet. Green money would be like the dollar in this system, an additional currency or unit of account with global reach and acceptance. However, imbued with another spirit, the green currency would aim to be as complementary as the dollar has been extractive for any country outside of the US.

The idea of having two currencies in circulation, one that is not seen but is dominant and another that is seen but subservient, has been the reality for almost every Latin American country (and other regions) for decades. Alain Parguez (2010) identifies it as "the predatory double monetary circuit". For example, in Mexico a new peso is born when the government spends on, for example, social assistance programmes. However, the fresh bill does not originate in the debit card credited by the government or in the ATM where the bill is received or in the central bank that has the right to print it. The conception of pesos occurs mainly outside the country, in talks between the largest banks in the world and in dollar terms. How much to invest in Mexico is decided based upon the criteria of expected profitability. Dollars are sent as an investment to Mexico, and depending on the volume of these, the government can print a commensurate number of pesos. Seen as a bird, the peso created for programmes of social assistance spends its youth in Mexico, in the hands of workers and then businesses. But as it matures, (almost) every peso returns to its native territory to die as a dollar. When the peso is spent in commerce, sooner rather than later it goes to the purchase of a foreign good or services, and in this way it returns to the form of the dollar. Even when local businesses accumulate pesos, when they enter the financial system in the form of investments in capital markets, they end up in the dominant financial circuit.

Just as the great personal fortunes of the region are converted into dollars and escape north through private banking, narco money also enters the same circuit, and also flies north. In more licit markets, the (successful) investment in stocks or bonds has a more direct lifecycle: it enters in the form of dollars, grows as pesos, and when it is converted into profit, it returns again to the form of the dollar. For decades this type of speculative capital has been called *capital golondrina* in the Spanish-speaking world. The structure of this system determines it to be predatory, as more capital leaves the region than enters. Beginning with the ultimate alchemy of turning shit into gold, the institutional framework of the green monetary system would not pull money up the pyramid but rather push it down; instead of transferring resources from the poor to the rich and from poor regions to the rich regions, the flow would be inverted, from the top to the bottom and from the centre to the periphery.

Under ideal conditions, the green financial circuit would not only be funded exogenously by the dominant monetary circuit, but could also create money endogenously through local green banks.

7.   THE LOCAL GREEN BANK

By having green money in global circulation, like the dollar in the current system, it would be the local green banks that would connect local ecological efforts – both at the household and business level – with the global monetary circuit. The central function of the local green bank would be to report to the GCB how much money it needs per day, week, and so on to pay the amounts and prices necessary to maintain a private market for waste. The GCB would guarantee the necessary money for the local green banks, and these to the processing centres. This is the same hierarchy and set of operations that exists in the current system.

Under this scheme, green businesses, such as our featured plastic and human waste processing centres, would operate under the motive of money, like any commercial bank client today. These centres would have commercial income, as they could sell building blocks or other recycled plastic products, and in the case of human waste, fertilizer or other products (Wald, 2017). Just as in the current system, private commerce thrives on credit. The green commercial bank can lend to the recycling centre for the purchase of an initial installation of green toilets, or for the construction of the very centre.

The green commercial bank would also be the financial connecting point with households, just as commercial banking is today, and just as today's commercial banks reward those who contribute the most to the common interest of financial rent, under the green system those who contribute the most to the common ecological cause would be most rewarded. As stated, once the egg reaches the processing centre, the bird is born and leaves the nest. However, the lifecycle would not have to be so short. Instead of forcing the young bird to abandon the nest right away, the nest could be accommodated to convince it to stay a while longer. As in any commercial bank, the worker could be encouraged not to withdraw all income immediately but to continue business with the bank in the form of savings, loans, or mortgages. Thus, the green worker could receive payment in the local currency, and could leave a part in the bank in a green savings account or a green mortgage. The payments of the green market would therefore be in the local currency, but the credit system would be in the realm of another currency. Again, this is nothing new for Latin America and other peripheral countries.

The green bank can also offer favourable terms between currencies. For example, a unit of green money can be equivalent to one Mexican peso that is withdrawn at the moment, but if it enters the green credit system, it could be worth twice as much. Similar incentives could be attached to green credits or mortgages. If mechanisms are put in place for green money to be converted into green credit, there are ways to expand and direct green credit towards green activities. For example, for initial expenses for toilets, trucks, and processing centres, long-term, zero-rate credits can be granted; and for green workers, the construction of new homes from recycled material sold by the recycling centre can be incentivized. Employing the money motive, but without the ultimate goal of financial rent, opens up many possibilities, albeit with important limitations.

The limits of the credit generosity of the green system – or how much monetary creation would come from outside the system or from within it – would ultimately depend on the ability to control green prices, which in turn would depend on the ability to fund the GT. Like any central bank, the GCB would have to fix the value of green money with respect to other currencies and try to maintain a certain stability. It is worth mentioning that these tasks could be carried out under conditions much more favourable than those faced today by central banks in peripheral countries. As a supranational bank with a global currency, the "impossible trilemma" would not exist, and the GCB could operate under conditions more akin to those of the Federal Reserve than those of the Mexican Central Bank. It would therefore be able to set the value of its currency in accordance with its overall strategy and not as a response to external pressure.

Under the ideal situation of a closed global circuit in which polluting companies must pay the fines or taxes in green currency, the treasury would not have a difficult job. By ensuring this flow of payment, each dollar of green taxes could be sent to pay for waste at a price that would allow the private green market to prosper. Upon the establishment of such a system, the GT could be capitalized with the green money taxes and a certain number of dollars could be raised, or the GT could simply act like any other national treasury and sell bonds in advance of its revenue. As mentioned, in a world of negative rates, the profit motive could attract many buyers even at a zero rate.

8. WHEN SITUATIONS BECOME LESS IDEAL

Until this point, the green financial system proposal has followed conventional accounting between commercial banks, the treasury, and the central bank. Operating with a central bank and a treasury, there is a way to establish a self-sustaining ebb and flow of money, using a system similar to the current monetary system. On the treasury side, taxes on polluters can be raised or lowered, while on the GCB side, green money flows can be adjusted both in volume and velocity. The value of waste relative to green money can also be changed, as well as the exchange rates between green and other currencies. All such operations had been undertaken by global central banks for decades before the 2007–2008 crisis.

The policies undertaken by the same institutions in the last decade – prominently QE – have been guided by conventional thinking (Rochon and Vallet, 2019), but have led to very unconventional results. Envisioning the same policies but guided by less conventional thinking opens up a wide gamut of possibilities of financial (social) engineering that can be used for the green financial system if possibilities diminish for the ideal scenario of plentiful carbon revenues.

Within the outline of a plan that includes green money, a GT, a GCB, and a network of collection centres/banks, operations can be scaled up and down and variations of all types can be made. As has become ever more evident in recent years, under the right social conditions money can be created from nothing and without technical limit. Similarly, if the correct social conditions were to exist, there would also be no limits on the capitalization of a green financial system. But although the system can grow to the size that society wants, it can also operate in a reduced way if political conditions do not exist at the global, national, or regional level. In the remainder of this short section, pieces will be removed from the presented ideal situation to argue that, although with limited capacity, a green system could work even in its simplest of forms: the social creation of green money and a bank to manage its creation and distribution.

The biggest piece to remove would be the carbon market, and with it the constant revenue stream from carbon taxes. Without its reflux mechanism, green money could still be issued, but it would no longer return; that is to say, the circuit would not be closed but rather open and global: there would be monetary issuance, but no income. Yet losing the income stream and the integrity of the circuit would not necessarily have to doom the proposal. As mentioned, there are trillions of dollars in bonds yielding negative interest rates in Europe and Japan, and other trillions in toxic assets on (and off) the books of the world's largest banks and central banks. A simple change in legislation to make these eligible to be held by the GT could offer a sufficient capital base from which to be drawn down, with no expectation of recovery, for decades.

If proposals for financial recycling do not gain acceptance, self-financing is also an option. With the existence of a GT and a GCB, the GT can simply sell green bonds to the GCB, for it to "print" the corresponding amount of green money: "one hand washing the other," as Adam Smith (1776) said centuries ago. It would be nothing more than another version of current QE, but instead of the mission of channelling money towards financial rent, it would be towards the ecological market.

Without the reflux mechanism in the monetary circuit in the form of the carbon market, what is left is a perpetual money creation machine that never receives an input – something impossible in the physical world but not in the social world: the dollar again offers the example. In recent times, the relationship between the Fed and the Treasury is much more perverse than in Smith's time. With the Fed converted into a financial black hole and the US Treasury an *ex nihilo/ad infinitum* credit machine, today one hand strengthens the dynamics of debt deflation, while the other partially recompenses them.

Today, digging and filling a bottomless black hole is a profitable task. But precisely because the design of the task is to produce financial rent, the current system also lacks a reflux mechanism. The enormous financial rents produced by QE are born in the form of American treasury paper, and are grown and nurtured in capital markets around the world, but instead of returning home, they largely escape to tax havens or other private stashes. If the lifecycle of the dollar were closed, speculative profits would die where they are born: in the treasury by paying taxes on capital gains. However, by charging minimal taxes and allowing off-shore accounts for financial rentiers, the circuit is left open and financial rentiers' money escapes death, just like they escape taxes.

Under a system with an infinite capacity to create money with little attempt to have it return, the national debt grows vertiginously, but with no apparent technical limit. The lack of a closed circuit and a reflux mechanism does not make the dollar or Latin American currencies unviable, and it should not sink green money either. To the contrary, the addition of a new financial system and its corresponding assets could offer various mechanisms to combat global financial deflation.

While international green money can exist without third-party funding and without a reflux mechanism, it still depends on the acceptance of individual countries. So the next big piece to take away is the international acceptance of green money. An international financial system can exist without the inclusion of all countries; it would simply be reduced to a bloc of those who accept it and those who do not. If there is no international initiative, any sole country could create its reduced domestic system, made up of a GCB, GT, green money, and green commercial banking.

If there is no international interest, and no national interest in a green financial system, a state or even a city could consolidate banking and treasury functions under the same roof as a state or municipal public bank and issue green money, putting a green financial system in place, albeit on a smaller scale and with less potential. This is as far down as a proposal can be scaled, though, as a green currency would need at least both a currency and an issuing bank.

9.   CONCLUSIONS

This chapter has outlined a proposal attending to the financial aspect of the ecological crisis, and has no doubt omitted many viable proposals, both financial and ecological. The great social energy awakened by ecological concern has been generating a wide range of alternative proposals of great interest – from nuclear energy to new forms of social organizations. The few green projects mentioned here are not to exclude others. Rather, the financial proposal is made for a transformation of the financial system that allows the most promising green projects to flourish based on a framework that can change prices towards desired goals.

NOTES

1.   Ingham only gives passing mentions to Polanyi, who did manage to make this "decisive break" through his arguments against any notion of a natural market or economic determinism (Polanyi Levitt, 2013).

2.   The line between endogenous and exogenous is the line between the market and the state, and a difficult one to trace. Here another line is drawn between the green market and the other markets.

REFERENCES

Black, M., and Fawcett, B. (2008) *The Last Taboo: Opening the Door on the Global Sanitation Crisis*. London: Earthscan/Routledge.
Black, W. K. (2010) Statement by William K. Black, Associate Professor of Economics and Law, University of Missouri–Kansas City, before the Committee on Financial Services United States House of Representatives regarding "Public Policy Issues Raised by the Report of the Lehman Bankruptcy Examiner", 20 April (Washington, DC: US Government Printing Office) [http://www.gpo.gov/fdsys/pkg/CHRG-111hhrg57742/html/CHRG-111hhrg57742.htm].
Davidson, P. (2008) "Post WW II Politics and Keynes's Aborted Revolutionary Economic Theory". *Economia e Sociedade*. Vol. 17. Campinas. December.
Galbraith, J. K. (1975) *Money: From Whence It Came, Where It Went*. Boston, MA: Houghton Mifflin.
Graeber, D. (2014) *Debt: The First 5000 Years*. New York: Melville House.
Guttmann, R. (2018) *Eco-Capitalism: Carbon Money, Climate Finance, and Sustainable Development*. London: Palgrave Macmillan.
Henry, J. (2003) "What Egypt Tells Us About the Origins of Money". In *Credit and State Theories of Money: The Contributions of A. Mitchell Innes*, ed. L. Randall Wray. Northampton, MA: Routledge.
Henry, J. (2017) "Brutus es un hombre honorable". *Ola Financiera*. Vol. 10, No. 28.
Hudson, M. (2018) ... *And Forgive Them Their Debts: Lending, Foreclosure and Redemption from Bronze Age Finance to the Jubilee Year*. Glashütte: ISLET – Verlag.
Ingham, G. (2004) *The Nature of Money*. Cambridge: Polity Press, Ltd.
Kaldor, N. (1982) *The Scourge of Monetarism*. New York: Oxford University Press.
Keynes, J. M. (2013 [1933]) "La Auto-Suficiencia Nacional". *Ola Financiera*. Vol. 13. No. 25.
Keynes, J. M. (1936) *The General Theory of Employment, Interest, and Money*. London: Macmillan.
Lee, F. (2009) *A History of Heterodox Economics: Challenging the Mainstream in the Twentieth Century*. London: Routledge.
Newman, A. (2019) "Where Rent Is $13,500, She Lives Off What's Left at the Curb". *New York Times*. 26 December. https://www.nytimes.com/2019/12/26/nyregion/collecting-cans-collectors-nyc.html.
Parguez, A. (2010) "El doble circuito monetario depredador: los costos de la plena integración al sistema financiero y productivo multinacional". *Ola Financiera*. No. 6.
Polanyi, K. (1944) *The Great Transformation*. Boston: Beacon Press.
Polanyi, K. (1945) "Universal Capitalism or Regional Planning". *The London Quarterly of World Affairs*. Enero.
Polanyi, K. (2014 [1950]) "The Contribution of Institutional Analysis to the Social Sciences". In *For a New West: Essays, 1919–1958*, ed. G. Resta and M. Catanzariti. London: Polity Press.
Polanyi Levitt, K. (2013) *From the Great Transformation to the Great Financialization*. London: Zed Books.

Rochon, L. P., and Vallet, G. (2019) "Economía del Ave María: El modelo teórico detrás de las políticas monetarias no convencionales". *Ola Financiera.* Vol. 12. No. 34: 1–24.

Smith, A. (1994 [1776]) *An Inquiry into the Nature and Causes of the Wealth of Nations.* New York: The Modern Library.

Volcker, P. (1978) "The Political Economy of the Dollar". The Fred Hirsch Lecture. Coventry, UK. *Federal Reserve Bank of New York Quarterly Review.* Vol. 3. No. 4 (Winter 1978–1979): 1–12.

Wald, C. (2017) "The New Economy of Excrement: Entrepreneurs Are Finding Profits Turning Human Waste into Fertilizer, Fuel and Even Food". *Nature.* 13 September.

Wallace, D. F. (2005) "What Is Water?" Kenyon College Commencement Speech.

8. Financial regulation, uncertainty and the transition to a net-zero-carbon economy

Josh Ryan-Collins

1. INTRODUCTION

Central banks and finanical supervisers' now accept that climate change is material to their mandates given the financial stability risks it may generate (Campiglio et al., 2018; Giuzio et al., 2019; NGFS, 2020c; Brunetti et al., 2021; BIS, 2021). These include physical climate risks and transition risks driven by changes to policy, technology and consumer behaviour that may result in a disorderly transition (Carney, 2015). To meet a 1.5-degree temperature threshold, carbon emissions need to decline by about 45% from 2010 levels by 2030 to reach net zero around 2050 (IPCC, 2018), requiring major structural shifts in the economy in a short timeframe. Huge new investments are required into green energy, transport and infrastructure whilst unsustainable sources of financing need to be rapidly phased out, in particular fossil-fuel-intensive activities.

The dominant policy framework that has emerged for dealing with climate-related financial risks (CRFRs) is to treat them essentially as forms of market failure. CRFRs are perceived to be under-priced in existing financial markets – or not priced at all – and as a result financial markets are viewed as too short-term in their outlook. Accordingly, the role of policy is to encourage financial institutions to measure and disclose their perceived CRFRs to enable price discovery and resulting shifts in the allocation of capital. The most notable initiative along these lines has been the Task Force on Climate-Related Financial Disclosures (TCFD, 2017). More recently, perhaps in recognition that voluntary disclosures have either not happened fast enough or are not leading to required shifts in investment, central banks have begun to shift towards mandatory disclosure frameworks, scenario analysis to examine the impacts of different climate policy trajectories on banks' balance sheets and, relatedly, climate stress testing (Bank of England, 2019; NGFS, 2020b; ECB, 2020b).

Underlying this approach is an assumption that CRFRs are measurable or at least can be meaningfully estimated, independently of the actions of market participants, including regulators. In contrast, this chapter argues that CRFRs are better thought of as endogenous and systemic, themselves generated by policy changes, technological innovation, changing consumer preferences and their complex interactions with each other, the real economy and a highly interconnected financial system. This means CRFRs are subject to radical uncertainty (Keynes, 1937; Kay and King, 2020), rendering standard probabilistic quantitative assessments of risk and resulting price discovery problematic. Instead of a market-failure framework, a 'market-shaping', precautionary policy approach to financial regulation is proposed which recognises financial regulators' endogenous role in the climate transition and strives to actively steer market actors in a clear *direction* – towards a managed transition. Two regulatory traditions – the precautionary principle from environmental policy and modern macroprudential policy – are discussed as the basis of this alternative regulatory framework.

The remainder of the chapter is structured as follows. In section 2, the nature of climate-related financial risks is set out and section 3 makes a case for why they are subject to radical uncertainty. In section 4, the precautionary policy framework is outlined and some policy interventions based on capital requirements and negative screening are proposed. Section 5 discusses how such a policy might create challenges for central banks' existing time horizons, mandates and notions of independence. Section 6 concludes.

2.   CLIMATE-RELATED FINANCIAL RISKS AND THE CURRENT POLICY RESPONSE

Climate change involves two main categories of financial risk. Physical risks stem from the increase in frequency and severity of extreme weather events and long-term environmental changes. Transition risks originate from the socioeconomic reaction to mitigate and adapt to climate change, for example the introduction of climate-change-related policies such as carbon taxes, new regulations or rules around production of certain goods, technological breakthroughs and deployment, the evolution of consumer preferences, and litigation.

Physical climate risk initially materialises at physical asset and company levels, either through companies' own operations or from others, via the market or the supply chain. These impact the assets, collateral and/or cash flows of the companies, which then affect their access to capital and financial values, which in turn can impact on investors in those firms. For example, sea-level rises and extreme weather could cause significant losses for commercial real-estate investment companies with damaged or possibly unusable properties along coastlines (Ambrosio, 2018). If the company is unable to meet its financial obligations because of these additional costs or lost rental income, it could then transmit losses to mortgage-backed securities investors or banks with real-estate loans on their balance sheets, posing systemic risk to the wider financial system.

Transition risk is also becoming material. Big energy companies are beginning to face the prospects of transition-related write-downs of hydrocarbon assets. For example, BP wrote down \$17.5 billion in assets in June 2020 after lowering its long-term fossil fuel price assumptions (Hurst, 2020), and Total SE wrote down \$7 billion on Canadian oil sands assets in July 2020 (Bousso, 2020).

Recognising the materiality of these CRFRs, central banks have invested considerable energy into researching and attempting to measure them. This includes the formation of a new international network – the Network for Greening the Financial System (NGFS) – made up of over 90 institutions and 13 observers, representing the vast majority of the world's systemically important financial institutions,[1] which has published a number of reports on the topic as well as guidance on how central banks and financial supervisors should conceptualise CRFRs (NGFS, 2019b, 2019a, 2020c, 2020a).

But there has been little in the way of concrete policy interventions to deal with CRFRs in high-income economies. This may seem surprising given the recognised urgency of the threats posed by climate change. However, it is in keeping with the wider approach to financial regulation that has dominated economic theory and practice since the 1980s. This essentially views competitive financial markets and the pricing system as the most efficient and welfare-optimising tool for coordinating economic activities and capital allocation. The view has its origins in Friedrich Hayek's (1945) work on the coordination of capitalist markets and the efficient markets hypothesis (Fama, 1970), which argues that (stock) market prices capture all publicly available information, making them highly efficient and superior to any single market actor or public planner. The role of policy and regulation should be limited under such conditions to instances of clear 'market failure' when price discovery is being impaired.

The 'impairment' that prevents the efficient price discovery of CRFRs, in this view, is a lack of disclosure of information about the risks market actors face. The disclosure narrative lies at the centre of policy efforts by financial regulators to meet the challenge of climate change financial risks. By encouraging corporations to disclose their actual or perceived exposures and plans to deal with these exposures, more effective price discovery can occur, 'market discipline' can be imposed and capital allocation can be optimised (Christophers, 2017; Ryan-Collins, 2019).

The market-failure framework has been through several iterations. The initial phase was to encourage firms to voluntarily measure and disclose their self-defined CRFRs with the setting up of the international TCFD (2017), coming out of the Financial Stability Board (FSB) and in partnership with private financial institutions. The TCFD recommendations have been widely embraced, with most large banks, asset managers and pension funds, credit rating agencies and accountancy firms having signed up to them. However, whilst many firms have published information about their exposures, fewer have disclosed their views on the forward-looking financial risks they face or considered the longer-term strategic resilience of their business models to the reality of the massive structural change needed to shift to a net-zero-carbon economy (e.g. ECB, 2020c). Moreover, the evidence suggests the voluntary approach to risk disclosure will be sufficient to generate a step change in investment and bank lending behaviour (Ameli et al., 2019; Christophers, 2019; Mooney et al., 2019).

Presumably recognising the limits of voluntary disclosure approaches, the second, current phase of the market-failure approach has involved central banks and supervisors delineating potential future scenarios for market actors and then 'stress testing' the impact of such scenarios on financial balance sheets (NGFS, 2019b). The NGFS has developed three main scenarios – an orderly transition, a disorderly transition (with more rapid and sudden shifts in policy) and 'hot-house world' with no policy shifts – upon which banks then assess their vulnerabilities (ibid.). In 2021, the European Central Bank (ECB) became the first central bank to implement an economy-wide stress test, based on the NGFS's three scenarios over a 30-year period, encompassing 4 million companies and 2,000 banks in the Euro area (de Guindos, 2021). Preliminary results from their analysis suggested serious risks building up in banks liquidity and capital ratios, stating that

> there are clear benefits in acting early. The short-term costs of the transition pale in comparison to the costs of unfettered climate change in the medium to long term. The early adoption of policies to drive the transition to a zero-carbon economy also brings benefits in terms of investing in and rolling out more efficient technologies. These results underline the crucial and urgent need to transition to a greener economy, not only to ensure that the targets of the Paris Agreement are met, but also to limit the long-run disruption to our economies, businesses and livelihoods. (de Guindos, 2021, n.p.)

In one sense, this scenario/stress-testing approach already admits the limits of any kind of pure, market-led solution to the problem of CRFRs, as effectively policymakers are setting the parameters of what is appropriate or not appropriate to measure. However, the ECB does not, it appears, consider this step sufficient to justify taking regulatory action to fulfil the urgent need to transition to a greener economy. It has made no commitment to adjust either banks' capital or liquidity requirements to account for the 'unpriced' carbon risks in the financial system, presumably still assuming the market will, at some point, re-orientate itself. In that sense, the market-failure framework and the possibility of price discovery remain the underlying conceptual assumptions. Or, to put it another way, to measure CRFRs *is* to manage them.

3.   DISTINGUISHING BETWEEN RISK AND UNCERTAINTY

Risk is generally understood in economics and financial modelling to mean 'probabilistic risk', meaning unknowable outcomes with knowable probabilities (Knight, 1921). Because the probabilities are knowable, market actors can adjust their strategies and capital allocation policies to optimise their profits and resilience to shocks, even if they cannot predict eventual outcomes. If I'm going out for the day, I can look at the weather forecast and see the percentage chance of rain and choose to take an umbrella or not. The weather can be seen as an *exogenous* risk; whether or not I take an umbrella does not affect the chance of rain. Fundamental to this is the efficient-market-hypothesis assumption that markets are affected by so many heterogeneous participants such that no individual market participant can move the markets. The risk manager is thus perceived as being in a 'game against nature' (Danielson, 2003).

But climate risk is actually closer to being in a state of uncertainty, involving random outcomes with *unknowable probabilities* (Christophers, 2017). This distinction was first identified by the economist Frank Knight (1921) as the actual source of profit in economies under conditions of imperfect information and was later developed by Keynes (1937, pp. 213–215) as a key element of his theory of macroeconomic fluctuations driven by 'animal spirits' (Keynes, 1936). Transition risk can involve technological innovations (e.g. a sudden breakthrough in battery technology), changes in legislation and regulation (e.g. the rapid implementation of a carbon tax following the surprise election of a progressive political party) and changes in consumer behaviour (e.g. a shift in attitudes towards the purchase of plastics). These types of risk are all inherently uncertain in terms of their impact, their time horizon and how they will manifest.

Added to this is that CRFRs are typically *endogenous* to the system they affect rather than exogenous. For example, a policy change (e.g. a carbon tax) may occur because of a shift in consumer sentiment that makes such a tax more politically feasible or a technological breakthrough that will lower the cost of renewable energy. These types of interactions can create non-linear dynamics with high potential for positive feedback loops, covariance of risk probabilities and 'fat tails', creating model uncertainty (Thomä and Chenet, 2017). Standard statistical approaches – for example, Value at Risk (VaR) evaluation – are unable to deal with these kinds of dynamics (Danielsson and Shin, 2003; Lamperti et al., 2018). Indeed, standard financial risk analysis is backward-looking, usually based on less than five years of data observations, and uses linear pricing techniques (Naqvi et al., 2017). A recent survey by the Bank of England on the preparedness of UK banks for climate change found their planning horizons averaged four years, likely too short even to account for probable physical and liability risks (Bank of England, 2018). Another recent study of 21 major investors found that most were still using conventional discounted-cash-flow analysis to value fossil fuel firms' assets rather than examining the carbon-intensity of their resource base, making them reluctant to divest (Christophers, 2019).

Further uncertainty is created by the highly interconnected nature of the modern financial system. Interlinkages among financial institutions – both banks and non-banks – can amplify both positive and negative shocks and significantly decrease the accuracy of default probabilities (Battiston et al., 2012). For example, although European banks typically only have low direct exposures to high-carbon sectors, they have exposures to pension funds and insurance companies that have larger direct exposures (Battiston et al., 2017). Unexpected policy reforms or technological breakthroughs can cause rapid shifts in market sentiment, leading to a network of adverse cascade effects (e.g. large-scale fire-sale of assets or hoarding of cash) between market players, creating a potentially unanticipated redistribution of economic resources across multiple sectors (Cahen-Fourot et al., 2019). Such an upheaval of our current economies and propagation to the deeply interlinked network of financial intermediaries constitutes systemic risk to the financial system.

The scenario analysis and stress-testing strategies outlined in section 2 can be seen as attempts to bring some order to the uncertainties surrounding climate change and to give financial institutions some parameters around which to consider their exposures. However, they have clear limits when it comes to climate change. Climate change involves a situation where many options are 'possible' or 'plausible'. The Intergovernmental Panel on Climate Change (IPCC), for example, considers a set of 222 scenarios that are compatible with the 1.5°C or 2°C global warming target, plus 189 scenarios representing a variety of non-desirable warmer futures (Masson-Delmotte et al., 2018). And those only represent *global* emission pathways, not the multiple variations at regional and national levels that interact with each other and are the responsibility of local and national governments, central banks and supervisors. These are simply the multiple scenarios of climate pathways, which have not been mapped onto highly complex interconnected modern financial systems – which would engender yet more potential scenarios, which are somehow supposed to inform financial supervisors.

A simple example – the Australia bushfires of 2019–2020 – serves to illustrate the limits of scenario analysis. With the benefit of hindsight, the long drought and very high temperatures that Australia endured in 2020 – both associated with climate change – created unusually dangerous conditions. But in New South Wales, one of the worst-affected areas, fire detections in January 2020 were *four times* higher than the previous highest (2002–2003) and almost eight times the seasonal average (see Figure 8.1). The country was understandably unprepared. It is questionable whether regulators would have been taken seriously had they presented such a scenario to banks as one that should be 'stress-tested' for a year or two before 2020.

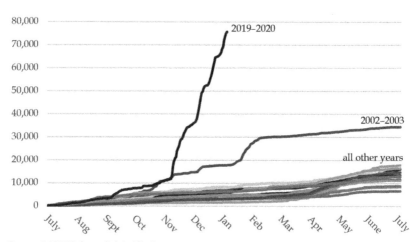

Source: MODIS, https://globalfiredata.org.

Figure 8.1   *Cumulative fire detections in New South Wales, Australia, 2002–2020*

Another problem arises around appropriate time horizons. As an example, the recent Bank of England (2019) discussion paper '2021 Biennial Exploratory Scenario on the Financial Risks from Climate Change' is illustrative of this analytical challenge relative to the time dimension in stress testing. It proposes scenario analysis exercises with a 2050 (30-year) horizon, with a fixed 2020 balance sheet. The physical consequences of climate change are proposed to be explored on the same 2020 balance sheet, but with an impact level that is supposed to be material for a 2070 horizon; that is, 50 years. This constitutes a heroic set of 'all else remaining equal' assumptions. Bank balance sheets in advanced economies have doubled in overall size relative to GDP since 1980 and their make-up has transformed completely with the majority of credit supporting households rather than firms (Jordà et al., 2017). A rapid low-carbon transition can potentially be more easily captured by shorter time windows and would certainly be more compatible with fixed current balance sheets, but presently such an outcome seems highly unlikely. This questions to what extent fixed balance sheets are relevant assumptions for climate stress testing. More generally, it is questionable whether it is possible and meaningful to model dynamic balance sheets over extended periods.

The existing market-failure-orientated risk management paradigm implicitly bets on the eventual materiality of CRFRs for financial institutions and that this market signal is both appropriate in timing and credible in intensity. At present, there is little sign of such a materialisation, despite significant falls in asset valuation of fossil fuel firms and falls in price of green assets in some sectors such as renewable energy. A recent study analysing fossil fuel financing from the world's 60 largest commercial and investment banks found they had lent or underwritten $3.8 trillion into fossil fuels from 2016 to 2020 (aggregating both equity and debt issuances) (Rainforest Action Network, 2021). The 2020 figure was a drop of 6% compared to 2019, matching the global drop in fossil fuel demand and production due to the COVID-19 pandemic but still higher than in 2016 (the year after the 2015 Paris Agreement). Further research has found the world's largest investment banks have provided more than $1.9tn of financing for the fossil fuel companies most aggressively expanding in new coal, oil and gas projects since the first launch of the TCFD (Greenfield, 2019a), whilst the thermal coal, oil and gas reserve holdings of the 'big three' asset managers (Blackrock, Vanguard and State Street) have surged by 34.8% since 2016 (Greenfield, 2019b). A detailed review of equity markets by the International Monetary Fund (IMF) (2020, p. 85) concluded that aggregate equity valuations in 2019 did not 'reflect the predicted changes in physical risk under various climate change scenarios. This suggests that equity investors may not be paying sufficient attention to climate change risks'. In its latest Financial Stability Review, the ECB notes that Eurozone bank lending to carbon-intensive firms, as a percentage of total lending, has increased since 2015 (ECB, 2020a, p. 73). It also notes that whilst the market for green bonds has been expanding rapidly, there is no evidence of the yields on green bonds being lower than on conventional bonds of a similar risk profile, which 'may reflect the fact that investors do not fully price in climate-related risks' (ECB, 2020a, p. 93).

In summary, whilst the reality of climate change is met with much less scepticism than it was even a few years ago in the financial community, it would appear the severest impacts are still not material today to the shorter-term time horizons of financial actors and policymakers. The 'tragedy of the horizon' that Mark Carney (2015) warned about seven years ago still appears to apply. The existing approach to CRFRs is thus not fit for purpose. Uncertainty makes conventional, backward-looking, financial risk-modelling approaches inefficient. Scenarios and stress testing are useful tools in the face of this uncertainty, but they are not forecasts and cannot compensate for the 'unknown unknowns' attached to underlying socioeconomic phenomena and mechanisms. Therefore, they cannot act as the sole guide for actual decision-making. An ontologically different approach to financial regulation is needed.

4.   A PRECAUTIONARY FINANCIAL POLICY APPROACH TO CLIMATE CHANGE

4.1   Theoretical Approach

The problem of uncertainty in the realm of finance and economics is not a new one. Central banks can draw on two regulatory traditions to develop alternatives to the market-failure/disclosure policy framework. One is the 'precautionary principle' which encourages preventative policies that protect human health and the environment in the face of scientific uncertainty. This has its roots in the German *Vorsorgeprinzip* which distinguishes between human activity with dangers of catastrophic consequences which must be prevented at all costs and human activity with potentially harmful consequences where preventative measures should be assessed using a more conventional assessment of costs and benefits (Henry and Henry, 2002). Commitments within the Kyoto Protocol and the Paris Agreement to keep global warming temperatures well below 2°C are prime examples of the precautionary principle applied in practice. The precautionary component involved establishing a well-defined threshold in the face of ongoing scientific uncertainty surrounding the effects of climate change, as well as the costs and feasibility of a significant cut in greenhouse emissions (Gee et al., 2013). Indeed, it acts as a cornerstone for multilateral organisations such as the IPCC (IPCC, 2014) and World Health Organization (WHO, 2004). It was further endorsed by the European Union (EU) Commission and formally adopted in an EU (2000) treaty. Across the EU, the precautionary principle has been applied to regulations across a range of different sectors beyond climate change including health and safety, biodiversity, consumer protection, chemicals, novel foods, pesticides, nanoproducts and pharmaceuticals.

Given the radical uncertainty attached to CRFRs, it would appear to be a good fit for precautionary-type policy interventions. Conventional economic decision-making based on static efficiency models and cost–benefit analysis (CBA) to determine the optimum mitigation pathway are of little use under a situation where the 'all else remaining equal' assumption, which such approaches rest on, no longer applies (Mazzucato et al., 2020). Rather, climate change is a 'ruin' problem: it will result in a system exposed to irreversible harm that can eventually lead to a risk of total failure, meaning negative outcomes may have infinite costs (Weitzman, 2012; Taleb et al., 2014). In the absence of a relevant CBA, it makes more sense to think in terms of insurance, where strong mitigation action would represent a collective strategy against the catastrophic outcomes of climate change (Weitzman, 2009; Aglietta and Espagne, 2016; Svartzman et al., 2020). Importantly, whilst the precise timing and magnitude of potential impacts of climate change on the financial system and economy are unpredictable, the fact that they will occur at some point is *increasingly* likely and will be affected by actions taken by agents now. They thus need to be distinguished from standard exogenous fat-tail risks. The Bank for International Settlements has designated such radically uncertain environmental threats as 'Green Swans' (Bolton et al., 2020).

A second important regulatory tradition is macroprudential policy. This has been the main policy innovation by central banks and supervisors in reaction to the financial crisis of 2007–2008. The crisis exposed the weakness of microprudential regulation-based backward-looking financial risk analysis, which was unable to capture endogenous and systemic risks, in particular the feedback between rising house prices, mortgage credit and the spread of risk via mortgage-backed securities and related innovations (Haldane and May, 2011; Nijskens and Wagner, 2011). Instead of regulating the soundness of individual institutions, macroprudential policy focuses on mitigating the systemic financial risks to the macroeconomy through pre-emptive interventions (De Nicoló et al., 2012; Favara and Ratnovski, 2014). Notably, macroprudential policy empowers central banks and supervisory authorities to reduce the likely emergence of instability *ex ante*; that is, before market participants recognise the emergence of risk and adjust their behaviours. The macroprudential policymaker is forward-looking, not backward-looking, and incentivised to intervene to prevent worst-case scenarios and 'lean against the wind'; for example, raising loan-to-value ratios on mortgages if house prices are rising rapidly against incomes.

Macroprudential policy thus favours precautionary but active policies that avoid large losses across scenarios regardless of the likelihood of any given scenario (Foulis and Bahaj, 2016; Webb et al., 2017). This ensures that the financial system is resilient enough to withstand and recover from (unforeseen) shocks, for example by increasing capital buffers or developing robust resolution procedures) (Borio, 2011; Claessens et al., 2013). Macroprudential policy is also intentionally not 'sector-' or 'market-neutral'. It recognises that certain sectors (e.g. real estate, foreign exchange) are more prone to the creation of systemic risk than others (e.g. lending to small firms) and develops sector-specific tools accordingly. In the case of housing, policies have included tighter loan-to-value and loan-to-income ratios for households on the demand side, whilst on the supply side they have required banks to hold more capital against certain types of real-estate lending.

The introduction of macroprudential tools in the aftermath of the 2007–2008 financial crisis was not the endpoint of a long and sophisticated attempt to accurately model the optimal quantity of mortgage credit in the economy in terms of financial stability. It was more a simple recognition that the previous intellectual framework – focused on microprudential risk – was not fit for purpose (Borio, 2011). Furthermore, the decisions on when and how to intervene are equally not based upon sophisticated risk modelling but on the observing of a set of core indicators (e.g. mortgage credit to GDP ratios at the national level, debt-servicing ratios), as well as regulator discretion and judgement (see, for example, Bank of England, 2016). A climate-aligned macroprudential policymaker would not view themselves as exogeneous to the emergence of CRFRs, or their sole job as helping the efficient flow of information from agents in the economy. Rather, they would view themselves as active participants in shaping their nature, timing and impact.

Precautionary policies to address environmental financial risks should shift towards a more qualitative risk management approach, where discretion, experience, heuristics and general direction-setting replace complicated mathematical models in the face of radical uncertainty (Chenet et al., 2021). Where there is little doubt as to the potential magnitude of a threat or the speed and direction of a harmful trend, fixating on precise quantitative results does not necessarily improve insights for decision makers, and at worst can distract from the best course of action (Kay and King, 2020; Saltelli et al., 2020). As former Bank of England governor Mervyn King has argued, in opposition to banks determining their own capital adequacy ratios using models: 'If the nature of the uncertainty is unknown … it is better to be roughly right than precisely wrong, and to use a simple but more robust measure of required capital' (King, 2016, chapter 4).

The financial system is better understood not as being in a state of equilibrium perturbed by market failures due to mispricing of risks but as a complex adaptative system (Anderson, 2018), the behaviour of which is determined in a highly decentralised fashion and subject to feedback loops, tipping points and threshold behaviour (Haldane and May, 2011; Monasterolo et al., 2019). Initial conditions and path dependency are hence important phenomena shaping how markets, sectors, institutions and green and consumer behaviours will evolve, meaning marginal changes to prices are unlikely to have large effects. Instead of focusing on the identification of *plausible* scenarios, precautionary approaches focus on *worst-case* outcomes and construct policies in order to avoid them (Dupuy, 2002). By recognising that 'what appear to be small and reasonable risks accumulate inevitably to certain irreversible harm' (Taleb et al., 2014), precautionary policymaking is better suited to managing the non-linear risks presented by ecological thresholds. Indeed, ecological 'tipping points' are obvious *worst-case* outcomes around which to design preventative policies for environmental breakdown (Neumayer, 2013).

A recent body of literature has also focused upon harnessing tipping-point dynamics to achieve transformative change in socio-ecological systems (Milkoreit et al., 2018; Farmer et al., 2019; Otto et al., 2020). If a tipping point represents a system sitting at the boundary of two different states, a small intervention could trigger non-linear dynamics (e.g. desirable feedback loops and positive spill-over effects) that generate a controlled regime shift towards sustainability (Westley et al., 2011) – or the opposite. One prominent example is how carbon pricing and subsidy policy has tipped the costs of new coal power plants over the threshold of new renewable investments in all major markets (Gray and Sundaresan, 2020). To build directional certainty in the sustainability transition and minimise potential market dislocations, central banks and supervisors should focus on discouraging the financing of clearly harmful business practices. Carefully targeted interventions may effectively act as 'social tipping points' (Farmer et al., 2019), enabling the financial system to shift to more sustainable patterns in capital allocation.

4.2 Precautionary Policy Implementation

In terms of actual policy, a good starting point for a precautionary policy approach would be capital requirements. The current Basel III international capital requirements framework completely neglect CRFRs, with all corporate loans receiving the same 100% risk weight by prudential regulators. The EU has been considering the idea of a 'green supporting factor' capital framework whereby capital requirements could be reduced on activities defined as green in accordance with the EU's newly developed green finance taxonomy (EU TEG SF, 2020). Whilst an argument can be made that lower capital requirements for green assets could be justified if these loans are deemed less risky than others, there is currently no evidence of lower risk for green loans (Boot and Schoenmaker, 2018; Dankert et al., 2018). In addition, the evidence suggests such 'supporting factors' make little difference to the issuance of loans (Dankert et al., 2018; Van Lerven and Ryan-Collins, 2018). Lowering prudential regulatory requirements for exposures that are not less risky would undermine the safety and soundness of financial institutions and could pose financial stability risks.

A precautionary approach would instead seek to increase capital requirements for dirty loans – a dirty loan 'penalising factor'. A sufficiently high capital requirement (a higher risk weight) for loans carrying carbon risk, or entities that are severely reliant on fossil fuels, would reflect the real and growing systemic risk of investing in carbon-intensive activities and could discourage further investment that contributes to climate change. It would also give banks a greater buffer to withstand losses related to climate-related transition risks and potential sudden value losses due to the repricing of assets. Regulators are already increasingly requiring fossil fuel companies to post additional financial resources to cover the eventual retirement costs associated with safely decommissioning their assets to avoid leaving these costs to the government after the company fails and becoming 'stranded liabilities' (Carbon Tracker, 2020). Regulators should first focus on the financial exposures that face the clearest transition-related risks: fossil fuel assets and infrastructure. Bonds, loans and derivative transactions for companies that derive more than, for example, 20% of their revenue from the extraction, exploration, transportation, storage, exporting or refining of oil, natural gas or coal should face higher capital risk weightings. These could be calibrated according to the type of fossil fuel (e.g. coal would attract a higher risk weighting), the maturity of the loan and the extent to which the borrowing firm is dependent for its revenue on fossil-fuel-related activities (Gelzinis, 2021).

From a macroprudential perspective, larger, systemically important banks at risk from transition risk could also be forced to hold an additional capital buffer or surcharge to increase their resilience to future shocks and internalise the cost their activities are placing on the rest of the financial system, in much the same way as post-crisis regulation has seen surcharges placed on globally systemically important banks (G-SIBs) (BCBS, 2013).

A more radical intervention would be a form of negative screening of the financing of certain activities. An obvious place would be new lending that enables fossil fuel extraction (including tar sands, Arctic and ultra-deep-water oil, liquefied natural gas (LNG) export, coal mining and coal power) (also proposed by Cullen, 2018). Such an approach can also be applied to existing assets (ongoing loans or securities), which makes sense for the technologies and industries that are already overexposed relative to climate targets. Such an approach opens questions relative to the choice of those precise activities to penalise or to favour reciprocal approaches, and in terms of coordination with fiscal policy. The situation of existing assets is potentially much more sensitive in terms of legal feasibility and acceptability. But in both cases, the reversal of the onus on the financier to prove their activity is 'safe' – a key element of the precautionary principle described above – can be a way to not be overly prescriptive: the regulator can issue and regularly update a list of a priori undesirable activities that financial institutions must then cease, or demonstrate to the supervisors' satisfaction that they do not reduce the chances of following a net-zero-carbon pathway (typically by demonstrating that lending to a specific brown company will contribute to greening).

Given the urgency of the climate crisis, central banks and supervisors should also be considering how they can more directly support the massive increase in sustainable finance that is required to meet the transition to a net-zero-carbon economy, beyond purely financial stability considerations. 'Credit guidance' – policy tools aimed at steering credit flows (encouraging or discouraging) towards particular sectors of the economy – has fallen somewhat out of fashion in advanced economies since the 1980s. However, it was commonly used in the post-war period and in East Asia during the 1980s to support rapid economic growth and ambitious industrial transition (Monnet, 2016; Bezemer et al., 2018), and is currently used in many emerging market economies to support green finance, including in China, India and Bangladesh (Dikau and Ryan-Collins, 2017; Dikau and Volz, 2018; D'Orazio and Popoyan, 2019). Use of such tools may require greater coordination between central banks and governments, in particular ministries of finance and industrial policy. This is certainly a field where further research is needed to examine what types of policies will be effective in a world where market-based finance (or 'shadow-banking') also plays an important role and is often not within the purview of central bank regulators.

5.   DISCUSSION

What challenges does the kind of market-shaping, precautionary policy approach to climate change laid out in this chapter create for central banks? One issue may be the time horizon. For monetary policy (i.e. interest-rate setting), the focus of central banks is normally on the 'business cycle' – typically two to three years, although central banks have begun to lengthen their policy horizons in the post-crisis period since taking on a stronger financial stability mandate, focusing on the 'credit' or 'financial cycle', which is typically estimated to be anywhere between 10 and 16 years (Aikman et al., 2014; Borio, 2014). The policies discussed in section 4.2 would naturally heighten short-term transition risks. Adopting a precautionary approach, supervisors would need to 'see through' this, having in mind the longer-term catastrophic losses arising from physical risks associated with a more drawn-out transition which may materialise over a 30–50-year period. Of course, a first-best scenario would be that environmental legislation would also prohibit such activity in its entirety, but given the lack of such an intervention, a precautionary approach would advocate intervention now on the assumption that such action may not occur (i.e. a worst-case scenario). Currently, as mentioned above, financing for greenhouse gas industries continues unabated and is even expanding, despite national and international agreements on reducing carbon emissions. The longer-term scenarios and stress testing being implemented by some central banks clearly illustrates their awareness of this 'tragedy of the horizon' problem. Now it is time for them to follow through with policy interventions to match in the short term.

Another challenge centres on central banks' mandate and independence from governments. Recent studies of central bank mandates and climate change make clear that different jurisdictions have very different mandates related to how far they support national economic priorities beyond price and financial stability (D'Orazio and Popoyan, 2019; Dikau and Volz, 2021). Indeed, in addition to price stability, the mandates of central banks often cover general economic welfare, which would appear to be compatible with consideration of climate change (Krogstrup and Oman, 2019; Dikau and Volz, 2021). For example, the People's Bank of China has a 'structural changes' objective in its mandate and the Chinese government views this as a tool for the implementation of national economic priorities, which now includes the environment. In Europe, Article 2 of the European System of Central Banks statutes mentions explicitly the objective of supporting economic policies in the community. Recently the new ECB president, Christine Lagarde, put forward the objective of fighting climate change as a priority in the ECB's agenda (ECON, 2019).

One argument against a precautionary approach to policy is that it is the job of the government, not the independent central bank or financial supervisor, to impose policies to repress or support particular sectors of the economy. This argument, drawing on the concept of 'market neutrality', may have had some force pre-crisis (van 't Klooster and Fontan, 2020). However, post-crisis it is less convincing. Central banks in most advanced economies have taken on a clear financial stability mandate, along with their traditional focus on price stability. If a precautionary policy approach is viewed as reducing financial risks, then it would not appear to be stretching a mandate or reducing independence. Senior central bankers have recently acknowledged that the traditional interpretation of market neutrality may need reconsidering where there is clear evidence of the failure of financial markets to price in environmental risks (Arnold, 2020). Central banks should strive for coherence with government transition policy rather than market neutrality as the guiding operational principle for regulatory policymaking for the green transition (Robins et al., 2021; Barkawi and Zadek, 2021). The rationale is that (1) government transition policy is less likely to be successful if private financial dynamics are pushing against it; and (2) alignment with government transition policy is the most effective way for central banks to minimise systemic risks to financial stability. Again, this recognises that central banks are not exogenous to the financial system; rather, they are participating economic actors whose policy decisions help shape markets.

Furthermore, the argument for central bank independence was originally justified on the existence of a 'time-inconsistency problem' (Kydland and

Prescott, 1977). The aim was to push back against the tendency of incumbent governments to ramp up spending in the run-up to elections and pressure central banks to ease monetary policy to stimulate growth and employment. This would generate inflation and inflationary expectations that only an independent central bank could credibly prevent and reverse. In the aftermath of the 2007–2008 financial crisis, many advanced-economy central banks and supervisors were given (or asked for) greater responsibility for interventions in the mortgage market using macroprudential policy, precisely because, given political pressures, it was felt politicians, ministries of finance and the market itself would find it harder to 'take away the punchbowl'. For example, in countries where the majority of voters are home-owners or would like to become so, policies that restrict mortgage credit or reduce house price growth in the upturn are likely to be highly unpopular, and the electoral cycle often dictates the time horizons of governments (Holmes, 2018).

The same issues apply to the problem of CRFRs. Politicians and ministers of finance are under significant political pressure not to regulate against large companies (e.g. energy companies) engaged in unsustainable activities which will enhance both physical and transition-related CRFRs. The lobbying power of these organisations is evident in the still enormous subsidies they receive, which far outweigh the subsidies flowing in to renewable energy (Gençsü et al., 2020). There is, as with house prices, also pressure from voters. The introduction of a carbon tax, for example, would almost certainly push up the cost of the majority of households' energy bills and increase the cost of transport with potentially severe political ramifications, as was seen with the *gilet jaunes* protests in France (Chamorel, 2019). In these circumstances, a central bank that did not act to reduce the financial risks relating to climate change could be accused of not being independent or at the very least of not justifying the privilege of independence.

None of this is to say that governments should not also be going much further, much faster, to address the risks from climate change (Bolton et al., 2020). It is rather to say that financial policymakers have a duty to take systemic financial stability risk seriously, whatever sector of the economy it is coming from, and not to wait until the crisis arrives before taking action.

6.   CONCLUSION

Significant progress has been made by central banks in analysing the challenges for financial stability posed by climate change and a net-zero-carbon transition. There is increasing recognition of the problem of uncertainty and the difficulty for financial institutions in measuring it and adjusting their time horizons accordingly. However, the lack of actual policy interventions to deal with CRFRs reveals an implicit and unfounded belief in the power of private capital and financial markets to enable a smooth transition – via efficient pricing of risks – once the quality of data on these risks improves. This chapter has argued this is a misguided approach given the radical uncertainty that characterises climate change and its interaction with the financial system, meaning conventional backward-looking probabilistic financial risk modelling is not fit for purpose in dealing with them. This market-failure approach creates a bias against the short-term market disruption from raised transition risk that is in fact needed to avoid longer-term, potentially catastrophic financial and economic damages created by physical climate change.

The proposed precautionary policy prioritises preventative action and qualitative approaches to managing risk above quantitative measurement and information disclosure. It aims to steer financial actors and the economy away from tipping points and build system resilience as a superior means of managing radical uncertainty. To operationalise such an approach, central banks should discourage the financing of clearly harmful business practices in order to address drivers of CRFRs where they intersect with the financial system via changes to capital requirements or negative screen approaches. Not all precautionary-type interventions will be successful. But, on balance, more valuable information can be found from intervening and studying the (endogenous) reactions that follow a particular intervention than can be gleaned from non-interventionist analysis, modelling and forecasting. As Federal Reserve Governor Lael Brainard (2021, n.p.) recently stated:

> Despite the challenges, it will be critical to make progress, even if initially imperfect, in order to ensure that financial institutions are resilient to climate-related financial risks and well-positioned for the opportunities associated with the transition to a more sustainable economy.

NOTE

1.   The Federal Reserve was a latecomer to the NGFS, joining in November 2020 following the election defeat of Donald Trump.

REFERENCES

Aglietta, M. and Espagne, E. 2016. *Climate and Finance Systemic Risks: More Than an Analogy? The Climate Fragility Hypothesis* [Online]. Centre d'etudes prospectives et d'informations internationales. Available from: http://www.cepii.fr/CEPII/en/publications/wp/abstract.asp?NoDoc=9079.
Aikman, D., Haldane, A.G. and Nelson, B.D. 2014. Curbing the credit cycle. *The Economic Journal.* **125**(585), pp. 1072–1109.
Ambrosio, N. 2018. Climate risk, real estate, and the bottom line. *Four Twenty Seven* [Online]. Available from: https://427mt.com/2018/10/11/climate-risk-real-estate-investment-trusts.

Ameli, N., Drummond, P., Bisaro, A., Grubb, M. and Chenet, H. 2019. Climate finance and disclosure for institutional investors: Why transparency is not enough. *Climatic Change.* **4**(160), pp. 565–589.

Anderson, P.W. 2018. *The Economy as an Evolving Complex System.* London: CRC Press.

Arnold, M. 2020. ECB to consider using climate risk to steer bond purchases, says Lagarde. *Financial Times* [Online]. Available from: https://www.ft.com/content/f5f34021-795f-47a2-aade-72eb5f455e09.

Bank of England. 2016. *The Financial Policy Committee's Powers Over Housing Policy Instruments – A Draft Policy Statement* [Online]. London. Available from: https://www.bankofengland.co.uk/-/media/boe/files/statement/2016/the-financial-policy-committee-powers-over-housing-policy-instruments.pdf.

Bank of England. 2018. *Enhancing Banks' and Insurers' Approaches to Managing the Financial Risks from Climate Change – Consultation Paper* [Online]. London: Bank of England. Available from: https://www.bankofengland.co.uk/prudential-regulation/publication/2019/enhancing-banks-and-insurers-approaches-to-managing-the-financial-risks-from-climate-change-ss.

Bank of England. 2019. *The 2021 Biennial Exploratory Scenario on the Financial Risks from Climate Change – Discussion Paper* [Online]. London. Available from: https://www.bankofengland.co.uk/paper/2019/biennial-exploratory-scenario-climate-change-discussion-paper.

Barkawi, A. and Zadek, S. 2021. *Governing Finance for Sustainable Prosperity* [Online]. Council on Economic Policies. Available from: https://www.cepweb.org/wp-content/uploads/2021/04/Barkawi-and-Zadek-2021.-Governing-Finance-for-Sustainable-Prosperity.pdf.

Battiston, S., Delli Gatti, D., Gallegati, M., Greenwald, B. and Stiglitz, J.E. 2012. Liaisons dangereuses: Increasing connectivity, risk sharing, and systemic risk. *Journal of Economic Dynamics and Control.* **36**(8), pp. 1121–1141.

Battiston, S., Mandel, A., Monasterolo, I., Schütze, F. and Visentin, G. 2017. A climate stress-test of the financial system. *Nature Climate Change.* **7**(4), pp. 283–288.

BCBS. 2013. *Global Systemically Important Banks: Updated Assessment Methodology and the Higher Loss Absorbency Requirement* [Online]. Basel: Bank for International Settlements. Available from: https://www.bis.org/publ/bcbs255.htm.

Bezemer, D., Ryan-Collins, J., van Lerven, F. and Zhang, L. 2018. Credit where it's due: A historical, theoretical and empirical review of credit guidance policies in the 20th century. [Online]. UCL Institute for Innovation and Public Purpose. Available from: https://www.ucl.ac.uk/bartlett/public-purpose/publications/2018/nov/credit-where-its-due.

BIS. 2021. *Climate-Related Risk Drivers and Their Transmission Channels* [Online]. Basel: Bank for International Settlements. Available from: https://www.bis.org/bcbs/publ/d517.htm.

Bolton, P., Després, M., Pereira da Silva, L., Samama, F. and Svartzman, R. 2020. *The Green Swan: Central Banking and Financial Stability in the Age of Climate Change* [Online]. Bank for International Settlements. Available from: https://www.bis.org/publ/othp31.pdf.

Boot, A. and Schoenmaker, D. 2018. Climate change adds to risk for banks, but EU lending proposals will do more harm than good. *Bruegel.* [Online]. Available from: http://bruegel.org/2018/01/climate-change-adds-to-risk-for-banks-but-eu-lending-proposals-will-do-more-harm-than-good.

Borio, C. 2011. Implementing a macroprudential framework: Blending boldness and realism. *Capitalism and Society.* **6**(1), art. 1.

Borio, C. 2014. The financial cycle and macroeconomics: What have we learnt? *Journal of Banking & Finance.* **45**, pp. 182–198.

Bousso, R. 2020. BP wipes up to $17.5 billion from assets with bleaker oil outlook. *Reuters.* [Online]. Available from: https://www.reuters.com/article/us-bp-writeoffs -idUSKBN23M0QA.

Brainard, L. 2021. Speech by Governor Brainard on the role of financial institutions in tackling the challenges of climate change. *Board of Governors of the Federal Reserve System* [Online]. Available from: https://www.federalreserve.gov/ newsevents/speech/brainard20210218a.htm.

Brunetti, C., Dennis, B., Gates, D., Hancock, D., Ignell, D., Kiser, E.K., Kotta, G., Kovner, A., Rosen, R.J. and Tabor, N.K. 2021. Climate change and financial stability. *FEDS Notes* (2021–03), pp. 19–23.

Cahen-Fourot, L., Campiglio, E., Dawkins, E., Godin, A. and Kemp-Benedict, E. 2019. Capital stranding cascades: The impact of decarbonisation on productive asset utilisation. *Energy Economics.* **103**, 105581.

Campiglio, E., Dafermos, Y., Monnin, P., Ryan-Collins, J., Schotten, G. and Tanaka, M. 2018. Climate change challenges for central banks and financial regulators. *Nature Climate Change.* **8**(6), pp. 462–468.

Carbon Tracker. 2020. *The Flip Side: Stranded Assets and Stranded Liabilities* [Online]. Available from: https://carbontracker.org/reports/the-flip-side-stranded -assets-and-stranded-liabilities.

Carney, M. 2015. *Breaking the Tragedy of the Horizon: Climate Change and Financial Stability.* London: Bank of England.

Chamorel, P. 2019. Macron versus the yellow vests. *Journal of Democracy.* **30**(4), pp. 48–62.

Chenet, H., Ryan-Collins, J. and van Lerven, F. 2021. Finance, climate-change and radical uncertainty: Towards a precautionary approach to financial policy. *Ecological Economics.* **183**, 106957.

Christophers, B. 2017. Climate change and financial instability: Risk disclosure and the problematics of neoliberal governance. *Annals of the American Association of Geographers.* **107**(5), pp. 1108–1127.

Christophers, B. 2019. Environmental beta or how institutional investors think about climate change and fossil fuel risk. *Annals of the American Association of Geographers*, pp. 1–21.

Claessens, S., Ghosh, S.R. and Mihet, R. 2013. Macro-prudential policies to mitigate financial system vulnerabilities. *Journal of International Money and Finance.* **39**, pp. 153–185.

Cullen, J. 2018. After 'HLEG': EU banks, climate change abatement and the precautionary principle. *Cambridge Yearbook of European Legal Studies.* Cambridge: Cambridge University Press.

Danielson, J. 2003. On the feasibility of risk based regulation. *CESifo Economic Studies.* **49**(2), pp. 157–179.

Danielsson, J. and Shin, H.S. 2003. Endogenous risk. In P. Field, ed. *Modern Risk Management: A History.* London: Risk Books, pp. 297–316.

Dankert, J., van Doorn, L., Reinders, H.J., Sleijpen, O. and De Nederlandsche Bank, N.V. 2018. A green supporting factor: The right policy? *SUERF Policy Note.*

de Guindos, L. 2021. Shining a light on climate risks: The ECB's economy-wide climate stress test. *The ECB Blog* [Online]. Available from: https://www.ecb.europa.eu/press/blog/date/2021/html/ecb.blog210318~3bbc68ffc5.en.html.

De Nicoló, M.G., Favara, G. and Ratnovski, L. 2012. *Externalities and Macroprudential Policy* [Online]. Available from: https://www.imf.org/external/pubs/ft/sdn/2012/sdn1205.pdf.

Dikau, S. and Ryan-Collins, J. 2017. *Green Central Banking in Emerging Market and Developing Country Economies* [Online]. New Economics Foundation. Available from: https://eprints.soas.ac.uk/24876/1/Green-Central-Banking.pdf.

Dikau, S. and Volz, U. 2018. *Central Banking, Climate Change and Green Finance* [Online]. Tokyo: Asian Development Bank Institute. Available from: https://core.ac.uk/download/pdf/161527987.pdf.

Dikau, S. and Volz, U. 2021. Central bank mandates, sustainability objectives and the promotion of green finance. *Ecological Economics*. **184**, 107022.

D'Orazio, P. and Popoyan, L. 2019. Fostering green investments and tackling climate-related financial risks: Which role for macroprudential policies? *Ecological Economics*. **160**, pp. 25–37.

Dupuy, J.-P. 2002. *Pour un catastrophisme éclairé: quand l'impossible est certain.* Paris: Seuil.

ECB. 2020a. *Financial Stability Review*. Frankfurt am Main: ECB.

ECB. 2020b. *Guide on Climate-Related and Environmental Risks: Supervisory Expectations Relating to Risk Management and Disclosure* [Online]. Frankfurt am Main: ECB. Available from: https://www.bankingsupervision.europa.eu/ecb/pub/pdf/ssm.202011finalguideonclimate-relatedandenvironmentalrisks~58213f6564.en.pdf.

ECB. 2020c. *ECB Report on Institutions' Climate-Related and Environmental Risk Disclosures* [Online]. Frankfurt am Main: ECB. Available from: https://www.bankingsupervision.europa.eu/press/pr/date/2020/html/ssm.pr201127~5642b6e68d.en.html.

ECON. 2019. *Draft Report on the Council Recommendation on the Appointment of the President of the European Central Bank (C9-0048/2019 – 2019/0810(NLE))* [Online]. Available from: https://www.europarl.europa.eu/doceo/document/A-9-2019-0008_EN.html.

EU. 2000. *Article 191(2) of the Treaty on the Functioning of the EU* [Online]. European Union. Available from: https://eur-lex.europa.eu/legal-content/EN/TXT/?uri=celex:12016E191.

EU TEG SF. 2020. *TEG Final Report on the EU Taxonomy* [Online]. Available from: https://ec.europa.eu/info/sites/info/files/business_economy_euro/banking_and_finance/documents/200309-sustainable-finance-teg-final-report-taxonomy_en.pdf.

Fama, E. 1970. Efficient capital markets: A review of theory and empirical work. *Journal of Finance*. **25**(2), pp. 383–417.

Farmer, J.D., Hepburn, C., Ives, M.C., Hale, T., Wetzer, T., Mealy, P., Rafaty, R., Srivastav, S. and Way, R. 2019. Sensitive intervention points in the post-carbon transition. *Science*. **364**(6436), pp. 132–134.

Favara, G. and Ratnovski, L. 2014. Externalities: An economic rationale for macroprudential policy. In D. Schoenmaker, ed. *Macroprudentialism* [Online]. Duisenberg School of Finance, VoxEU: CEPR Press. Available from: https://voxeu.org/sites/default/files/file/macroprudentialism_VoxEU_0.pdf#page=151.

Foulis, A. and Bahaj, S. 2016. Uncertainty is no excuse for not using macroprudential tools. *BankUnderground* [Online]. Available from: https://bankunderground.co.uk/2016/01/29/uncertainty-is-no-excuse-for-not-using-macroprudential-tools.

Gee, D., Grandjean, P., Hansen, S.F., MacGarvin, M., Martin, J., Nielsen, G., Quist, D. and Stanners, D. 2013. Late lessons from early warnings: Science, precaution, innovation. *EEA Report.* **1**.

Gelzinis, G. 2021. *Addressing Climate-Related Financial Risk Through Bank Capital Requirements* [Online]. Washington, DC: American Enterprise Institute. Available from: https://www.americanprogress.org/issues/economy/reports/2021/05/11/498976/addressing-climate-related-financial-risk-bank-capital-requirements.

Gençsü, I., Whitley, S., Trilling, M., van der Burg, L., McLynn, M. and Worrall, L. 2020. Phasing out public financial flows to fossil fuel production in Europe. *Climate Policy.* **20**(8), pp. 1010–1023.

Giuzio, M., Krušec, D., Levels, A., Melo, A.S., Mikkonen, K. and Radulova, P. 2019. *Climate Change and Financial Stability* [Online]. Frankfurt am Main: ECB. Available from: https://www.ecb.europa.eu/pub/financial-stability/fsr/special/html/ecb.fsrart201905_1~47cf778cc1.en.html.

Gray, M. and Sundaresan, S. 2020. *How to Waste Over Half a Trillion Dollars: The Economic Implications of Deflationary Renewable Energy for Coal Power Investments* [Online]. Carbon Tracker. Available from: https://carbontracker.org/reports/how-to-waste-over-half-a-trillion-dollars.

Greenfield, P. 2019a. Top investment banks provide billions to expand fossil fuel industry. *The Guardian.*

Greenfield, P. 2019b. World's top three asset managers oversee $300bn fossil fuel investments. *The Guardian.*

Haldane, A.G. and May, R.M. 2011. Systemic risk in banking ecosystems. *Nature.* **469**(7330), pp. 351–355.

Hayek, F.A. 1945. The use of knowledge in society. *The American Economic Review.* **35**(4), pp. 519–530.

Henry, C. and Henry, M. 2002. Formalization and applications of the precautionary principles. *SSRN Electronic Journal*, March 1.

Holmes, D.R. 2018. A tractable future: Central Banks in conversation with their publics. In J. Beckert and R. Bronk, eds. *Uncertain Futures: Imaginaries, Narratives, and Calculation in the Economy.* Oxford: Oxford University Press, pp. 173–193.

Hurst, L. 2020. 'Stranded assets' risk rising with climate action and $40 oil. *Bloomberg. com* [Online]. Available from: https://www.bloomberg.com/news/articles/2020-08-11/why-climate-action-40-oil-create-stranded-assets-quicktake.

IMF. 2020. Climate change: Physical risk and equity prices. In *Global Financial Stability Report: Markets in the Time of COVID-19.* Washington, DC: International Monetary Fund.

IPCC. 2014. *Mitigation of Climate Change: Contribution of Working Group III to the Fifth Assessment Report of the Intergovernmental Panel on Climate Change* [Online]. Available from: https://www.ipcc.ch/report/ar5/wg3.

IPCC. 2018. *Global Warming of 1.5°C.* Geneva: Intergovernmental Panel on Climate Change.

Jordà, Ò., Schularick, M. and Taylor, A.M. 2017. Macrofinancial history and the new business cycle facts. *NBER Macroeconomics Annual.* **31**(1), pp. 213–263.

Kay, J. and King, M. 2020. *Radical Uncertainty: Decision-Making for an Unknowable Future.* London: The Bridge Street Press.

Keynes, J.M. 1936. *The General Theory of Employment, Interest, and Money* [Online]. Cham: Springer International Publishing. Available from: http://link.springer.com/ 10.1007/978-3-319-70344-2.

Keynes, J.M. 1937. The general theory of employment. *The Quarterly Journal of Economics.* **51**(2), pp. 209–223.

King, M. 2016. *The End of Alchemy: Money, Banking and the Future of the Global Economy.* London: W.W. Norton and Company.

Knight, F. 1921. *Risk, Uncertainty and Profit.* New York: Harper Torchbook.

Krogstrup, S. and Oman, W. 2019. *Macroeconomic and Financial Policies for Climate Change Mitigation: A Review of the Literature* [Online]. Washington, DC: International Monetary Fund. Available from: https://www.imf.org/en/Publications/ WP/Issues/2019/09/04/Macroeconomic-and-Financial-Policies-for-Climate-Change -Mitigation-A-Review-of-the-Literature-48612.

Kydland, F.E. and Prescott, E.C. 1977. Rules rather than discretion: The inconsistency of optimal plans. *Journal of Political Economy.* **85**(3), pp. 473–491.

Lamperti, F., Dosi, G., Napoletano, M., Roventini, A. and Sapio, A. 2018. Faraway, so close: Coupled climate and economic dynamics in an agent-based integrated assessment model. *Ecological Economics.* **150**, pp. 315–339.

Masson-Delmotte, V., Zhai, P., Pörtner, H.-O., Roberts, D., Skea, J., Shukla, P.R., Pirani, A., Moufouma-Okia, W., Péan, C., Pidcock, R., Connors, S., Matthews, J.B.R., Chen, Y., Zhou, X., Gomis, M.I., Lonnoy, E., Maycock, T., Tignor, M. and Waterfield, T. 2018. *Global Warming of 1.5°C – An IPCC Special Report on the Impacts of Global Warming of 1.5°C Above Pre-Industrial Levels and Related Global Greenhouse Gas Emission Pathways, in the Context of Strengthening the Global Response to the Threat of Climate Change.* Geneva: Intergovernmental Panel on Climate Change.

Mazzucato, M., Kattel, R. and Ryan-Collins, J. 2020. Challenge-driven innovation policy: Towards a new policy toolkit. *Journal of Industry, Competition and Trade.* **20**(2), pp. 421–437.

Milkoreit, M., Hodbod, J., Baggio, J., Benessaiah, K., Calderón-Contreras, R., Donges, J.F., Mathias, J.-D., Rocha, J.C., Schoon, M. and Werners, S.E. 2018. Defining tipping points for social-ecological systems scholarship: An interdisciplinary literature review. *Environmental Research Letters.* **13**(3), 033005.

Monasterolo, I., Roventini, A. and Foxon, T.J. 2019. Uncertainty of climate policies and implications for economics and finance: An evolutionary economics approach. *Ecological Economics.* **163**, pp. 177–182.

Monnet, E. 2016. *Monetary Policy without Interest Rates: The French Experience with Quantitative Controls (1948 to 1973).* Paris: Banque de France.

Mooney, A., Hook, L. and McCormick, M. 2019. BlackRock, Vanguard, Axa raise coal holdings despite climate fears. *Financial Times.*

Naqvi, M., Burke, B., Hector, S., Jamison, T. and Dupré, S. 2017. *All Swans Are Black in the Dark: How the Short-Term Focus of Financial Analysis Does Not Shed Light on Long Term Risks.* The Generation Foundation [Online]. Available from: https://2degrees-investing.org/wp-content/uploads/2017/02/All-swans-are-black-in -the-dark.pdf.

Neumayer, E. 2013. *Weak versus Strong Sustainability: Exploring the Limits of Two Opposing Paradigms.* Cheltenham: Edward Elgar Publishing.

NGFS. 2019a. *Macroeconomic and Financial Stability – Implications of Climate Change.* Network for Greening the Financial System. Technical supplement to the

first comprehensive report [Online]. Available from: https://www.ngfs.net/sites/
default/files/medias/documents/ngfs-report-technical-supplement_final_v2.pdf.

NGFS. 2019b. *NGFS First Comprehensive Report. A Call for Action: Climate Change
as a Source of Financial Risk* [Online]. Available from: https://www.ngfs.net/sites/
default/files/medias/documents/ngfs_first_comprehensive_report_-_17042019_0
.pdf.

NGFS. 2020a. *Guide for Supervisors: Integrating Climate-Related and Environmental
Risks into Prudential Supervision* [Online]. Available from: https://www.ngfs.net/
sites/default/files/medias/documents/ngfs_guide_for_supervisors.pdf.

NGFS. 2020b. *Guide to Climate Scenario Analysis for Central Banks and Supervisors
– Technical Document* [Online]. Available from: https://www.ngfs.net/sites/default/
files/medias/documents/ngfs_guide_scenario_analysis_final.pdf.

NGFS. 2020c. *The Macroeconomic and Financial Stability Impacts of Climate Change:
Research Priorities – Technical Document* [Online]. Available from: https://www
.ngfs.net/sites/default/files/medias/documents/ngfs_research_priorities_final.pdf.

Nijskens, R. and Wagner, W. 2011. Credit risk transfer activities and systemic risk:
How banks became less risky individually but posed greater risks to the financial
system at the same time. *Journal of Banking & Finance.* **35**(6), pp. 1391–1398.

Otto, I.M., Donges, J.F., Cremades, R., Bhowmik, A., Hewitt, R.J., Lucht, W.,
Rockström, J., Allerberger, F., McCaffrey, M., Doe, S.S.P., Lenferna, A., Morán,
N., van Vuuren, D.P. and Schellnhuber, H.J. 2020. Social tipping dynamics for stabilizing Earth's climate by 2050. *Proceedings of the National Academy of Sciences.*
117(5), pp. 2354–2365.

Rainforest Action Network. 2021. Banking on climate chaos. Rainforest Action Network
[Online]. Available from: https://www.ran.org/bankingonclimatechaos2021.

Robins, N., Dikau, S. and Volz, U. 2021. *Net-Zero Central Banking: A New Phase in
Greening the Financial System.* Grantham Research Institute on Climate Change and
the Environment, London School of Economics.

Ryan-Collins, J. 2019. *Beyond Voluntary Disclosure: Why a 'Market-Shaping' Approach
to Financial Regulation Is Needed to Meet the Challenge of Climate Change* [Online].
SUERF. Available from: https://www.suerf.org/policynotes/4805/beyond-voluntary
-disclosure-why-a-market-shaping-approach-to-financial-regulation-is-needed-to-meet-
the-challenge-of-climate-change.

Saltelli, A., Bammer, G., Bruno, I., Charters, E., Di Fiore, M., Didier, E., Nelson
Espeland, W., Kay, J., Lo Piano, S., Mayo, D., Pielke Jr, R., Portaluri, T., Porter,
T.M., Puy, A., Rafols, I., Ravetz, J.R., Reinert, E., Sarewitz, D., Stark, P.B., Stirling,
A., van der Sluijs, J. and Vineis, P. 2020. Five ways to ensure that models serve
society: A manifesto. *Nature.* **582**(7813), pp. 482–484.

Svartzman, R., Bolton, P., Després, M., Pereira Da Silva, L.A. and Samama, F. 2020.
Central banks, financial stability and policy coordination in the age of climate
uncertainty: A three-layered analytical and operational framework. *Climate Policy.*
21, pp. 1–18.

Taleb, N., Read, R., Douady, R., Norman, J. and Bar-Yam, Y. 2014. The precautionary principle (with application to the genetic modification of organisms) [Online].
Available from: https://arxiv.org/pdf/1410.5787.pdf.

TCFD 2017. *Final Report – Recommendations of the Task Force on Climate-Related
Financial Disclosures* [Online]. Available from: https://assets.bbhub.io/company/
sites/60/2020/10/FINAL-2017-TCFD-Report-11052018.pdf.

Thomä, J. and Chenet, H. 2017. Transition risks and market failure: A theoretical
discourse on why financial models and economic agents may misprice risk related

to the transition to a low-carbon economy. *Journal of Sustainable Finance & Investment.* **7**(1), pp. 82–98.

Van Lerven, F. and Ryan-Collins, J. 2018. *Adjusting Banks' Capital Requirements in Line with Sustainable Finance Objectives.* London: New Economics Foundation.

van 't Klooster, J. and Fontan, C. 2020. The myth of market neutrality: A comparative study of the European Central Bank's and the Swiss National Bank's corporate security purchases. *New Political Economy.* **25**(6), pp. 865–879.

Webb, I., Baumslag, D. and Read, R. 2017. *How Should Regulators Deal with Uncertainty? Insights from the Precautionary Principle* [Online]. Available from: https://bankunderground.co.uk/2017/01/27/how-should-regulators-deal-with-uncertainty-insights-from-the-precautionary-principle.

Weitzman, M.L. 2009. On modeling and interpreting the economics of catastrophic climate change. *Review of Economics and Statistics.* **91**(1), pp. 1–19.

Weitzman, M.L. 2012. GHG targets as insurance against catastrophic climate damages. *Journal of Public Economic Theory.* **14**(2), pp. 221–244.

Westley, F., Olsson, P., Folke, C., Homer-Dixon, T., Vredenburg, H., Loorbach, D., Thompson, J., Nilsson, M., Lambin, E., Sendzimir, J., Banerjee, B., Galaz, V. and van der Leeuw, S. 2011. Tipping toward sustainability: Emerging pathways of transformation. *AMBIO.* **40**(7), pp. 762–780.

WHO. 2004. *The Precautionary Principle: Protecting Public Health, the Environment and the Future of Our Children* [Online]. Available from: http://citeseerx.ist.psu.edu/viewdoc/download?doi=10.1.1.177.1936&rep=rep1&type=pdf.

9.   Money and the environment

Eric Kemp-Benedict

1.   INTRODUCTION

The two halves of this essay's title – "money" and "the environment" – share a feature in common: most people think they know what the words mean, yet they are notoriously difficult to pin down. Following the post-Keynesian tradition as presented by Lavoie (2014, chap. 4), money herein will be treated as a social relation. More narrowly, it will be viewed as credit money, which "requires a property-based society where pledges based on legal property – collateral – permit the expansion of loan contracts" (Lavoie 2014, 188). In this view, money arises endogenously from the extension of credit. Credit, in turn, is crucial for capitalist economies, in which private actors pursuing diverse activities must spend money before they can earn it. From among the many theories of endogenous credit money, particular attention will be paid to the theory of the monetary circuit as presented by Graziani (2003) and his followers.

Regarding "the environment," those who study it tend not to use the term except as a convenient catch-all designation. Instead, the operative concept is the "ecosystem," which the *Dictionary of Ecology* defines as "a discrete unit that consists of living and non-living parts, interacting to form a stable system" (Allaby 2015a). Like economies (Jespersen 2009, 138), ecosystems are open systems that exchange energy and materials with their surroundings. Taking a holistic view, "the environment," although it must remain perpetually in quotation marks, can be seen as the vast and interconnected web of ecosystems throughout the world. But the ecosystem is the proper object of analysis.

With these concepts as a starting point, the title to this essay might perhaps be reframed as "points of contact between the monetary circuit and ecosystems."

Economics and ecology are brought together under the broad heading of "ecological economics." Those who identify as ecological economists are, for the most part, not interested in money per se. Rather, they are driven by pressing problems in ecological sustainability. A fundamental, even defining, research agenda for the field is to identify possible structures for economic activity that are consistent with robust ecological functioning (Røpke 2004).

In the pursuit of such structures, the relationship between monetary and material flows has been a central concern, with Soddy (1934), Georgescu-Roegen (1971), and Odum (1973) often credited as pioneers.

A recurrent question, from Jevons (1865) to today (Alcott 2008), is the relationship between the growth in economic output and material and energy flows. The global economy as a whole is already placing unsustainable pressures on ecosystems (Rockström et al. 2009; Steffen et al. 2015), raising the question of how to constrain and control material and energy flows so as to remain well within the provisioning and regulating capacity of ecosystems while meeting human needs (Raworth 2013). As there is no historical evidence of persistent absolute decoupling of energy and material flows from economic output (Ayres and Warr 2010), many ecological economists use GDP growth as a proxy for growth in material and energy flows.

An increasing number of ecological economists align themselves at least in part with notions of endogenous credit money by identifying money as the counterpart to credit (Ament 2020; Cobb 2016; Farley et al. 2013; Rezai and Stagl 2016, 183–4). This leads to a focus on the issuance of credit, rather than of money, as the variable of interest (Fontana and Sawyer 2016a). Given the goal of this essay, such developments seem promising, but they have not yet borne much fruit. For some ecological economists, the supply of credit can be curtailed by introducing interest-free local currency – money as pure exchange – to meet day-to-day demands for liquidity (Douthwaite 2012; Michel and Hudon 2015). However, Cahen-Fourot and Lavoie (2016) have shown that zero interest is not necessary for a steady-state economy; the rate of growth is controlled by other factors. For ecological economists, full (or at least high) reserve banking (FRB) can serve to restrain bank lending (Lawn 2010; Farley et al. 2013). However, Fontana and Sawyer (2016b) argue that, as with interest rates, other factors drive economic growth and reserve requirements will be circumvented in order to achieve them.

The contact between theorists of the monetary circuit and ecological economists has thus been largely negative, with ecological economists incorporating theories of money and banking that post-Keynesian monetary theorists reject. As a positive contribution, post-Keynesian theorists have offered thoughtful proposals for ecological economists to consider, in particular Fontana and Sawyer (2016a) and Cahen-Fourot and Lavoie (2016). These contributions are useful and move in the direction of building an analytical toolkit to better understand how economic activity can be made compatible with robust ecosystem functioning. However, in this author's view, at least, the connection to ecosystems is as yet too thin to address the myriad questions raised by ecological economists.

This essay offers reflections on a research agenda addressing points of contact between the monetary circuit and ecosystems. It starts by showing where those interactions occur, with the main message being that they are pervasive and unavoidable. Two connections stand out: the incorporation of raw materials into the economy and the expulsion of waste materials and heat from the economy. Both are important to the sustainability debate, but this essay focuses on the first, paying particular attention to the operation of commodity futures markets.

2.   POINTS OF CONTACT BETWEEN THE MONETARY CIRCUIT AND ECOSYSTEMS

An essential fact about economies is that, regardless of whether they ever achieve an equilibrium in terms of macroeconomic variables, they are certainly far from *thermodynamic* equilibrium. That is true of all living things, as well as all systems in which living things interact – including ecosystems and economies. Such systems need a regular inflow of energy and materials to maintain a net production of entropy (Glucina and Mayumi 2010; Ruth 2005). Within those systems there may be a local decrease in entropy, but entropy-reducing processes require energy and are more than offset by dissipative (entropy-generating) processes. For example, plants use sunlight – a source of energy – to create sugars out of water and carbon dioxide. Those sugars provide chemical energy for the growth of the plant. Yet, overall, there must, of necessity, be a net generation of entropy. To remain alive, the plant requires a regular, if intermittent, flow of energy in the form of sunlight.

Figure 9.1 shows the monetary circuit with no government sector adapted from Fontana and Sawyer (2016a). The thin arrows indicate payments, and hence flows of money. In the circuit, initial finance is provided to firms in advance of production. Firms use the money to buy inputs and pay workers, who then either spend their income on goods and services, thereby providing income to firms, or save it. Workers' savings take the form of deposits, which are the counterpart to loans, or purchases of securities on financial markets, which provide final finance to firms, allowing firms to pay down the principal on their bank loans.

In Figure 9.1, the monetary circuit is superimposed on a sketch of biophysical flows and annotated by the four types of ecosystem services identified in the Millennium Ecosystem Assessment (MA 2005): *provisioning*; *regulating*; *cultural*; and *supporting*. Ecosystem services are defined in the *Dictionary of Ecology* as the "material and psychological benefits that humans derive from the functioning of natural ecosystems" (Allaby 2015b).[1]

As shown in Figure 9.1, energy and materials from natural sources – the provisioning services of ecosystems – are drawn into production, where they provide the raw materials for goods and the energy for both goods and services. They are passed to households as energy and materials embodied in goods and

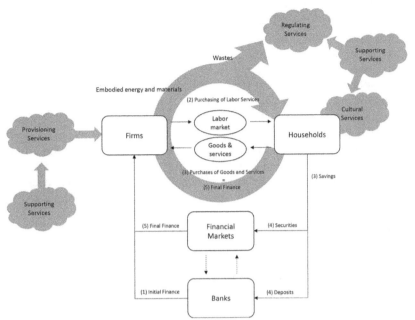

Source: Author's elaboration based on Fontana and Sawyer (2016a).

Figure 9.1   *The monetary circuit for a closed economy with no government sector superimposed on biophysical flows and annotated by ecosystem services*

services – flowing in the opposite direction to payments[2] – and embodied energy and materials are then returned to the firms in the form of human labor (e.g., see Costanza 1980, 1220; Costanza and Herendeen 1984, 151–6). The laws of thermodynamics guarantee a flow of waste material and heat, which impact upon ecosystems, which then absorb and buffer waste flows through regulating services. Households also derive benefits from the cultural services of ecosystems, such as religious or spiritual activities, recreational activities, and aesthetic experiences. The ecosystems themselves are maintained through supporting services, which indirectly benefit humans by maintaining the other services. While supporting services are an afterthought for humans, they are essential, often dominate provisioning services, and are frequently unobserved and underappreciated.

An example can help clarify the roles of different ecosystem services. Fossil carbon contains carbon atoms from carbon dioxide fixed by early plants through photosynthesis hundreds of millions of years ago.[3] Heat from radio-active elements in the Earth's interior drives tectonic activity, while sunlight drives both the water cycle and the winds, weathering the rocks on the Earth's surface. Together, those processes buried the remains of the dead plants deep underground, where intense pressure and heat transformed the carbohydrates built by the plants into hydrocarbons, which have a high energy density per unit mass.

Fossil fuel extraction is thus made possible by ecosystem *provisioning services* playing out on geological time scales. Humans have created legal systems that assign ownership of fossil reserves to people or institutions, who earn rents from extraction. Extractors sell futures contracts for crude oil and other fossil raw materials, which are bought by firms and investors. From those futures contracts that end in delivery, or from purchases on the spot market, firms process the raw material to produce refined fuels and chemical feedstocks, which are purchased by other firms for their own production, in a production chain that eventually reaches final consumers.

At each link in the chain, the use of processed fossil materials produces waste products and heat, among them carbon dioxide. The carbon dioxide is taken up mainly by the oceans, but also by forests and wetlands, a key example of a *regulating service*. Ecosystems have a finite absorptive capacity for carbon dioxide, which is evident even in the vast oceans. Humans enjoy coral reefs – a *cultural service* – but they are being irreversibly harmed by the rise in ocean temperature and acidity arising from excess carbon dioxide. Meanwhile, by cutting down forest and draining wetlands, humanity is undermining the *supporting services* it relies on to buffer rising carbon dioxide emissions.

This short discussion suggests that ecosystems and the energy and materials they provide touch the monetary circuit at every stage, mainly through regulating services and embodied provisioning services. These act to the detriment of supporting services and often to the detriment of cultural services. Among the most salient issues today are our reliance on non-renewable sources of energy and materials for economic activity and, of even more immediate concern, the extreme strains placed on regulating ecosystem services. Transitioning to renewable natural resources, in particular agricultural products and timber, will place new demands on ecosystem services.

The initial point of contact is in provisioning services – the production of natural resource commodities. The rest of this essay focuses on the financial transactions that facilitate commodity production, processing, and use.

3.   COMMODITIES, COMMODITY MARKETS, AND FUTURES

Ecosystem services, despite the name, include flows of both goods and services. Those flows are valued by humans, suggesting that they might be analogous to the income from a financial asset. The corresponding asset is often termed "natural capital." Schumacher (1973) introduced the term as a metaphor, to try to convince business-oriented stakeholders and policymakers that the environment (or, in current terms, "ecosystem function") was worth preserving. Just as one should not spend down principal, humanity should preserve the natural capital that provides it with valued benefits.

Subsequently, the metaphor took on a life of its own, with expanding efforts to quantify the value of ecosystem services and the underlying natural capital (Pearce, Markandya, and Barbier 1989; Costanza et al. 1997; 2014). The policy goal is to maintain the stock of natural capital at a steady level; a "constant capital" bequest to the future (Pearce, Markandya, and Barbier 1989, 48). However, monetary valuation of flows suggests erroneously that they are appropriable. That is true of very few ecosystem services (Kemp-Benedict and Kartha 2019), and not true at all of the critical supporting services that ensure ecosystem function. A key implication within a credit money economy is that natural capital as defined by environmental and ecological economists cannot serve as collateral against loans.[4]

Investopedia has a completely different definition of natural capital, as "the inventory of natural resources held by companies, such as water, gold, natural gas, silver, or oil," noting that any inventory must be certified to be placed on futures markets (Mitchell 2021). This definition is far from ecological economists' concepts of ecosystem services and ecosystem function, but is more consistent with the behavioral assumptions underpinning the monetary circuit. Most importantly, inventory, mineral and land leases, or futures contracts can act as collateral on loans.

Incorporating natural resources into post-Keynesian macroeconomic models, particularly of the stock-flow consistent variety (Godley and Lavoie 2007), requires the introduction of some new economic actors. This essay distinguishes four types for firms, which are shown in Figure 9.2: producers, processors, users, and those in the rest of the economy. Producers harvest or extract the resource (for example, crude oil) and sell it as a commodity[5] to processors, a catch-all category that includes warehousing and storage. Processors sell it on to firms that use the (cleaned and graded) raw material to make goods. Those are often intermediate goods, such as the "platform chemicals," like ethylene, that are the building blocks of more complex chemicals (Smiley and Jackson 2002), but may be final products, such as canned tomato sauce. The users of raw materials then sell their products to downstream firms, either as an intermediate input to manufacturing and services industries or to wholesalers and retailers.

An additional class of actor in Figure 9.2 is the natural resource owners. They may also be producers, for example an oil company that owns the mineral resources it is extracting, or a farmer that owns her own land. Producers thus either earn implicit resource rents or explicitly make rental payments to the

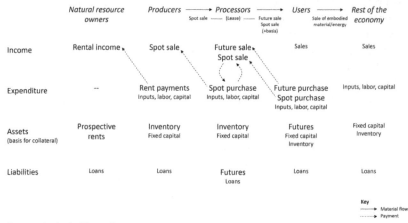

Source: Author's illustration.

*Figure 9.2   Natural resources in the economy: larger font emphasizes the
particular features of raw and processed materials*

owner of the resource. Producers may also have storage facilities of their own,
but for many sectors, grading, cleaning, storage, and distribution are carried
out by third parties, the processors.

    Processors buy from producers at the spot price prevailing at the time of sale
(for example, when farmers deliver their harvest to a grain elevator). The processor then typically immediately sells the shipment into the futures market.
The counterparties to those futures contracts are, in the first instance, users of
the commodity who wish to ensure supply. However, and crucially, the users
have bought a promise of delivery of an amount of a particular commodity of
a particular grade, and not the actual physical commodity sitting in the processors' elevators, warehouses, tanks, trucks, or railway cars (the different grades,
locations, and so on affect the price and are referred to as the "basis"). Futures
contracts are therefore fungible, and can be rolled over, so they can be traded
by financial actors who see an opportunity for arbitrage but would be severely
inconvenienced by physical delivery of the commodity. For that reason, the
volume of open positions for a given commodity normally far exceeds physical
production of the commodity.[6] The financial actors are referred to as "speculators," and they play an essential role in commodity markets.

4.   HEDGERS, SPECULATORS, AND THE IMPLICIT MARKET IN COMMODITY LOANS

In the language of commodity markets, "hedging" is trade in commodities and derivatives as part of the normal course of business, while "speculation" is trade in commodity derivatives to benefit from price differentials. A single actor (in particular, large firms) may engage in both hedging and speculation (Irwin et al. 2009, 380). Speculation, when it does not dominate, plays an essential role in commodity markets by rapidly erasing arbitrage opportunities and thus helping to establish prices that take into account supply and demand conditions (Working 1948).[7]

Figure 9.2 is presented from a hedging perspective. That is intentional. As noted in the review by Working (1962, 432), the available evidence at the time showed that "futures markets depend for their existence primarily on hedging." In the 2000s, rapidly expanding speculative market activity threw that conclusion into doubt. The new actors were financial intermediaries offering swaps to their clients using over-the-counter products based on commodity indexes (Sanders, Irwin, and Merrin 2010). The impact of index traders could not be readily ascertained using the data collected by the US Commodity Futures Trading Commission (CFTC). Beginning in 2006, the CFTC has produced statistics of index trading activity. On the basis of that data, the consensus is that Working's conclusion still stands. The volume of speculative activity is well within historical bounds relative to the volume of hedging (Irwin et al. 2009; Sanders, Irwin, and Merrin 2010; Mixon, Onur, and Riggs 2018).

An important implication of Working's conclusion for post-Keynesian theory is that behavioral assumptions for commodity market actors can, to a first approximation, be based on hedging behavior. Changes in speculative positions can propagate through the financial system, flowing from commodity markets to the broader economy, but the reflux back into the commodity markets themselves is a second-order phenomenon.

The key step in the commodity production chain that connects it to financial markets is processors' simultaneous purchase on the spot market accompanied by a sale into the futures market. These actions are conventionally viewed as a risk management strategy (hence "hedging"), a notion that underlies the "portfolio" theory of hedging (Stein 1961). In that view, the fundamental position for processors is the spot market purchase, a "long" position, since processors will profit if the price rises. Processors then offset the risk arising from potentially adverse price changes by taking short positions in futures markets.

The portfolio theory argument appears plausible on its face, and references to risk management pervade the literature on commodities. However, Williams (1986, 111) points out that processors' need to control stocks of the commodity as part of doing business is sufficient motivation to enter into futures contracts. The idea that processors want to hold stocks they do not own originated with Kaldor (1939) in his theory of the "convenience yield," an implicit payment by processors for holding stocks. Indeed, for active participants in commodity markets, a fully hedged position is risk-free (Gray 1984; Williams 1986, 94); as a futures contract approaches maturity, the spot–futures spread may vary widely, but at maturity they must coincide, because a futures contract at maturity is a contract for spot delivery. At any time between the first issuance and maturity, the processor may buy and sell on either the spot or futures market. The implication is that the risk-neutral position – and therefore the fundamental position for processors – is to be fully hedged.

Building on this idea, Williams (1986) notes that when actors nearly always take simultaneous positions in two markets, they are not truly interested in either market by itself. Instead, they are taking positions within an implicit market. In the case of commodity spot and futures markets, processors are expressing a desire for the loan of commodities owned by others. Elaborating on this idea, he writes (Williams 1986, 111):

> The theory for holding inventory presented in this chapter consciously parallels the analysis of the reasons firms hold money at the cost of forgone interest. The reasons for holding money not only resemble the reasons firms hold inventories but also illuminate the existence of spreads below full carrying charges, interest, after all, being a use charge for money expressed in percentage terms. Perhaps most significant, conventional models of the demand for money demonstrate that even risk-neutral firms desire to hold cash.

On a conceptual level, Williams thus directly connects the normal operation of commodity markets to the market for loans, a connection that could be explored further by post-Keynesian monetary theorists. For stock-flow consistent models (Godley and Lavoie 2007), Williams' thesis provides a behavioral rule: the neutral position for processors is to be fully hedged, with short and long positions exactly balanced. Any departure from that position amounts to speculative activity by processors.

5.   CONTANGO AND BACKWARDATION

Before summing up, it is worth spending some time on terms and topics that appear in the literature on commodity markets. In an efficient commodity market, in which speculators are active but not dominant, the future price should equal the expected spot price plus the cost of storage (including interest charges). In this case, the price of a futures contract exceeds the expected spot price, a condition called "contango" (or a "normal market"). However, that is not always true, and sometimes the futures price lies below the expected spot price, a condition called "backwardation" (or an "inverted market").

Keynes made an ultimately unproductive contribution to the literature with his theory of "normal backwardation," in which he claimed that futures prices for agricultural commodities are biased downward, so that taking the long side in futures contracts would invariably yield profits. However, Gray and Rutledge (1971, 63) showed that his theory did not stand up to empirical scrutiny. Kaldor's (1939) concept of the convenience yield was more durable. Because there is a value to holding stocks, when stocks are low, the value of holding on to stocks rises, and with it the spot price. This gives rise to a characteristic curve (see Figure 9.3), in which the difference between the future price and the spot price is: (a) negative when stocks are low, thereby exhibiting backwardation; (b) approximately constant and positive when stocks are in a normal range, exhibiting contango; and (c) positive and rising at very high storage levels as storage facilities become full. This was termed the "storage supply curve" by Working (1949). In an influential paper, Fama and French (1987) found empirical evidence for the storage theory.

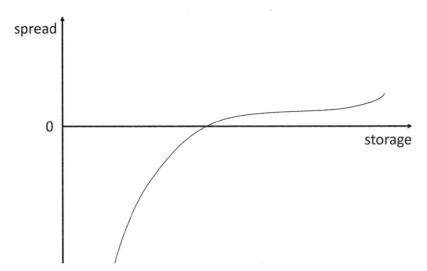

Source: Author's illustration.

Figure 9.3   *The supply-of-storage curve: the future–spot spread plotted against aggregate storage*

In a subsequent development, Wright and Williams (1989) argued, using both theory and data, that the storage supply curve is purely an aggregate phenomenon. Individual processors and production units pay only storage costs. The storage supply curve emerges because it is costly to transport, elevate (in a grain elevator), and process commodities. In the face of uncertainty or stochastic variability at the level of the individual unit, rational expectations give rise in the aggregate to the storage supply curve. The implication is that the curve in Figure 9.3 is not stable, although its qualitative features are persistent. The price at any moment depends on the distribution of commodities of a given type at different processing stages or locations. Based on their analysis, Wright and Williams (1989, 12) offer the term "total transformation cost minimization" as a replacement for Kaldor's "convenience yield," while noting its comparative inelegance. Their theory is a refinement of Working's theory of storage that systematically incorporates rational expectations. Partial support for the rational expectations storage model was provided by Deaton and Laroque (1992), although they failed to satisfactorily reproduce all the features of the commodity price time series they considered. Cafiero et al. (2011) refined and updated their analysis and showed that the storage model matches the historical data well.

6.   REFLECTIONS ON A RESEARCH PROGRAM

Post-Keynesian theory, as represented in Lavoie's (2014) textbook, has much to bring to analysis and debates within ecological economics. Indeed, potential connections have long been recognized (Gowdy 1991; Holt, Pressman, and Spash 2009; Kronenberg 2010). There is currently active work in the area of "ecological macroeconomics" (Rezai and Stagl 2016) and, within that broad classification, contributions specifically on monetary theory (Cahen-Fourot and Lavoie 2016; Fontana and Sawyer 2016a). Without taking anything away from any prior work, this essay has presented a personal view on the questions a research program on links between ecosystems and the monetary circuit might address.

The primary goal of the proposed program is to answer a central question within ecological economics: what institutions and relationships are compatible with robust ecosystem function, and hence with ecological sustainability? A sustainable *capitalist* economy is a counterfactual, as none has ever been observed. The analytical task is thus not only to understand how things are but also to say how they could be. One possible leverage point, not explored in this essay, is the structure of ownership and availability of collateral for the different economic actors in Figure 9.2, including the receipt of natural resource rents. At the same time, a sustainability analysis must take account of the way economies work today, if only to anticipate challenges and opportunities in the transition from current, unsustainable, practices to sustainable ones.

Regardless of how an economy and its supporting institutions is structured, it necessarily relies on pervasive and predictable interactions with ecosystems. On purely physical grounds, any economic activity requires a regular flow of energy and materials provided by ecosystems, and is accompanied by the generation of waste materials and heat, which are processed and buffered by ecosystems. As a consequence, the finite capacity of the Earth's ecosystems constrains the material and energy footprint of global economic activity. That is a non-negotiable fact about the world, for which there truly is no alternative. Either we solve the problem of transitioning to sustainable modes of living, producing, consuming, and working, or a solution will be imposed upon us out of physical necessity.

There are multiple potential points of entry for post-Keynesian and related analysis, as suggested by Figure 9.1. For example, tracking embodied energy and materials is well suited to neo-Ricardian analysis (Kemp-Benedict 2014), while neo-Kaleckian models have been used to explore climate mitigation (Rezai, Taylor, and Mechler 2013), depletion of finite resources (Fontana and Sawyer 2016a), and "no-growth capitalism" (Cahen-Fourot and Lavoie 2016, 167). The most immediate impacts of economic activity on ecosystems arise from extraction and waste production. This essay focused on the first of these: the process by which raw materials enter the monetary circuit through commodity markets.

This essay offers some reflections for post-Keynesian theory. The first is that insights can be gained from the tradition in commodity market theory pioneered by Kaldor (1939) and Working (1948; 1949), and further developed by Gray and Rutledge (1971) and Williams (1986), among others. The papers by Irwin et al. (2009) and Sanders et al. (2010) are in this tradition. A competing neoclassical theory builds off of the portfolio theory of commodity markets. Higinbotham (1976) argued that spreads are frequently below carrying cost because if stocks are ever zero due to a general shortage, the price can rise as high as the market will bear, while futures prices will reflect a return to normal conditions. On average, spreads will be below carrying cost. However, as Williams (1986, 33–4) points out, total stocks have *never* been zero (a "general stock-out" has not been observed), so Higinbotham's theory cannot be sustained. Nevertheless, Pirrong (2012) created a fully neoclassical model of commodity prices using Higinbotham's idea. Pirrong argues that the convenience yield cannot be derived from an optimizing representative agent model, while Higinbotham's model is susceptible to that sort of analysis. Pirrong showed that an optimizing representative agent model can be adapted to generate some of the standard empirical results, but not all of them. However, regardless of whether requiring a rational agent model is a sensible approach economic analysis, Pirrong was incorrect. The convenience yield *has* been derived from a rational expectations model by Wright and Williams (1989), albeit without assuming that market actors know the future. There is some irony here; commodity markets act as marginalist theory claims all markets to act, but the unrealistic superstructure erected by neoclassical theory renders it unsuitable for analyzing commodities.

Second, despite the seeming complexity of commodity markets – and the institutions surrounding them are indeed complex and the terminology obscure – the underlying behavior is straightforward. Even with the recent rapid expansion of futures markets and the rise of commodity index trading, commodity markets continue to be dominated by hedging rather than speculation (Mixon, Onur, and Riggs 2018). The implication is that prices – both spot and future – are driven by conditions of supply and demand for the commodity itself and not for financial derivatives. Moreover, there is no need to invoke different tolerance for risk among market actors to understand the operation of futures markets. The standard practice of taking balanced positions simultaneously in spot and futures markets is risk-free (Gray 1984). As argued by Williams (1986), commodity processors are effectively taking positions in an implicit market in loans of commodities.

Williams (1986, chap. 4) takes some pains to draw a connection between the demand for loans of commodities and the demand for money. It is unclear how readily a connection can be drawn between the theory of commodity markets and the theory of credit money. The most direct link is through collateral, for example via the assets listed in Figure 9.2. However, one parallel is that processors and users must gain access to raw and processed materials prior to production, either by storing them or by securing delivery through a futures contract. In our fossil resource-based economies, resource production has been accommodationist, expanding in response to observed and anticipated demand. In a renewables-based economy, while flows of materials and energy can in principle be sustained indefinitely, the amount available over any given period is finite. Accommodation will thus eventually be impossible and rationing will ensue. It is an open question what institutions might be best suited to mediate between competing claims to finite resource flows. Elinor Ostrom's (2015) work on governing the commons may provide some insights.

7.   CONCLUSION

This essay has presented a personal view on the links between the environment and money – or, more precisely, points of contact between the monetary circuit and ecosystems. Links are not hard to find, and are indeed pervasive. The greatest environmental impact occurs at the points of extraction of raw materials and of emission of wastes. Both processes are thermodynamically necessary and inescapable. A "circular economy," if one is ever achieved, will only be possible by diverting unidirectional, and non-circular, energy flows, whether directly from sunlight or indirectly from wind, water, and biomass.

When natural resources enter the economy, they do so through commodity markets. This essay has sought to make the case that commodity markets have features of interest to post-Keynesian monetary theorists. One of the most enduring concepts in the theory of commodity markets is Kaldor's "convenience yield," which inspired a considerable subsequent literature. Research within that tradition, in particular as inspired by Working (1948; 1949), has shown that commodity markets are dominated by non-financial motivations (hedging) rather than financial ones (speculation), a conclusion that continues to hold despite the recent growth in commodity index trading. That means that disturbances tend to propagate from conditions of demand and supply for commodities to financial markets, rather than the reverse.

A further insight is an explanation for the near-universal phenomenon of commodity processors simultaneously buying on the spot market and selling on the futures market. Williams (1986) argued that this is a sign that processors are taking a position in an implicit market for loans of commodities, observing that they need the loan of commodities to carry out their business, analogous to the demand for loans of money.

The prospects for a sustainable future depend on commodities. From the winding down of fossil fuel extraction (Erickson, Lazarus, and Piggot 2018) to the ramping up of the "bio-economy" (German Presidency of the Council of the European Union 2007), links between commodity markets, financial markets, and the rest of the economy will rise in importance. There is much that post-Keynesian monetary theory can bring to the discussion.

NOTES

1. This is clearly anthropocentric (Farber, Costanza, and Wilson 2002, 376). Whether or not such an instrumental position is ethically justified, it is a plausible starting assumption regarding economic behavior.
2. The ubiquity of counter-flows of money against flows of energy and materials is a general feature of economies, as noted by Odum (1973; 2007). Counter-flows even appear in the seemingly immaterial world of computer-mediated deposits and purchases of securities, where transactions are carried out on very material computers, which consume energy and generate heat in the process of executing programs.
3. Photosynthesis is the only known way to produce complex carbon compounds at ambient temperature and pressure. Whether in fossil or contemporary form, there are no substitutes for plants and other primary producers (Ayres 2007).
4. For the most part, "green finance" seeks competitive returns from a portfolio representing environmentally benign or beneficial activities. "Greenness" is ensured through criteria for inclusion in the portfolio, rather than through valuing the ecosystem services or natural capital maintained by the assets underlying

the portfolio. In some cases, such as carbon markets or payments for ecosystem services, ecosystem services valuation does provide the underlying value of financial assets, but only because a market has been created to determine a price (Kemp-Benedict and Kartha 2019).

5. The term "commodity" is often used loosely by economists to refer to any good. However, to an investor, a commodity is a basic good, nearly always used in the production of other goods, that is interchangeable with any other good of the same type. This means that commodities cannot be distinguished between different producers, ruling out non-price competitive factors. Basic goods undergo multiple processing steps or types, and each step or type represents a separate commodity. For example, rice may be unhulled, hulled, or polished, while West Texas Intermediate crude oil is sweet (low sulfur) and light (mostly consisting of low-molecular-weight constituents).

6. Net open positions are canceled on a regular schedule (e.g., weekly or daily) through a clearinghouse.

7. The operation of commodity markets closely resembles the neoclassical ideal of an efficient market. However, the causality in the history of economic thought almost certainly goes from empirical study of commodity markets to neoclassical theory, and not the other way around. Pasinetti (1981, 5–11) makes that case in his exegesis of classical and marginalist writings, arguing that the marginalists focused on an aspect of economic production that classicals, and Ricardo in particular, thought was relatively unimportant. Inappropriate extrapolation from commodity markets to the whole economy is particularly evident in Debreu (1959, 29–32), in which he passes rapidly, if not glibly, from a graded commodity (No. 2 Red Winter Wheat) to manufactures and services, claiming that they can all be treated within the same framework. However, futures markets are rare (Williams 1986, 180). They only appear when the underlying market has flexible prices, rather than administered prices (Gray and Rutledge 1971, 85), and do not exist for many commodities.

REFERENCES

Alcott, Blake. 2008. "Historical Overview of the Jevons Paradox in the Literature." In *The Jevons Paradox and the Myth of Resource Efficiency Improvements*, edited by John M. Polimeni, Kozo Mayumi, Mario Giampietro, and Blake Alcott, 7–78. Earthscan.

Allaby, Michael. 2015a. "Ecosystem." In *A Dictionary of Ecology*. Oxford University Press. http://www.oxfordreference.com/view/10.1093/acref/9780191793158.001.0001/acref-9780191793158-e-1785.

Allaby, Michael. 2015b. "Ecosystem Services." In *A Dictionary of Ecology*. Oxford University Press. http://www.oxfordreference.com/view/10.1093/acref/9780191793158.001.0001/acref-9780191793158-e-6377.

Ament, Joe. 2020. "An Ecological Monetary Theory." *Ecological Economics* 171 (May): 106421. https://doi.org/10.1016/j.ecolecon.2019.106421.

Ayres, Robert U. 2007. "On the Practical Limits to Substitution." *Ecological Economics* 61 (1): 115–28. https://doi.org/10.1016/j.ecolecon.2006.02.011.

Ayres, Robert U., and Benjamin Warr. 2010. *The Economic Growth Engine: How Energy and Work Drive Material Prosperity*. Edward Elgar Publishing.

Cafiero, Carlo, Eugenio S. A. Bobenrieth H., Juan R. A. Bobenrieth H., and Brian D. Wright. 2011. "The Empirical Relevance of the Competitive Storage Model." *Journal of Econometrics* 162 (1): 44–54. https://doi.org/10.1016/j.jeconom.2009.10.008.

Cahen-Fourot, Louison, and Marc Lavoie. 2016. "Ecological Monetary Economics: A Post-Keynesian Critique." *Ecological Economics* 126 (Supplement C): 163–8. https://doi.org/10.1016/j.ecolecon.2016.03.007.

Cobb, John B., Jr. 2016. "Making Money." In *Beyond Uneconomic Growth: Economics, Equity and the Ecological Predicament*, edited by Joshua Farley and Deepak Malghan, 233–43. Advances in Ecological Economics. Edward Elgar Publishing.

Costanza, Robert. 1980. "Embodied Energy and Economic Valuation." *Science* 210 (4475): 1219–24. https://doi.org/10.1126/science.210.4475.1219.

Costanza, Robert, and Robert A. Herendeen. 1984. "Embodied Energy and Economic Value in the United States Economy: 1963, 1967 and 1972." *Resources and Energy* 6 (2): 129–63. https://doi.org/10.1016/0165-0572(84)90014-8.

Costanza, Robert, Ralph d'Arge, Rudolf de Groot, Stephen Farber, Monica Grasso, Bruce Hannon, Karin Limburg et al. 1997. "The Value of the World's Ecosystem Services and Natural Capital." *Nature* 387 (6630): 253–60. https://doi.org/10.1038/387253a0.

Costanza, Robert, Rudolf de Groot, Paul Sutton, Sander van der Ploeg, Sharolyn J. Anderson, Ida Kubiszewski, Stephen Farber, and R. Kerry Turner. 2014. "Changes in the Global Value of Ecosystem Services." *Global Environmental Change* 26 (Supplement C): 152–8. https://doi.org/10.1016/j.gloenvcha.2014.04.002.

Deaton, Angus, and Guy Laroque. 1992. "On the Behaviour of Commodity Prices." *The Review of Economic Studies* 59 (1): 1–23. https://doi.org/10.2307/2297923.

Debreu, Gerard. 1959. *Theory of Value: An Axiomatic Analysis of Economic Equilibrium*. Cowles Foundation for Research in Economics at Yale University. Monograph 17. Yale University Press.

Douthwaite, Richard. 2012. "Degrowth and the Supply of Money in an Energy-Scarce World." *Ecological Economics* 84 (December): 187–93. https://doi.org/10.1016/j.ecolecon.2011.03.020.

Erickson, Peter, Michael Lazarus, and Georgia Piggot. 2018. "Limiting Fossil Fuel Production as the Next Big Step in Climate Policy." *Nature Climate Change* 8 (12): 1037–43. https://doi.org/10.1038/s41558-018-0337-0.

Fama, Eugene F., and Kenneth R. French. 1987. "Commodity Futures Prices: Some Evidence on Forecast Power, Premiums, and the Theory of Storage." *The Journal of Business* 60 (1): 55–73.

Farber, Stephen C., Robert Costanza, and Matthew A. Wilson. 2002. "Economic and Ecological Concepts for Valuing Ecosystem Services." *Ecological Economics* 41 (3): 375–92. https://doi.org/10.1016/S0921-8009(02)00088-5.

Farley, Joshua, Matthew Burke, Gary Flomenhoft, Brian Kelly, D. Forrest Murray, Stephen Posner, Matthew Putnam, Adam Scanlan, and Aaron Witham. 2013. "Monetary and Fiscal Policies for a Finite Planet." *Sustainability* 5 (6): 2802–26. https://doi.org/10.3390/su5062802.

Fontana, Giuseppe, and Malcolm Sawyer. 2016a. "Towards Post-Keynesian Ecological Macroeconomics." *Ecological Economics* 121 (January): 186–95. https://doi.org/10.1016/j.ecolecon.2015.03.017.

Fontana, Giuseppe, and Malcolm Sawyer. 2016b. "Full Reserve Banking: More 'Cranks' Than 'Brave Heretics.'" *Cambridge Journal of Economics* 40 (5): 1333–50. https://doi.org/10.1093/cje/bew016.

Georgescu-Roegen, Nicholas. 1971. *The Entropy Law and the Economic Process.* Harvard University Press.

German Presidency of the Council of the European Union. 2007. "The Cologne Paper: En Route to the Knowledge-Based Bio-Economy." www.europabio.org.

Glucina, Mark David, and Kozo Mayumi. 2010. "Connecting Thermodynamics and Economics." *Annals of the New York Academy of Sciences* 1185 (1): 11–29. https://doi.org/10.1111/j.1749-6632.2009.05166.x.

Godley, Wynne, and M. Lavoie. 2007. *Monetary Economics: An Integrated Approach to Credit, Money, Income, Production and Wealth.* Palgrave Macmillan.

Gowdy, John M. 1991. "Bioeconomics and Post Keynesian Economics: A Search for Common Ground." *Ecological Economics* 3 (1): 77–87. https://doi.org/10.1016/0921-8009(91)90049-K.

Gray, Roger W. 1984. "Commentary." *Review of Research in Futures Markets* 3 (11): 80–1.

Gray, Roger W., and David J. S. Rutledge. 1971. "The Economics of Commodity Futures Markets: A Survey." *Review of Marketing and Agricultural Economics* 39 (4): 57–108.

Graziani, Augusto. 2003. *The Monetary Theory of Production.* Federico Caffè Lectures. Cambridge University Press. https://doi.org/10.1017/CBO9780511493546.

Higinbotham, Harlow N. 1976. "The Demand for Hedging in the Grain Futures Markets." Ph.D., University of Chicago.

Holt, Richard P. F., Steven Pressman, and Clive L. Spash, eds. 2009. *Post Keynesian and Ecological Economics: Confronting Environmental Issues.* Edward Elgar Publishing.

Irwin, Scott H., Dwight R. Sanders, Robert P. Merrin et al. 2009. "Devil or Angel? The Role of Speculation in the Recent Commodity Price Boom (and Bust)." *Journal of Agricultural and Applied Economics* 41 (2): 377–91. http://ageconsearch.umn.edu/bitstream/53083/2/jaaeip3.pdf.

Jespersen, Jesper. 2009. *Macroeconomic Methodology: A Post-Keynesian Perspective.* Edward Elgar Publishing.

Jevons, William Stanley. 1865. *The Coal Question: An Inquiry Concerning the Progress of the Nation, and the Probable Exhaustion of Our Coal-Mines.* Macmillan and Co.

Kaldor, Nicholas. 1939. "Speculation and Economic Stability." *The Review of Economic Studies* 7 (1): 1–27. https://doi.org/10.2307/2967593.

Kemp-Benedict, Eric. 2014. "The Inverted Pyramid: A Neo-Ricardian View on the Economy–Environment Relationship." *Ecological Economics* 107 (November): 230–41. https://doi.org/10.1016/j.ecolecon.2014.08.012.

Kemp-Benedict, Eric, and Sivan Kartha. 2019. "Environmental Financialization: What Could Go Wrong?" *Real-World Economics Review* 87: 69–89.

Kronenberg, Tobias. 2010. "Finding Common Ground between Ecological Economics and Post-Keynesian Economics." *Ecological Economics* 69 (7): 1488–94. https://doi.org/10.1016/j.ecolecon.2010.03.002.

Lavoie, Marc. 2014. *Post-Keynesian Economics: New Foundations.* Edward Elgar Publishing.

Lawn, Philip. 2010. "Facilitating the Transition to a Steady-State Economy: Some Macroeconomic Fundamentals." *Ecological Economics* 69 (5): 931–6. https://doi.org/10.1016/j.ecolecon.2009.12.013.

Michel, Arnaud, and Marek Hudon. 2015. "Community Currencies and Sustainable Development: A Systematic Review." *Ecological Economics* 116 (August): 160–71. https://doi.org/10.1016/j.ecolecon.2015.04.023.

Millennium Ecosystem Assessment (MA), ed. 2005. *Ecosystems and Human Well-Being: Synthesis: A Report of the Millennium Ecosystem Assessment*. Island Press.

Mitchell, Cory. 2021. "Natural Capital." Investopedia. January 28. https://www.investopedia.com/terms/n/natural-capital.asp.

Mixon, Scott, Esen Onur, and Lynn Riggs. 2018. "Integrating Swaps and Futures: A New Direction for Commodity Research." *Journal of Commodity Markets* 10 (June): 3–21. https://doi.org/10.1016/j.jcomm.2017.06.001.

Odum, Howard T. 1973. "Energy, Ecology, and Economics." *Ambio* 2 (6): 220–7. http://www.jstor.org/stable/4312030.

Odum, Howard T. 2007. "Energy and Economics." In *Environment, Power, and Society for the Twenty-First Century: The Hierarchy of Energy*, 252–80. Columbia University Press.

Ostrom, Elinor. 2015. *Governing the Commons: The Evolution of Institutions for Collective Action*. Canto Classics. Cambridge University Press. https://doi.org/10.1017/CBO9781316423936.

Pasinetti, Luigi L. 1981. *Structural Change and Economic Growth: A Theoretical Essay on the Dynamics of the Wealth of Nations*. Cambridge University Press.

Pearce, D., Anil Markandya, and Edward Barbier. 1989. *Blueprint for a Green Economy*. Earthscan.

Pirrong, Craig. 2012. *Commodity Price Dynamics: A Structural Approach*. Cambridge University Press.

Raworth, Kate. 2013. "Defining a Safe and Just Space for Humanity." In *State of the World 2013: Is Sustainability Still Possible?*, edited by Worldwatch Institute, 28–38. Island Press. http://link.springer.com.ezproxy.library.tufts.edu/chapter/10.5822/978-1-61091-458-1_3.

Rezai, Armon, and Sigrid Stagl. 2016. "Ecological Macroeconomics: Introduction and Review." *Ecological Economics* 121 (January): 181–5. https://doi.org/10.1016/j.ecolecon.2015.12.003.

Rezai, Armon, Lance Taylor, and Reinhard Mechler. 2013. "Ecological Macroeconomics: An Application to Climate Change." *Ecological Economics* 85: 69–76. https://doi.org/10.1016/j.ecolecon.2012.10.008.

Rockström, Johan, Will Steffen, Kevin Noone, Asa Persson, F. Stuart Chapin III, Eric F. Lambin, Timothy M. Lenton et al. 2009. "Planetary Boundaries: Exploring the Safe Operating Space for Humanity." *Ecology and Society* 14 (2). http://www.ecologyandsociety.org/vol14/iss2/art32.

Røpke, Inge. 2004. "The Early History of Modern Ecological Economics." *Ecological Economics* 50 (3): 293–314. https://doi.org/10.1016/j.ecolecon.2004.02.012.

Ruth, Matthias. 2005. "Insights from Thermodynamics for the Analysis of Economic Processes." In *Non-Equilibrium Thermodynamics and the Production of Entropy*, edited by Axel Kleidon and Ralph D. Lorenz, 243–54. Understanding Complex Systems. Springer. http://link.springer.com.ezproxy.library.tufts.edu/chapter/10.1007/11672906_18.

Sanders, Dwight R., Scott H. Irwin, and Robert P. Merrin. 2010. "The Adequacy of Speculation in Agricultural Futures Markets: Too Much of a Good Thing?" *Applied Economic Perspectives and Policy* 32 (1): 77–94. https://doi.org/10.1093/aepp/ppp006.

Schumacher, E. F. 1973. *Small Is Beautiful: Economics as If People Mattered.* Harper & Row.

Smiley, Robert A., and Harold L. Jackson. 2002. *Chemistry and the Chemical Industry: A Practical Guide for Non-Chemists.* CRC Press.

Soddy, Frederick. 1934. *The Role of Money: What It Should Be, Contrasted with What It Has Become.* 2003 reprinting. Routledge.

Steffen, Will, Katherine Richardson, Johan Rockström, Sarah E. Cornell, Ingo Fetzer, Elena M. Bennett, R. Biggs et al. 2015. "Planetary Boundaries: Guiding Human Development on a Changing Planet." *Science* January: 1259855. https://doi.org/10.1126/science.1259855.

Stein, Jerome L. 1961. "The Simultaneous Determination of Spot and Futures Prices." *The American Economic Review* 51 (5): 1012–25.

Williams, Jeffrey C. 1986. *The Economic Function of Futures Markets.* Cambridge University Press. https://doi.org/10.1017/CBO9780511571848.

Working, Holbrook. 1948. "Theory of the Inverse Carrying Charge in Futures Markets." *Journal of Farm Economics* 30 (1): 1–28. https://doi.org/10.2307/1232678.

Working, Holbrook. 1949. "The Theory of Price of Storage." *The American Economic Review* 39 (6): 1254–62. http://www.jstor.org/stable/1816601.

Working, Holbrook. 1962. "New Concepts Concerning Futures Markets and Prices." *The American Economic Review* 52 (3): 431–59. http://www.jstor.org/stable/1810553.

Wright, Brian D., and Jeffrey C. Williams. 1989. "A Theory of Negative Prices for Storage." *The Journal of Futures Markets (1986–1998)* 9 (1): 1. http://search.proquest.com/docview/225498737/abstract/2482E66EBC4C4B7APQ/1.

10. A green mandate: The Central Bank of Nigeria and sustainable development

Salewa Olawoye-Mann

1.   INTRODUCTION

The Nigerian economy is heavily dependent on income from its oil and gas industry. This comes at a great cost to the environment and health of the indigenes of the resource-rich communities. A lot of the environmental and health effects come from oil-spill pollutions and the flaring of associated gas. Historically, Nigeria has been one of the top gas-flaring countries in the world with an estimate of about 40% of the gas produced in Nigeria being flared (Ejiogu, 2013; NNPC, 2021). This has been detrimental to the health of its citizens. It does not help that Nigeria's public health expenditure has not contributed meaningfully to the quality of life of its citizens (Nathaniel and Khan, 2020). So, climate change issues are an additional contribution to the decreasing quality of life of Nigerians.

In response, the government of Nigeria has set dates to end flaring, but these dates have been repeatedly changed for about three decades. In addressing other environmental-related issues, the Federal Government of Nigeria set up an Ecological Fund in 1981 to attend to soil erosion, flood control, drought, desertification and pollution. This fund was set up through the Federation Account Act of 1981 but its office was not set up until 1985. In September 2016, the Nigerian president, Mohammadu Buhari, along with several country leaders, signed the Paris Agreement to commit to reversing the negative effects of climate change. Nigeria committed to reducing carbon emissions by 20% through environmentally efficient energy, transport and agricultural projects. The fight for the environment and sustainable development has not been successfully handled by the Federal Government. Thus, highlighting the need for the central bank also plays a significant role. Both units, the Federal Government and the central bank, need to work independently and together in order to successfully reverse the negative effects of climate change.

Gas flaring, spillage and other environmental-related issues have monetary effects and they affect the financial system of a country. Climate change has major effects on the stability of the financial system (Aglietta and Espagne, 2016; Batten et al., 2016; Scott et al., 2017). Like central banks around the world, the Central Bank of Nigeria (CBN) has a responsibility towards stakeholders in the economy such as investors, regulators and citizens. As one of the top six greenhouse emitters in Africa, Nigeria has to address the effects of climate change on the financial, health, energy and economic sectors (Usman and Dije, 2013). As a result, climate change management cannot be left to the Federal Government alone; the central bank has a role to play.

A central bank has a stake in climate change because climate change-related droughts and floods may have a significant impact on agricultural output. This could lead to supply shocks and cost-push inflation. For economies such as Nigeria where agricultural production is a central pillar of the economy, anything that affects the agricultural sector affects the aggregate economy. Thus, climate change can lead to supply-side shocks that may cause a trade-off for central banks between stabilising inflation and stabilising output fluctuations (Cœuré, 2018). Different climate change policy regimes such as carbon policies could affect different monetary policy regimes, so if central banks only respond to the inflationary component without considering climate change-related rising prices and decreasing output, the economy may experience large output losses (McKibbin et al., 2017). So, the Nigerian central bank has much at stake with climate change as a developing country.

The CBN has tackled the issue of climate change through development finance initiatives such as the creation of a conducive environment for financial institutions to deliver effective services. These services are targeted at rural development, agriculture and small and medium enterprises. However, more can still be done by the CBN regarding climate change-related issues. In order to address the roles of the CBN and a green mandate for its operations, the next section will analyse climate change issues in Nigeria and the opportunities for central bank intervention. Then, the CBN initiatives towards climate change and environmental issues are analysed in the third section. Finally, we provide a green mandate for the CBN and a conclusion.

2.   TACKLING CLIMATE CHANGE IN NIGERIA

Nigeria borders the North Atlantic ocean in West Africa and has a total land area of 923,773 square kilometres. According to the 2019 World Bank Database, Nigeria has an estimated population size of 201 million and is the most populous country in Africa. The 2019 Statista data shows that agriculture, which includes forestry, livestock, crops and fishing, contributed 21.91% to Nigeria's GDP. However, the major source of revenue in Nigeria has been crude oil. Fossil fuels such as oil and gas are used extensively for exports in Africa, especially in Nigeria. This is a threat to the increase in greenhouse gases and global warming. Also, global climate change patterns are largely attributed to increased levels of carbon dioxide in the atmosphere produced by fossil fuels. An Intergovernmental Panel on Climate Change (IPCC) report in 2007 detailed increased carbon emissions from fossil fuel burning. So, as one of the leading producers and users of fossil fuel in the world, Nigeria faces a threat to its environmental sustainability and climate change (Achike and Onoja, 2014; Ebele and Emodi, 2016). Therefore, steps have to be taken towards sustainable environmental management such as a reduction in greenhouse gas emission and climate change adaptation strategies (Achike and Onoja, 2014). With a heavy reliance on crude oil and agriculture, climate-related issues need to be given more attention in Nigeria.

However, addressing climate change issues in Nigeria requires a pluralistic approach because Nigeria has a varying climate system and so the climate concerns differ. While the climate is equatorial in the south, it is tropical in the centre and arid in the north. The average rainfall ranges from 500 to 1800 mm at an average of about 1282.2 mm (Apata, 2011).

The ecosystem in Nigeria varies as well. It ranges from mangroves and rainforests in the south to the savannah in the north. Climate issues affect the ecosystems in the regions of Nigeria in different ways. The excessive flooding in the south has affected farming in the coastal areas of the south, while the north has been affected by desertification. Both excessive flooding and desertification have been harmful to people's livelihoods and have contributed to impoverishing citizens. From grains lost to a loss of land for animal grazing (ANAP, 2005; Akinyosoye, 2006), Nigeria's agriculture has been affected. Climate change has led to a shift in crop cultivation in the north (Scoones et al., 2005). Also, increasing temperatures have affected livestock production and increased livestock mortalities, while excessive rainfalls increase the distribution of disease vectors such as malaria and dengue fever (Ebele and Emodi, 2016). Because of the loss of land for grazing, climate change has further led to conflict in Nigeria. Evidence has shown that climate change has already affected crop yields in many countries (IPCC, 2007). This is particularly true in low-income countries like Nigeria, where climate is the primary determinant of agricultural productivity and adaptive capacities are low (Apata et al., 2009).

Climate change has led to a reduction in yields for farmers, so they have had to cultivate more land in Nigeria, thereby leaving little land for cattle grazing. This has led to a clash between nomadic pastoralists, mostly Fulanis in northern Nigeria, and farmers. The Fulani herdsmen have had to leave their normal grazing routes, to the dismay of farmers. This conflict started in northern Nigeria and has moved down to southern Nigeria. These Fulani herdsmen have been known to destroy farmlands and kill farmers in a bid to have their cattle graze the land. So, the ongoing Fulani herdsmen crisis has its roots in climate change (Odoh and Chilaka, 2012).

Apart from the continuous herdsmen crisis, climate change has effects on rural poverty through its effects on agriculture (Ebele and Emodi, 2016). With a forced shift in crop cultivation, many farmers cannot afford to buy new seedlings and other necessary resources. Also, with an invasion of their crops by Fulani herdsmen, these farmers lose out on their harvest and from the revenue they could have received for these harvests, thus encouraging more rural poverty.

Reversing the negative effects of climate change has required input from various stakeholders including non-governmental organisations, not just the Federal Government and the central bank. To curb the threat posed by forest degradation in the country, the Nigerian Conservation Foundation (NCF) signed a collaborative agreement with the International Institute of Tropical Agriculture (IITA) on tree planting in 2018. This agreement aimed to help the Federal Government's Green Recovery Initiative in managing and replanting felled trees in the mangrove forest, thereby reversing the effects of climate change that had impacted negatively on the environment and human lives. In the same year, the Federal Government introduced the National Gas Flaring Commercialisation Programme (NGCP) and approved the Flare Gas (prevention of waste and pollution) Regulations 2018. The goal of the programme is to end gas flaring, reduce carbon emission and minimise the effects of climate change. To accelerate sustained economic growth, the Federal Ministry of Environment and its sub-agencies in the review period aligned their key environmental policies and projects to the Economic Recovery and Growth Plan (ERGP) and Nationally Determined Contributions (NDCs) to include green initiatives as captured in the Climate Change Paris Agreement. These policies and projects were the Great Green Wall (GGW), Nigeria Erosion and Watershed Management Project (NEWMAP), Reducing Emissions from Deforestation and Forest Degradation (REDD+), Ogoni Cleanup Project and green bonds. These projects were designed to prevent and reverse land degradation by curbing gully erosion in Niger-Delta areas, a collection of oil-producing regions that had been a threat to infrastructural development and livelihood existence in those areas. Clean-up activities started in the Ogoni land of the Niger-Delta areas. The clean-up activities of the Ogoni land involved the selection of 21 companies by the Hydrocarbon Pollution Remediation Project (HYPREP) agency and a Federal Government funding of US$177 million out of the estimated US$1 billion required for the project. Yet, the Federal Government of Nigeria has not been able to tackle climate change issues alone.

All these climate-related issues have led to the creation of climate refugees around Nigeria (Apata, 2011). If climate change issues are ignored by the

CBN, it will have to deal with the resulting effects of an impending general increase in the price level of agricultural products and any product affected by agriculture. In an interview with the News Agency of Nigeria (NAN) in Minna, the chairman of the Niger state chapter of the All Farmers Association of Nigeria (AFAN) with 1.6 million members warned about the impending price hike to offset the losses caused by COVID-19, flooding and banditry. As a result of these environmental issues and other issues with roots in the environment, he said, "we should expect increase in the prices of food and agricultural produce this year because the farmers have lost a lot to natural and man-made disasters." He also said that COVID-19, flooding and banditry affected many farmers in the north, while farmers from other parts of the country were affected by COVID-19 and flooding (News Agency of Nigeria, 2020).

According to a Consumer Price Index (CPI) report of July 2020, the composite food index rose to 15.48% in July 2020 compared to 15.18% in June 2020. Compared to the downward trend of core inflation, the "All items less farm produce", or core inflation, which excludes the prices of volatile agricultural produce, stood at 10.10% in July 2020, down by 0.03% when compared with the 10.13% recorded in June 2020. Overall, inflation rose to 12.82% in July 2020 from 12.56% in June 2020. Of the items in the CPI, the highest increase was recorded in agricultural products such as oil and fats, fish, tubers such as potatoes and yams, meats, bread and cereals and fruits. Thus, agriculture is a major sector in reversing the negative effects of climate change and an important focus sector in carrying out a green mandate.

The climate change effects on agriculture have led to an increasing composite food index (Figure 10.1), which influences the inflation rate and level of poverty in Nigeria. This could make it more difficult for central banks to measure underlying inflationary pressures and maintain inflation close to the target (Batten et al., 2016). So, the CBN has a stake in curbing climate change in Nigeria.

Climate change is subtle yet affects livelihoods, social order, health, peace and stability (Ezirim and Onuoha, 2008). People depend on the environment for sustenance and their existence. Humanity cannot exist without the environment. So, climate change is an issue that affects humanity. It is a global issue, not a Western one, and like the rest of the world, it affects Nigeria in many ways and has become an important issue that requires the appropriate policy actions to combat it.

3.   THE CBN AND CLIMATE CHANGE

Climate change poses two risks to the financial system. First, it poses a physical risk through damage to the balance sheets of households, corporations, banks

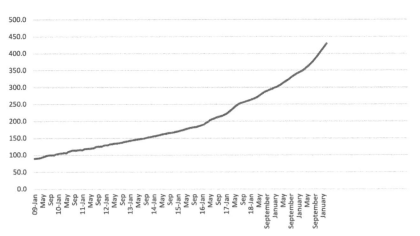

Figure 10.1   Climate change effect on agriculture in Nigeria

and insurance companies; then it poses a transition risk through the effects of unexpected tightening of carbon emission policies on carbon-intensive assets (Batten et al., 2016). Climate change can increase the rate of default of corporate loans if it destroys the capital of firms and affects their profitability and liquidity. This could affect the stability of a country's entire banking system. Then, climate change damages can lead to a gradual decline in the price of corporate bonds through a portfolio reallocation (Dafermos et al., 2018). Overall, climate change can lead to an overall crippling of the financial system. This makes it impossible for the CBN to ignore the dangers of climate change on the financial system and overall economy of Nigeria. In reversing the negative effects of climate change, the CBN has taken internal measures within the institution and external measures for different units in the financial system.

With respect to internal activities carried out by the CBN towards combating climate change, it has created awareness sessions and taken steps towards recycling with a goal of enhancing sustainable banking principles among staff. On World Environment Day, 5 June 2018, the CBN conducted awareness sessions on plastic pollution and began to recycle paper waste as a step towards reducing its greenhouse gas emissions. Here, the CBN received a first batch of recycled waste paper in the form of toilet papers and distributed them across all Strategic Business Units. However, the CBN is responsible for creating change that goes beyond creating awareness internally.

There is a call for urgent policy action because of the effects that climate change can have on economies (IPCC, 2018). Climate change has serious implications for output, employment and price developments, so much so that central banks cannot ignore it. In recent times, the CBN has popularised climate change issues through raising awareness and developing policies centred around climate change. In making a commitment to economic growth that is environmentally sustainable, the CBN became a member of the Sustainable Banking Network (SBN) in 2012. Then, together with the Nigerian Banking Association, it adopted sustainable banking principles that provide guidelines for green central banking activities. First, the CBN issued a memo addressed to all banks, discount houses and development finance institutions in 2012. This memo included nine sustainable banking principles that the financial institutions must adhere to. Of the nine principles given, three of them directly affect climate change. They are:

> Principle 1: To integrate environmental and social considerations into decision-making processes relating to business activities so as to avoid, minimise or offset negative impacts.
> Principle 2: To avoid, minimise or offset negative impacts of business operations on the environment and local communities and, where possible, promote positive impacts.
> Principle 6: To implement robust environmental and social governance practices in the respective institutions and assess the environmental and social governance practices of clients.

These principles also provided guidelines for banking business with the agricultural and oil and gas sector. They ensured financial involvement in ensuring environmentally sustainable practices in these sectors.

Since the core task of central banks is maintaining price stability through the trade of government bonds and change of interest rates (Schoenmaker, 2021; Goodhart, 1995), the CBN has adopted green financial policies that target the management and reversal of climate change-related damages to the environment and the entire financial system. In order to do this, the CBN has adopted green policies through the inclusion of green bonds and financial inclusion that are environmentally conscious and target price stability, through projects that are environmentally sustainable.

3.1   Green Bonds

Green bonds are fixed-income instruments targeted at the support of specific new or existing climate-related or environmental projects (Fender et al., 2020). They are instruments used for implementing sustainability objectives (Fender et al., 2019). These bonds are a financing option available to private firms and public entities. They are designed to encourage environmental sustainability by supporting projects that are energy efficient, that protect the aquatic and terrestrial ecosystem, and that provide clean transportation, clean water and sustainable agriculture, forestry and fishery. These green bonds are designed to target the management of climate-related damages to the environment and the economy. The first multilateral development institution green bond was issued by the European Investment Bank (EIB) in 2007, while the World Bank issued the second green bond in 2008 (Banga, 2019). In Nigeria, the first green bond was issued in 2017.

According to the CBN's 2018 monetary policy review, its green bond initiative is an "environmentally conscious instrument of economic management" and a "debt security, issued to raise capital and specifically to enhance environmental sustainability by supporting climate-related or environmental projects" (CBN, 2018, 67) determined on climate-related financial risk such as the physical risks of climate events, liabilities from parties that have suffered a loss and transitional risk from the process of adjusting to a lower-carbon economy. These bonds are issued based on four criteria that follow the Green Bond Principle (GBP). GBPs focus on the use of proceeds, processes for project evaluation and selection, the management of proceeds and the reporting of these bonds to ensure that they are truly environmentally friendly:

– The first criterion has to do with defining the type of "green" project the green bonds would be used for.
– The second criterion involves an extremely thorough project review and approval process. Here, the potential environmental and/or social implications of the project are analysed.
– The third criterion involves separating proceeds from green bonds and making periodic allocations to eligible investors.
– The fourth criterion involves the CBN monitoring the implementation of the green projects and giving periodic reports on the environmental sustainability impacts.

In December 2017, the Federal Government of Nigeria issued its first green bond totalling N10.69 billion for a five-year tenure at 13.48%. Through the issuance of green bonds, the Nigerian government ensures that it achieves the twin objectives of fiscal efficiency and environmental sustainability. In approving green bonds, the CBN has to ensure that debt instruments were offered for the purpose of financing or refinancing projects which yielded positive environmental impact. Also, the management of issues proceeds and a process for refinancing has to be on environmentally friendly projects.

3.2   The CBN's Financial Inclusion

In implementing Principle 1 of the principles of sustainable banking, the financial inclusion strategy was launched in 2012. It is a development initiative aimed at poverty reduction, wealth creation, employment generation and improving the welfare of citizens. According to the CBN, the major tools for driving the strategy include agent banking, tiered know-your-customer requirements, financial literacy, consumer protection, linkage banking, the implementation of the Micro, Small and Medium Enterprises (MSME) Development Fund, and credit enhancement programmes.

The credit enhancement programmes target agriculture, entrepreneurship and small and medium enterprises (SMEs). They include:

– The Agricultural Credit Guarantee Scheme (ACGS)
– The Commercial Agricultural Credit Scheme (CACS)
– The Nigeria Incentive-Based Risk Sharing System for Agricultural Lending (NIRSAL)
– Refinancing and Rediscounting Facilities for SMEs
– The SME Credit Guarantee Scheme
– Entrepreneurship Development Centres.

These tools help financial institutions integrate environmental and social considerations into decision-making processes relating to business activities and operations. Through grassroots financial inclusion in the agricultural and MSME sectors, the CBN ensures an environmental initiative that can be easily monitored and reported by the financial institutions. In addition, these credit facilities provide empowerment that is crucial in enhancing farmers' awareness about environmentally friendly ways that will aid in the reversal of the negative effects of climate change. This is particularly useful for the adaptation, decision-making and planning processes by farmers (Apata, 2011). However, at the time of writing, the central bank is still working on the framework for consumer protection and has recently set up a Financial Inclusion Secretariat to coordinate the implementation of this strategy. Many of the policies are still at the initial stage of decision-making and implementation.

4.   A GREEN MANDATE: CBN POLICY RECOMMENDATIONS

Although the CBN's actions towards reversing the negative effects of climate change are still in the early stages, with some still being discussed and not yet implemented, there is still room for implementation and more policy recommendations. There is a call for urgent policy action due to the impending disastrous effects climate change can have on the economy (IPCC, 2018). The Department for International Development (DFID) in the United Kingdom has concluded that the cost of climate change in Nigeria would be between 6% and 30% of its GDP by 2050. This is estimated at a cost of $100 billion to $460 billion. So, there is an urgent need for the CBN to operate with more mandates that explicitly promote sustainable growth and development through green policies and strategies for implementation. However, the margin given by the DFID on the cost of climate change in Nigeria is large. As uncertain as climate change is, a lack of proper data makes it more difficult to estimate its cost in Nigeria. With a lack of proper data and effective access to climate information in Nigeria (Apata, 2011), it is quite impossible to provide and analyse policy recommendations empirically.

4.1   Green Data

There is a paucity of data on development issues in Nigeria and this extends to data on climate change. There is an urgent need for data generation for the effective monitoring and evaluation of key performance indications. Proper data would help with the monitoring of response rates and attrition for policies administered (Warburton and Warburton, 2004). Without adequate information through data, the CBN may not be fully aware of the extent of climate change effects on the financial system and economy as a whole. Also, it would be difficult to monitor the progress and results of each green policy implemented. In order to achieve a sustainable economy in Nigeria, there has to be a full understanding of the connections of the economic systems and the well-being of the people in the environment and the drivers and responders to change (Carpenter et al., 2006). This leads to the first step towards a "Green Mandate", which is data collection. The power consumption of data centres affects the environment heavily. It is counterproductive to implement green policies, then implement them and monitor them in ways that are more destructive to the environment. It is worse to implement these policies without the right data as this is tantamount to applying treatments to a disease without knowing where the disease is or its seriousness. It could lead to underestimating the seriousness of climate change and misapplying policies. Since the different parts of Nigeria have different kinds of climate – equatorial in the south, tropical in the centre and arid in the north – the treatments will differ and having the right data will help in determining and implementing the right policies for the reversal of climate change effects.

Without the right data, green policies would be operating blind and could be ineffective or, worse, cause more damage to the environment. However, the process of gathering and sorting data has contributed negatively to climate change. From the cars driven to gather data to the computers used to input and sort data, data collection has typically not been environmentally friendly. Murugesan (2008) opines that each computer in use produces about a ton of carbon dioxide every year. Gathering and sorting out data for the reversal of the negative effects of climate change should not contribute more than necessary to the issue being addressed. Green data will provide significant energy saving for data collection and processing (Liu et al., 2009). It also provides financial and non-financial added benefits of reducing power consumption and saving on costs (Murugesan, 2008). As a result, the CBN has to begin with an investment in a "green data centre" on energy-efficient information for environmental and sustainable issues (Wu et al., 2016). This investment in a sustainable data centre uses an energy-efficient technology in the collection and processing of data and is also in line with a green mandate. This centre will also be responsible for monitoring the implementation, progress and results of green policies and projects within Nigeria. By investing in green data, the CBN will lay a solid foundation on which it can implement and monitor green policies that will build a green nation. Also, the benefits of the green data extend beyond the central bank usages (Bholat, 2015). It will flow into other institutions such as financial and educational centres and can be used for policy purposes.

The availability of green data to educational institutions provides an added benefit of encouraging university lecturers and researchers in different fields to carry out research on issues relating to climate change. These innovative research projects can lead to practical solutions in combating climate change which stem from the CBN green data. The ensuing effects of an investment in green data geared towards reversing the effects of climate change are numerous and are a worthwhile investment for the CBN. The benefits accrue to the CBN for its policymaking, as well as other sectors in the economy. Thus, green data is a beneficial starting point towards the CBN's green mandate.

4.2   Greening Monetary Policies

The central bank has accommodative and defensive roles in monitoring money supply through interest rates and the trading of securities (Rochon and Rossi, 2007). These are used to create endogenous money through the demand from the actions of the non-bank public and the banking system, respectively (Rochon and Rossi, 2004). Since the CBN cannot set environmental policies, it can create awareness of climate change issues and switch its operations and policies to be more environmentally friendly and leave a smaller carbon footprint. To achieve this, the CBN sets interest rates with a bias for low-carbon projects and applies this low-carbon bias to the trade of securities. This will have a ripple effect in banking projects, loans and the economy as a whole. The carbon bias would encourage farmers, producers, businesses and institutions to make investment and business decisions that are green and reverse climate change effects. This carbon bias can be applied and enforced in new and existing central bank projects that encourage environmentally friendly production and agriculture. This can include a lower interest rate to fund proper grazing, which would reverse the negative effects of climate change, including the Fulani herdsmen crisis.

Despite claims of market neutrality, evidence shows that central banks have typically had a bias towards industries that have been called "capital intensive" in order to stimulate the economy (Matikainen et al., 2017). These capital-intensive sectors, such as the oil and gas sector, have also been carbon intensive in their operations (Doda, 2016). To reverse the negative effects of climate change, the central bank has to adopt a gradual low-carbon bias that shifts the allocation of assets and collateral gradually from high-carbon companies to low-carbon companies. This bias and gradual shift will lower the cost of capital in low-carbon companies compared to those of high-carbon companies without interfering in the smooth conduct of monetary policy (Schoenmaker, 2021). Through this gradual shift, the CBN avoids the effects of a total high-carbon to low-carbon change-induced shock in the economy while addressing the carbon bias in its monetary operation. Overall, with this gradual shift to a low-carbon bias, the CBN reduces the carbon emission in its corporate and bank bond portfolio (Schoenmaker, 2021), stabilises the economy and contributes to the reversal of climate change effects. Through these actions, Nigeria can foster a sustainable economy and environment.

5.   CONCLUSION

This chapter has shed light on the climate change issues in Nigeria and the efforts the CBN has made to address these issues. Climate change is not a new phenomenon and its effects have been felt in varying degrees in Nigeria for decades. While the climate change issues have largely been the responsibility of the Federal Government, the central bank has adjusted its policies to address these issues. This is because climate change has had negative effects on people and inflation through the volatility of food prices, which shows why the reversal of the effects of climate change cannot be left to the Federal Government alone. These rapidly increasing food prices make inflation targeting difficult for the CBN. Though CBN green policies are still in the early stages, this chapter pinpoints areas of urgency that need to be addressed for the effective application and monitoring of green policies by the CBN.

One of the setbacks in providing a green mandate is the availability of data, which also poses an opportunity for environmentally friendly data collection and sorting. This green data is the foundation for proper policy implementation and monitoring. The availability of data ensures that research is encouraged, proper solutions are found and the right policies are implemented. Once green data exists, the process of greening monetary policy becomes more effective through proper implementation and monitoring.

Greening monetary policies in Nigeria would require a low-carbon bias to reduce the carbon emission in the CBN's portfolio. In tackling climate change, the CBN can implement a gradual shift in its asset portfolios to favour low-carbon over high-carbon assets in its mix of assets. Through its credit enhancement schemes, the CBN can tackle climate change directly by making climate change education and credit more accessible to people in the agricultural sector and other sectors. Then, through green bonds, the CBN can issue environmentally conscious instruments of economic management and support climate-related projects that ensure environmental sustainability while providing price stability in the economy. Overall, though a green mandate cannot be empirically analysed in Nigeria because of insufficient data, this chapter has addressed what currently exists and policy recommendations that can begin a discussion on a green mandate in Nigeria's central bank.

REFERENCES

Achike, A. I., and Onoja, A. O. (2014). Greenhouse gas emission determinants in Nigeria: Implications for trade, climate change mitigation and adaptation policies. *British Journal of Environment and Climate Change* 4(1), pp. 114–125.

Aglietta, M., and Espagne, É. (2016). *Climate and Finance Systemic Risks, More Than an Analog? The Climate Fragility Hypothesis.* CEPII (Centre d'etudes prospectives et d'informations internationales), Paris.

Akinyosoye, V. O. (2006). *Government and Agriculture in Nigeria: Analysis of Policies, Programme and Administration.* Macmillan Nigeria Publishers Limited, Ibadan.

Apata, T. G. (2011). Effects of global climate change on Nigerian agriculture: An empirical analysis. *CBN Journal of Applied Statistics* 2(1), pp. 31–50.

Apata, T. G., Samuel, K. D., and Adeola, A. O. (2009). *Analysis of Climate Change Perception and Adaptation among Arable Food Crop Farmers in South Western Nigeria* (No. 1005-2016-79140). Contributed paper prepared for presentation at the International Association of Agricultural Economists' 2009 Conference, Beijing, China, 16–22 August.

Assessment of Nigeria Agricultural Policy (ANAP) (2005). *Agriculture in Nigeria: Identifying Opportunities for Increased Commercialization and Investment.* IITA Press, Ibadan.

Banga, J. (2019). The green bond market: A potential source of climate finance for developing countries. *Journal of Sustainable Finance and Investment* 9(1), pp. 17–32.

Batten, S., Sowerbutts, R., and Tanaka, M. (2016). Let's talk about the weather: The impact of climate change on central banks. *Bank of England Working Paper* No. 603.

Bholat, D. (2015). Big data and central banks. *Big Data and Society* 2(1), 2053951715579469.

Carpenter, S. R., DeFries, R., Dietz, T., Mooney, H. A., Polasky, S., Reid, W. V., and Scholes, R. J. (2006). Millennium ecosystem assessment: Research needs. *Science* 314, pp. 257–258.

CBN (2018). *Monetary Policy Review*. Central Bank of Nigeria, Abuja.

Cœuré, B. (2018). Monetary policy and climate change. Speech at the NGFS Conference "Scaling Up Green Finance: The Role of Central Banks" at the Deutsche Bundesbank, Berlin, 8 November.

Dafermos, Y., Nikolaidi, M., and Galanis, G. (2018). Climate change, financial stability and monetary policy. *Ecological Economics* 152, pp. 219–234.

Doda, B. (2016). Sector-level carbon intensity distribution. *Centre for Climate Change Economics and Policy Working Paper*, 281.

Ebele, N. E., and Emodi, N. V. (2016). Climate change and its impact in Nigerian economy. *Journal of Scientific Research and Report* 10(6), pp. 1–13.

Ejiogu, A. R. (2013). Gas flaring in Nigeria: Costs and policy. *Energy and Environment* 24(6), pp. 983–998.

Ezirim, G. E., and Onuoha, F. C. (2008). Climate change and national security: Exploring the theoretical and empirical connections in Nigeria. *Journal of International Politics and Development* 4(1&2).

Fender, I., McMorrow, M., Sahakyan, V., and Zulaica, O. (2019). Green bonds: The reserve management perspective. *BIS Quarterly Review*. Retrieved from https://www.bis.org/publ/qtrpdf/r_qt1909f.htm.

Fender, I., McMorrow, M., Sahakyan, V., and Zulaica, O. (2020). Reserve management and sustainability: The case for green bonds? *BIS Working Papers*, no. 849, March.

Goodhart, C. (1995). *The Central Bank and the Financial System*. Springer, New York.

IPCC (2007). Climate change 2007 synthesis report: Contribution of Working Groups I, II, and III to the fourth assessment report of the Intergovernmental Panel on Climate Change. Cambridge University Press, Cambridge.

IPCC (2018). *Global Warming of 1.5 °C: Summary for Policymakers*. IPCC, Incheon.

Liu, L., Wang, H., Liu, X., Jin, X., He, W. B., Wang, Q. B., and Chen, Y. (2009, June). Green cloud: A new architecture for green data center. In *Proceedings of the 6th International Conference Industry Session on Autonomic Computing and Communications Industry Session* (pp. 29–38). Association for Computing Machinery, New York.

Matikainen, S., Campiglio, E., and Zenghelis, D. (2017). The climate impact of quantitative easing. Policy Paper, Grantham Research Institute on Climate Change and the Environment, London School of Economics and Political Science.

McKibbin, W. J., Morris, A. C., Panton, A., and Wilcoxen, P. (2017). Climate change and monetary policy: Dealing with disruption. Brookings Discussion Paper in *Climate and Energy Economics*, December. CAMA Working Paper 77/2017, Australian National University.

Murugesan, S. (2008). Harnessing green IT: Principles and practices. *IT Professional* 10(1), pp. 24–33.

Nathaniel, S., and Khan, S. (2020). Public health financing, environmental quality, and the quality of life in Nigeria. *Journal of Public Affairs* 20(3), e2103.

News Agency of Nigeria (2020). Nigeria: Farmers warn against impending increase in prices of food, agricultural produce. Retrieved from https://worldstagenews.com/nigeria-farmers-warn-against-impending-increase-in-prices-of-foods-agricultural-produce.

NNPC (2021). Nigerian gas. Retrieved from https://nnpcgroup.com/NNPC-Business/Business-Information/Pages/Nigeria-Gas.aspx.

Odoh, S. I., and Chilaka, F. C. (2012). Climate change and conflict in Nigeria: A theoretical and empirical examination of the worsening incidence of conflict between Fulani herdsmen and farmers in Northern Nigeria. *Oman Chapter of Arabian Journal of Business and Management Review* 34(970), pp. 1–15.

Rochon, L.-P., and Rossi, S. (2004). Endogenous money: The evolutionary versus revolutionary views. Paper presented at the EAEPE 2004 annual conference on Economics, History and Development, Crete, 28–31 October.

Rochon, L.-P., and Rossi, S. (2007). Central banking and post-Keynesian economics. *Review of Political Economy* 19(4), pp. 539–554.

Schoenmaker, D. (2021). Greening monetary policy. *Climate Policy*, pp. 1–12.

Scoones, I., Devereux, S., and Haddad, L. (2005). Introduction: New directions for African agriculture. *IDS Bulletin: Institute of Development Studies* 36(2), pp. 1–12.

Scott, M., Van Huizen, J., and Jung, C. (2017). The bank's response to climate change. *Bank of England Quarterly Bulletin* Q2, pp. 97–109.

Usman, Y. D., and Dije, B. I. (2013). Potential challenges of climate change to the Nigeria economy. *IOSR Journal of Environmental Science, Toxicology and Food Technology* 6(2), pp. 7–12.

Warburton, R. N., and Warburton, W. P. (2004). Canada needs better data for evidence-based policy: Inconsistencies between administrative and survey data on welfare dependence and education. *Canadian Public Policy/Analyse de politiques* 30(3), pp. 241–255.

Wu, J., Guo, S., Li, J., and Zeng, D. (2016). Big data meet green challenges: Greening big data. *IEEE Systems Journal* 10(3), pp. 873–887.

11. Mind the gap: Monetary policy and financial regulations for supporting green finance

Lilit Popoyan and Giorgos Galanis[1]

1. INTRODUCTION

Climate change has been recognized as one of the defining challenges human-kind faces in the 21st century. It is now acknowledged that the rise of global temperature to 2°C requires a structural shift to bring the global economy from a high- to a low-carbon path. On its way, the policy responses to climate change challenges have been predominantly fiscal. Accordingly, a carbon tax and cap-and-trade policies were recommended as the first line of defence against environmental externalities (see Stern and Stern, 2007; Krogstrup and Oman, 2019).

The Paris Agreement in 2015 braked this monotonicity in climate policy response, sending a crucial message to policymakers and the international community. It called for an alignment of financial flows with a pathway towards a low-carbon economy (COP, 2016), using it as a major tool to meet climate targets. Indeed, besides traditional environmental themes (e.g. reduction of greenhouse gas emissions and climate change adaptation), COP21 acknowledged the challenges related to the financing of a green transition. For the first time, central banks and financial supervisors have been called to contribute through "making finance flows consistent with a pathway towards low greenhouse gas emissions and climate-resilient development" (COP, 2016, Article 2). In particular, COP21 posed the question of how central banks and financial regulators can align the finance sector with the sustainable transition roadmaps, thus closing the "green finance gap".

At the same time, there is increasing acknowledgement and shared awareness of climate change as a significant threat to monetary policy and financial stability, thus on macro and financial dynamics. On the monetary policy side, climate change can directly or indirectly affect a central bank's ability to meet its price stability objectives, posing both supply and demand shocks to the economy (Batten et al., 2020). Therefore, central banks are not immune to the risks posed by climate change. Monetary authorities will need to identify the nature, persistence, and magnitude of the climate-induced shocks to the economy and prepare an adequate instrumental setup to address them (Cœuré, 2018). Instead, on the regulatory policy side, climate-induced physical damages and abrupt policy interventions are among the primary sources of financial imbalances with the potential systemic implication of financial stability (Hsiang et al., 2017; Semieniuk et al., 2021).

Despite the rising awareness of the adverse impact of climate-related risk on monetary policy and financial stability (Carney, 2015; NGFS, 2020), so far, few central banks and financial regulators have decided to take significant action to protect their balance sheets (D'Orazio and Popoyan, 2019a, b). One of the main hurdles to facilitating meaningful policy change is the absence of a green taxonomy, resulting in a lack of access to better climate risk data to assess its exposure (Bolton et al., 2020). Moreover, many central banks hesitate to commit to climate change aligning monetary policy instruments to avoid departure from the "market neutrality" principle (Cochrane, 2020). On the financial regulation side, there are no internationally agreed-upon regulatory schemes to withstand the potential losses caused to the financial sector (D'Orazio and Popoyan, 2019b).

Since the Paris Agreement, there is clear evidence that monetary authorities worldwide, either in their monetary stability or supervisory responsibilities, have started to consider the possibility of incorporating the policies mitigating the climate-related financial risks in their operational remit. However, policy commitment strongly differs across countries, posing several fundamental research questions. What is the current level of commitment of monetary and financial supervisory authorities in aligning with green policy mandates? How green are the monetary and financial regulatory policies? How can they be made "green" to favour the low-carbon transition and contain the possible financial instability? What might be the consequences of such policies?

In this chapter, we shed light on the monetary policy and financial regulatory instruments that can be implemented and their possible effects on the low-carbon transition path and on protecting the financial sector from climate-related financial risks. Moreover, we explore the state of the art in green monetary and financial regulatory tool usage and take a prospective look at its future development. The remainder of the chapter is organized as follows. Section 2 discusses central banks' involvement in low-carbon transition, relying on their two main functions – monetary and supervisory – as well as their role in tackling climate change and the state of the art. Section 3, building on the previous section and the current state of green finance, looks forward to the future. Finally, Section 4 concludes the discussion.

2.   CENTRAL BANKS AND CLIMATE CHANGE: WHERE ARE WE NOW?

Until recently, climate policies have been predominantly thought about in fiscal terms, mainly relying on such policy solutions as the carbon tax and cap-and-trade policies with little (if any) place for monetary policy. One reason for this is the mismatch of policy windows. If central banks' operational objectives (manly price stability) are short term, climate change policies and effects, on the contrary, are about long-term horizons (Batten et al., 2016). This unilateral policy preference changed with the Paris Agreement, requiring parties to limit global warming to well below 2°C above pre-industrial levels. Most central banks acknowledge that climate change is a significant threat to monetary stability, consequently translating into adverse macro and financial dynamics. However, opinions vary on whether they should take action, and some are finding it difficult to accommodate their climate ambitions with their mandates (Krogstrup and Oman, 2019). Considering historical differences in central banks' policy traditions and the evolution of institutions' mandates worldwide (Goodhart et al., 2011), this may not be unexpected.

Figure 11.1, indicating the structure of Organisation for Economic Co-operation and Development (OECD) and G20 countries' central bank mandates, shows a heterogeneity picture in terms of objectives. While the operational scope varies widely across central banks, what makes them alike is the price stability objective as a necessary component of the central banks' institutional mandate. As the data shows, sustainability is far from being an explicit mission statement by central banks. However, the most striking example comes from the UK where, since 3 March 2021, the Bank of England (BoE) mandate was updated to explicitly promote "sustainable and balanced growth that is also environmentally sustainable and consistent with the transition to a net zero economy" (see BoE, 2021). Figure 11.1 also shows that monetary authorities in advanced economies are assigned a narrower mandate than emerging economies' experience. For example, in China, Brazil, Argentina and Turkey, having a broader monetary policy and frequently developmental objectives gives them certain flexibility in their interpretations of the mandate. Accordingly, in these jurisdictions, green financial instruments directed to canalization of credit flows to more environmentally friendly sectors have been employed as part of economy-wide sustainable development objectives.

The second most commonly used operational target is the financial stability objective. The financial crisis of 2007–2009 triggered an extensive transformation in monetary policymaking, reshaping central banks' institutional role, governance and mandate structures (Baker, 2013; Quaglia, 2013). As a result, in 2020, 62% of central banks in the G20 and OECD countries had financial

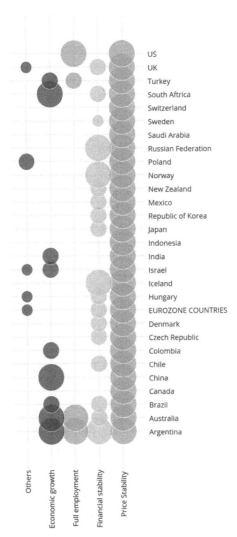

US
UK
Turkey
South Aftrica
Switzerland
Sweden
Saudi Arabia
Russian Federation
Poland
Norway
New Zealand
Mexico
Republic of Korea
Japan
Indonesia
India
Israel
Iceland
Hungary
EUROZONE COUNTRIES
Denmark
Czech Republic
Colombia
Chile
China
Canada
Brazil
Australia
Argentina

Others
Economic growth
Full employment
Financial stability
Price Stability

Source: Authors' calculations based on International Monetary Fund central banks' legislation database, double-checked with central bank laws and statutes.

Figure 11.1   Structure of Organisation for Economic Co-operation and Development (OECD) and G20 central bank mandates

stability as an integrative part of the mandate, against 17% observed in 2000. This shift was mainly driven by high-income countries, which saw the role of economic stability in the hierarchical contest, keeping the primary focus on price stability (see Figure 11.1). In emerging economies, financial stability is either present at the same level as the price stability mandate or is de facto absent. However, as mandated to assure sustainable economic growth, the latter group of countries, because of its broad definition, assign central banks supervisory objectives to safeguard the financial system's stability to reach the final goal.

Relying on the insights provided by Figure 11.1, we will separate our analysis of the possible actions of central banks in managing climate-related risks based on their two principal objectives – monetary and financial stability. Although none of the above reported central banks has yet explicitly or implicitly included the management of climate-related risks in their operational objectives, an increasing number of monetary authorities from advanced (e.g. the UK, France, Germany) and emerging (e.g. Brazil, China, India) economies nowadays identify climate change as a significant threat to financial stability; even three years ago, hardly any made that claim. Since climate-related risks became of utmost interest for central banks, they have urged the creation of voluntary central bank collaboration networks (e.g. the Network for Greening the Financial System (NGFS) created in December 2017 by Banque de France) and expert groups (e.g. the high-level expert group on sustainable finance established by the European Commission in December 2016) to thoroughly incorporate climate-related financial risk into monetary policy actions.

3.   MONETARY POLICY AND CLIMATE-RELATED FINANCIAL RISKS

Together with messages sent to the international community, the Paris Agreement has also been a whistle-blower for many central banks worldwide, urging them to take action. Since the Agreement was signed, many central banks have started to take seriously the challenges posed by climate change, acknowledging that climate-related risks could affect their ability to meet their principal operational mandate, the monetary stability thus posing both supply and demand shocks to the economy (McKibbin et al., 2017). In particular, extreme weather events, through the physical risk transmission channel, can result in supply-side shocks driving the shortage of commodities with consequent price volatility and erosion of productive capital stock, hence slowing economic growth.[2] Losses induced by extreme climate events can also cause demand-side shocks at one end, having a negative wealth effect and follow-up reduction in private consumption, and at the other end bring adverse financial shock driven by high uncertainty, stranded assets, and financial loss. Thus, the shocks mentioned above can, directly or indirectly, affect precautionary saving, credit spreads, real interest rates, and financial instability, hence affecting inflationary pressures, for which monetary policy is responsible (Bolton et al., 2020).

Moreover, while demand-side shocks with a current armoury of central bank tools are manageable, the same is not true for supply-side shocks that pull output and inflation in opposite directions, thus inducing the trade-off between stabilizing inflation and output fluctuations (see McKibbin et al., 2017; Cœuré, 2018).[3] Hence, being directly or indirectly exposed to climate-related risks that hinder monetary policy mandate achievement, the monetary authority is forced to identify the nature, magnitude, and persistence of climate-induced shocks, evaluate their impact, and prepare an adequate instrumental toolkit to deal with them. However, as noted by Cœuré (2018), traditional policy instruments may be less effective at smoothing these shocks, to the extent that these are more or less permanent biophysical shocks rather than transitory economic shocks. Accordingly, the monetary policy line should rely on non-traditional measures to deal with these shocks.

The literature has pointed to several paths in which monetary policy could be a tool of (i) protection of the economy from green financial risks and (ii) support towards the green transition (for example, see Krogstrup and Oman, 2019; Dafermos et al., 2020; Dafermos, 2021). We can split the green financial action among central banks and regulators between "market-fixing" (i.e. passive) and "market-shaping" (more active) approaches.[4] Those approaches, first and foremost, highlight the necessity of adequate assessment of the climate risk impact on central banks' collateral frameworks and asset portfolios (see Matikainen et al., 2017). The second line calls for a recalibration of asset purchase programmes through eliminating high-carbon assets from central bank portfolios in favour of low-carbon assets (primarily known as "green quantitative easing (QE)"), supported by the idea of adjusting risk weights to reflect climate risks correctly (see Olovsson, 2018; Van Lerven and Ryan-Collins, 2017). All in all, this suggests that central banks should step beyond conventional monetary policy operations internalizing climate risks in central banks' unconventional monetary policy practices, such as "green" QE and climate-aligned criteria in central bank collateral frameworks and portfolio management.

A restricted group of countries has already taken this route. However, we should note that this type of policy focuses more on financial risks than greening the central banks' mandates, as has been the case in the Bank of England. Since 2018, the People's Bank of China (PBoC) has revised and expanded the collateral list it accepts for medium-term lending. In particular, it was announced that the PBoC accepts commercial banks' green bonds, loans and asset-backed securities with a double-A rating and above as eligible collateral. Another country in the queue is Japan – since 2012 the Bank of Japan has been supporting lines of credit to green activities achieved through a "Loan Support

Programme". The latter provides preferential liquidity at low interest to financial institutions lending to socially and environmentally beneficial projects.
Other countries, such as Brazil, India, and Indonesia, similarly to Japan, have
adopted credit allocation measures to priority and environmentally friendly
sectors, such as green lending quotas and concessional loans.

After Christine Lagarde became president of the European Central Bank
(ECB), the European Union (EU) also started to show its ambitions in this
field. In particular, defining climate change as "mission critical" for the ECB,
its most significant suggestion includes adopting "green QE" programmes.
Disregarding the created agiotage, few works discuss the efficiency of
green monetary policies. Dafermos et al. (2018), building on the DEFINE
stock-flow-fund macro model (Dafermos et al., 2017), find that implementing
a green QE programme can reduce climate-induced financial instability and
restrict global warming. However, green QE is not by itself capable of preventing a substantial reduction in atmospheric temperature.

These proposals found very controversial reaction – while many central
banks have been very enthusiastic about it (Financial Times, 2021), the
academic world has criticized it heavily, considering that in both cases, these
interventions are considered a massive departure from one of the main principles of traditional monetary policymaking, namely "market neutrality", while
responding to climate change-induced market failures (see Cochrane, 2020;
Weidmann, 2019). Moreover, several scholars (see Campiglio et al., 2018;
Olovsson, 2018; Dikau and Volz, 2018) emphasize that incorporating sustainability goals into monetary policy's operational remit is prone to overstretching
its mandate and engendering its institutional independence. However, this
criticism was met with the conviction that the degree of discretion the many
monetary authorities have in interpreting their mandates will smooth down the
possible effects. Moreover, the COVID-19 pandemic has already prompted
mandate reinterpretations to sustain broad economic objectives in coordination
with fiscal authorities. Accordingly, a strong argument emerges in favour of
coherent coordination between different policy wings for green transition
rather than chasing "market neutrality" as the central postulate for monetary
and financial regulatory policymaking in the way of green transition (see
Barkawi and Zadek, 2021).

3.1   Climate Change and Financial Regulations: Exploring the Field in Between

The financial sector is frequently seen as key to enhancing a "green structural change" via directing financial resources towards green investments
to close the "green finance gap" (see Bolton et al., 2020; Dikau and Volz,
2021). At the same time, climate-related risks and a disorderly transition from

a high- to low-carbon economy may hinder the financial system's stability. Climate-induced physical damages and sharp policy interventions are among the primary sources of economic imbalances with the potential systemic implication of financial stability (see Diaz and Moore, 2017; Hsiang et al., 2017). Accordingly, the literature classifies the risks posed by climate change to financial stability into two main categories: physical and transition risks. The former is associated with the economic cost of actual or expected extreme climate events that can provoke erosions and high volatility of physical and financial assets' monetary value, thus increasing overall uncertainty in financial markets. The latter instead is connected to a disorderly transition to a low-carbon economy that could have a destabilizing effect on the financial system through sharp changes in public policy not anticipated by market participants (FSB, 2020).

Even if the mission is clear and the risks material, in the current state the financial regulations are far from giving tangible results, since in the existing Basel III regulatory setup, climate-related financial risks are narrowly defined and financial intermediaries are not explicitly required to assess the impact of climate-related risks on its exposures (Gros et al., 2016; D'Orazio and Popoyan, 2019b). Financial regulatory frameworks also contain an intrinsic "carbon bias" that creates barriers to aligning the finance sector with sustainable transition roadmaps (see Campiglio et al., 2018). Moreover, the Basel III requirements (in particular capital and liquidity) reinforce short-termism in financial markets (Haldane, 2011), hence hindering the capital mobilization aimed at green investment projects (see Spencer and Stevenson, 2013; Bhattacharya et al., 2015).

We believe that by "greening" the Basel III regulatory instruments (BCBS, 2017), including both lender and borrower side requirements, it is possible to retrieve the regulatory toolkit available to policymakers to address climate-related financial risks.[5] These measures can be divided into three categories targeting banks' capital, liquidity, and credit limits, respectively. The capital management tools are the most discussed among the three categories mentioned above in both policymaking and academic debates because of their potential to align the finance sector with sustainable transition targets. These include the minimum capital requirement with two applications for sustainable finance – the Green Supporting Factor (GSF) and the Brown Penalizing Factor (BPF) – together with countercyclical, conservation capital buffer and leverage requirements. According to the working mechanism of GSF, the banks will be allowed to apply a lower risk weight to low-carbon assets, thus exerting less pressure on the intermediaries' balance sheets, therefore directing their investments more towards finance climate-related projects. However, the proposal received considerable criticism considering that the looser regulatory capital requirement for green assets can underestimate possible real financial risks associated with those and thus threaten financial stability. The risk associated with GSF leads to the BPF proposal, mainly from academic circles, requiring banks to conserve higher capital for carbon-intensive assets (Schoenmaker and Van Tilburg, 2016; Thomä et al., 2016; 2DII, 2018; D'Orazio and Popoyan, 2019b).

In the set of capital instruments, the leverage ratios, particularly those applied in sectoral bases, could be the easiest to implement to curb the financial sector's exposure to carbon-intensive assets, thus addressing potential threats from a low-carbon transition. Instead, the countercyclical capital buffer, even if essential to limit excessive credit growth to carbon-intensive assets, could be challenging to implement. This difficulty is mainly connected to the lack of data and information on the carbon-intensive credit cycle (Carney, 2019) and the absence of a green taxonomy (NGFS, 2020) to distinguish between green (sustainable) and unsustainable assets.

Concerning liquidity regulations, following D'Orazio and Popoyan (2019b), three main instruments can be identified: liquidity coverage ratios (LCRs), net stable funding ratios (NSFRs), and reserve requirements (RRs). Empirical studies evidence the efficiency of LCRs and NSFRs in managing a liquidity crisis (Li et al., 2017; Papadamou et al., 2021). Still, they could hinder financial intermediaries' capacity to allocate capital to long-term climate-related assets. RRs instead represent one of the most used instruments by financial institutions actively involved in the green transition. Among those, Lebanon is a successful example of a country using the RR to support the low-carbon credits by lowering the RRs of commercial banks by 100–150% if the bank can provide a certificate of energy-saving potential of the financial project (BDL, 2010). Another example is PBoC, which uses differentiated RR regulatory policy tools to align intermediaries' portfolios to green growth objectives (Chang et al., 2019). In the case of "greened" RR, the level of obligatory reserves to hold against the attracted deposits depends on the bank's asset portfolio structure. Accordingly, the required reserves rate can be reduced in relation to a green portfolio, hence freeing financial resources to direct to green sectors.

The third category of regulatory tools is used either to limit or channel the financial flows to specific segments. It includes such widely used regulatory tools as minimum credit floors, maximum credit ceilings, and large exposure limits. Volz (2017) noticed that credit limits offer a very straightforward mechanism to channel investments to "green" projects. The maximum credit ceilings will structure the portfolios so limit certain carbon-intensive or polluting activities (sectors), while minimum credit floors would force the banks to allocate a certain fraction of their credit exposure portfolio to low-carbon sectors.

Climate-related stress tests and disclosure requirements hugely support the three groups of instruments mentioned above. Climate-related stress tests aim at testing the resilience of individual financial institutions and the financial system as a whole to hypothetical climate shocks (Battiston et al., 2017; NGFS, 2019). Climate-related stress tests produce valuable information about exposures of financial actors to climate-related risks (see Vermeulen et al., 2018). This information can be used to calibrate and evaluate climate-related macroprudential tools. Finally, disclosure requirements of the physical, liability, and transition risks associated with climate change are also relevant to develop a credible green financial system and avoid a so-called "green washing" (TCFD, 2018).

One could ask: what is the state-of-the-art usage of green financial regulatory tools? The increasing awareness of climate-related financial risks both in the policy and academic debates (see Dietz et al., 2016; Campiglio et al., 2018; Dafermos et al., 2018; Dafermos and Nikolaidi, 2021; Carney, 2018; Nieto, 2019) pushes for the integration of those risks under the prudential regulations radar and shifting the policy agenda from whether financial regulators should act on the climate crisis to what measures they should take.

After the famous speech of the Governor of the Bank of England, Mark Carney (2015), in the EU, a new wave of discussion started with the creation of the Task-Force on Climate-Related Financial Disclosures (TCFD, 2017) advocated by the Financial Stability Board, and the High-Level Expert Group by the European Commission. These initiatives and further steps towards creating the NGFS provide evidence of intensified political debates and action after 2015 (Carney, 2015; NGFS, 2017; HLEG, 2018) that could provide effective guidance for building capacity and understanding of risks in the field of green prudential policy tools. However, direct policy actions towards managing climate-related financial risks, at least in developed economies, mainly meet the "all talk, no walk" approach, relying only on discussions about financial regulatory tool adoptions. In fact, trusting the updated data collected by D'Orazio and Popoyan (2019a) on country-level diffusion of green prudential instruments listed above, Southern and East Asian regions (particularly China, India, Pakistan, Bangladesh, Vietnam, and Indonesia) appear as the forefront adopters of mandatory financial regulations. Other examples of successful application of green financial regulations are in Nigeria and Brazil, for which mandatory and voluntary regulations are adopted. Instead, such countries as France, Mexico, Turkey and others (marked with medium-grey in Figure 11.2) opted for the voluntary requirement.

What is the reason for such heterogeneity? All in all, as one can note from Figure 11.2, low-income countries and emerging economies are more involved in pursuing policies to green the banking sector than developed countries. This can be connected to three main factors. First, as noted at the beginning of section 2, central banks in emerging and low-income countries have a larger spectrum of goals and more flexibility in defining the policy periphery than high-income countries. Second, low-income countries are more exposed to climate change; therefore, they must shape timely and effective responses. The third reason could be connected to the lack of data to identify and assess climate-related risks. The latter builds a burden towards creating a common taxonomy to facilitate more consistent and targeted green finance policies and investment. The creation of taxonomies could empower financial regulators to develop green credit allocation policies to encourage the banking sector to lend directly to environmentally friendly sectors. Such an approach could comprise credit quotes in the form of either credit ceilings for minimum lending requirements to green sectors or, conversely, credit ceilings that limit loans to carbon-intensive industries. Another critical concern that, so far, slows down the process of incorporation of climate-related risks to financial intermediaries' risk radar is an already "carbon-biased" financial system; if not correctly addressed, this can compromise the financial system's safety and soundness (D'Orazio and Popoyan, 2019b).

Considering the instruments defined in section 3.1 and data provided by D'Orazio and Popoyan (2019a), we observe no usage of green capital instruments. Instead, as expected, lending limits are more widely adopted and mainly on mandatory bases in countries such as Bangladesh, Brazil, China, India, Indonesia, Nigeria, South Korea, and Vietnam, and are voluntary in Japan. The climate-related stress test has been effectively conducted on a mandatory basis only in China. However, few central bankers and regulators, namely the Bank of Canada and the macroprudential authorities in China, France, the Netherlands, and the UK, have started to consider integrating physical and transition risks in their stress-testing scenarios (BoE-PRA, 2019; BdF-ACPR, 2019).

The French supervisor conducted a voluntary stress-test exercise in July 2020 to identify vulnerabilities in addressing climate-financial risks (Allen et al., 2020). A similar schedule was adopted by De Nederlandsche Bank (Vermeulen et al., 2019), while the Bank of England performed the stress test in June 2021 (BoE-PRA, 2019). The European Central Bank (ECB) plans to conduct a supervisory stress test, including climate-related risks, in 2022.

Lastly, climate risk assessment and disclosure requirements in applications gather much interest, perhaps because of the necessity of having enough data to acknowledge the problem and later to react. Relying on D'Orazio and Popoyan (2019a), they are implemented as a mandatory requirement in India, Indonesia, Nigeria, Indonesia, Pakistan, South Korea, and Vietnam, whereas they are voluntary in Colombia, Ecuador, France, Japan, Kenya, Mexico, Mongolia, Morocco, Nepal, Peru, South Africa, and Turkey. Argentina, Canada, Denmark, Laos, Sweden, Switzerland, and the United Kingdom are currently discussing the possibility of implementing them.

As evidenced by D'Orazio and Popoyan (2020), frequently a "green financial mandate" is delivered by the central banks (47% of all active cases) through their financial regulatory functions. The 11% of countries active in green financial regulations store the contribution to the green transition in the hands of separate financial regulators. However, it is essential to highlight that central banks and financial regulators are frequently not alone carrying the burden of green objectives. We observe that the leading authorities collaborating with central banks in greening the financial sector (21% of active cases) are bank associations in Cambodia and Mongolia, capital market authorities in India and Morocco, regulatory authorities in China and Finland, and government in Denmark and Italy. In the rest of the active cases, the responsible authority is either a banks' association (Ecuador, Luxembourg, Mexico, South Africa, and Turkey) or a separated prudential regulatory body (Australia, Chile, Indonesia, Norway, and Peru). Two authorities active in the green finance debate are the government (Argentina, Sweden, and the US) and the Ministry of Environment (Colombia, South Korea, and Switzerland). All in all, Figure 11.2 highlights the dominant role of central banks (either in the role of the regulator or not) and independent financial regulators in delivering the green finance mandate.

Source: Authors' calculations based on publicly available information and D'Orazio and Popoyan (2019a).

Figure 11.2   *The adoption of green prudential requirements in 2020*

3.2   The Future of Green Finance: A Look Forward

Although monetary authorities have recently demonstrated greater interest and engagement in climate-related issues, only a few central banks have decided on considerable climate action. Here two essential aspects need to be considered. Central banks are unelected delegates, and their actions are tightened to their operational mandates (Masciandaro and Romelli, 2015). Therefore, many central banks possess significant institutional and operational independence compared to other policy entities. However, they are required to exercise those powers following "market neutrality" (Vonessen et al., 2020). Henceforth, guiding financial flows to low-carbon activities without having an explicit mandate could endanger the credibility and independence of the monetary authorities (Cochrane, 2020). This explains why some perceive intervention by central banks in long-term sustainability issues with a degree of diffidence and as a "second-best" intervention instead of other policy actions such as taxation and fiscal policy. In this, a critical question arises of how monetary authorities and financial regulators could get out of this institutional deadlock.

Second, the operational scope to support the climate agenda varies widely across central banks, with sustainability far from being a universally explicit mission statement (see Figure 11.1). Some monetary and prudential authorities have relatively narrow interpretations of their mandate to address climate issues. For instance, in 2015, Bank of England Governor Carney's call for central bankers to engage in a policy area outside their traditional charter was met with accusations of "mission creep" (Financial Times, 2019). Other central banks (such as PBoC, Central Bank of Brazil, Central Bank of Argentina) possess relatively broader policy remits to support green finance measures and climate policy.

This evidence brings a green monetary policy "dilemma" to the attention of policymakers and researchers. On the one hand, there is an urgency for central banks to contribute to keeping global warming below 2°C by closing the green finance gap and maintaining financial stability (i.e. macroprudential objective). On the other hand, the dilemma is concerned with preserving the central bank's mandate and independence while "leaning against climate-related risks" (Campiglio et al., 2018; Schoenmaker and Van Tilburg, 2016; de Galhau, 2019). Additionally, conflicts between the joint conduct of green monetary policy and prudential policy tools are possible because of intertwined transmission mechanisms (D'Orazio and Popoyan, 2020).

In fact, the goals and toolkits of green prudential regulation and monetary policy differ substantially (Svensson, 2018). Whereas the former focuses on green financial stability – that is, reducing systemic risks posed by climate change, decarbonizing banks' balance sheets, favouring the flow of funds to green sectors, and choosing green tools (Lamperti et al., 2019) – the latter relies, in the majority of the cases, on the policy rate to ensure price stability. However, since their field of influence passes through the financial system, they are characterized by an intertwined transmission mechanism (Barnea et al., 2015; Brunnermeier and Sannikov, 2014).

Moreover, considering that one policy is shaping the playground of the other, their respective impacts should be taken into consideration in their implementation. Thus, the existence of climate-related financial risks, together with the need to scale up green finance, calls for the development of a "synthesis" between monetary and green prudential policymaking. The latter boils down to Tinbergen's (1939, 1952) well-known principle, according to which "for each policy objective, at least one policy instrument is needed".

Relying on Tinbergen's "*n* objectives – *n* tools" formula, incorporating green financial goals into the central bank's price stability mandate could, on the one hand, endanger the principle itself and, on the other, overstretch the mandate, making it too broad and less explicit, thus undermining the authority's independence (Cochrane, 2020). However, as noted by D'Orazio and Popoyan (2020), if the green prudential regulation were treated as a composite part of a more general prudential policy, the "leaning against the climate-related risk" function could be fulfilled without violating the Tinbergen principle. In particular, looking at the mappings of central banks' financial regulatory governance models in Figure 11.3, we can see a governance model where the financial regulations are given either to a separate authority (i.e. separate model) or to a separate committee (i.e. committee model) guided by central banks and the ones that are most spread. Moreover, putting together Figures 11.2 and 11.3, one can note that the countries that have adopted tools to align the financial sector to sustainable objectives mainly belong to separate models (D'Orazio and Popoyan, 2020). While this arrangement safeguards the Tinbergen principle, it will require a greater level of coordination between the monetary and prudential authorities since the "distribution" of the green prudential regulation among several authorities may hamper decision-making, reduce accountability, and increase the risk of an inaction bias.

Proceeding with analysis and putting together the obtained results of green financial policy adoptions with the structure of central banks' mandates (see Figure 11.1), we can see that monetary authorities that have no financial stability in their structural mandates or have it "at the bottom" of the hierarchy frequently chose the separated models. Alternatively, monetary authorities with an implicit financial stability mandate chose models with greater central bank participation; that is, central bank or committee models. Accordingly, among active countries in the green finance debate, the most common central bank governance setups in the presence of climate-related financial policy are the separated models.

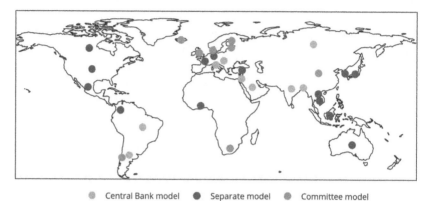

Central Bank model   ● Separate model   Committee model

Source: Authors' calculations based on International Monetary Fund central banks' legislation database, double-checked with central bank laws and statutes.

Figure 11.3   Central bank financial regulatory governance models in the active countries

4.   CONCLUSIONS

The last five years have seen increasing consideration from scholars, policy analysts, and practitioners on central banks' role and their policy responses in dealing with the climate change challenge. While the debate on the urgency of interventions by central banks and financial regulatory authorities stalls, the number of central banks moving in this direction has been rising; however, the overall number is still limited. Despite the mounting knowledge and advances made in quantifying the adverse impact of climate-related risk on price and financial stability, there are no internationally agreed-upon regulatory schemes to withstand the potential losses caused to the financial sector.

This chapter has sought to provide a state-of-the-art analysis of the current debate on the involvement of central banks and financial regulators in the green debate and their contribution in aligning the finance sector with sustainable transition roadmaps. It summarizes the possible tools available to central banks and macroprudential authorities and their consecutive usage. We study how the central bank has adopted its structures to cope with climate uncertainty. Additionally, we identify the conflict areas between the joint conduct of green monetary and financial policies and propose how to solve them.

For the sake of analysis, a critical distinction must be introduced between the two responsibilities that central banks undertake in most countries: the implementation and conduct of monetary policy and the supervision, regulation, and oversight of financial institutions' activities. Furthermore, the literature has pointed to paths in which monetary policy could support the green transition through market-shaping approaches. However, as our analysis demonstrates, the central banks are leaning towards market-fixing instruments that are called to incentivize financial market participants to internalize the inherent mispricing of assets. In fact, according to a recent survey conducted by OMFIF (2020), most central banks are worried about the usage of market-shaping tools. They are concerned that these tools could have distortionary, unintended consequences when applied to the current myopic state where the climate-related financial risks are neatly measured. In particular, the central banks that responded to the survey identify two significant obstacles to the incorporation of climate risks into supervisory practice: (1) missing green taxonomy (Carney, 2019) and (2) a lack of climate risk data. Similar conclusions were reached by the NGFS survey of 26 central banks from 51 countries (NGFS, 2020) and highlight the need for consistent, comparable, and reliable climate risk data. In the shadow of these drawbacks, only a small set of central banks have implemented far-reaching climate risk mitigation policies. So far, only a few countries have proceeded down this path, with only the BoE taking an active step towards a green transition. Since 2018 the PBoC has expanded its eligible collateral, including green assets for lending; since 2012 the Bank of Japan has been supporting lines of credit to green activities, while recently the ECB is showing increasing interest in relevant policies, pointing in the direction of "green QE".

There is a critical issue in the debate of central banks involved in the battle against climate change in the quality of monetary authority that explains their lesser effective involvement. As highlighted by Cochrane (2020) and Tooze (2020), this will have grave implications for central banks' independence and the maintenance of market neutrality because of the possible overstretching of their mandate. Accordingly, most central banks see their contribution to the green debate through their financial regulatory and oversight function, considering that most of them have adopted financial stability in their institutional mandates in the aftermath of a financial crisis. As we discussed above, most of the effectively adopted green finance tools are of a financial regulation and macroprudential nature. We can also notice that developing and emerging economies are more active in their effective adoption than the developed world. Moreover, in many cases, this green mandate is jointly delivered by multiple agencies.

However, we also point out that the joint conduct of green financial regulatory and monetary policies is prone to conflicts because of existing intertwined transmission mechanisms. We highlight that the conflict can be less pronounced in a specific policy arrangement than the others respecting Tinbergen's principle. We found that the governance structures where the prudential mandate is not embedded in a monetary one, but rather is separate either in terms of delegated authority or in a separate committee with central banks' participation, can help avoid conflicts, but will require higher coordination efforts. Our study emphasizes that even if these arrangements are already prevailing on the world-map after the post-crisis arrangements and can embrace climate-related risk management schemes, further research is needed on the advantages and disadvantages of the climate-related financial instruments and green monetary policy options, taking into account country-specific characteristics.

NOTES

1. We thank Yannis Dafermos for providing useful comments on an earlier draft of this chapter. Any mistakes are solely ours.
2. Note that the supply-side shocks can also arise through the transition from a high- to a low-carbon economy.
3. Few studies investigating the impact of climate-related shocks on inflation indicate that commodity prices tend to increase in the short term following natural disasters and weather extremes inducing upward pressure on the inflation rate (see Klomp, 2020; Heinen et al., 2019; Parker, 2018).
4. The literature also proposes other classifications of policy reactions to climate-related risks. For example, Baer et al. (2021) classify those policies depending on either different objectives the policy means to reach (i.e. prudential and promotional) or mechanisms (i.e. informational, incentive, or coercive).
5. Extensive analysis of the greened Basel III macro and macroprudential regulatory tools can be found in D'Orazio and Popoyan (2019b).

REFERENCES

2DII (2018), "The green supporting factor: Quantifying the impact on European banks and green finance", Technical Report, 2 degrees Investing Initiative.
Allen, T., S. Dees, V. Chouard, L. Clerc, A. de Gaye, A. Devulder, S. Diot, N. Lisack, F. Pegoraro, M. Rabate et al. (2020), "Climate-related scenarios for financial stability assessment: An application to France", Banque de France. https://publications.banque-france.fr/en/climate-related-scenarios-financial-stability-assessment-application-france.
Baer, M., E. Campiglio, and J. Deyris (2021), "It takes two to dance: Institutional dynamics and climate-related financial policies", Grantham Research Institute on Climate Change and the Environment.
Baker, A. (2013), "The new political economy of the macroprudential ideational shift", *New Political Economy*, 18(1): 112–139.
Barkawi, A. and S. Zadek (2021), "Governing finance for sustainable prosperity", Council on Economic Policies.
Barnea, E., Y. Landskroner, and M. Sokoler (2015), "Monetary policy and financial stability in a banking economy: Transmission mechanism and policy tradeoffs", *Journal of Financial Stability*, 18: 78–90.
Batten, S., R. Sowerbutts, and M. Tanaka (2016), "Let's talk about the weather: The impact of climate change on central banks", Technical Report, Bank of England.

Batten, S., R. Sowerbutts, and M. Tanaka (2020), "Climate change: Macroeconomic impact and implications for monetary policy", in *Ecological, Societal, and Technological Risks and the Financial Sector*, Springer, 13–38.

Battiston, S., A. Mandel, I. Monasterolo, F. Schütze, and G. Visentin (2017), "A climate stress-test of the financial system", *Nature Climate Change*, 7: 283–288.

BCBS (2017), "Range of practices in implementing the countercyclical capital buffer policy", Technical Report, BCBS – Basel Committee on Banking Supervision.

BdF-ACPR (2019), "French banking groups facing climate change-related risks", Technical Report, Banque de France – ACPR.

BDL (2010), "Intermediate circular on reserve requirements", Technical Report, Intermediate Circular No. 236.

Bhattacharya, A., J. Oppenheim, and N. Stern (2015), "Driving sustainable development through better infrastructure: Key elements of a transformation program", *Brookings Global Working Paper Series*.

BoE (2021), "Remit for Monetary Policy Committee, 3 March, 2021". https://www.bankofengland.co.uk/-/media/boe/files/letter/2021/march/2021-mpc-remitletter.pdf?la=en&hash=C3A91905E1A58A3A98071B2DD41E65FAFD1CF03E

BoE-PRA (2019), "A general insurance stress test 2019 scenario specification, guidelines and instructions", Technical Report, Bank of England – Prudential Authority Regulation.

Bolton, P., M. Després, L. A. P. da Silva, F. Samama, and R. Svartzman (2020), "The green swan", Banque de France. https://www.bis.org/publ/othp31.pdf.

Brunnermeier, M. K. and Y. Sannikov (2014), "Monetary analysis: Price and financial stability", in *Proceedings ECB Forum on Central Banking, Sintra*, 61–80.

Campiglio, E., Y. Dafermos, P. Monnin, J. Ryan-Collins, G. Schotten, and M. Tanaka (2018), "Climate change challenges for central banks and financial regulators", *Nature Climate Change*, 8: 462–468.

Carney, M. (2015), "Breaking the tragedy of the horizon: Climate change and financial stability", Speech given at Lloyds of London, 29: 220–230.

Carney, M. (2018), "A transition in thinking and action", Bank of England, speech.

Carney, M. (2019), "Fifty shades of green", *Finance & Development*. Washington, DC, 12–15.

Chang, C., Z. Liu, M. M. Spiegel, and J. Zhang (2019), "Reserve requirements and optimal Chinese stabilization policy", *Journal of Monetary Economics*, 103: 33–51.

Cochrane, J. (2020), "Central banks and climate: A case of mission creep", *Hoover Institutions Publications*.

Cœuré, B. (2018), "Monetary policy and climate change", speech by B. Cœuré, Member of the Executive Board of the ECB, at a conference on "Scaling Up Green Finance: The Role of Central Banks", European Central Bank.

COP (2016), "Marrakech action proclamation for our climate and sustainable development", UN-Framework Convention on Climate Change.

Dafermos, Y. (2021), "Climate change, central banking and financial supervision: Beyond the risk exposure approach", Working Papers 243, Department of Economics, SOAS, University of London, UK.

Dafermos, Y. and M. Nikolaidi (2021), "How can green differentiated capital requirements affect climate risks? A dynamic macrofinancial analysis", *Journal of Financial Stability*, 54, 100871.

Dafermos, Y., M. Nikolaidi, and G. Galanis (2017), "A stock-flow-fund ecological macroeconomic model", *Ecological Economics*, 131: 191–207.

Dafermos, Y., M. Nikolaidi, and G. Galanis (2018), "Climate change, financial stability and monetary policy", *Ecological Economics*, 152: 219–234.

Dafermos, Y., D. Gabor, M. Nikolaidi, A. Pawloff, and F. van Lerven (2020), *Decarbonising Is Easy: Beyond Market Neutrality in the ECB's Corporate QE*, London.

de Galhau, V. (2019), "Climate change: Central banks are taking action", Banque de France. https://publications.banque-france.fr/sites/default/files/media/2019/06/12/fsr_villeroy.pdf.

Diaz, D. and F. Moore (2017), "Quantifying the economic risks of climate change", *Nature Climate Change*, 7: 774–782.

Dietz, S., A. Bowen, C. Dixon, and P. Gradwell (2016), "Climate value at risk of global financial assets", *Nature Climate Change*, 6: 676.

Dikau, S. and U. Volz (2018), "Central banking, climate change and green finance", Asian Development Bank Institute. https://core.ac.uk/download/pdf/161527987.pdf.

Dikau, S. and U. Volz (2021), "Central bank mandates, sustainability objectives and the promotion of green finance", *Ecological Economics*, 184: 107022.

D'Orazio, P. and L. Popoyan (2019a), "Dataset on green macroprudential regulations and instruments: Objectives, implementation and geographical diffusion", *Data in Brief*, 24: 103870.

D'Orazio, P. and L. Popoyan (2019b), "Fostering green investments and tackling climate-related financial risks: Which role for macroprudential policies?", *Ecological Economics*, 160: 25–37.

D'Orazio, P. and L. Popoyan (2020), "Taking up the climate change challenge: A new perspective on central banking", Technical Report, LEM Working Paper Series.

Financial Times (2019), "Central banks are finally taking up the climate change challenge", 25 April.

Financial Times (2021), "Central banks should turn green", 5 April.

FSB (2020), "The implications of climate change for financial stability", Financial Stability Board.

Goodhart, C. et al. (2011), "The changing role of central banks", *Financial History Review*, 18: 135–154.

Gros, D., P. Lane, S. Langfield, S. Matikainen, M. Pagano, D. Schoenmaker, J. Suarez et al. (2016), "Too late, too sudden: Transition to a low-carbon economy and systemic risk", Technical Report, European Systemic Risk Board.

Haldane, A. (2011), "The short long, 29th Société Universitaire Européene de Recherches Financiéres Colloquium: New Paradigms in Money and Finance? Brussels", Technical Report, Bank of England.

Heinen, A., J. Khadan, and E. Strobl (2019), "The price impact of extreme weather in developing countries", *The Economic Journal*, 129: 1327–1342.

HLEG (2018), "Final report on financing a sustainable European economy", Interim Report – High-Level Expert Group on Sustainable Finance.

Hsiang, S., R. Kopp, A. Jina, J. Rising, M. Delgado, S. Mohan, D. Rasmussen, R. Muir-Wood, P. Wilson, M. Oppenheimer et al. (2017), "Estimating economic damage from climate change in the United States", *Science*, 356: 1362–1369.

Klomp, J. (2020), "Do natural disasters affect monetary policy? A quasi-experiment of earthquakes", *Journal of Macroeconomics*, 64: 103164.

Krogstrup, S. and W. Oman (2019), *Macroeconomic and Financial Policies for Climate Change Mitigation: A Review of the Literature*, International Monetary Fund.

Lamperti, F., V. Bosetti, A. Roventini, and M. Tavoni (2019), "The public costs of climate-induced financial instability", *Nature Climate Change*, 9: 829–833.

Li, B., W. Xiong, L. Chen, and Y. Wang (2017), "The impact of the liquidity coverage ratio on money creation: A stock-flow based dynamic approach", *Economic Modelling*, 67: 193–202.

Masciandaro, D. and D. Romelli (2015), "Ups and downs of central bank independence from the Great Inflation to the Great Recession: Theory, institutions and empirics", *Financial History Review*, 22: 259–289.

Matikainen, S., E. Campiglio, and D. Zenghelis (2017), "The climate impact of quantitative easing", Technical Report, London School of Economics.

McKibbin, W. J., A. C. Morris, A. Panton, and P. Wilcoxen (2017), "Climate change and monetary policy: Dealing with disruption", Brookings. https://www.brookings.edu/wp-content/uploads/2017/12/es_20171201_climatechangeandmonetarypolicy.pdf.

NGFS (2017), "Charter of the Central Banks and Supervisors Network for Greening System", Network for Greening the Financial System.

NGFS (2019), "A call for action: Climate change as a source of financial risk, first comprehensive report", Network for Greening the Financial System.

NGFS (2020), "Survey on monetary policy operations and climate change: Key lessons for further analyses", Network for Greening the Financial System.

Nieto, M. J. (2019), "Banks, climate risk and financial stability", *Journal of Financial Regulation and Compliance*, 27: 243–262.

Olovsson, C. (2018), "Is climate change relevant for central banks?", *Sveriges Riksbank Economic Commentaries*, 13.

OMFIF (2020), "Tackling climate change: The role of banking regulation and supervision". https://www.omfif.org/tacklingclimatechange.

Papadamou, S., D. Sogiakas, V. Sogiakas, and K. Toudas (2021), "The prudential role of Basel III liquidity provisions towards financial stability", *Journal of Forecasting*, 40(7): 1133–1153.

Parker, M. (2018), "The impact of disasters on inflation", *Economics of Disasters and Climate Change*, 2: 21–48.

Quaglia, L. (2013), "Financial regulation and supervision in the European Union after the crisis", *Journal of Economic Policy Reform*, 16(1): 17–30.

Schoenmaker, D. and R. Van Tilburg (2016), "What role for financial supervisors in addressing environmental risks?", *Comparative Economic Studies*, 58: 317–334.

Semieniuk, G., E. Campiglio, J.-F. Mercure, U. Volz, and N. R. Edwards (2021), "Low-carbon transition risks for finance", *Wiley Interdisciplinary Reviews: Climate Change*, 12: e678.

Spencer, T. and J. Stevenson (2013), "EU low-carbon investment and new financial sector regulation: What impacts and what policy response?", IDDRI Sciences Po, Paris.

Stern, N. and N. H. Stern (2007), *The Economics of Climate Change: The Stern Review*, Cambridge University Press.

Svensson, L. E. (2018), "Monetary policy and macroprudential policy: Different and separate?", *Canadian Journal of Economics/Revue canadienne d'économique*, 51: 802–827.

TCFD (2017), "Final report: Recommendations of the Task Force on Climate-Related Financial Disclosures", Task Force on Climate-Related Financial Disclosures.

TCFD (2018), "TCFD: 2018 Status Report", Task Force on Climate-Related Financial Disclosures.

Thomä, J., C. Weber, M. Fulton, S. Dupré, M. Allison, and H. Chenet (2016), "Transition Risk Toolbox: Scenarios, Data, and Models", 2 Degree Investing

Initiative. https://2degrees-investing.org/wp-content/uploads/2016/12/Transition-risk
    -toolbox-scenarios-data-and-models-2017.pdf.
Tinbergen, J. (1939), *Business Cycles in the United States of America: 1919–1932*,
    League of Nations.
Tinbergen, J. (1952), "On the theory of economic policy", *Contributions to Economic
    Analysis*, 1.
Tooze, A. (2020), "The death of the central bank myth", *Foreign Policy*, 13: 2020.
Van Lerven, F. and J. Ryan-Collins (2017), "Central banks, climate change and the
    transition to a low carbon economy: A policy briefing", New Economics Foundation.
Vermeulen, R., E. Schets, M. Lohuis, B. Kölbl, D.-J. Jansen, and W. Heeringa (2019),
    "The heat is on: A framework for measuring financial stress under disruptive energy
    transition scenarios", De Nederlandsche Bank Working Paper.
Vermeulen, R., E. Schets, M. Lohuis, B. Kölbl, D.-J. Jansen, W. Heeringa et al. (2018),
    "An energy transition risk stress test for the financial system of the Netherlands",
    Technical Report, Netherlands Central Bank, Research Department.
Volz, U. (2017), "On the role of central banks in enhancing green finance", *UN
    Environment Inquiry Working Paper 17/01*.
Vonessen, B., K. Arnold, R. D. Mas, and C. Fehlker (2020), "The case for central bank
    independence: A review of key issues in the international debate", ECB Occasional
    Paper.
Weidmann, J., "Climate change and central banks", in *Welcome Address at the
    Deutsche Bundesbanks Second Financial Market Conference, Frankfurt am Main*,
    volume 29.

Index